MASTERING EXCEL VBA AND MACHINE LEARNING

A Complete, Step-by-Step Guide To Learn and Master Excel VBA and Machine Learning From Scratch

TABLE OF CONTENTS

Excel VBA

*A Step-By-Step Tutorial For Beginners To Learn
Excel VBA Programming From Scratch*

Excel VBA

*Intermediate Lessons in Excel VBA Programming
for Professional Advancement*

Excel VBA

A Step-By-Step Comprehensive Guide on Advanced Excel VBA Programming Techniques and Strategies

Excel VBA

A Comprehensive, Step-By-Step Guide On Excel VBA Finance
For Data Reporting And Business Analysis

Excel VBA

A Step-by-Step Comprehensive Guide on Excel VBA Programming Tips and Tricks for Effective Strategies

Machine Learning

A Comprehensive, Step-by-Step Guide to Learning and Understanding Machine Learning Concepts, Technology and Principles for Beginners

Machine Learning

A Comprehensive, Step-by-Step Guide to Intermediate Concepts and Techniques in Machine Learning

Machine Learning
*A Comprehensive, Step-by-Step Guide to Learning and Applying
Advanced Concepts and Techniques in Machine Learning*

Machine Learning
*A Complete Exploration of Highly Advanced Machine Learning
Concepts, Best Practices and Techniques*

Excel VBA

A Step-By-Step Tutorial For Beginners To Learn Excel VBA Programming From Scratch

Introduction

Congratulations on purchasing *Excel VBA: A Step-By-Step Tutorial For Beginners To Learn Excel VBA Programming From Scratch*

and thank you for doing so. Despite the fact that most people don't know all that much about it, Excel is an extremely useful and versatile tool and taking this first step towards utilizing it to the fullest is sure to pay serious dividends in the future.

In order to ensure you have all the tools you need at your disposal, the following chapters will discuss everything you need to know about VBA, starting with the basics including accessing this feature in modern spreadsheets. Next, you will learn how to make the most of macros by using existing Excel data. You will then learn about the many ways both variables as well as If/Then statements can be used to take your macros to the next level.

From there, you will learn about some more complicated concepts include looping, as well as a number of additional tools that are sure to prove useful from time to time. You will then learn about common errors to watch out for while debugging and some additional tips for success to keep in mind while working with VBA to ensure you get started on the right foot.

There are plenty of books on this subject on the market, thanks again for choosing this one! Every effort was made to ensure it is full of as much useful information as possible, please enjoy!

Chapter 1

VBA Primer

While you can manipulate Excel to a fair degree through the use of formulas alone, there are always going to be tasks that require you to move and sort data in ways that are limited through the use of this knowledge alone. In these situations, it will generally be much more efficient time-wise to just create a program that can automate the task you are attempting. In Excel, these programs are known as Macros and Excel offers an easy means of creating your own through its own programming language known as Visual Basic for Applications or VBA for short.

The language operates via Visual Basic 6 which was a programming language in vouge before Microsoft standardized things with the .NET languages. While it was once quite popular, these days VBA is the last place most people will encounter it and even then in newer versions of Excel you have to manually activate the feature to even get a peek at it. If you pursue it, however, you will find that once you get used to it you will be able to easily create macros that will easily complete a wide variety of different functions.

While the language struggles with more complicated actions, as long as you don't push the limits of what's possible you will find that a little bit of studying will help to save a significant amount of time in the long-run. VBA can be found throughout the Microsoft Office suite of programs as well which means your new skill can have a wide variety of uses indeed.

First thing's first

If you are using a version of Excel from 2010 or later, you will need to enable VBA functionality before you can get started. This is due to the fact that some macros could, hypothetically, lead to security issues so Microsoft puts the responsibility of enabling it on the user. Luckily, the process to do so isn't difficult, all you need to do is go to FILE, then OPTIONS and choose the option for CUSTOMIZE RIBBON. From the resulting screen, you will then want to find the box marked DEVELOPER as doing so will provide a space for developer icons to appear on the main screen.

This won't do you any good on its own, however, as you have to use a separate option to allow Macros to be run within Excel. Specifically, you will want to select FILE, then OPTIONS, then TRUST CENTER and finally TRUST CENTER SETTINGS. From the resulting screen, you will then want to choose the option for MACROS SETTINGS. Finally, you will want to check the box marked ENABLE ALL MACROS.

Assuming you have followed these steps correctly you should now see the space for developer tools on the main screen and also run a program. If you can't do both successfully then you will know that you need to repeat the steps above.

Write your first program

If you have ever programmed something before then you likely know what is coming next. This is due to the fact that programming tradition demands that the first program you write is one that causes the message "Hello world" to appear on the screen. While this isn't the most useful program to run multiple times, creating it will help to get you used to the basics of VBA while at the same time ensuring you don't get into anything too complex which can make it difficult to determine where any errors might have come from.

In order to write your first VBA program, however, you will need to operate in something outside of the standard worksheet interface. You will be working in what's commonly referred to as a module which is a special type of workbook page. To get started you will want to locate the VBA icon in the newly visible developer tab.

To start creating your program you are going to want to use the command INSERT MACRO MODULE which will create an entirely blank page. Once you click on this option you will also find a new set of options near the arrows for REDO and UDNO. These new options include stop, play and pause and they will work just as you expect them to. Each module is also automatically named, starting with Module1. In order to change the name to something more descriptive, all you need to do is to locate the PROPERTIES box in the lower left corner of the screen and change the name you find there.

While working with modules, it is important to understand that they operate quite differently than your more run of the mill spreadsheet. The biggest differences you will notice right away is that the new page won't contain any cells and it also won't automatically calculate provided formulas. When you start typing what you will see are more traditional lines of text that you can then use the traditional paste, copy and cut functionality that you would expect from a Microsoft product. The module will save normally when you save the workbook as a whole.

One of the most important differences you will notice about the module is that it seems to complain about the text you type, regardless of whether or not what you are typing is grammatically correct. This is because the module isn't checking for spelling or grammar mistakes, it is checking for accurate VBA commands. This tool will be invaluable during the early days of your time with VBA when mistakes are likely to be far more common.

In order to ensure that you create a program that the module is sure to read, you will need to start the first line of every program in the same fashion by typing:

Sub *name* () with the name of your program replacing *name*. To create the program discussed above you will want to begin by typing Sub hell () which will serve to tell the module that the name of the program in question is hello. When you are finished creating a program you will want to ensure the final line of your program reads: End Sub. Without this line, Excel will assume that it is waiting for additional input.

You will be able to tell if you have entered a command correctly because it will automatically turn blue. This process will also include proper capitalization if you did not provide it as well. This will occur with any VBA keyword, which is a fixed set of commands that the VBA is programmed to automatically recognize. Luckily, the VBA is also programmed to recognize and correct common errors, such as failing to include the bracket in Sub hell () or forgetting to end the program with End Sub. It is important to be aware that this is the case as otherwise, you may end up creating even more errors by accidentally fixing errors twice. As you get more used to the language and what can be added via a module you are sure to find that it speeds things up a great deal.

Once you have the name, as well as the end and start point of the program, all that you are left with now is filling in the remaining middle bits. When working on a VBA program it is useful to think about what you are doing in terms of creating a list of instructions for the program to follow. As such, if your goal is to create a greeting at the top of the page then you need to give it an instruction to create a message box as well as what to fill it with. The easiest way to create a message box is via the MsgBox command. This command signals the module that you want to create a message box meanwhile following the MsgBox command

7

with text in quotation marks like so MsgBox "message" will display the message in question in the message box.

With all of the pieces now in play, the process of display a message box that says hello becomes relatively straightforward. The program would look like so:

Sub hell ()

MsgBox "Hello World"

End Sub

In order to double check that the program is going to run successfully, all you will need to do is to click on the play button on the toolbar. If this part of the toolbar isn't immediately visible, you will need to check that it has been turned on. You can find the relevant option by selecting VIEW, then TOOLBARS, then VBA. You can also get the program going by using the command RUN, Start.

Assuming everything works as it should, you should now see a dialog box appear that will show you all of the programs you can run from within the current module. All you need to do is select the hello program and then select the RUN option. Assuming everything is working properly this will now cause the Hello World message to be displayed. You can then click on OK to dismiss the message and also end the program. However, if you had instead entered additional details after the first message, hitting OK would have brought up the next part of the message instead. However, if despite your best efforts, no message is displayed, then you will want to go back and retry the steps outlined above as well as check your code to ensure it doesn't contain any extra spaces.

Additional input

Once the starter program is up and running, the next thing you will want to do is to create a means for the user to interact with the program so they can add information as needed. To do so, you will need to use the VBA command InputBox which is similar to a message box just more complex.

The command for the InputBox is A = InputBox ("message). This will cause the input box to ask a question ("message") and also allow the user to generate their own response. The answer to the question needs to be numerical, however, something like "what is the number of pets you have". Any answer is then going to be confirmed via the Enter key. Based on the above command, the number given as the answer would then be saved as variable A, if it was written a B = InputBox then the variable would be saved as B.

Variables are an extremely important part of most macros and you can think of each as operating in much the way that a named cell operates. The biggest difference here, however, is the fact that the VBA variable isn't tied to one worksheet as it will work throughout the full workbook.

When creating a VBA variable, the module will automatically track and store any details without you having to issue any additional commands. You can name a variable anything you like, though letters are used most commonly in situations where a full name is impractical. Once you have stored a value, you can then return to it again from any module in the workbook and it will be recognized.

As an example, if you were interested in finding out how many pets the user owns you would write the program as:

Sub hello()

    Pets = InputBox("How many pets do you have")

    MsgBox Pets

End Sub

When run, this will generate a message asking the user to indicate the number of pets they have before saving the results under the variable labeled "pets". While this might seem pretty basics on the surface, the truth of the matter is that it requires several things to happen at the same time. For starters, the MSgBox isn't displaying the word Pets and is instead displaying the number that was saved as the pets variable. This distinction is similar to adding a number to the A1 cell and then referring to it after the fact.

Taking things up a notch

While being able to generate simple avenues for output and input is certainly enough to allow you to create a wide variety of macros, it is still really just scratching the surface when it comes to everything VBA can do. The real fun will begin in the way it interacts with Excel directly, which you will learn more about in future chapters. Nevertheless, there is still more you can do with what you have already learned.

One prime example of this is a solution to the problem that arises when it comes to generating numerous sheets at once and making sure everyone using then understand what types of data need to go where. This is where a particularly useful feature of VBA, creating prompts, comes into play as it will generate a prompt at each place when someone needs to enter specific data.

With the following example, you will notice that the code has been simplified by ignoring the component that would involve the spreadsheet.

Sub loan()

    MsgBox "This program works

      out the total cost of the interest on a home loan."

Amount = InputBox("The amount you will be borrowing from the bank ")

Interest = InputBox("What is the amount you will pay in interest each month")

Months = InputBox("What is the length of the loan")

pay = Application.Pmt (Interest, Months, -Amount)

MsgBox "Your total interest will be " & pay

End Sub

While these lines are written normally for the sake of legibility, while typing them into the module you may very well find yourself at the end of a specific line without finishing a specific command. If this happens you will then need to continue the command on the following line to ensure it is read properly by the module when the time comes.

If you have set everything up properly to this point then when you run the above program you should see a message box that shows the goal of the program along with a series of boxes for inputs as well as the rest of the important information. You should also receive an answer once all the boxes have been filled in. You should not, however, just copy and paste the above code for use in a real-world scenario as it is missing check that makes sure users put in realistic values.

The important new feature in this example is the PMT function that is used to accurately figure out the full amount of the loan. This function also needs to be written as follows: Application.pmt (. This allows the VBA to understand that the listed function is generated via a spreadsheet as opposed to a command that came from within the VBA.

While this is a simple example, it serves to show an example of what a VBA macro can accomplish. What's more, it will make it possible for you to more likely accurately determine what is going to happen as well as what will cause it.

Chapter 2

Making Use of Data from Excel

Once you start working in VBA successfully, you will find that it becomes far easier to understand all of the possibilities of doing so. The trouble can being, however, if you find that you are having a hard time accessing information found elsewhere in the workbook. This works in stark contrast to a majority of traditional workbook functions where finding specific data is an extremely easy task.

Typically this process can be completed by typing something simple like =B4+B5 into a given cell and letting the worksheet sort out the rest. If you try this same approach in the module, however, you will find that the way this process works in the VBA is a remnant of its roots as a programming language. Thus, while its commands aren't quite as simple, they can be used in a wider variety of scenarios.

Locating data within a given cell

The easiest way to determine how these processes work is to start by referring to data that is stored in specific cells in a way that the VBA will understand. It is important to keep in mind, however, that there are going to be easier ways of reaching this data in the end, which makes this portion more of a thought exercise. In the following example, it is assumed that you were interested in accessing whatever is in Workbooks 2, cell G2 of Sheet 17.

temp= Application.Workbooks("Book2"). _

Worksheets("Sheet17"). _

Range("G2").Value

While this can be a lot of work to access the data in a single cell, it serves to illustrate how the code works as a type of address, starting with the most general information and getting more specific as it progresses. You will see this same type of pattern repeated numerous times as you work with VBA. It is also important to keep in mind the fact that various parts of the address are separated by a period while at the same time being read left to right as you might expect. To read the above address you would look at the application, which is Excel in this case, before finding the active workbook number, which is crucial when telling the program what to limit its search too. Finally, each workbook can then have any number of worksheets as well as cells within those sheets so the remaining information is honed in on even more easily.

You will also need to take note of the underscores that are placed at the end of certain lines of the code. These are simply used as a means of ensuring that the module reads the two lines of code as one complete thought. If you need to split a command between two lines splitting them with an underscore and a space is recommended. Underscores are what is known as a continuation character which means they indicate if a given instruction is spread across more than one line. While the module will most likely read the code properly regardless, it is often easier to insert these line breaks yourself to ensure everything remains nice and clear.

There are also a variety of different properties for cells that can be utilized, including color, height, width and more which is why Value is necessary in order to guarantee you end up with the correct value when everything is said and done. While all of this will certainly be useful as the groundwork for additional information, later on, it is only going to be needed in its entirety in very rare occasions.

Objects and properties

While this approach to finding the data in a specific cell can feel cumbersome to start, it is actually inline with a variety of modern programming languages so it certainly bears learning, even if you won't be using it all that frequently at the moment. The basic idea is that when working in VBA you will be working with Objects and these objects all have Properties. For example, if a specific cell in a spreadsheet is an object, and the properties within that cell are its values which means that the range B2 applies specifically to a cell that is also an object named B2 as well as the range ("B2"). Value can then be used to tell you if the value has a specific property.

While this is fairly straightforward to start, it can quickly become more and more complicated based on the fact that objects can also have other objects as properties as well. For example, if you are looking for an Application as an object then it can include a variety of different workbooks which are also objects in their own right while still being part of the Application's associated properties. Each of these workbooks could then contain a variety of worksheets which are then objects in their own right even though they contain cells which are objects as well.

This nestled functionality goes by the name object hierarchy and it goes application, workbook, worksheet, cell range. Each cell could also have additional objects associated to its properties though it is rare you will need to get that granular with anything. While this system might seem cumbersome at first, it is important to persevere as once you get a better feel for the arrangement of most objects your speed is bound to increase. VBA also features an object viewer that will allow you to easily view the hierarchies that exist within your module while also choosing objects from the list if you prefer. This will, as an example, make it possible for you to press F2 to look at the range for a given worksheet.

Simplify: After you are familiar with the general principles at play within the object hierarchy, you can then simplify things, even more, starting with the process for finding specific detail more quickly. To begin you will want to write your references with a specific set of properties so that you don't need to write out full names as you can count on several factors to be included automatically. These default phrases will naturally relate to the object of the required type that is currently active.

As an example, if you were to start out: temp = Worksheets("Sheet4").

Range("B4").Value

This would tell the module that Excel is the application that is currently active and it would remember that fact moving forward. The same can be said if you use the VBA in other Office products like Word. The same level of assumption can be applied to workbooks that are currently active, assuming it is part of the same module. You can also let the worksheet autofill but this can be tricky in certain instances as it can become difficult to determine which sheet is currently active in a given model.

If you want to remove the need for a given worksheet reference you can write it as such: = Range("B1").Value. You will then want to ensure you runt eh code at least once to watch everything work properly. As you do so, it is important to watch and make sure the correct sheet is picked up. This will require to use the Activate method. Beyond properties, a majority of objects have methods as well. A method is simply something an object is asked to do. For example: worksheets ("Sheet4").Activate. This would, in turn, give the fourth sheet the activate method which would set it to the active sheet. This will be the fourth sheet in the current workbook, however, so it is important to set the workbook accordingly as well.

16

When it comes to creating something entirely new, you would include it like so:

```
ub newvalue()
        Worksheets("Sheet2").Activate
        temp = Range("C2").Value
        MsgBox temp
End Sub
```

This will then help to ensure that things work as expected and that you are leaving nothing to chance as a result. This will ensure you see the contents of the specific cell on the specific sheet no matter what the state of things happened to be prior to starting the module. A side effect of this is that if you happen to close the module you will find that the sheet you indicated is now the active sheet.

The same overall process can be used to generate the correct workbook and would look something like this:

```
Sub findvalue()

        Workbooks("Example1").Activate

        Worksheets("Sheet2").Activate

        temp = Range("C2").Value

        MsgBox temp

End Sub
```

This will, in turn, help to ensure that the workbook with the given name is active, before then activating its second worksheet and then circling in on the cell C2.

With

After you have worked to make sure the module is looking for the specified data in the right place, you will then be able to go ahead and leave out those references moving forward as you can count on the module to fill them in automatically. This will not be the case, however, if you go ahead and reference several different workbooks or worksheets in short order. Luckily, as taking the time to switch them all over on your own can be extremely time consuming, you can do it without having to write out entire names. This involves the use of the command With – End With.

The goal here is that you can successfully quote a long string of names that you will eventually be using at the very start with a list inside a block. Doing so would look something like this:

```
Sub findvalue()

    With Worksheets("Sheet3")

    temp = .Range("C3").Value

    End With

    MsgBox temp

End Sub
```

After the "with" the reference

.Range("C3").Value

is expanded to

Worksheets("Sheet3").Range("C3").Value

From there, any reference that is placed between the With and the End With commands will need to be proceeded by a "." they can then be expanded upon in much the same way. The "." works as a type of invitation for the WITH command to include the rest of the name. it is also important to keep in mind that the above example takes advantage of the workbook that is currently active. You can then further specify the object that you want to focus on by using the With-End With command. For example, you would be able to indicate that Workbook3 and Sheet3 are the defaults for future With-End With instructions like so:

```
Sub getvalue()

    With Workbooks("Book3").Worksheets("Sheet3")

    temp = .Range("C3").Value

    End With

    MsgBox temp

End Sub
```

This can then be used with any object that is going to be considered the default With object...End With statement.

Using it: With this option on the table, you should now have a general idea of the best way to get at any of the values that you may have already added to a specific worksheet which means you are now ready to begin thinking about the many ways in which VBA and Excel can successfully work together. In most scenarios where you are choosing whether to implement what happens with the VBA or if a spreadsheet can do the job more quickly, some things are always going to need to remain on the spreadsheet in order to truly be effective.

One such instance is with the starter program discussed in the first chapter. It utilized inputs as well as a message box in order to utilize data entered by the user who was asked to provide an answer. The process was then taken care of by the VBA program and the data didn't actually utilize a spreadsheet in a meaningful fashion. As such, it could have been created in much the same way using any other programming language. Often, however, you will find that you are working with specifics that deal with Excel far more directly.

Back to the starter program, it could have been altered in such a way that it utilized data that was originally stored in the spreadsheet and had its calculations done directly through the spreadsheet as well. To do this all you would have needed to do was to create a new workbook before opening up the module and then using the INSERT command, then MACRO and MODULE before using the following:

```
Sub loan()

        MsgBox "This program works out the interest paid on a loan."

        With Workbooks("Book3").Worksheets("Sheet3")

        .Range("C3") = InputBox( _

            "The amount you will be borrowing ")

        .Range("C1") = InputBox( _

            "Monthly interest")

        .Range("C2") = InputBox( _

            "How long is the loan for")

        .Range("C4") = "=Pmt(C2, C1, -C3)"

        .Activate

        MsgBox "Monthly repayments " & .Range("C4")

        End With

End Sub
```

As written, this program does much the same thing as the program found in Chapter 1, except that it now uses values that were input from the cells in the relevant sheet and book. It is also important to take note of the With command in this scenario; generally speaking, it will be used to indicate specific books and sheets to act as defaults for any future references, here, however, the .Activate line helps to ensure the proper sheet is currently active. Finally, the message box displays any relevant information.

You should also be aware of the .Range command as it is useful when it comes to placing a full formula into a specific cell. Doing so successfully requires a bit of work, however, as the formula will need to be written with quotation marks to help ensure the VBA doesn't work to solve prior to placing the details in the specific cell. With this done, you can then switch to the worksheet and you will see the formula in question in the appropriate cell, just as you initially entered it.

You can get the same effect by adding the formula you wish to use to the cell manually, prior to opening the module. This will then require that the module make a handful of assumptions about the things that are stored in the worksheet, but certainly no more than most programs. In most instances, the module will begin by building as much of the automation for the given spreadsheet as possible right from the start prior to writing the part of the program that will require its functionality to be extended to an even greater degree.

The greatest advantage of this course of action is doing things in this fashion is that once a program has been properly executed you can still access the formula or data from the spreadsheet as normal which means you are free to change variables on the fly before running the program again to see what's changed as a result. This is where much of the true power of the spreadsheet comes from and where it provides a significant advantage when compared to utilizing pure VBA functionality.

If the program outlined above were written in its final form then it would have included additional titles and formatting to the spreadsheet side of things to help present all of the available information as effectively as possible. It would almost certainly have pre-included the secondary formula as well which means the macro would have been able to simply pull the data and show the results. In fact, these are two of the more commonly used roles that VBA programs play when it comes to working with spreadsheets that have a more complicated agenda. This doesn't mean that guiding the user isn't an important function, however, and you can easily use the VBA to provide relevant values and also check to ensure they are added properly to the worksheet.

Utilizing Ranges

Range object: The range object is arguably the main object you'll be using to interact with ranges. When you record macros in VBA and select a range of cells, Excel uses the range object. So if you selected cell A1 while recording a macro, Excel would record the action like so:

> Range("A1").select

In this example, range is the object. The parameter (argument) we're providing to this object is a valid cell reference (A1 in this case) which is provided as a string (i.e. in double quotes.) And the method (action) we're performing is "select" to select the cell, or range of cells, that was provided as a parameter to the range object. So we're telling Excel to find the range A1 in the worksheet (in this case, in the activesheet) and select that cell.

If you selected a range of cells while recording a macro, say the cells in the A1 through C3, Excel would record the action like so:

> Range("A1:C3").select

In addition to selecting a cell, or a range of cells, you can also select a range of non-continuous cells. For example, you can select cells A1, B4, and D8 like so:

Range("A1,B4,D8").select

In addition to passing ranges, you can also pass variables that contain valid range references like so:

Dim addy as string

Addy = "A1,B4,D8"

Range(addy).select

All of these examples have shown the range object taking one parameter (a range of cells). However, the range object can take up to two parameters. The previous example of selecting cells A1:C3 can be written like so:

Range("A1","C3").select

You may be wondering why you would want to do this over the previous example since it requires more typing. In this example, the first approach would make more sense. But this flexibility can be useful as you'll see later when I discuss the current region property.

It is important to note in all of these examples the select method has been consistently used. This is how you typically work in the Excel worksheet. You select the cell, or range of cells, you'd like to work with, and then you perform some action on that range (e.g. insert a value, insert a formula, etc.) Because this is how you work in Excel, people typically bring this line of thinking when they start working in VBA. However, it is not necessary to select ranges to work with them in VBA.

Because it is not necessary, selecting cells is actually discouraged when writing VBA code unless it's absolutely necessary (unnecessarily selecting cells will slow down your macros.) Let's look at the previous example, but instead of selecting those cells, let's give them the value of 5. A property we can use to assign values to a cell, or range of cells, is the value property. So if we wanted to assign a value of 5 to all of those cells, we could write the example like so:

Range("A1,B4,D8").value = 5

This will input the value of 5 into cells A1, B4, and D8 without doing any selecting. Since no selecting is done, this macro is faster than a macro that does do selecting since it has less instructions to execute.

Cell property: The cells property is similar to the range object in that it can be used to interact with cells in a worksheet. The cells property is not an object like the range object. It's actually a property of the worksheet object. One big difference between the cells property and the range object is that the cells property can only interact with one cell at a time. Another difference is how the cell reference is provided. The cells property has two arguments: One argument is required for the row, and another is required for the column. Selecting cell B3 in a range would be done like so:

cells(3,2).value = 5

In this example, the row parameter is provided first (3 in this case), and then the column parameter is provided a second (2 in this case.) Alternatively, the second argument in the cells property can use a column letter that's provided as a string. Here's the previous example, rewritten using a column letter:

Cells(3,"B").value = 5

Used range property: The used range property is useful for determining the range of non-empty cells in a worksheet. Unlike many of the previous examples we've discussed, it is not a property of the range or activecell objects, but of a sheet object. So, you can see the usedrange property of the worksheet Sheet1 like so:

Msgbox Worksheets("Sheet1").UsedRange.Address

The used range of a particular worksheet is determined by the upper-leftmost non-empty cell to the lower-rightmost non-empty cell. So, if you ran the previous macro, and only two cells in that sheet had values (e.g. A1 and E5) the previous macro would return A1:E5 in a messagebox.

When you want to use the usedrange property though, you can also invoke it on the activesheet object like so:

Msgbox activesheet.usedrange.address

If you used the activesheet object, one thing to note is that Excel does not provide intellisense whereas it does for the worksheets object. This is because Excel does not know what type of sheet the activesheet will be referring to until runtime. This is because the activesheet does not need to refer to a worksheet. The activesheet can also refer to a chart sheet for example. If that were the case, the previous macro would fail whereas it would not with worksheets.

One last thing to note is that, even though the cells between a used range may be empty, they're still included as cells in the range. In the previous example, using only cells A1 and E5 with values in the used range, only two cells have values. However, if you ran this macro:

Msgbox activesheet.usedrange.count

You'd see that it says that 25 cells are included in the used range. So, if you run a macro that processed all of the cells in a used range, it would be processing a lot of empty cells. This may not be an issue for a small group of cells like in this example. But let's say you had a used range with tens or hundreds of thousands of cells to process, with many of the cells being empty. In that case, using the used range would be very inefficient and the macro would likely be slow. There are a few strategies you can use to make the range in the used range more precise.

Chapter 3

If/Then Statements and Variables

Variables

The goal of this chapter is to teach you the easiest ways to initialize, declare and display different variables in VBA. Declaring a variable is the way you indicate to a given system that it should pay special attention to a given variable. Initializing is the name given to the process that assigns a primary value to a specific variable.

Naming variables: You're given freedom on how to name your variables, but there are some restrictions:

1. The first character in a variable name must be alphabetic

2. You can use alphabetic, numeric, and certain punctuation characters in VBA code

3. Variable names can be no longer than 254 characters

4. Certain words are classified as keywords and are not capable of being used as variable names.

Although these are not restrictions, here are a few other things to note about naming variables:

You can't write two different variables in VBA that differ only by case. If you create a variable named hw, and then later create a variable named HW, these variables will have the same value. This is important to note because some other languages allow this (e.g. C#).

Function names in VBA are not reserved keywords. So you can use the "left" name for the left function as a variable in VBA. It's recommended that you don't do this. If you do, you'll have to use vba.left to access the left function.

While you don't need to name your variables anything in particular, it's good practice to try to name them something appropriate for their purpose in your code so that others, or even yourself, can understand why you created them if they read your code. For example, assume you want a variable to represent the number 24. You can call this variable "b", but b in no way indicates why it's representing the value 24. You could also call it "hoursInADay" which is much more descriptive. This tells you that you're creating this variable because you want to represent the hours in a day.

Variable data types: All variables in VBA have a data type. VBA is known as a dynamically typed language. This means that you can either declare your own datatype or have VBA do it for you. If you don't declare a datatype, VBA will declare the datatype as variant and will try to make its best guess as to what datatype to assign it if a more specific one is available. However, this is not recommended for a few reasons:

By explicitly assigning a datatype, you can put restrictions on the types of data a variable will store. If you don't do this, the value of the datatype can be one you did not expect which can lead to bugs in your code.

One of the datatypes that VBA may try to use is the variant data type. The variant datatype is one of the largest datatypes in terms of bytes used in VBA. The variant datatype is large because it has the ability to handle any type of data. However, large use of the variant datatype can lead to poor performance. It's generally recommended NOT to use the variant datatype unless it's explicitly needed. (e.g. in variant arrays)

VBA supports several datatypes including the following categories:

Boolean: The Boolean (1 byte) datatype is a datatype that can store one of two values: True or False

Numeric: VBA supports a number of numeric datatypes such as Integer (2 bytes), Long (4 bytes), Single (4 bytes), and Double (8 bytes). These numeric datatypes differ by the range of values they can store. In these datatypes, an integer has the smallest range whereas double has the largest range. It's generally recommended that you use the smallest filesize capable of handing the range of numbers you want to use (or one above it.)

String: The string (10 bytes + string length) datatype can store text. So you can use the string datatype to store values like "Hello world"

Object: The object datatype is capable of storing any object reference

Variant: The variant (varies) datatype is capable of supporting many different values types, like string, numeric, etc.

Declaring a variable and assigning a type: To declare your variables, start by writing the "Dim" statement. You can write this anywhere in your procedure, but I tend to write mine on the first line in the procedure. To declare a datatype, you simply use the dim statement and the variable name like so:

    Dim hw

Although this variable is declared, it has not been given an explicit datatype. To give it an explicit datatype, you use the "as" statement and then its datatype like so:

    Dim hw as string

You only need one dim statement per line for your variable declarations. All variable datatypes in VBA must be explicitly named. VBA does not support declaring multiple variables with one datatype like so:

Dim a, b, d as string

Although all of these variables are declared, only d is given the datatype of string. The a and b variables have a datatype of variant. So to properly declare all of these variables as string, you have to write the procedure like so:

Dim a as string, b as string

Dim c as string

Forcing variable declaration (option explicit): VBA allows you to use variables and assign them values without declaring them. However, this is considered poor practice as it can lead to bugs in your code. It's generally recommended to turn on option explicit to force you to declare all of your variables. You can do this in the visual basic editor by going to Tools, options, and checking "Require variable declaration". If you turn this on, whenever you create a new module, the words "option explicit" will appear at the very top. You will get an error if you try to use any variable that you have not explicitly declared.

Determining a variable's type: Sometimes, it's useful to know what the type of a variable is. This can be very useful for both debugging and for using it in conditional execution statements. To find the datatype of a variable, you use the typename function and the variable name like so:

Dim a as string

Typename(a)

This will return the type of the variable (in this case, string)

Command button: The first thing you need to understand is that this process uses a command button which means in order for it to work properly you will need to insert one in your worksheet. To start, you will need to go to the Developer Tab prior to clicking on the Insert option. Next, you will need to locate the ActiveX control options prior to clicking on the selection titled Command Button. You can then drag the resulting button anywhere on the worksheet that you like.

At this point, the button won't be connected to a specific macro which means that it won't actually do much of anything. To link it to a given macro you will need to activate Design Mode. From there, you will want to right-click on the command button and then chose the option to View Code. Assuming this has been done correctly, this command should then open the Visual Basic Editor directly to the secion of code regarding the button. Next, you will need to locate the line that starts with Private Sub CommandButton1-Click () EndSub. In that space, you will want to enter the following: Range ("A1") .Value = "Hello:

Now, when you open the VBE a second window should also open that provides you with a variety of additional sheet names. This window is called Project Explorer and it will make it easier for you to see what sheet you are adding code to. If Project Explorer isn't automatically visible, you can find it in the view option by selecting the option for Project Explorer.

After you have entered the code you can then close the VBE, though you will need to save manually before doing so. The next step is to clear Design Mode and then click on the command button. Assuming the code was entered correctly the word Hello should now appear in the A1 cell of the current worksheet. Assuming everything worked properly that means you are now ready to move on to using more complex variables.

Integer variables: In order to store a variety of numbers for use at a later point you can use this code:

```
Dim x As Integer

z = 8

Range("B2").Value = z
```

The code above would then place the number 8 into the B2 cell. More specifically, the primary line of the code indicates a precise variable called Z in addition to the number 8. With that done, it will then initialize the value of x which is 6 as well as determine the location of the resulting equation which was A1. This means you will be able to change the range, integer, or value as needed. At the same time, an even more complicated formula for the button to solve could be included as well as variables from numerous cells as opposed to just one. You can also then add further variables as the need arises.

String variables: String variables come in handy when you need to store text instead of integers. Using the following code, for example:

```
Dim book As String

dog = "Labradoodle"

Range("A1").Value = dog
```

Would then add the word dog to A1. Additionally, if you had already used the word dog in a cell it would then be changed to Labradoodle. When you use this code you are declaring the first line which includes the string variable. The second line then indicates the variable as well as the additional change. When creating string variables it is important to keep in mind that quotation marks around the word are important. The final line will then indicate the new location for the variable in question.

Adding another variable: Doubling up on variables is useful when you need something more accurate than a single integer as it can store additional numbers after the decimal point. An example of this type of code would be:

Dim x As Integer

x = 6=2

MsgBox "value is " & z

Using this code would cause Excel to generate a dialogue box which will display the selected value of 6. This is not the correct answer, of course, which is why you need the double variable type beyond the standard integer type. To further make sure you generate the correct answer in this scenario you would want to write the code as:

Dim x As Double

x = 6.2

MsgBox "value is " & z

This code will let Excel know that it needs to check for a decimal place in addition to the primary integer and return the proper answer of 6.2. If you are looking to go past the first decimal point then you will need to use a long variable to do so. It is important that you use variables that are always of the right length in order to help your code run as smoothly as possible.

Boolean variable: In order to indicate a variable that can either be true or false, you will want to use a Boolean variable. An example of this type of code looks like:

Dim continue As Boolean

continue = True

> If continue = True Then MsgBox "Boolean variables are cool"

Assuming it is written correctly, this code will then create a dialog box that expresses the proven fact that Boolean variables are cool. The first like of this code declares a Boolean Variable which is then initialized with a true value and the only Boolean variable is then utilized to help display the message correctly assuming the variables is considered true.

Statement types

If/then statements: An if/then statement is especially useful if you want a given line of code to activate only when specific conditions are met. In order to ensure this happens successfully, you will want to start by creating a button before then connecting it to the following code.

```
Dim score As Integer, result As String

score = Range("B3").Value


If score >= 70 Then result = "pass"


Range("B3").Value = result
```

The end result here is that if the score ends up being 70 or above it will be automatically labeled as a pass. This means if the integer in the first cell is 80 then pressing the button will add the word pass to the next cell over. As written the cells that are less than 70 would remain blank, though you can add an additional result written as < 60 = fail to have the word fail be displayed by those that did not pass.

Else statements: While secondary results can be added using the method above, an even easier way of doing so is by using an else statement which looks like so:

```
Dim score As Integer, result As String

score = Range("A1").Value

If score >= 70 Then

    result = "pass"

Else

    result = "fail"

End If

Range("B1").Value = result
```

This will, in turn, make it possible to assign a value of pass to the appropriate cells in the range that are above the determined value and a value of fail to the rest. It is important to keep in mind that this will only really work if there is an additional line of code after the portion of the statement and also if the statement doesn't contain any additional Else sections. If this ends up being the case then you can successfully add code to the line directly beneath the then statement as well as omit the End If line. This will, however, require that you start on a new line after the Else and then and also make sure you place the End line in the new appropriate location.

Chapter 4

Looping

Looping is an immensely useful programming technique that will make it possible for you to run through several ranges quickly while only requiring the addition of a small amount of extra code.

Single loop: The first type of loop, the single loop, can be sued to easily move through ranges of cells that are one-dimensional. An example of this can be connected to the command button with the following code:

```
Dim i As Integer


For j = 2 To 7

    Cells(j, 1).Value = 75

Next i
```

Assuming everything is written properly, pressing the button at this junction will place the integer (75) in J2 – J7. This occurs because the line of code between For and Next is then executed five additional times. The first time that J = 1, the VBA knows to place the integer 75 into the cell where the column and row meet one another. From there, you will need for the VBA to hit the second j in order to increase the amount by 1 and thus reset everything to the For statement. Next, when j = 2, the VBA then provides a value in the form of 75 into the cell that exists at the next point where the row and column intersect. This then continues for all of the various cells and rows between 2 and 7. While this is not expressly required, with this type of code you are going to need to be in the habit of indenting to keep things as legible as possible. Specifically, this will comes into play between the words For and Next as this should make things easier to read when it comes time to find errors.

Double loop: A double loop is, as the name implies, a loop that makes a movement through a full two-dimensional cell range. In order to use one, you can use the following code and attach it to your command button:

```
Dim j As Integer, k As Integer


For j = 2 To 7
    For k = 1 To 2
        Cells(j, k).Value = 75
    Next k
Next j
```

Assuming everything has been done correctly you will then find that this fills rows 2 – 7 of the columns k and j with the number 75. This code can then tell the VBA that when j = 2 and k =1 then it needs to enter 75 wherever the two meet initially, from there, it increases by 1 before returning to For in the k statement. Next, when j = 2 and k =2 then VBA knows to place 75 where they intersect again. Based on the code, the VBA will then ignore j moving forward as it will only be running between 1 and 2. This is then repeated until the VBA has run through all of the j columns that meet the desired criteria.

Triple loop: A triple loop is much the same as a double loop with the exception that it works across numerous worksheets. In order to use one effectively, you can use the following code:

```
Dim d As Integer, j As Integer, k As Integer

For d = 2 To 4

    For j = 2 To 7

        For k = 2 To 3

            Worksheets(d).Cells(j, k).Value = 75

        Next k

    Next j

Next d
```

When comparing this to the double loop code, the biggest difference you should see comes in the form of the variety of worksheets being used thanks to (Worksheets(c)). It is important to place it before Cells in order to properly ensure the first sheet has a two-dimensional range when it comes to c = 1, c = 2 for the second sheet and c = 4 on the third.

Do while loop: The loops listed above are what are known as For Next loops, another type of loop is the Do While Loop which can be used to make a given action repeat indefinitely as long as the process as a whole remains true. You can try one yourself like so:

```
Dim i As Integer

J = 2


Do While j < 7
```

```
Cells(j, 2).Value = 25

    j = j + 1

Loop
```

With the code inserted properly into the command button, you will find that the number 25 is placed in the cells of the given rows. This works by looking for a j that is less than 7, in any instance where this is the case then the VBA will know to place 25 in the cell instead. When working with VBA, the = symbol means "becomes" rather than "equals". This means that j = j +1 is akin to the point where j becomes j + 1 or if the value of j is increased by 1. For example, if j = 1, j really becomes 1 + 1 = 2. This means that integer 25 will be adding into the column as many times as possible until j equals 7.

Now for a more advanced example, assume that you entered the integers 27, 35, 56, 59, 85 and 84 into the first six cells of column A. Next, place the following code into your command button:

```
Dim i As Integer

    j = 1


Do While Cells(j, 1).Value <> ""

    Cells(j, 2).Value = Cells(j, 1).Value + 10

    j = j + 1

Loop
```

When done properly this should generate date within the first six lines of the column in question using the number 94, 69, 95, 66, 45, 37. The reason that this is the case is that for the length of time that the j and 1 cells value is not empty (<> is short for not equal to(, then the VBA will enter the value into the cell at the point where the column and the various rows intersect. The number that is entered is then ultimately going to be greater than 10 above the value of the cell at the relative point on the column/row intersection. Furthermore, the VBA will then stop auto-filling when j equals 7 as this is where the future cells will begin to empty. This process can then be used to generate a loop that is used for generating an almost limitless number of rows for a specific worksheet.

Chapter 5

Additional Tools

Autofilters

Creating the Autofilter: Creating an autofilter is extremely simple. You'll either need to have a header row or create one before proceeding. The following example creates an autofilter in the modules parent workbook on the first sheet from columns A to H.

```
Sub CreateFilter()

    With ThisWorkbook.Sheets(1)

        .Range("A1:H1").AutoFilter

    End With
```

'or simply

```
        ThisWorkbook.Sheets(1).Range("A1:H1").AutoFilter

    End Sub
```

Filter the Autofilter: You can filter any column of data by anything contained in the column. If you filter it by a value that is not contained in the column, it will simply filter everything out and you'll be left with only the header. In the following example, you will see the table filtered by a known value. Assume it's the table that was created in the above example.

```
Sub FilterATable()


With ThisWorkbook.Sheets(1).Range("A1")


    .AutoFilter Field:=1, Criteria1:="yes"

    .AutoFilter Field:=2, Criteria1:="blue", _

        Operator:=xlOr, Criteria2:="red"


End With


End Sub
```

Notice here that the column has been filtered "A" for "yes" by choosing Field:= 1 and Criteria1:= "yes". Similarly, in the next line, the column has been filtered "B" for "blue" and "red". As you see above, an "Operator" has to be used to filter a column for more than one item and each subsequent criteria has to be followed with a number; first criteria is "Criteria1", second is "Criteria2" and so on.

The "Operator" is simple stating "I want to filter items that are "red" OR "blue". The most important thing to take from this example is that the range object only needs to specify a single cell in the header.

Autofilter with Variables: Here's where we can do some interesting things by integrating dictionaries into our macro. The situation is that you need to do multiple filters and do calculations with each set of filters i.e. you need to do some sums for each item category for each month. If you have 30 item categories and two months you're already at 60 manual filters and if you need to do 4 sums per filter, you can do the math. Check out the example:

```
Sub DataToDash()


    Dim oRow As Long

    Dim i As Integer

    Dim oCell As Range

    Dim oWB As Workbook, xWB As Workbook

    Dim oDict, oItem, oKey, xDict, xKey, errChk


    Set oWB = Workbooks("Your Book")

    Set oDict = CreateObject("scripting.dictionary")

    Set xDict = CreateObject("scripting.dictionary")


    With oWB.Sheets("Your Sheet")

        oRow = .UsedRange.Rows.Count
```

```vba
For Each oCell In .Range("A2:A" & oRow)

    oDict(oCell.Value) = 1

Next oCell


For Each oCell In .Range("B2:B" & oRow)

    xDict(oCell.Value) = 1

Next oCell


i = 1

For Each xKey In xDict

    .Range("A1").AutoFilter _

        Field:=2, _

        Criteria1:=xKey

    For Each oKey In oDict.keys

        .Range("A1").AutoFilter _

            Field:=1, _

            Criteria1:=oKey


        On Error GoTo next1

        errChk =
Application.WorksheetFunction.Sum(.Range("D2:D" &
oRow).SpecialCells(xlCellTypeVisible))
```

```
        On Error GoTo 0


        .Range("A" & oRow + i) = oKey

        .Range("B" & oRow + i) = xKey

        .Range("C" & oRow + i) = "Top 25"

        .Range("D" & oRow + i) =
Application.WorksheetFunction.Sum(.Range("D2:D" &
oRow).SpecialCells(xlCellTypeVisible))

        .Range("F" & oRow + i) =
Application.WorksheetFunction.Sum(.Range("F2:F" &
oRow).SpecialCells(xlCellTypeVisible))

        .Range("G" & oRow + i) =
Application.WorksheetFunction.Sum(.Range("G2:G" &
oRow).SpecialCells(xlCellTypeVisible))

        .Range("E" & oRow + i).FormulaR1C1 = "=RC[1]/RC[-1]"


        For Each oCell In .Range("H2:H" & oRow + i -
1).SpecialCells(xlCellTypeVisible)

            oCell = oCell.Offset(0, -4) / .Range("D" & oRow + i)

        Next oCell

        i = i + 1

next1:

        Next oKey

      Next xKey

    End With
```
45

The basic concept here is to create a "Top 25" (luckily all of the accounts in these reports are top 25 accounts so we don't worry about filtering out non-top 25 accounts) category in the "National Account Name" column that does multiple sums for each "Item cat 1" per "Year/Month". This issue, then, is that we don't know how many or what item categories we have and we don't know how many months the data spans.

The simplest way to find out what we're dealing with is to roll these columns into a dictionary and see what unique values we're left with. That's exactly what the first part of this macro does, it finds unique "Item cat 1" and "Year/Month" values. Once we have these, all we have to do is loop the "Item cat 1" values inside of the "Year/Month".

Manipulating tables can be extremely time consuming and there's no reason why you shouldn't automate calculations that you need to do on a regular basis. By utilizing the Range.Autofilter method it allows you to write code that does not have to take the whole dataset into consideration when attempting to do calculations.

Collections

Collections are not only easy to use but can be utilized in a wide variety of applications. When you discover collections and the power they have, it will change your approach to VBA drastically.

Declaring & Setting: Declare a collection simply:

      Dim aCollection As Collection

Setting a collection is just as simple:

      Set aCollection = New Collection

The neat thing about collections is you can dim & set at the same time:

Dim aCollection as New Collection

Adding/Removing from a Collection: Adding to a collection is quite simple and it involves Items and Keys. To add an item with a key:

aCollection.Add aItem, aKey

Keys are not necessary and for most applications will not be used:

aCollection.Add aItem

It's important to note that you can add any variable type to a collection. this includes ranges, sheets, books, and files.

In the same way remove from:

aCollection.Remove aKey

aCollection.Remove(index number)

Remove everything:

aCollection = nothing

or

Set aCollection = New Collection

Looping Through a Collection

For Each Item in aCollection

   Debug.Print Item

Next Item

For i = 1 to aCollection.Count

   Debug.Print aCollection(i)

Next i

Find something and perform an action

```vba
Sub Find_Add_DoSomething()

    Dim Type_Match As Range

    Dim Match_Collection As New Collection

    Dim First_Address As String

    With Sheets("Your Sheet").Range("Your Range")

        Set Type_Match = .Find("Your Find", , , xlWhole)

        If Not Type_Match Is Nothing Then

            First_Address = Type_Match.Address

                Do

                    Match_Collection.Add Type_Match

                    Set Type_Match = .FindNext(Type_Match)

                Loop    While    Not    Type_Match    Is    Nothing    And
Type_Match.Address <> First_Address

        End If

    End With

    For Each Item In Match_Collection

    'Do something to each item

    'Ex. Rows(Item.Row).Hidden = True

    Next
```

End Sub

Dig through folder/subfolder/files

Dim fso, oFolder, oSubfolder, oFile, queue As Collection

```
    Set fso = CreateObject("Scripting.FileSystemObject")

    Set queue = New Collection

    queue.Add fso.GetFolder("C:\test")


    Do While queue.Count > 0

        Set oFolder = queue(1)

        queue.Remove 1
    '....insert folder processing here....

        For Each oSubfolder In oFolder.SubFolders

        queue.Add oSubfolder

        Next oSubfolder


        For Each oFile In oFolder.Files
    '....insert file processing here....

        Next oFile

    Loop


End Sub
```

Dictionaries

A dictionary, like a collection, is a powerful tool to have in your VBA toolbox. Dictionaries are similar to collections and although a dictionary is a bit more complicated to manipulate than a collection, dictionaries offer some unique properties that are advantageous over collections like .keys, .items, and unique keys.

Declaring and Setting: Because dictionaries are not in the standard VBA library, a connection has to be made to the library. This can be done in two ways: late binding, and early binding.

Late binding is the easiest way to create a dictionary. This can be done in two ways:

With CreateObject("scripting.dictionary")

   .Add Key, Item

End With

or

Set dictNew = CreatObject("scripting.dictionary")

dictNew(Key) = Item

In both examples, the item is added with a key into the dictionary.

To use early binding it is required that you activate "Microsoft Scripting runtime" in the Tools-References tab. After this, declaring and setting becomes standard.

Dim dictNew as Dictionary

Set dictNew = New Dictionary

or

Dim dictNew as New Dictionary

Adding/Removing: To add an item/key pair to the dictionary

Set dictNew = CreateObject("scripting.dictionary")

dictNew(KeyAsVariable) = ItemAsVariable

or

dictNew("KeyAsString") = "ItemAsString"

of course you can mix and match AsVariable/"AsString"

It is important to note that a key can only be entered once in a dictionary. If you add a key/item pair with a non-unique key, the original item will be written over.

To remove a key/item pair: Set dictNew = CreateObject("scripting.dictionary")

dictNew.Remove KeyAsVariable

or

dictNew.Remove "KeyAsString"

CompareMode property of the Dictionary: This can only be set when the Dictionary is empty but allows you to control how the Dictionary accepts keys.

Dim dictNew As Dictionary

Set dictNew = New Dictionary

' Compare new key with existing keys based on a binary match. Essentially, case sensitive

dictNew.CompareMode = vbBinaryCompare

51

```
dictNew("Donut").Add "Sprinkles"

dictNew("donut").Add "Chocolate Glaze"

dictNew("donuT").Add "Maple Walnut"

' Remove all keys

dictNew.RemoveAll

' Set the CompareMode to Text. Case inSensITiVe. Donut ==
DONUT == donUt == dONUt

dictNew.CompareMode = vbTextCompare

dictNew("Donut").Add "Sprinkles"

' ERROR! Duplicate key

dictNew("donut").Add "Chocolate Glaze"

' ERROR! Duplicate key

dictNew("donuT").Add "Maple Walnut"
```

You can also test if an item Exists in a Dictionary, which you cannot do as easily in a Collection

```
If dictNew.Exists("Donuts") Then Call EatEmAll(dictNew)

Sub EatEmAll(ByRef someDict)

    someDict.RemoveAll

End Sub
```

To do the same with a Collection

```
Set existsInColl = someColl("Donuts")

    If existsInColl = Nothing Then
```

```vba
        Call BuyDonuts(someColl)

    End If


    Sub BuyDonuts(ByRef someColl)

    someColl.Add 12, "Donuts"

    End Sub
```

Examples: This first example splits a notes section into 25 character sections while retaining the index number for each split up string and then prints the newly formatted data onto the sheet. The index number is in column A, comments in column B.

```vba
Sub String_Split()

    Set dictNew = CreateObject("scripting.dictionary")

    For Each cell In Range("B1:B" &
Range("B1").End(xlDown).Row)

        For i = 1 To Len(cell) Step 25

        dictNew(Mid(cell, i, 25)) = cell.Offset(0, -1)

        Next i

    Next cell

    Range(Cells(1, 3), Cells(dictNew.Count, 3)).Value =
Application.Transpose(dictNew.Items)

    Range(Cells(1, 4), Cells(dictNew.Count, 4)).Value =
Application.Transpose(dictNew.Keys)

    Set dictNew = Nothing

End Sub
```

This second example creates a dictionary with the values in column A excluding duplicate values because they are set as the keys. It then sums all the values in the adjacent column and prints the unique values along with their summed values.

```
Sub Take_The_Cake()

    Dim rngAdd As Range

    Dim intSum As Integer

    Dim strAddress As String

    Set dicNew = CreateObject("scripting.dictionary")

    For Each cell In Range("A1:A" & Range("A1").End(xlDown).Row)

        dicNew(cell.Value) = 1

    Next cell


    For Each Key In dicNew.Keys
        With Sheets(1).Columns("A")
            Set rngAdd = .Find(Key, , , xlWhole)
            If Not rngAdd Is Nothing Then
                strAddress = rngAdd.Address
                Do
                    intSum = intSum + rngAdd.Offset(0, 1)
                    Set rngAdd = .FindNext(rngAdd)
```

```vba
        Loop While Not rngAdd Is Nothing And rngAdd.Address
<> strAddress

            dicNew(Key) = intSum

            intSum = 0

        End If

    End With

  Next Key


  Range(Cells(1, 3), Cells(dicNew.Count, 3)).Value =
Application.Transpose(dicNew.Keys)

  Range(Cells(1, 4), Cells(dicNew.Count, 4)).Value =
Application.Transpose(dicNew.Items)

  Set dicNew = Nothing

End Sub
```

Chapter 6

Errors to Watch out for While Debugging

You might find some problems with your VBA code, but how can you debug the error? There are cases that your VBA code may require you to debug. Error handling refers to a code that you write to handle some of these errors when your application is running. These errors can occur as a result of missing a file, invalid data, a missing database, and many other reasons.

If you have a feeling that an error may occur at a given point in your code, it is advised to write a specific code that can handle the error when it shoots up.

Other VBA errors one can apply a generic code to handle them. This the time when the VBA error handling statement is important. It will enable an application to handle any error that is not expected.

To understand how to debug VBA errors, one must first know the different types of errors that exist in VBA.

Errors in VBA

The three types of errors in VBA include:

1. Compilation errors

2. Runtime errors

3. Syntax errors

Error handling is used to debug runtime errors. Let's now discuss each of these errors so that it becomes clear to everyone what a runtime error is.

Syntax errors

In VBA programming, if you type a line and press return, VBA will determine the syntax and in case it is not correct it will show an error message. For instance, when a user types an if statement and forgets to include the Then keyword, VBA will show the following error message.

Other examples of syntax errors include:

• Missing a right parenthesis i.e. c = left ("ABCD", 1)

• Missing an equal after I i.e. For i 4 to 8

Syntax errors are associated with one line alone. It occurs when the syntax of one-line is wrong. However, if you don't want to see the syntax errors, you can still switch off the Syntax error dialog box by navigating to Tools>Options and check off "Auto Syntax Check". This means that the line with a syntax error will appear red but the dialog box won't show up.

Compilation errors

Compilation errors will happen in multiple lines. The syntax is correct on a single line but wrong when the entire code is examined. Some examples of compilation errors include:

- A For without Next

- Calling a Function that does not exist

- Calling a Function using the wrong parameters

- Assigning a Function similar name to a module

- An if statement that does not have an End If statement

- Undeclared variables appearing at the top of a module

The screenshot below demonstrates a compilation error when a For loop does not have a matching Next statement.

The Debug> Compile

If you want to identify compilation errors, the Debug > Compile VBA Project from the Visual Basic menu is important.

Once you select Debug>Compile, VBA will show the first error that it comes across. If the error is fixed, run the Compile again for VBA to determine the next error.

The Debug> Compile also has a syntax error in its search that is very important.

If there are no more errors left when the Debug> Compile runs, it might look like nothing has happened. But "Compile" will show up in the Debug menu. In this case, the application does not have compilation errors at the current time.

The Debug> Compile Usage

It is a good practice to always use the Debug>Compile before you can run your code. This will make sure that your code does not have compilation errors when you run it.

However, failing to run Debug>Compile means that VBA might come across compile errors when it runs. Don't confuse this with Runtime errors.

Runtime errors

As the name suggests, runtime errors happen when the application is running. These are the type of errors which you have no control. Runtime errors occur as a result of errors in your code.

For instance, assume that your application is going to read from an external workbook. If this file is deleted, VBA will shoot up an error when the code attempts to open it. Other examples of runtime errors include:

- A user typing invalid data

- A cell with a text instead of a number

- A missing database

Expected and Unexpected Errors

When you have a feeling that a runtime error may occur, it is important to write a code in place to handle it. For example, a code is always written to deal with a missing file. The code below first determines if the code is available before it opens it. If the file is missing, a message is displayed to the user before the code exits.

```vba
Sub OpenFile()

    Dim sFile As String
    sFile = "C:\docs\data.xlsx"

    ' Use Dir to check if file exists
    If Dir(sFile) = "" Then
        ' if file does not exist display message
        MsgBox "Could not find the file " & sFile
        Exit Sub
    End If

    ' Code will only reach here if file exists
    Workbooks.Open sFile

End Sub
```

Therefore, if you think that an error is likely to happen at some point, it is advised to add a code to deal with the situation. This kind of errors is referred to as expected errors. If there is no specific code that can deal with the error, it is considered an unexpected error. VBA error handling statements are important to use to deal with the errors.

The On Error Statement

So far you have learned the two ways you can treat runtime errors.

1. Write specific code to handle expected errors

2. Use VBA error handling statements to deal with unexpected errors

The VBA On Error statement is important to use to handle errors. This statement shoots a response when an error appears during runtime.

There are four different ways that one can use this statement

1. **The On Error Resume Next**. This code moves to the next line. There is no error message that appears.

2. **The On Error Goto-1.** This will clear the current error.

3. **The Error Goto 0-** This code will stop at the line with the error and display a message.

4. **The On Error Goto[label]-**This code moves to a particular line or label.

There is no error message that is displayed. This is mostly used for error handling.

Let's examine each of the above statements briefly

On Error Goto 0

This is the default response of VBA. Anyone who doesn't use On Error will see this response.

Once an error has happened, VBA will stop on the line that has the error and display the error message. Therefore, the application will need some user interaction with the code before it can resume. This may involve fixing the error or restarting the application. In this case, there is no error handling that happens.

Let's now look at an example:

In the code shown below, there is no On Error line applied. This means that VBA is going to use On Error Goto O response by default.

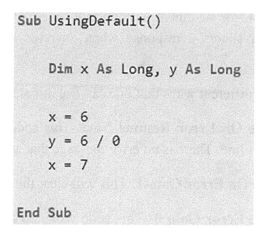

```
Sub UsingDefault()

    Dim x As Long, y As Long

    x = 6
    y = 6 / 0
    x = 7

End Sub
```

The second assignment line is a divide by zero error. If this code runs, an error message will show up on the screen as shown below:

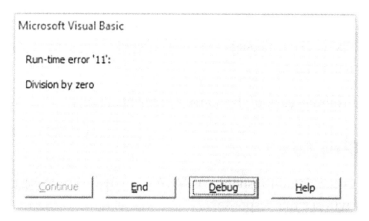

When this error shows up, you can either choose to end or debug. If you click End, the application terminates. On the other hand, if you click Debug, the application highlights the error line as shown below:

```
(General)

    Option Explicit

    Sub UsingDefault()

        Dim x As Long, y As Long

        x = 6
⇨       y = 6 / 0
        x = 7

    End Sub
```

This type of response is good when you are writing your VBA code because it highlights the exact line with an error. However, this is not suitable for applications that are created for users. They appear unprofessional and make an application unsuitable. This kind of error results in the application crashing. A user cannot continue without first restarting the application. In this case, users will not be able to use the application until the error is fixed.

But using the **On Error [label]** gives the user a more controlled error message. Furthermore, it prevents the application from stopping. This means that it is possible to force the application to behave in a given way.

The On Error Resume Next

The On Error Resume Next makes the VBA ignore the error and continue.

There are certain occasions when this is important. In most cases, you need to avoid using it. Adding Resume Next in the previous example causes VBA to ignore the divide by zero error.

```
Sub UsingResumeNext()

    On Error Resume Next

    Dim x As Long, y As Long

    x = 6
    y = 6 / 0
    x = 7

End Sub
```

Even though this makes VBA ignore the divide by zero, it is not advised to do this. If you choose to ignore the error, then the response may be unpredictable. The error is likely to affect the application in many different ways. Therefore, you could end up with the wrong data. Another thing is that you will not be aware that something has gone wrong because of suppressing the error.

The On Error Go to [label]

This is the correct way to handle errors in VBA. It is equivalent to Try and Catch function in C# and Java language. If an error happens, the error is sent to a specific label. This often appears at the bottom of the sub. Let's use this in the example:

```
Sub UsingGotoLine()


    On Error Goto eh


    Dim x As Long, y As Long


    x = 6
    y = 6 / 0
    x = 7


Done:
    Exit Sub
eh:
    MsgBox "The following error occurred: " & Err.Description
End Sub
```

Below is what happens when an error takes place.

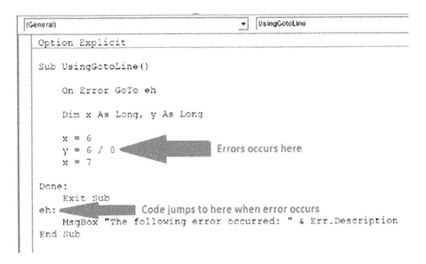

VBA shifts to eh because it has been specified in the On Error Goto line.

Note

1. The label that you apply in the On...Goto statement should be in the current Function. If it misses, a compilation error will occur.

2. If an error happens when the On Error Goto[label] is applied, the error handling picks up the default behavior. The code will remain on the line with the error and show the error message.

The On Error Goto-1

This is a different statement from the ones discussed previously. Usually, it clears the current error instead of setting a particular behavior.

When an error happens while using On Error Goto[label], the error handling routine returns to the default response. This means that when a different error happens, the code will appear on the current line.

This response only happens to the current sub. The moment the sub is exited; the error is automatically cleared.

Using On Error

So far you have learned that VBA will perform any of the following three things when an error happens.

1. Jump to a specific line

2. Ignore the error and continue

3. Stop and show the error

VBA will always assume any of the above situations. If you use On Error, VBA will change to the behavior that you specified and forget any previous action.

The Err Object

When an error takes place, you can review the details of the error using the Err object. If a runtime error happens, VBA will automatically fill the Err object with the details. To debug an error using Err. Study the screenshot below:

```
Sub UsingErr()

    On Error Goto eh

    Dim total As Long
    total = "aa"

Done:
    Exit Sub
eh:
    Debug.Print "Error number: " & Err.Number _
                & " " & Err.Description
End Sub
```

Err. Description: This contains the details of the error. This is the text that you will see when an error happens.

Err. Number: This is the ID number of the error. The time that you need this is when you are searching for a specific error.

Err. Source: The source will display the object name.

Get a Line number

The Erl function is perfect for displaying the number where the error happened. In the code below, Erl will return zero.

```
Sub UsingErr()

    On Error Goto eh

    Dim val As Long
    val = "aa"

Done:
    Exit Sub
eh:
    Debug.Print Erl
End Sub
```

There are no line numbers in this code, and that is why it displays zero. Many people aren't aware that with VBA, you can use line numbers.

The Err. Raise

This will allow one to create errors. You can use it to define custom errors for the application. It is similar to the Throw statement in Java and C#.

It has the following format:

```
Err.Raise [error number], [error source], [error description]
```

The Err. Clear

This is used to clear text and numbers from the Err. Object. In short, it clears the number and description. It is rare that you may need to use this in your VBA.

Simple Debugging Strategy in VBA

VBA has countless ways that you can debug an error. This means that it is easy to get confused about the type of error handling to apply in VBA. This section provides you with a simple error debugging strategy that you can apply in all your applications.

A basic implementation

1. Place the On Error Goto Label line at the beginning of the top sub

2. Place the Error Handling Label at the end of the top Sub

3. When an expected error happens, handle it and continue.

4. If the application cannot continue, use Err. Raise and jump to the error handling label

5. When an unexpected error happens, the code will jump to the error handling label.

The flowchart below shows how this happens:

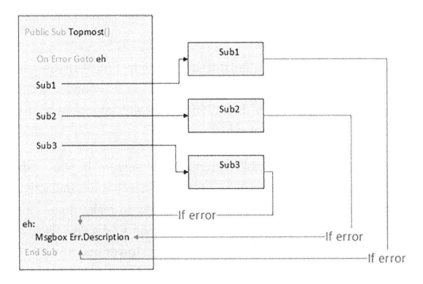

Chapter 7

Easy Mistakes To Avoid

When you program with VBA, it is easy to find yourself making mistakes. Most of these mistakes can cost you a lot. You will lose a lot of time as well as get frustrated. There are a lot of mistakes made in VBA code. If you go to forums such as CodeReview and StackOverflow, you will see many incidences of VBA code with mistakes. Usually, these mistakes are the same but committed with different people. Below are some of the common mistakes made by VBA programmers.

1. Use. select/. Activate

Did you know that it is not a must to apply? Select or. Activate? In fact, the reason why people use it is that they see it produced when you use the Macro Recorder. But, 99.9% it is not important to use it. Why? Here are two reasons why?

- It causes the workbook to repaint the screen. If you write Sheets ("Sheet1"). Activate, suppose Sheet1 is not the active worksheet, it means that Excel will have to make it so. This will result in Excel redrawing the screen to display Sheet1. This is inefficient and might result in a slower macro.

- It makes the user to get confused because they manipulate the workbook while they use it. Other users can think that they are getting hacked.

The only moment and occasion when you may need to use. Select or. Activate is when you want to direct your user to a particular worksheet. If not, delete any line of code that has these. It is doing more harm than good.

2. Failing to use Application. ScreenUpdating=False

When you make changes to a cell, Excel has to update/repaint the screen to display the changes. This can definitely slow down your macro than the way it is supposed to be. The next time you are creating a macro, try and add the following VBA lines:

```
Public Sub MakeCodeFaster()
    Application.ScreenUpdating = False

    ' do some stuff

    ' Always remember to reset this setting back!
    Application.ScreenUpdating = True
End Sub
```

3. Failing to Qualify a Range Reference

One of the most popular bugs that people find that can be very painful to debug happens when the VBA code does not fully qualify the range reference. To understand what tot qualifying a range reference means, consider this code Range("A1"). What worksheet does it refer to?

Well, it points to the ActiveSheet. This is the worksheet that is currently seen by the user.

In most cases, this is harmless. But as time goes, you add more features into your VBA code and it takes a longer time to process. This means that when you run the code and click on a different worksheet, you will find unexpected behavior. This example may look contrived, but it demonstrates the point.

```
Public Sub FullyQualifyReferences()
    Dim fillRange As Range

    Set fillRange = Range("A1:B5")

    Dim cell As Range

    For Each cell In fillRange
        Range(cell.Address) = cell.Address
        Application.Wait (Now + TimeValue("0:00:01"))
        DoEvents
    Next cell
End Sub
```

If you use Range () and forget to highlight the worksheet, Excel will assume it is the active sheet. So, the way to avoid this is by fully qualifying the worksheet. You can change this part of the code:

Range (Cell. Address) = cell. Address to Data. Range (cell. Address) = cell. Address

4. Use the Variant Type

Another common VBA mistake is thinking that you are using one Type but the truth is that you have another one. If you look at the code below, would you say that a, b, and c belong to type Long?

Dim a, b, c, as Long

However, they aren't. In fact, a and b are of type Variant. This means that they can be of any type as well as a change from one type to another.

Any variable of type Variant is risky because it has been found to make it difficult to debug an application in VBA. It is important to avoid using Variant variables so that you don't make critical mistakes. There are certain functions which need Variant and you may not have any other option but to use them. However, if you can avoid using Variant types, it will save you time and cost to debug.

5. Reference a worksheet name using a String

It is normal to see people making a reference to a worksheet name in VBA by using a string. You can take a look at the following code:

```
Public Sub SheetReferenceExample()
    Dim ws As Worksheet

    Set ws = Sheets("Sheet1")
    Debug.Print ws.Name
End Sub
```

It looks like it has no issues, right?

Well, let's now assume that you submit your workbook to an accountant. The accountant decides to change the "Sheet1" to give it a more meaningful name such as "Report". Once the worksheet name is changed, the accountant attempts to run the macros using Sheets("Sheet1") and they find out that it doesn't work.

A simple way to fix this problem is to reference the sheet via the object directly, instead of doing it via Sheets collection. If you look in the VBE project window, you will see worksheets and correct names.

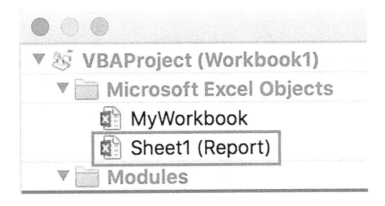

The name of the sheet that people see in Excel is "Report" and the name of the object that you can reference in VBA is Sheet1. Let's now update this code.

Now the sheet name is updated. What you can use is Sheet1 instead of Sheets("Sheet1").

But, what if one wants to make the name look meaningful? What if you want sheet1 to describe its action? Once Sheet1 was renamed to Report, it is a requirement to update the VBA code.

6. Make your Sub / Function Very Long

One rule of thumb is that if your function is very long such that one must scroll to see it, then you need to organize your VBA code. It is important to ensure that both the Sub and Function are short by creating sub procedures and helper functions.

7. Move Down the nested for / If Rabbit Hole

It is not a good practice to have a longer nesting. More than 3+ levels of nesting are considered long.

Whether you are a VBA guru who develops dashboards in Excel, or new to VBA, you only know how to write simple scripts that perform basic cell calculations, by learning the above mistakes increases the odds of writing a clean and bug-free code.

Conclusion

Thanks for making it through to the end of *Excel VBA: A Step-By-Step Tutorial For Beginners To Learn Excel VBA Programming From Scratch*, let's hope it was informative and able to provide you with all of the tools you need to achieve your goals, whatever it is that they may be. Just because you've finished this book doesn't mean there is nothing left to learn on the topic, and expanding your horizons is the only way to find the mastery you seek.

While much of what you have read in the proceeding chapters likely seems confusing now, never fear, with practice your skill with VBA will grow and you will find that you are able to automate a wide variety of useful tasks with ease. Don't forget, there is a reason that VBA is called a programming *language* as like any other language it is important to start slowly and take things one step at a time. As such, learning VBA is much like a marathon as opposed to a sprint which means slow and steady win the race every time.

Finally, if you found this book useful in anyway, a review on Amazon is always appreciated!

Excel VBA

Intermediate Lessons in Excel VBA
Programming for Professional
Advancement

Introduction

Thank you for purchasing the book, '*Excel VBA - Intermediate Lessons in Excel VBA Programming for Professional Advancement.*'

Excel VBA is an extremely helpful way to automate a routine task like copying data, creating your functions to reduce manual effort and increase productivity. When you use VBA, you can manipulate and customize data that is present in an Excel sheet. If you have read my previous book, you will have gathered some information on what VBA is. You would have learned about the different variables in VBA and data types, and how you can use them.

In this book, we will go one step further and focus on some important aspects of VBA. When you use VBA in Excel, you must also learn how to source data from one workbook to another without having to open the file. You also need to know more about working with loops and conditional statements. These statements make it easier to simplify iterative tasks. If you are eager to learn more about these aspects of VBA, you have come to the right place. Along with the points mentioned above, you will also learn about how you can manipulate strings and handle errors.

There are many examples given across the book that will help you understand the concepts better. Practice these examples before you begin to write your own code. You must remember that practice will make you a better programmer.

I hope you will find all the information you were looking for.

Chapter One

VBA, A Primer

Microsoft Office products like PowerPoint, Word, Outlook, FrontPage, Visio, Access, Project, Excel and some other third-party programs support VBA. If you have Microsoft Office on your device, you have VBA. VBA works similarly on all Microsoft products except for Access. The differences only relate to the specific objects of every application. For example, if you are using a spreadsheet object, you can only use it in Excel. VBA is currently based on VB 6.0, but there is a possibility that the future releases will migrate towards .net.

The focus of this book is how you can use VBA in Excel. VBA enhances the use of Excel by providing valuable features that you will not find with Excel formulas.

Macro Recorder

You can write macros in VBA in the same way that you would write a code in VB. The concepts of structures, variables, expressions, subprocedures, etc. are the same for both VB and VBA. The problem with VBA is that you will need to refer to every object you are writing a code for. For example, if you were writing a code for a specific cell in a worksheet, you would need to refer to that specific cell in your code. You are often unaware of what the names of these objects are and the attributes that you can control. The Macro Recorder solves this problem.

The macro recorder helps you develop a new macro in Excel quickly and easily. You must start the recorder and perform the necessary actions. The macro recorder will write the code for you. Alternatively, you can also run the VBA editor, which will allow you to insert a new module. This will give you a blank sheet on which you can write your macro. If you have already written the macro, you do not have to insert a new module. You will only need to add code to an existing module.

You will need to make some changes to the code written by the macro recorder. This is important to do when you need to change the cell references from absolute to relative or when you need the user form to interact with the user. If you have read the earlier version of the book, you will be familiar with VBA in Excel and some of the syntaxes and structures. Additionally, you must understand the differences between relative and absolute addressing.

VBA is different from VB in the sense that it is not a standalone language. VBA can only run through another product. For example, every VBA application you write in Excel can only run within Excel. This means that you will need to run Excel, then load the macro, after which the compiler will execute the macro. The VBA applications are all stored in the spreadsheet that they were written in. You can also store VBA applications in a way that will allow you to refer to them in other worksheets or workbooks.

When the application is loaded into Excel, you can invoke the application in many ways. Let us look at a few ways to run the macro:

1. You can assign a key to the macro when you record the macro. You can then invoke the macro by pressing Ctrl-"key." If the key is "a," your shortcut will be Ctrl+a. You must remember that the macro shortcut will override the default meaning of the Ctrl+a shortcut. You should also note that Ctrl/a and Ctrl/A are different.

2. You can either include an object or a button on the spreadsheet to call the macro. Go to the Forms window using the path Menu->View->Toolbars->Forms and select the command button. Now, draw the button on the spreadsheet. Choose the macro that you want to link to the button when the dialog box or prompt opens. You can also include pictures and other objects and assign macros to them.

3. Select the macro from the menu and run it. Go to the Macros section using the following path Menu->Tools->Macro->Macros and choose the macro you want to run.

4. You can also use the VBA editor to run the macro. You can either click on the run button to run the macro or go through each line of the code while giving yourself time to debug the code. When you are debugging the code, you should move the VBA editor into a pane adjacent to the spreadsheet and execute the code to see what is happening.

If you choose to name a macro "Sub Auto_Open()," this macro will run when you load or open the spreadsheet. This will only happen if you have enabled macros.

Security and Macro Storage

For every Microsoft Office application, there are three security levels for macros. The macro security level is always set to high by default. To change the security of your macro, go to the security tab and make your selection. Go to Menu->Tools->Security Tab->Macro Security.

The three security levels for macros are:

1. High: The macros that are signed by a trusted source will run in Excel. If there is any unsigned macro, it will automatically be disabled.

2. Medium: This is the recommended setting since you can choose to enable or disable a macro.

3. Low: This is not recommended since the macros are loaded into the workbook without notifying the user.

If you know you will be using macros, you should set the security of the macros to medium. When you load the spreadsheet, Excel will ask you if you want to enable or disable a macro. If you know that a specific sheet contains a macro and you know who wrote it, you can enable it.

Since there are some macros that are set to run when you open a spreadsheet, it is not possible for you to always have the chance to examine the macro before you enable it. It is important to remember that an Excel Macro virus is very rare. This is because a macro is only available on the spreadsheet where it was written. Macros are always stored in the workbook by default and every time you load the workbook, the macros are loaded.

When you create a macro for the first time, you can decide where to store the macro. The best choices are:

1. This Workbook: The macro is stored in the worksheet where it is written. Anybody who has access to the worksheet can access the macro.

2. Personal Macro Workbook: All the macros on your PC are stored in this workbook. Only when you copy the macro and save it with the spreadsheet will others be able to view the macro.

You can use the VBA editor to see where the macros are stored. The Project Explorer Window, on the upper left of the screen, shows you where the files are placed and their hierarchy. You can use the Explorer to view, move, copy or delete a macro.

Chapter Two

How to Use Data from Excel

There will be times when you do not want to manually copy data from one Excel file to another. If you automate this procedure, you can ensure that the data is entered accurately, there is no duplication in the data and the figures will not be entered in an incorrect location. This will also save time.

You can write the code to perform this function in the Workbook_Open() event or function in ThisWorkBook object in VBA. When you write this code in the Workbook_Open() function, the compiler will ensure that the figures are updated correctly when the source Excel file is open.

To develop the code, open the destination excel file and press Alt+F8. You will find the ThisWorkbook module under the Microsoft Excel Objects in Project Explorer. Open the window and from the object dropdown list, choose "Workbook."

Option Explicit

```
        Private Sub Workbook_Open()

            Call ReadDataFromCloseFile

        End Sub
```

```vba
Sub ReadDataFromCloseFile()

    On Error GoTo ErrHandler

    Application.ScreenUpdating = False

    Dim src As Workbook

    ' OPEN THE SOURCE EXCEL WORKBOOK IN
    "READ ONLY MODE."

    Set src = Workbooks.Open("C:\Q-SALES.xlsx", True,
    True)

    ' GET THE TOTAL ROWS FROM THE SOURCE
    WORKBOOK.

    Dim iTotalRows As Integer

    iTotalRows = src.Worksheets("sheet1").Range("B1:B" &
    Cells(Rows.Count, "B").End(xlUp).Row).Rows.Count

    ' COPY DATA FROM SOURCE (CLOSE
    WORKGROUP) TO THE DESTINATION WORKBOOK.

    Dim iCnt As Integer      ' COUNTER.

    For iCnt = 1 To iTotalRows

        Worksheets("Sheet1").Range("B" & iCnt).Formula =

        src.Worksheets("Sheet1").Range("B" &
    iCnt).Formula

    Next iCnt

    ' CLOSE THE SOURCE FILE.

    src.Close False          ' FALSE - DON'T SAVE THE
    SOURCE FILE.

    Set src = Nothing

    ErrHandler:
```

Application.EnableEvents = True

Application.ScreenUpdating = True

End Sub

Property Application.ScreenUpdating

In the first line of the code, you will see that the Application.ScreenUpdating property is set to false. This is done to increase the speed of the macro that you have written.

Open the Source File and Read Data

We are then opening the source workbook to read or copy the data from it. Excel will only open the file in the read only state. This means that it will make no changes to the source file.

Set src = Workbooks.Open("C:\Q-SALES.xlsx", True, True)

Once you have obtained the data, the compiler will count the number of rows present in the source workbook. The loop will run and the data will be copied from the source and pasted into the destination workbook.

' COPY DATA FROM SOURCE (CLOSE WORKGROUP) TO THE DESTINATION FILE.

For iCnt = 1 To iTotalRows

Worksheets("Sheet1").Range("B" & iCnt).Formula =

src.Worksheets("Sheet1").Range("B" & iCnt).Formula

Next iCnt

You should then close the source file and finally set the property Application.ScreenUpdating to true.

Chapter Three

Working With Loops

One of the most powerful and basic programming tools available in VBA is a loop. This tool is used across many programming languages where the programmer wants to repeat a block of code until a condition holds true or until a specific point. If the condition is false, the loop will break and the section of code after the loop is executed. By using loops, you can write a few lines of code and achieve significant output.

The For Loop

For…Next Statement

The For…Next Loop will repeat a statement or a block of code for a specific number of iterations. The syntax for the loop is as follows:

```
For counter_variable = start_value To end_value

[block of code]

Next counter_variable
```

Let us look at a simple example of how to use this loop.

```
Sub forNext1()

Dim i As Integer

Dim iTotal As Integer
```

```
iTotal = 0

For i = 1 To 5

iTotal = i + iTotal

Next i

MsgBox iTotal

End Sub
```

The For Each ... Next Statement

If you want to repeat a block of code for every object or variable in a group, you should use the For Each...Next Loop. This statement will repeat the execution of a block of code or statements for every element in the collection. The loop will stop when every element in the collection is covered. The execution will immediately move to that section of code that is immediately after the Next statement. The syntax of the loop is as follows:

```
For Each object_variable In group_object_variable

        [block of code]

        Next object_variable
```

Example 1

In the example below, the loop will go through every worksheet in the workbook. VBA will execute the code which will protect the worksheets with a password. In this example, the variable ws is the Worksheet Object variable. The group or collection of worksheets is present in this workbook.

```
Sub forEach1()

Dim ws As Worksheet
```

```
For Each ws In ThisWorkbook.Worksheets

ws.Protect Password:="123"

Next ws

End Sub
```

Example 2

In the example below, the VBA will iterate through every cell in the range A1:A10. The code will set the background color of every cell to yellow. In this example, rCell is the Range Object variable, and the collection or group of cells is present in Range("A1:A10").

```
Sub forEach2()

Dim rCell As Range

For Each rCell In ActiveSheet.Range("A1:A10")

rCell.Interior.Color = RGB(255, 255, 0)

Next rCell

End Sub
```

Nesting Loops

If you want to include more than one condition in a loop, you can use nesting. You can create a nested loop by adding one loop to another. You can add an infinite number of loops if you are creating a nested loop. You can also nest one type of a loop inside another type of loop.

If you are using a For Loop, it is important that the inner loop is completed first. It is only after the inner loop is fully complete that the statements below the Next statement of the inner loop are executed. Alternatively, you can nest one type of control structure in another.

In the example below, we will use an IF statement in a WITH statement that is within a For...Each Loop. VBA will go through every cell in the range A1:A10. If the value of the cell exceeds 5, VBA will color the cell as Yellow. Otherwise, it will color the cells red.

```
Sub nestingLoops()

Dim rCell As Range

For Each rCell In ActiveSheet.Range("A1:A10")

With rCell

If rCell > 5 Then

.Interior.Color = RGB(255, 255, 0)

Else

.Interior.Color = RGB(255, 0, 0)

End If

End With

Next rCell

End Sub
```

The Exit For Statement

You can use the Exit For statement to exit the For Loop without completing the full cycle. This means that you will be exiting the For Loop early. This statement will instruct VBA to stop the execution of the loop and move to the section or block of code at the end of the loop, or the code that follows the Next statement. If you are using Nested loops, VBA will stop the execution of the code in the inner level and move to the outer level. You should use this statement wen you want to terminate the loop once it has satisfied a condition or reached a specific value. You can also use this statement to break an endless loop after a certain point.

Let us look at the following example:

In the example below, if the value of Range("A1") is blank, the value of the variable iTotal will be 55. If Range("A1") has the value 5, VBA will terminate the loop when the counter reaches the value 5. At this point, the value of iTotal will be 15. You should note that the loop will run until the counter value reaches 5, after which it will exit the loop.

```
Sub exitFor1()

Dim i As Integer

Dim iTotal As Integer

iTotal = 0

For i = 1 To 10

iTotal = i + iTotal

If i = ActiveSheet.Range("A1") Then

Exit For

End If

Next i

MsgBox iTotal

End Sub
```

The Do While Loop

You can use the Do While Loop to repeat a block of code or statements indefinitely as long as the condition is met and the value is True. VBA will stop executing the block of code when the condition returns the value False. You can test the condition either at the start or at the end of the loop. The Do While…Loop statement is where the condition is tested at the start while the Do…Loop While statement is the condition that is tested at the end of the loop. When the condition at the start of the loop is not met, the former loop will not execute the block of code in the loop. The latter statement will function at least once since the condition is at the end of the loop.

Do While…Loop Statement

The syntax for the loop is:

    Do While [Condition]

    [block of code]

    Loop

Do…Loop While Statement

The syntax for the loop is:

    Do

    [block of code]

    Loop While [Condition]

The loops are explained below with the help of examples.

Example 1

In the example below, the condition is tested at the beginning of the loop. Since the condition is not met, the loop will not execute, and the value of iTotal will be zero.

    Sub doWhile1()

```
Dim i As Integer

Dim iTotal As Integer

i = 5

iTotal = 0

Do While i > 5

iTotal = i + iTotal

i = i - 1

Loop

MsgBox iTotal

End Sub
```

Example 2

In the example below, the condition is only tested at the end of the function. Since the condition is true, the loop will execute once. It will terminate after that since the value of I will reduce to 4, and the variable iTotal will return the value 5.

```
Sub doWhile2()

Dim i As Integer

Dim iTotal As Integer

i = 5

iTotal = 0

Do

iTotal = i + iTotal

i = i - 1
```

```
Loop While i > 5

MsgBox iTotal

End Sub
```

Example 3

In this example, we will replace the blanks in a range of cells with underscores.

```
Sub doWhile3()

Dim rCell As Range

Dim strText As String

Dim n As Integer

'rCell is a Cell in the specified Range which contains the
strText

'strText is the text in a Cell in which blank spaces are to be
replaced with underscores

'n is the position of blank space(s) occurring in a strText

For Each rCell In ActiveSheet.Range("A1:A5")

strText = rCell

'the VBA InStr function returns the position of the first
occurrence of a string within another string. Using this to
determine the position of the first blank space in the strText.

n = InStr(strText, " ")

Do While n > 0

'blank space is replaced with the underscore character in the
strText
```

```vba
strText = Left(strText, n - 1) & "_" & Right(strText,
Len(strText) - n)
```

'Use this line of code instead of the preceding line, to remove all blank spaces in the strText

```vba
'strText= Left(strText, n - 1) & Right(strText, Len(strText) -
n)
```

```vba
n = InStr(strText, " ")
```

```vba
Loop
```

```vba
rCell = strText
```

```vba
Next
```

```vba
End Sub
```

The Exit Do Statement

You can use the Exit Do Statement to exit the Do While Loop before you complete the cycle. The Exit Do statement will instruct VBA to stop executing the lines of code in the loop and move to the block of code that is immediately after the loop. If it is a nested loop, the statement will instruct VBA to execute the lines of code in the outer loop. You can use an infinite number of Exit Do statements in a loop, and this statement is useful when you want to terminate the loop once you obtain the desired value. This is similar to the Exit For statement.

Let us look at the following example. In the example below, the iTotal will be 55 is Range("A1") is blank. If it contains the number 5, VBA will terminate the loop when the value of the counter is 5. The value of iTotal will increase to 10.

```vba
Sub exitDo1()
```

```
Dim i As Integer

Dim iTotal As Integer

iTotal = 0

Do While i < 11

iTotal = i + iTotal

i = i + 1

If i = ActiveSheet.Range("A1") Then

Exit Do

End If

Loop

MsgBox iTotal

End Sub
```

The Do Until Loop

When you use the Do Until Loop, VBA will repeat the block of code indefinitely until the specified condition is true. You can use this statement to test the condition either at the start or at the end of the loop. The Do Until...Loop statement will test the condition at the start of the loop while the Do...Loop Until statement will test the condition at the end of the loop. In the former statement, if the condition is false, VBA will not execute the block of code within the statement since the condition has to hold true right from the start. In the latter statement, the block of code in the loop will execute at least once since the condition is at the end of the loop.

Do Until...Loop Statement

The syntax for the statement is below:

Do Until [Condition]

[block of code]

Loop

Do...Loop Until Statement

The syntax for the statement is below:

Do

[block of code]

Loop Until [Condition]

Let us look at the following statements using the following examples.

Example 1

In this example, VBA will color every empty cell yellow until it encounters a non-empty cell. If there is a non-empty cell at the start, the code will not execute since the condition is mentioned at the beginning of the loop.

```
Sub doUntil1()

Dim rowNo As Integer

rowNo = 1

Do Until Not IsEmpty(Cells(rowNo, 1))

Cells(rowNo, 1).Interior.Color = RGB(255, 255, 0)
```

```
rowNo = rowNo + 1

Loop

End Sub
```

Example 2

In this example, VBA will color every empty cell yellow until it encounters a non-empty cell. If there is a non-empty cell at the start, the code will execute at least once since the condition is mentioned at the end of the loop.

```
Sub doUntil2()

Dim rowNo As Integer

rowNo = 1

Do

Cells(rowNo, 1).Interior.Color = RGB(255, 255, 0)

rowNo = rowNo + 1

Loop Until Not IsEmpty(Cells(rowNo, 1))

End Sub
```

The Exit Do Statement

You can use the Exit Do statement to exit the Do Until Loop without completing a full cycle. This is similar to the Do While Loop that we looked at earlier.

Chapter Four

Working With Conditional Statements

There are two conditional statements that you can use in VBA:

1. If...Then...Else

2. Select...Case

In both these conditional statements, VBA will need to evaluate one or more conditions after which the block of code between the parentheses is executed. These statements are executed depending on what the result of the evaluation is.

If...Then...Else Statements

This conditional statement will execute a block of statements or code when the condition is met.

Multiple-line Statements

> *If condition Then*
>
> *statements*
>
> *ElseIf elseif_condition_1 Then*
>
> *elseif_statements_1*
>
> *ElseIf elseif_condition_n Then*
>
> *elseif_statements_n*
>
> *Else*

else_statements

End If

Let us break the statements down to understand what each part of the block of code written above means.

If Statement

If you want to write a multiple-line syntax, like the example above, the first line of the code should only contain the 'If' statement. We will cover the single-line syntax in the following section.

Condition

This is an expression that could either be a string or numeric. The compiler will evaluate this condition and return either true or false. It is necessary to define a condition.

Statements

These statements make up the block of code that the compiler will execute if the condition is true. If you do not specify a statement, then the compiler will not execute any code even if the condition is true.

ElseIf

This is a clause that can be used if you want to include multiple conditions. If you have an ElseIf in the code, you need to specify the elseif_condition. You can include an infinite number of ElseIf and elseif_conditions in your code.

elseif_condition

This is an expression that the compiler will need to evaluate. The result of the expression should either be true or false.

Elseif_statements

These statements or blocks of code are evaluated if the compiler returns the result true for the elseif_condition. If you do not specify a statement, then the compiler will not execute any code even if the condition is true.

The Else -> condition and elseif_conditions are always tested in the order they are written in. If any condition is true, the block of code that comes immediately after the condition will be executed. If no conditions in the elseif_conditions returns the value the true, the block of code after the **Else** clause will be executed. You can choose to include the Else in the If…Then…Else statement.

else_statements

These statements are the blocks of code written immediately after the Else statement.

End If

This statement terminates the If…Then…Else block of statements and it is important that you mention these keywords at the end of the block.

Nesting

You can nest the If…Then…Else statements in a loop using the Select…Case or VBA Loops (covered in the previous chapter), without a limit. If you are using Excel 2003, you can only use 7 levels of nesting, but if you use Excel 2007, you can use 64. The latest versions of Excel allow a larger level of nesting.

Let us look at the following example:

Example 1

```
Sub ElseIfStructure()

'Returns Good if the marks are equal to 60.

Dim sngMarks As Single

sngMarks = 60

If sngMarks >= 80 Then

MsgBox "Excellent"

ElseIf sngMarks >= 60 And sngMarks < 80 Then

MsgBox "Good"

ElseIf sngMarks >= 40 And sngMarks < 60 Then

MsgBox "Average"

Else

MsgBox "Poor"

End If

End Sub
```

Example 2

In this example, we will use Multiple If...Then Statements. This is an alternative to the ElseIf structure, but is not as efficient as the ElseIf Structure. In the Multiple If...Then Statements, the compiler will need to run through every If...Then block of code even after it returns the result true for one of the conditions. If you use the ElseIf structure, the subsequent conditions are not checked if one condition is true. This makes the ElseIf structure faster. If you can perform the function using the ElseIf structure, you should avoid using the Multiple If...Then Structure.

```
Sub multipleIfThenStmnts()

"Returns Good if the marks are equal to 60.

Dim sngMarks As Single

sngMarks = 60

If sngMarks >= 80 Then

MsgBox "Excellent"

End If

If sngMarks >= 60 And sngMarks < 80 Then

MsgBox "Good"

End If

If sngMarks >= 40 And sngMarks < 60 Then

MsgBox "Average"

End If

If sngMarks < 40 Then

MsgBox "Poor"

End If

End Sub
```

Example 3

In this example, we will nest the If...Then...Else statements within a For...Next Loop.

```
Sub IfThenNesting()
```

'The user will need to enter 5 numbers. The compiler will add the even numbers and subtract the odd numbers.

Dim i As Integer, n As Integer, iEvenSum As Integer, iOddSum As Integer

```
    For n = 1 To 5

    i = InputBox("enter number")

    If i Mod 2 = 0 Then

    iEvenSum = iEvenSum + i

    Else

    iOddSum = iOddSum + i

    End If

    Next n

    MsgBox "sum of even numbers is " & iEvenSum

    MsgBox "sum of odd numbers is " & iOddSum

    End Sub
```

Example 4

You can use the following options to test multiple variables using the If...Then statements.

Option 1: ElseIf Structure

Sub IfThen1()

'this procedure returns the message "Pass in maths and Fail in science"

```
Dim sngMaths As Single, sngScience As Single

sngMaths = 50

sngScience = 30

If sngMaths >= 40 And sngScience >= 40 Then

MsgBox "Pass in both maths and science"

ElseIf sngMaths >= 40 And sngScience < 40 Then

MsgBox "Pass in maths and Fail in science"

ElseIf sngMaths < 40 And sngScience >= 40 Then

MsgBox "Fail in maths and Pass in science"

Else

MsgBox "Fail in both maths and science"

End If

End Sub
```

Option 2: If...Then...Else Nesting

```
Sub IfThen2()

'this procedure returns the message "Pass in maths and Fail in science"

Dim sngMaths As Single, sngScience As Single

sngMaths = 50

sngScience = 30

If sngMaths >= 40 Then
```

If sngScience >= 40 Then

MsgBox "Pass in both maths and science"

Else

MsgBox "Pass in maths and Fail in science"

End If

Else

If sngScience >= 40 Then

MsgBox "Fail in maths and Pass in science"

Else

MsgBox "Fail in both maths and science"

End If

End If

End Sub

Option 3: Multiple If...Then Statements

As mentioned earlier, this may not be the best way to perform the operation.

```
Sub IfThen3()

'this procedure returns the message "Pass in maths and Fail
in science"

Dim sngMaths As Single, sngScience As Single

sngMaths = 50

sngScience = 30
```

```vba
If sngMaths >= 40 And sngScience >= 40 Then

MsgBox "Pass in both maths and science"

End If

If sngMaths >= 40 And sngScience < 40 Then

MsgBox "Pass in maths and Fail in science"

End If

If sngMaths < 40 And sngScience >= 40 Then

MsgBox "Fail in maths and Pass in science"

End If

If sngMaths < 40 And sngScience < 40 Then

MsgBox "Fail in both maths and science"

End If

 End Sub
```

Example 5

In this example, we will use the If Not, If IsNumeric and IsEmpty functions in the Worksheet_Change event.

```vba
Private Sub Worksheet_Change(ByVal Target As Range)

'Using If IsEmpty, If Not and If IsNumeric (in If...Then statements) in the Worksheet_Change event.

'auto run a VBA code, when content of a worksheet cell changes, with the Worksheet_Change event.

On Error GoTo ErrHandler

Application.EnableEvents = False
```

'if target cell is empty post change, nothing will happen

If IsEmpty(Target) Then

Application.EnableEvents = True

Exit Sub

End If

'using If Not statement with the Intersect Method to determine if Target cell(s) is within specified range of "B1:B20"

If Not Intersect(Target, Range("B1:B20")) Is Nothing Then

'if target cell is changed to a numeric value

If IsNumeric(Target) Then

'changes the target cell color to yellow

Target.Interior.Color = RGB(255, 255, 0)

End If

End If

Application.EnableEvents = True

ErrHandler:

   Application.EnableEvents = True

   Exit Sub

End Sub

Using the Not Operator

When you use the Not operator on any Boolean expression, the compiler will reverse the true value with the false value and vice versa. The Not operator will always reverse the logic in any conditional statement. In the example above, If Not Intersect(Target, Range("B1:B20")) Is Nothing Then means If Intersect(Target, Range("B1:B20")) Is Not Nothing Then or If Intersect(Target, Range("B1:B20")) Is Something Then. In simple words, this means that the condition should not be true if the range falls or intersects between the range ("B1:B20").

Single Line If…Then…Else Statements

If you are writing a short or simple code, you should use the single-line syntax. If you wish to distinguish between the singly-line and multiple-line syntax, you should look at the block of code that succeeds the Then keyword. If there is nothing succeeding the Then keyword, the block of code is multiple-line. Otherwise, it is a single-line code.

The syntax for Single-line statements is as follows:

If condition Then statements Else else_statements

These blocks of statements can also be nested in a single-line syntax within each other. You can insert the clause Else If in the code, which is similar to the ElseIf clause. You do not need to use the End If keywords in the single-syntax block of code since the program will automatically terminate.

Let us look at some examples where we will use the single-line syntax for the If…Then…Else statements.

If sngMarks > 80 Then MsgBox "Excellent Marks"

If sngMarks > 80 Then MsgBox "Excellent Marks" Else MsgBox "Not Excellent"

'add MsgBox title "Grading":

If sngMarks > 80 Then MsgBox "Excellent Marks", , "Grading"

'using logical operator And in the condition:

If sngMarks > 80 And sngAvg > 80 Then MsgBox "Both Marks & Average are Excellent" Else MsgBox "Not Excellent"

'nesting another If...Then statement:

If sngMarks > 80 Then If sngAvg > 80 Then MsgBox "Both Marks & Average are Excellent"

Example 1

```
Sub IfThenSingleLine1()

Dim sngMarks As Single

sngMarks = 85
```

'Execute multiple statements / codes after Then keyword. Code will return 3 messages: "Excellent Marks - 85 on 90"; "Keep it up!" and "94.44% marks".

```
If sngMarks = 85 Then MsgBox "Excellent Marks - 85 on 90": MsgBox "Keep it up!": MsgBox Format(85 / 90 * 100, "0.00") & "% marks"

End Sub
```

Example 2

```
Sub IfThenSingleLine1()

Dim sngMarks As Single

sngMarks = 85
```

'Execute multiple statements / codes after Then keyword. Code will return 3 messages: "Excellent Marks - 85 on 90"; "Keep it up!" and "94.44% marks".

If sngMarks = 85 Then MsgBox "Excellent Marks - 85 on 90": MsgBox "Keep it up!": MsgBox Format(85 / 90 * 100, "0.00") & "% marks"

End Sub

Example 3

Sub IfThenSingleLine2()

Dim sngMarks As Single, sngAvg As Single

sngMarks = 85

sngAvg = 75

'nesting If...Then statements. Code will return the message: "Marks are Excellent, but Average is not"

If sngMarks > 80 Then If sngAvg > 80 Then MsgBox "Both Marks & Average are Excellent" Else MsgBox "Marks are Excellent, but Average is not" Else MsgBox "Marks are not Excellent"

End Sub

Example 4

Sub IfThenSingleLine3()

Dim sngMarks As Single

sngMarks = 65

'using the keywords Else If (in single-line syntax), similar to ElseIf (in multiple-line syntax). Procedure will return the message: "Marks are Good".

If sngMarks > 80 Then MsgBox "Marks are Excellent" Else If sngMarks >= 60 Then MsgBox "Marks are Good" Else If sngMarks >= 40 Then MsgBox "Marks are Average" Else MsgBox "Marks are Poor"

End Sub

Select...Case Statement

The Select...Case statement will execute statements or a block of code depending on whether some conditions have been met. It will evaluate an expression and executes one of the many blocks of code depending on the result of the expression. This statement is similar to the If...The...Else statement.

Syntax

Select Case expression

Case expression_value_1

statements_1

Case expression_value_n

statements_n

Case Else

else_statements

End Select

Expression

This can be a range, field or a variable. The expression can be expressed by using a VBA function -> as "rng.HasFormula" or "IsNumeric(rng)" where the 'rng' is the range variable. The expression can return a String value, Boolean Value, Numeric Value or any other data type. It is important that you specify the expression. It is the value of the expression that the compiler will test and compare with each case in the Select...Case statement.

When the values match, the compiler will execute the block of code under the matching Case.

Expression_value

The data type of the expression_value should be the same as the expression or a similar data type. The compiler will compare the value of the expression against the expression_value in each case. If it finds a match, the block of code under the case or the statements will be executed. You must specify at least one expression_value, and the compiler will test the expression against these values in the order they are mentioned in. The expression_values are similar to a list of conditions where the condition must be met for the relevant block of code to be executed.

Statements

The compiler will execute the block of code or statements under a specific case if the value of the expression and the expression_value are the same.

Case Else -> expression_value

When the compiler matches the value of the expression to the expression_value, it will execute the block of code under that case. It will not check the value of the expression against the remaining expression_value. If the compiler does not find a match against any expression_value, it will move to the Case Else clause. The statements under this clause are executed. You do not have to use this clause when you write your code.

Else_statements

As mentioned earlier, the else_statements are included in the Case Else section of the code. If the compiler cannot match the value of the expression to any expression_value, it will execute these statements.

End Select

These keywords terminate the Select...Case block of statements. You must mention these keywords at the end of the Select...Case statements.

Let us look at an example of the Select...Case statements.

```
Sub selectCase1()

'making strAge equivalent to "young" will return the
message "Less than 40 years"

Dim strAge As String

strAge = "young"

Select Case strAge

Case "senior citizen"

MsgBox "Over 60 years"

Case "middle age"

MsgBox "Between 40 to 59 years"

Case "young"

MsgBox "Less than 40 years"

Case Else

MsgBox "Invalid"

End Select

End Sub
```

Using the To Keyword

You can use the To keyword to specify the upper and lower range of all matching values in the expression_value section of the Select...Case statements. The value on the left side of the To keyword should either be less than or equal to the value on the right side of the To keyword. You can also specify the range for a specified set of characters.

Let us look at an example.

Sub selectCaseTo()

'entering marks as 69 will return the message "Average"; entering marks as 101 will return the message "Out of Range"

Dim iMarks As Integer

iMarks = InputBox("Enter marks")

Select Case iMarks

Case 70 To 100

MsgBox "Good"

Case 40 To 69

MsgBox "Average"

Case 0 To 39

MsgBox "Failed"

Case Else

MsgBox "Out of Range"

End Select

End Sub

Using the Is Keyword

You can use the Is keyword if you want to include a comparison operator like <>, ==, <=, >=, < or >. If you do not include the Is keyword, the compiler will automatically include it. Let us look at the example below.

```
Sub selectCaseIs()

'if sngTemp equals 39.5, returned message is "Moderately Hot"

Dim sngTemp As Single

sngTemp = 39.5

Select Case sngTemp

Case Is >= 40

MsgBox "Extremely Hot"

Case Is >= 25

MsgBox "Moderately Hot"

Case Is >= 0

MsgBox "Cool Weather"

Case Is < 0

MsgBox "Extremely Cold"

End Select

End Sub
```

Using a comma

You can include multiple ranges or expressions in the Case clause. These ranges and expressions can be separated with a comma. The comma acts like the OR operator. You can also specify multiple expressions and ranges for character strings. Let us look at the example below.

Example 1

```
Sub selectCaseMultiple_1()

'if alpha equates to "Hello," the returned message is "Odd Number or Hello"

Dim alpha As Variant

alpha = "Hello"

Select Case alpha

Case a, e, i, o, u

MsgBox "Vowels"

Case 2, 4, 6, 8

MsgBox "Even Number"

Case 1, 3, 5, 7, 9, "Hello"

MsgBox "Odd Number or Hello"

Case Else

MsgBox "Out of Range"

End Select

End Sub
```

Example 2

In this example, we are comparing the strings "apples" to "grapes." The compiler will determine the value between "apples" and "grapes" and will use the default comparison method binary.

Sub SelectCaseMultiple_OptionCompare_NotSpecified()

'Option Compare is NOT specified and therefore text comparison will be case-sensitive

'bananas will return the message "Text between apples and grapes, or specifically mangoes, or the numbers 98 or 99"; oranges will return the message "Out of Range"; Apples will return the message "Out of Range."

```
Dim var As Variant, strResult As String

var = InputBox("Enter")

Select Case var

Case 1 To 10, 11 To 20: strResult = "Number is between 1
and 20"

Case "apples" To "grapes," "mangoes," 98, 99: strResult =
"Text between apples and grapes, or specifically mangoes,
or the numbers 98 or 99"

Case Else: strResult = "Out of Range"

End Select

MsgBox strResult

End Sub
```

Nesting

You can nest the Select...Case block of code or statements within VBA loops, If...Then...Else statements and within a Select...Case block. There is no limit on the number of cases you can include in the code. If you are nesting a Select...Case within another Select...Case, it should be a complete block by itself and also terminate with its End Select.

Example 1

> Sub selectCaseNested1()

Check if a range is empty; and if not empty, whether it has a numeric value and if numeric then if also has a formula; and if not numeric then what is the text length.

> Dim rng As Range, iLength As Integer
>
> Set rng = ActiveSheet.Range("A1")
>
> Select Case IsEmpty(rng)
>
> Case True
>
> MsgBox rng.Address & " is empty"
>
> Case Else
>
> Select Case IsNumeric(rng)
>
> Case True
>
> MsgBox rng.Address & " has a numeric value"
>
> Select Case rng.HasFormula
>
> Case True

```vba
MsgBox rng.Address & " also has a formula"

End Select

Case Else

iLength = Len(rng)

MsgBox rng.Address & " has a Text length of " & iLength

End Select

End Select

End Sub
```

Example 2

```vba
Function StringManipulation(str As String) As String

'This code customizes a string text as follows:

'1. removes numericals from a text string;

'2. removes leading, trailing & inbetween spaces (leaves single
space between words);

'3. adds space (if not present) after each exclamation, comma, full
stop and question mark;

'4. capitalizes the very first letter of the string and the first letter of a
word after each exclamation, full stop and question mark;

 Dim iTxtLen As Integer, iStrLen As Integer, n As Integer, i As
Integer, ansiCode As Integer

'--------------------------
```

'REMOVE NUMERICALS

'chr(48) to chr(57) represent numericals 0 to 9 in ANSI/ASCII character codes

For i = 48 To 57

'remove all numericals from the text string using vba Replace function:

str = Replace(str, Chr(i), "")

Next i

'--------------------------

'REMOVE LEADING, TRAILING & INBETWEEN SPACES (LEAVE SINGLE SPACE BETWEEN WORDS)

'use the worksheet TRIM function. Note: the TRIM function removes space character with ANSI code 32, does not remove the nonbreaking space character with ANSI code 160

str = Application.Trim(str)

'--------------------------

'ADD SPACE (IF NOT PRESENT) AFTER EACH EXCLAMATION, COMMA, DOT AND QUESTION MARK:

'set variable value to string length:

iTxtLen = Len(str)

For n = iTxtLen To 1 Step -1

'Chr(32) returns space; Chr(33) returns exclamation; Chr(44) returns comma; Chr(46) returns full stop; Chr(63) returns question mark;

If Mid(str, n, 1) = Chr(33) Or Mid(str, n, 1) = Chr(44) Or Mid(str, n, 1) = Chr(46) Or Mid(str, n, 1) = Chr(63) Then

'check if space is not present:

If Mid(str, n + 1, 1) <> Chr(32) Then

'using Mid & Right functions to add space - note that current string length is used:

str = Mid(str, 1, n) & Chr(32) & Right(str, iTxtLen - n)

'update string length - increments by 1 after adding a space (character):

iTxtLen = iTxtLen + 1

End If

End If

Next n

'---------------------------

'DELETE SPACE (IF PRESENT) BEFORE EACH EXCLAMATION, COMMA, DOT & QUESTION MARK:

'reset variable value to string length:

iTxtLen = Len(str)

For n = iTxtLen To 1 Step -1

'Chr(32) returns space; Chr(33) returns exclamation; Chr(44) returns comma; Chr(46) returns full stop; Chr(63) returns question mark;

If Mid(str, n, 1) = Chr(33) Or Mid(str, n, 1) = Chr(44) Or Mid(str, n, 1) = Chr(46) Or Mid(str, n, 1) = Chr(63) Then 'check if space is present:

If Mid(str, n - 1, 1) = Chr(32) Then

'using the worksheet Replace function to delete a space:

str = Application.Replace(str, n - 1, 1, "")

'omit rechecking the same character again - position of n shifts (decreases by 1) due to deleting a space character:

n = n - 1

End If

End If

Next n

'---------------------------

'CAPITALIZE LETTERS:

 'capitalize the very first letter of the string and the first letter of a word after each exclamation, full stop and question mark, while all other letters are lower case

iStrLen = Len(str)

For i = 1 To iStrLen

'determine the ANSI code of each character in the string

ansiCode = Asc(Mid(str, i, 1))

Select Case ansiCode

'97 to 122 are the ANSI codes equating to small cap letters "a" to "z"

Case 97 To 122

If i > 2 Then

'capitalizes a letter whose position is 2 characters after (1 character after, will be the space character added earlier) an exclamation, full stop and question mark:

If Mid(str, i - 2, 1) = Chr(33) Or Mid(str, i - 2, 1) = Chr(46) Or Mid(str, i - 2, 1) = Chr(63) Then

Mid(str, i, 1) = UCase(Mid(str, i, 1))

End If

'capitalize first letter of the string:

ElseIf i = 1 Then

Mid(str, i, 1) = UCase(Mid(str, i, 1))

End If

'if capital letter, skip to next character (ie. next i):

Case Else

GoTo skip

End Select

skip:

Next i

'----------------------------

'manipulated string:

StringManipulation = str

End Function

Sub Str_Man()

'specify text string to manipulate & get manipulated string

Dim strText As String

'specify the text string, which is required to be manipulated

strText = ActiveSheet.Range("A1").Value

'the manipulated text string is entered in range A5 of the active sheet, on running the procedure:

ActiveSheet.Range("A5").Value = StringManipulation(strText)

End Sub

Go To Statement

You can use the Go To statement to move to a different section of the code or jump a line in the procedure. There are two parts to the Go To statement:

1. The GoTo keywords that are followed by an identifier, also known as the Label.

2. The Label which is followed by a colon and the line of code or a few statements.

If the value of the expression satisfies the condition, the compiler will move to a separate line of code that is indicated in the GoTo statement. You can avoid this statement and use the If...Then...Else statement. The Go To function makes the code unreadable and confusing.

Select...Case Statements Versus the If...Then...Else Statements

The Select...Case and If...Then...Else statements are both conditional statements. In each of these statements either one or more conditions are tested and the compiler will execute the block of code depending on what the result of the evaluation is.

The difference between the two statements is that in the Select...Case statement only one condition is evaluated at a time. The variable that is to be evaluated is initialized or declared in the Select Case expression. The multiple case statements will specify the different values that the variable can take. In the If...Then...Else statement, multiple conditions can be evaluated and the code for different conditions can be executed at the same time.

The Select...Case statement will only test a single variable for several values while the If...Then...Else statement will test multiple variables for different values. In this sense, the If...Then... Else statement is more flexible since you can test multiple variables for different conditions.

If you are testing a large number of conditions, you should avoid using the If...Then...Else statements since they may appear confusing. These statements can also make it difficult for you to read the code.

Chapter Five

Working With Strings

Strings are an integral part of VBA, and every programmer will need to work with strings when he or she begins to automate functions using VBA. There are different types of manipulations that one can do on strings including

- Extracting some parts of a string

- Comparing different strings

- Converting a number into a string

- Formatting dates to include weekdays

- Finding the characters in a string

- Removing the blanks in a string

- Parsing the string into an array

There are many functions in VBA that you can use to perform these tasks. This chapter will act as a guide on how you can work with strings in VBA. There are some simple examples in the book that you can practice.

Points to Remember

There are two points that you need to keep in mind when you work with strings.

Original String Does Not Change

You must remember that the original string function does not change when you perform some operations on strings. VBA returns a new string with all the changes you have made to it. If you want to make a change to the original string, you should assign the result of the function to the original string. We will cover this concept later in this chapter.

Comparing Two Strings

There are some string functions like Instr() and StrComp() that allow you to include the **Compare** parameter. This parameter works in the following way:

- **vbTextCompare**: The upper and lower case letters in the string are considered the same.

- **vbBinaryCompare**: The upper and lower case letters in the string are treated differently.

Let us look at the following example to see how you can use the Compare parameter in the StrComp() function.

    Sub Comp1()

        ' Prints 0 if the strings do not match

        Debug.Print StrComp("MARoon", "Maroon", vbTextCompare)

        ' Prints 1 if the strings do not match

        Debug.Print StrComp("Maroon", "MAROON", vbBinaryCompare)

    End Sub

Instead of using the same parameter every time, you can use the Option Compare. This parameter is defined at the top of any module, and a function that includes the parameter Compare will use this setting as its default. You can use the Option Compare in the following ways:

Option Compare Text

This option makes uses the vbTextCompare as the default compare argument.

```
Option Compare Text

Sub Comp2()

    ' Strings match - uses vbCompareText as Compare argument

    Debug.Print StrComp("ABC", "abc")

    Debug.Print StrComp("DEF", "def")

End Sub
```

Option Compare Binary

This option uses the vbBinaryCompare as the default compare argument.

```
Option Compare Binary

Sub Comp2()

    ' Strings do not match - uses vbCompareBinary as Compare argument

    Debug.Print StrComp("ABC", "abc")

    Debug.Print StrComp("DEF", "def")

End Sub
```

129

If you do not use the Option Compare statement, VBA uses Option Compare Binary as the default. Please keep these points in mind when we look at the individual string functions.

Appending Strings

You can use the & operator to append strings in VBA. Let us look at some examples of how you can use this operator to append strings.

```
Sub Append()

    Debug.Print "ABC" & "DEF"

    Debug.Print "Jane" & " " & "Smith"

    Debug.Print "Long " & 22

    Debug.Print "Double " & 14.99

    Debug.Print "Date " & #12/12/2015#

End Sub
```

In the example above, there are different types of data that we have converted to string using the quotes. You will see that the plus operator can also be used to append strings in some programs. The difference between using the & operator and + operator is that the latter will only work with string data types. If you use it with any other data type, you will get an error message.

```
    ' You will get the following error:  "Type Mismatch"

    Debug.Print "Long " + 22
```

If you want to use a complex function to append strings, you should use the Format function which is described later in this chapter.

Extracting Parts of a String

In this section, we will look at some functions that you can use to extract information or data from strings.

You can use the Right, Left and Mid functions to extract the necessary parts in a string. These functions are simple to use. The Right function reads the sentence from the right, the Left function reads the sentence from the left and the Mid function will read the sentence from the point that you specify.

Sub UseLeftRightMid()

   Dim sCustomer As String

   sCustomer = "John Thomas Smith"

   Debug.Print Left(sCustomer, 4) ' This will print John

   Debug.Print Right(sCustomer, 5) ' This will print Smith

   Debug.Print Left(sCustomer, 11) ' This will print John Thomas

   Debug.Print Right(sCustomer, 12) ' This will print Thomas Smith

   Debug.Print Mid(sCustomer, 1, 4) ' This will print John

   Debug.Print Mid(sCustomer, 6, 6) ' This will print Thomas

   Debug.Print Mid(sCustomer, 13, 5) ' This will print Smith

End Sub

As mentioned earlier, the string functions in VBA do not change the original string but return a new string as the result. In the following example, you will see that the string "FullName" remains unchanged even after the use of the Left function.

```vba
Sub UsingLeftExample()

    Dim Fullname As String

    Fullname = "John Smith"

    Debug.Print "Firstname is: "; Left(Fullname, 4)

    ' The original string remains unchanged

    Debug.Print "Fullname is: "; Fullname

End Sub
```

If you wish to make a change to the original string, you will need to assign the return value of the function to the original string.

```vba
Sub ChangingString()

    Dim name As String

    name = "John Smith"

    ' The return value of the function is assigned to the
    original string

    name = Left(name, 4)

    Debug.Print "Name is: "; name

End Sub
```

Searching in a String

InStr and InStrRev are two functions that you can use in VBA to search for substrings within a string. If the compiler can find the substring in the string, the position of the string is returned. This position is the index from where the string starts. If the substring is not found, the compiler will return zero. If the original string and substring are null, the value null is returned.

InStr

Description of Parameters

The function is written as follows:

InStr() Start[Optional], String1, String2, Compare[Optional]

1. **Start**: This number specified where the compiler should start looking for the substring within the actual string. The default option is one.

2. **String1**: This is the original string.

3. **String2**: This is the substring that you want the compiler to search for.

4. **Compare**: This is the method we looked at in the first part of this chapter.

The Use and Examples

This function will return the first position in the string where the substring is found. Let us look at the following example:

```
Sub FindSubString()

  Dim name As String

  name = "John Smith"

  ' This will return the number 3 which indicates the
position of the first h

  Debug.Print InStr(name, "h")

  ' This will return the number 10 which indicates the
position of the first h starting from position 4

  Debug.Print InStr(4, name, "h")
```

' This will return 8

Debug.Print InStr(name, "it")

' This will return 6

Debug.Print InStr(name, "Smith")

' This will return zero since the string "SSS" was not found

Debug.Print InStr(name, "SSS")

End Sub

InStrRev

Description of Parameters

The function is written as follows:

InStrRev() StringCheck, StringMatch, Start[Optional], Compare[Optional]

1. **StringCheck**: This is the string that you need to search for.

2. **StringMatch**: This is the string the compiler should look for.

3. **Start**: This number specified where the compiler should start looking for the substring within the actual string. The default option is one.

4. **Compare**: This is the method we looked at in the first part of this chapter.

The Use and Examples

This function is the same as the InStr function except that is starts the search from the end of the original string. You must note that the position that the compiler returns is the position from the start of the sentence. Therefore, if the substring is available only once in the sentence, the InStr() and InStrRev() functions return the same value.

Let us look at some examples of the InStrRev function.

```
Sub UsingInstrRev()

    Dim name As String

    name = "John Smith"

    ' Both functions will return 1 which is the position of the only J

    Debug.Print InStr(name, "J")

    Debug.Print InStrRev(name, "J")

    ' This will return 10 which indicates the second h

    Debug.Print InStrRev(name, "h")

    ' This will return the number 3 and it indicates the first h as searches from position 9

    Debug.Print InStrRev(name, "h", 9)

    ' This will return 1

    Debug.Print InStrRev(name, "John")

End Sub
```

You should use the InStr and InStrRev functions when you want to perform basic searches in strings. If you want to extract some text from a string, the process is slightly complicated.

Removing Blanks

In VBA, you can use the trim functions to remove blanks or spaces either at the start or end of a string.

The Use and Examples

1. **Trim**: Removes the spaces from both the right and left of a string.

2. **LTrim**: Removes the spaces only from the left of the string.

3. **RTrim**: Removes the spaces from the right of the string.

Sub TrimStr()

    Dim name As String

    name = " John Smith "

    ' Will print "John Smith "

    Debug.Print LTrim(name)

    ' Will print " John Smith"

    Debug.Print RTrim(name)

    ' Will print "John Smith"

    Debug.Print Trim(name)

End Sub

Length of a String

You can use Len to return the length of the string since it is a simple function. This function will return the number of characters in the string. If you use different numeric data types like long, the function will return the number of bytes in the string.

```vb
Sub GetLen()

    Dim name As String

    name = "John Smith"

    ' This will print 10

    Debug.Print Len("John Smith")

    ' This will print 3

    Debug.Print Len("ABC")

    ' This will print 4 since the numeric data type Long is 4
bytes in size

    Dim total As Long

    Debug.Print Len(total)

End Sub
```

Reversing a String

The StrReverse function is another easy function to use. This will
return the original string with the characters reversed.

```vb
Sub RevStr()

    Dim s As String

    s = "Jane Smith"

    ' This will print htimS enaJ

    Debug.Print StrReverse(s)

End Sub
```

Comparing Strings

You can use the function StrComp to compare two strings.

Description of Parameters

The function is written as follows:

StrComp() String1, String2, Compare[Optional]

1. **String1**: The first string that needs to be compared.

2. **String2**: The second string that needs to be compared.

3. **Compare**: This is the method we looked at in the first part of this chapter.

The Use and Examples

Let us look at some examples of how to use the StrComp function:

```
Sub UsingStrComp()

    ' This will return 0

    Debug.Print StrComp("ABC", "ABC", vbTextCompare)

    ' This will return 1

    Debug.Print StrComp("ABCD", "ABC", vbTextCompare)

    ' This will return -1

    Debug.Print StrComp("ABC", "ABCD", vbTextCompare)

    ' This will return Null

    Debug.Print StrComp(Null, "ABCD", vbTextCompare)

End Sub
```

Comparing Strings Using Operators

VBA allows you to use the equal to sign to compare two strings. The differences between the StrComp and equal to sign are:

- The equal to sign will return either true or false.

- You cannot combine a Compare parameter with the equal sign since it will only use the Option Compare setting.

Let us look at a few examples where we use the equal to sign to compare two strings.

Option Compare Text

```
Sub CompareUsingEquals()

    ' This will return true

    Debug.Print "ABC" = "ABC"

    ' This will return True since the compare text parameter is
    at the start of the program

    Debug.Print "ABC" = "abc"

    ' This will return false

    Debug.Print "ABCD" = "ABC"

    ' This will return false

    Debug.Print "ABC" = "ABCD"

    ' This will return null

    Debug.Print Null = "ABCD"

End Sub
```

139

To see if two strings are not equal, you must use the "<>" operator. This operator performs a function that is opposite to the equal to sign.

Option Compare Text

Sub CompareWithNotEqual()

' This will return false

Debug.Print "ABC" <> "ABC"

' This will return false since the Compare Text parameter is at the start of the program

Debug.Print "ABC" <> "abc"

' This will return true

Debug.Print "ABCD" <> "ABC"

' This will return true

Debug.Print "ABC" <> "ABCD"

' This will return null

Debug.Print Null <> "ABCD"

End Sub

Comparing Strings Using Pattern Matching

Pattern matching is a VBA technique that helps you determine if a string has a specific pattern of characters. For instance, there are times when you need to check if a customer number has 3 numeric values and 3 alphabetic characters or if a specific string has the letters ABC followed by a set of numbers or characters. If the compiler deems that the string matches the pattern, it will return the value "True," otherwise, it will return the value "False."

Pattern matching is similar to the Format function. This means that you can use pattern matching in multiple ways. In this section, we will look at some examples that will help you understand how the pattern matching technique works. This will cover the common uses of pattern matching. Let us take the following string: [abc][!def]]?#X*

Let us look at how this string will work:

1. [abc]: This will represent a character – a, b or c.

2. [!def]: This will represent a character that is not d, e or f.

3. ?: This will represent any character.

4. #: This will represent any digit.

5. X: This represents the character X.

6. *: This means that the string is followed by more characters or zero.

Therefore, this is a valid string.

Now, let us consider the following string: apY6X.

1. a: This character is one of a, b and c.

2. p: This is not a character that is d, e or f.

3. Y: This is any character.

4. 6: This is a digit.

5. X: This is the letter X.

You can now say that the pattern for both strings is the same.

Let us look at a code that will show you a variety of results when you use the same pattern:

```vba
Sub Patterns()

    ' This will print true

    Debug.Print 1; "apY6X" Like "[abc][!def]?#X*"

    ' This will print true since any combination is valid after X

    Debug.Print 2; "apY6Xsf34FAD" Like "[abc][!def]?#X*"

    ' This will print false since the character is not a, b or c

    Debug.Print 3; "dpY6X" Like "[abc][!def]?#X*"

    ' This will print false since the character is one of d, e and f

    Debug.Print 4; "aeY6X" Like "[abc][!def]?#X*"

    ' This will print false since the character at 4 should be a digit.

    Debug.Print 5; "apYAX" Like "[abc][!def]?#X*"

    ' This will print false since the character at position 5 should be X.

    Debug.Print 1; "apY6Z" Like "[abc][!def]?#X*"

End Sub
```

Replacing Part of a String

You should use the replace function when you want to replace a substring in a string using another substring. This function will replace all the instances where the substrings are found.

Description of Parameters

The function is written as follows:

142

Replace() Expression, Find, Replace, Start[Optional], Count[Optional], Compare[Optional]

1. Expression: This is the original string.

2. Find: This is the substring that you want to replace in the Expression string.

3. Replace: This is the substring you want to replace the Find substring with.

4. Start: This is the start position of the string. The position is taken as 1 by default.

5. Count: This is the number of substitutions you want to make. The default is one, which means that all the Find substrings are replaced with the Replace substring.

6. Compare: This is the method we looked at in the first part of this chapter.

The Use and Examples

In the following code, we will look at some examples of how to use the Replace function.

```
Sub ReplaceExamples()

    ' To replace all the question marks in the string with semi colons.

    Debug.Print Replace("A?B?C?D?E", "?", ";")

    ' To replace Smith with Jones

    Debug.Print Replace("Peter Smith,Ann Smith", "Smith", "Jones")

    ' To replace AX with AB
```

```
Debug.Print Replace("ACD AXC BAX", "AX", "AB")
```

End Sub

The output will be as follows:

A;B;C;D;E

Peter Jones,Sophia Jones

ACD ABC BAB

In the next block of code, we will use the Count optional parameter to determine the number of substitutions you want to make. For instance, if you set up Count equal to one, it means that you want the compiler to only replace the first occurrence of the Find string.

```
Sub ReplaceCount()

    ' To replace only the first question mark

    Debug.Print Replace("A?B?C?D?E", "?", ";", Count:=1)

    ' To replace the first two question marks

    Debug.Print Replace("A?B?C?D?E", "?", ";", Count:=2)

End Sub
```

The output will be as follows:

A;B?C?D?E

A;B;C?D?E

You can return a part of the string if you use the Start optional parameter. The compiler will return the part of the string from the position that you specify in the Start parameter. When you use this operator, it will ignore all the words or the part of the string before the start position.

Sub ReplacePartial()

' This will use the original string from the position 4

Debug.Print Replace("A?B?C?D?E", "?", ";", Start:=4)

' This will use the original string from the position 8

Debug.Print Replace("AA?B?C?D?E", "?", ";", Start:=8)

' There are no items that will be replaced, but it will return the last two values

Debug.Print Replace("ABCD", "X", "Y", Start:=3)

End Sub

The output will be as follows:

;C;D;E

;E

CD

There may be times when you want to replace only the lower or upper case letters in a string. At such times, you can use the Compare parameter. This is a parameter that can be used in many string functions. To understand this better, you should refer to the section above.

Sub ReplaceCase()

' This will only replace the capitalized A's

Debug.Print Replace("AaAa", "A", "X", Compare:=vbBinaryCompare)

' This will replace all the A's

```vba
Debug.Print Replace("AaAa", "A", "X", _
Compare:=vbTextCompare)

End Sub
```

The output is as follows:

XaXa

XXXX

Multiple Replaces

You can nest the calls if you want to replace more than one value in a string. Let us look at the following example where we will replace the X and Y with A and B respectively.

```vba
Sub ReplaceMulti()

    Dim newString As String

    ' Replace the A with X

    newString = Replace("ABCD ABDN", "A", "X")

    ' Replace the B with Y in the new string

    newString = Replace(newString, "B", "Y")

    Debug.Print newString

End Sub
```

In the example below, we will make a few changes to the code above to perform this task. The return value of the first function is used as the argument or the original string for the second replacement.

```vba
Sub ReplaceMultiNested()

    Dim newString As String
```

' To replace A with X and B with Y

```
newString = Replace(Replace("ABCD ABDN", "A", "X"), "B", "Y")
```

Debug.Print newString

End Sub

The result of these replacements will be XYCD XYDN.

Chapter Six

Error Handling and Debugging

Error handling is a common programming practice where the programmer should anticipate and code for error conditions, which may arise when he or she runs the program. You will come across three errors – user entry data errors where the user enters a negative number instead of a positive number, run time errors which occur when VBA cannot execute a program statement and compiler errors where the programmer has not declared a variable. We will only worry about the run time errors in this chapter since the other two errors are easy for a programmer to solve. Typical errors include those where VBA is attempting to access a worksheet or workbook that is non-existent or attempting to divide a number by zero. The code in this chapter will use try to divide a number by zero since we want to raise an error.

You should include as many checks as you can when you write the code to ensure that you do not come across any run time errors when you execute the code. This includes ensuring that the worksheets and workbooks being referred to in the code are all present and the names are defined. When you constantly check the application when you write the code, you can ensure that the macro is stable. This is better than to detect an error when your application is running.

If a run time error occurs and you do not have a code written to handle the errors, VBA will display the run time error dialog box. When the application is in the development stage, you can welcome these errors. If the application is at the final stage or in the

148

production environment, you cannot expect to face these errors. The goal of an error handling code is to ensure that you identify the errors at run time and then correct them immediately. The goal should be to prevent the occurrence of any unhandled errors.

In this chapter, we will refer to Property procedure, Function and Sub as procedure and the words exit statement will mean Exit Property, Exit Function and Exit Sub. The words end statement will mean End Property, End Function, End Sub and End.

The On Error Statement

The heart of every error handling process in VBA is the On Error statement. When a run time error occurs, this statement will tell VBA what it must do to counter the error. The On Error statement takes the following forms:

1. On Error Goto 0

2. On Error Resume Next

3. On Error Goto <label>:

On Error Goto o is the default in VBA. This statement indicates that VBA should always display the standard run time error dialog box if it encounters a run time error when it executes the code. This will give you a chance to enter the debug mode and check the code. Alternatively, you can terminate the code. The On Error Goto o is the same as not including an error handling statement in your code. The error will prompt VBA to display the standard window.

The On Error Resume Next is the most misused and commonly used form. This statement will instruct VBA to ignore the line of code that has the error and move to the next line of code. You must remember that this statement does not fix the code in any way. It will only tell VBA to act as if there was no error in the code. This error can have a negative effect on the code. It is important that you test your code for any errors and then take appropriate actions to solve those errors. You can do this by executing the appropriate code when the value of Err.Number is not zero. For instance,

```
On Error Resume Next

N = 1 / 0    ' cause an error

If Err.Number <> 0 Then

    N = 1

End If
```

In the above code, we are assigning the value of 1/0 to a variable N. This is an incorrect approach, therefore VBA will raise the Division By Zero Error (Error 11). The code will continue to execute since we have used the On Error Resume Next statement. The statement will assign a value to the variable N after it tests the value of Err.Number.

The third form is the On Error Goto <lable>. This statement will tell VBA that it needs to execute the line of code after a specific line label if an error occurs. When the error occurs, VBA will ignore every line of code between the error line and the specified line label, including any loop statements.

```
On Error Goto ErrHandler:

N = 1 / 0    ' cause an error

'

' more code

'

Exit Sub

ErrHandler:

' error handling code

Resume Next

End Sub
```

Enabled and Active Error Handlers

When the On Error statement is executed, VBA will enable an error handler. It is important to remember that VBA will only enable on error handler at any given point, and it will behave according to that error handler. VBA will execute the code in this error handler when any error occurs. The execution is transferred to a different location using the On Error Goto <label>: statement. The code in the error handler should either resume execution in the main program or fix the error in the program. You an also use the error handler to terminate the execution of the program. You cannot use it like the second form of the On Error statement to skip a few lines. For example, the code below will not function correctly:

On Error GoTo Err1:

Debug.Print 1 / 0

' more code

Err1:

On Error GoTo Err2:

Debug.Print 1 / 0

' more code

Err2:

The execution of code transfers to Err1 when the first error occurs. Since the error handler is active when the next error occurs, the On Error statement will not trap the error.

The Resume Statement

The Resume statement will instruct VBA to resume the execution of the code at a specific point the code. You should use the Resume statement only in the error handling blocks of code. If you use it in another part of the program, it will cause an error. You should not use the Goto statement to direct the code execution out of the error handling section of code. If you do this, you will encounter some strange problems with error handlers.

There are three syntactic forms that the Resume statement takes:

1. Resume

2. Resume Next

3. Resume <label>

When Resume is used alone, it will instruct VBA to resume the execution of the program at the line of code that has the error. If you use this, you must ensure that the error handling code or block can fix the problem. Otherwise, the code will enter a loop that is endless since it will be jumping between the error handling block and the line that caused the error. In the example below, we will try to activate a worksheet that does not exist. VBA will give you an error (Subscript Out Of Range) and will immediately jump to the error handling code. This code will then create a sheet and solve the problems. The execution will then resume at the line of code that caused the error.

```
On Error GoTo ErrHandler:
Worksheets("NewSheet").Activate
Exit Sub
ErrHandler:
If Err.Number = 9 Then
    ' sheet does not exist, so create it
    Worksheets.Add.Name = "NewSheet"
    ' go back to the line of code that caused the problem
    Resume
End If
```

The second form of the Resume is Resume Next. This statement will instruct VBA to execute the line of code that immediately follows the line that caused the error. The following code sets a value to the variable N and it causes an error. The error handling code will assign the variable N a value 1, and will continue to execute the remainder of the program.

On Error GoTo ErrHandler:

N = 1 / 0

Debug.Print N

Exit Sub

ErrHandler:

N = 1

' go back to the line following the error

Resume Next

The third form is the Resume <label> form. This is similar to the On Error Goto <label> statement. The statement will instruct VBA to execute the code from the line label. This means that it will skip the part of the code where there is an error. For instance,

On Error GoTo ErrHandler:

N = 1 / 0

'

' code that is skipped if an error occurs

'

Label1:

'

```
' more code to execute

'

Exit Sub

ErrHandler:

' go back to the line at Label1:

Resume Label1:
```

Every form of the Resume statement will either clear or reset the error object.

Error Handling With Multiple Procedures

You do not need to include an error code in every procedure. If an error occurs while running a program, VBA will use the last On Error statement and act accordingly. If the code that is causing the error is in the same procedure as the On Error statements, the error is handled in the ways mentioned above. If the procedure does not have an error handling code, VBA will need to go back to the procedure and proceed backward until it reaches the line with the incorrect code. For example, a procedure A calls B and B calls C, and only procedure A has an error handling code. If an error occurs in C, VBA will go back to the error handling code in procedure A. It will skip all the code in procedure B.

A Note of Caution

You may want to use the On Error Resume Next statement when you are dealing with errors. This is a bad coding practice since you cannot run the code without solving the errors. You have to remember that this statement does not skip errors but ignores them.

Chapter Seven

Mistakes to Avoid

If you are reading this chapter, you will be familiar with Excel VBA. It is easy for anybody to make mistakes when they write a code in VBA. These mistakes will cost you greatly. This chapter lists the common mistakes that most VBA amateurs make.

Not Using Arrays

An interesting mistake that most VBA programmers make is that they try to process all the functions in a large nested loop. They filter the data down through the different rows and columns in the worksheet during the process of calculation. This method can work, but it can lead to performance troubles. If you have to perform the same function repeatedly, the efficiency of the macro will decrease. When you loop through the same column and you extract the values every single time, you are not only affecting the macro, but also affecting the processor. An efficient way to handle a list of numbers is to use an array.

If you have not used an array before, let me introduce it to you now. An array is a set of elements that have the same data type. Each element in the array is given an index. You must use this index to refer to the element in the array. An array can be defined by using the following statement: Dim MyArray (12) as Integer. This will create an array with 12 indices and variables that you will need to fill. Let us look at how a loop with an array will look like:

```
Sub Test1()

    Dim x As Integer

    intNumRows = Range("A2",
Range("A2").End(xldown)).Rows.Count

    Range("A2").Select

    For x = 1 To intNumRows

      arrMyArray(x-1) = Range("A" & str(x)).value

      ActiveCell.Offset(1, 0).Select

    Next

  End Sub
```

In this example, the code is processing through every cell in the range before it performs the calculation function.

Using .Select or .Activate

You do not have to always use the .Select or .Activate functions when you write code in VBA. You may want to use these functions since the Macro Recorder generates them. These functions are unnecessary for the following reasons:

- These functions may lead to the repainting of the screen. If you use the following function Sheets("Sheet1").Activate, Excel will redraw the screen so you can see Sheet1. This will lead to a slow macro.

- These functions will confuse users since you will be manipulating the workbook when the user is working on it. There are some users who will worry that they are being hacked.

You should use these functions only when you want to bring the user to a specific cell or worksheet. Otherwise, you should delete the line of code since it will be doing more harm than good.

Using Variant Type

Another mistake that most programmers make is to use one Type when they are actually using another. If you look at the following code, you will think that a, b and c are of the Long type. Well, that is incorrect since the variables a and b are of the Variant type. This means that they can be any data type, and can change from one type to another.

It is dangerous to have a variant type since it will become difficult for you to identify the bugs in your code. You should always avoid Variant types in VBA. There are some functions that will need the use of a Variant type, but you should avoid them if you can.

Not Using Application.ScreenUpdating = False

When you make a change to a cell or a group of cells in your code, Excel will need to repaint the screen to show the user the changes. This will make your macros slow. When you write a macro the next time, you should use the following lines of code:

```
Public Sub MakeCodeFaster()

Application.ScreenUpdating = False


' Block of code

' This setting should always be reset back

Application.ScreenUpdating = True

End Sub
```

Referencing the Worksheet Name with a String

People will refer to a worksheet using a String. Look at the following example:

```
Public Sub SheetReferenceExample()

    Dim ws As Worksheet

    Set ws = Sheets("Sheet1")

    Debug.Print ws.Name

End Sub
```

This does seem harmless does it not? In most cases, it is harmless. Imagine that you give another person this workbook, and that person decides to rename the sheet to "Reprot." When he tries to run the macro, the macro will look for "Sheet1," which no longer exists. Therefore, this macro will not work. You should choose to reference the sheet by using an object instead of using the "Sheets" collection. To be more resilient, let us use the following block of code:

```
Public Sub SheetReferenceExample()

    Dim ws As Worksheet

    Set ws = Sheet1 ' used to be Sheets("Sheet1")

    Debug.Print ws.Name

End Sub
```

If you want to rename Sheet1 to something more meaningful, you can go to the VBA Project properties window and make a change to the name of the module. Once you rename the module, you will also need to update the VBA code.

Not Qualifying the Range References

This is a common mistake that most people make when they write their code, and it is a real pain to debug this error. This error comes up when you do not qualify the range reference in the VBA code. You may wonder what I mean when I say range reference.

When you say Range("A1"), which sheet do you think the code is referring to? It is referring to the Activesheet. This means that the compiler will look at cell A1 in the worksheet that the user is referring to. This is harmless on most occasions, but there are times when you may add more features to your code. These features make it hard for the compiler to execute the code. When the user or even you run the code, and you click on another worksheet, the code will behave differently. Let us look at the following example:

```
Public Sub FullyQualifyReferences()

    Dim fillRange As Range

    Set fillRange = Range("A1:B5")

    Dim cell As Range

    For Each cell In fillRange

        Range(cell.Address) = cell.Address

        Application.Wait (Now + TimeValue("0:00:01"))

        DoEvents

    Next cell

End Sub
```

Run the code in VBA and see what happens. If you do not specify the worksheet when you use the Range() function, Excel will assume that you are looking at the active sheet. To avoid this, you should make a slight change to your code. All you need to do is change Range(cell.Address) = cell.Address to Data.Range(cell.Address) = cell.Address.

In the second statement, data refers to the sheet object. There are other ways to do this, but I wanted to use a simple example which did not need the addition of too much code.

Writing a Big Function

If you go back to some of the old functions you may have written, you will notice that they are very long. You will need to continue to scroll until you reach the end of the function.

You should remember that the function you write should fit your screen. You should be able to view the code without having to scroll. You must ensure that you keep the methods short by creating sub procedures or helper functions.

Using Nested For or If Statements

You may have read earlier that you can include many levels of nesting when you write your code. Do you think that is a good idea? You will need to add comments and indent the code to ensure that another user can read your code. If you are unsure of what I mean by nesting, let us look at the following example:

```
Public Sub WayTooMuchNesting()

    Dim updateRange As Range

    Set updateRange = Sheet2.Range("B2:B50")

    Dim cell As Range

    For Each cell In updateRange

        If (cell.Value > 1) Then
```

```vba
If (cell.Value < 100) Then

    If (cell.Offset(0, 1).Value = "2x Cost") Then

        cell.Value = cell.Value * 2

    Else

        ' do nothing

    End If

    End If

    End If

Next cell

End Sub
```

This is certainly not a clean code. If you use more than three levels of nesting, you have gone too far. To reduce the number of nesting levels, you should invert the condition in your If statement. In the example above, the code will make a change if a bunch of statements pass. You can invert this to ensure that the compiler will only execute the statements for the opposite case. That way you can skip the many levels of nesting.

Let us look at the updated version of the above example.

```vba
Public Sub ReducedNesting()

    Dim updateRange As Range

    Set updateRange = Sheet2.Range("B2:B50")

    Dim cell As Range

    For Each cell In updateRange

        If (cell.Value <= 1) Then GoTo NextCell
```

```
If (cell.Value >= 100) Then GoTo NextCell

    If (cell.Offset(0, 1).Value <> "2x Cost") Then GoTo
NextCell

    cell.Value = cell.Value * 2

NextCell:

    Next cell

End Sub
```

You can also combine the If statements in the code above if you wish.

Conclusion

Thank you once again for purchasing the book. If you have a good idea about VBA and how to write code in VBA you have come to the right place. This book provides information on some important concepts in VBA and will take you through the process of handling errors in your code.

I hope you have gathered all the information you are looking for. Thank you again for downloading the book !

If you're finding the information valuable so far, please be sure to leave **5-star feedback on Amazon.**

Sources

http://users.iems.northwestern.edu/~nelsonb/IEMS435/VBAPrimer.pdf

http://mcise.uri.edu/jones/ise325/vba%20primer.htm

http://ce270.groups.et.byu.net/syllabus/vbaprimer/intro/index.php

http://ce270.groups.et.byu.net/syllabus/vbaprimer/vb-variables/index.php

https://www.excel-easy.com/vba/variables.html

https://wellsr.com/vba/excel/vba-declare-variable/

https://www.excel-easy.com/vba/string-manipulation.html

https://www.tutorialspoint.com/vba/vba_strings.htm

http://codevba.com/learn/strings.htm#.W-RAHNUzaCg

https://excelmacromastery.com/vba-string-functions/#How_To_Use_Compare

https://excelmacromastery.com/vba-string-functions/#Searching_Within_a_String

https://excelmacromastery.com/vba-instr/#Example_3_Checkif_a_filename_is_valid

https://www.excel-easy.com/vba/loop.html

https://www.excelfunctions.net/vba-loops.html

https://powerspreadsheets.com/excel-vba-loops/#What-Is-An-Excel-VBA-Loop

https://www.contextures.com/excelvbatips.html

https://www.spreadsheetsmadeeasy.com/7-common-vba-mistakes-to-avoid/

https://www.encodedna.com/excel/copy-data-from-closed-excel-workbook-without-opening.htm

https://analysistabs.com/excel-vba/read-get-data-from-cell-worksheet/

http://www.globaliconnect.com/excel/index.php?option=com_content&view=article&id=361:excel-vba-activex-controls-form-controls-autoshapes-on-a-worksheet&catid=79&Itemid=475

http://codevba.com/learn/condition_statements.htm#.W-UNZ5MzbIU

https://analysistabs.com/excel-vba/conditional-statements/

http://www.cpearson.com/excel/errorhandling.htm

http://www.globaliconnect.com/excel/index.php?option=com_content&view=article&id=122:excel-vba-loops-with-examples-for-loop-do-while-loop-do-until-loop&catid=79&Itemid=475

Excel VBA

A Step-By-Step Comprehensive Guide on Advanced Excel VBA Programming Techniques and Strategies

Introduction

VBA is a tool that helps you perform tasks in the easiest way possible. You can perform these tasks in less than a minute when you automate them using VBA. For instance, you can create custom reports, add new toolbars or perform different types of data analysis using VBA. When you learn to write VBA codes, you will become an expert at all the tasks you perform, and you can absorb more work since you can finish a job quickly.

If you want to gather more information on VBA programming, you have come to the right place. This book provides more information about VBA and also talks about the different ways you can use VBA to automate processes. If you write code, you should also know what data types you should use and how you can use them in functions and modules. This book will provide all the information you need to know about VBA.

Over the course of the book, you will gather information on the different data types used in VBA, different types of collections in the VBA, some exercises on conditional and looping statements, arrays and other necessary information. You will also learn how to redirect the flow of programs and also how you should handle the errors.

To make the learning interesting, there are some exercises provided at the end of some chapters. You should try to write the code yourself before you look at the solutions provided to you at the end of the book. Remember that practice will make you better at coding. You will make errors, and these errors will help you become a better programmer. This book is a continuation of the beginner's book in the series and provides a little more information about VBA.

Thank you for purchasing the book. I hope you gather all the information you are looking for.

Chapter One

What Can You Do With VBA?

People use Excel and VBA for a variety of reasons. Some examples are:

- Analyzing data

- Creating lists

- Developing diagrams and charts using data

- Forecasting and Budgeting

- Creating forms and invoices

The list is endless since you can use Excel for many reasons, but I am sure you get the idea. In simple words, you can use Excel to perform different tasks, and I am sure you read the first book in the series and have picked up this book with a set of expectations. If there is any function in Excel that you want to automate, you can use VBA.

For instance, you may want to create or develop a program that will help you import some data or numbers and then format that data to print a report. Once you develop the code, you can execute the macro using a command or a button. This will ensure that Excel performs the task in a few seconds or minutes.

Common Uses of VBA

In the first book, you gathered information on the different functions in VBA. Before you apply those functions, you should understand why you want to use VBA. You have to take some time out of your day and write the code to automate processes. You must also look for different ways to use VBA. This section covers some processes that you can automate using VBA.

Automating Documents

People hate having to prepare documents, and if the documents they prepare always contain the same information, they will certainly not want to put more work into that document. In this instance, you can use the Excel Ad-in called Mail Merge, which is used to automate letters and documents, but this is not an option you can use when you need to write individual documents or letters. At such times, you should write a VBA code that will help you create a form, which will include common information. You can then include check boxes in your code to help you write the documents.

Word processing is not the only task you can automate using VBA. You can also automate the spreadsheet and there are numerous programs you can create for the same. For example, you can extract information or data from the internet into a spreadsheet by clicking a button. Therefore, you can limit the time you spend on simply copying the data from the web and pasting it according to the required format in your Excel worksheet.

Customizing Application Interfaces

There are some features in an application that will not help your cause, and you can learn to turn those features off. You cannot turn off these features if you need to use them for your other you work. Instead of disabling that feature, you can use VBA to create a new feature, which has all the functions that you need. For example, you can write a VBA code to help you if you want to use conditional formatting when you make some changes in your worksheet.

It is easy to change the interface of an application, so it works better for you. You can customize toolbars or menu systems, and can also move some elements around in the interface to make it look presentable. Additionally, you can use multiple interfaces and use a VBA code to shift between those interfaces.

A common application of VBA is to perform a variety of calculations in a few seconds. You can create different graphs and equations using the data that you store in Excel. You must make some changes or modifications to the data you are using so you can perform these calculations on it. If the equation is slightly complicated, you can use VBA and develop a code that will help to simplify the process. You can also use certain iterative functions to perform different calculations.

There are times when the numbers you obtain as a result of a calculation do not mean too much. This value is a just a number until someone decides what to do with that number. Some of the decisions a user makes are repetitive, and a smart application will save time and allow you to enjoy a nice game of Solitaire.

Adding new application features

Most developers and vendors do not use the applications they develop or build. Therefore, they forget to update the code for their application. You can tweak those applications by adding new features or develop a new application using VBA. When you develop these applications, you can complete some of your work in a few minutes or less, and you can impress your colleagues and your boss. This is an added use of VBA.

Chapter Two

VBA, A Primer

Macro Recorder

As mentioned in the previous book, the macro recorder is an important and useful tool in Excel. This tool will record every action that you perform in Excel. You only need to record a task once using the macro recorder, and you can execute that same task a million times by clicking a button. If you do not know how to program a specific task in Excel, you can use the Macro Recorder to help you understand what you need to do. You can then open the Visual Basic Editor once you have recorded the task to see how you can program it.

You cannot perform many tasks when you use the Macro Recorder. For instance, you cannot use the macro recorder to loop through data. The macro recorder also uses more code than you need, which will slow the process down.

Record a Macro

- Go to the Menu Bar and move the Developer Tab, and click the button to Record the Macro.

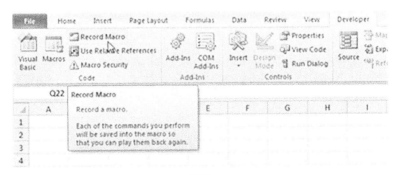

- Enter the name of the macro.

- Choose the workbook where you want to use the macro. This means that the macro can only be used in the current workbook.

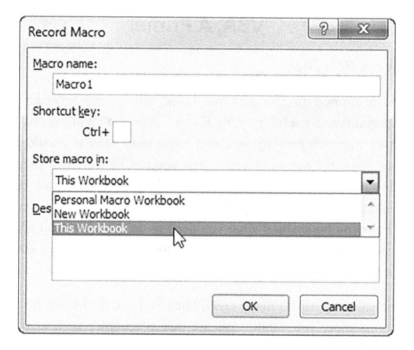

- If you store the macro in a personal macro workbook, you can access the macro in all your workbooks. This is only because Excel stores the macro in a hidden workbook, which will open automatically when it starts. If you store the macro in a new workbook, you can use the macro only in the opened workbook.

- Click OK.

- Now, right click on the active cell in the worksheet. Ensure that you do not select any other cell. Click format cells.

- Select the percentage.

- Click OK.

- Now, select the stop recording.

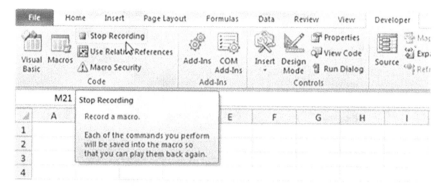

You have successfully recorded your macro using the macro recorder.

Run the Recorded Macro

You will now need to test the macro and see if you can change the format of the numbers to percentage.

- Enter any numbers between 0 and 1 in the spreadsheet.

- Select the numbers.

	A	B
1	percentages	
2	0.2	
3	0.6	
4	0.8	
5	0.6	
6	1	
7	0.4	
8		

- Move to the Developer tab, and click macros.

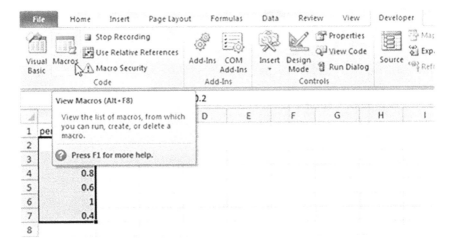

- Now click run.

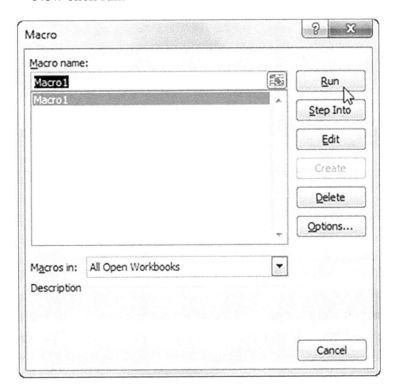

You will see the following result.

⚐	A	B
1	percentages	
2	20.00%	
3	60.00%	
4	80.00%	
5	60.00%	
6	100.00%	
7	40.00%	
8		

See The Macro

If you want to look at the macro, you should open the Visual Basic Editor.

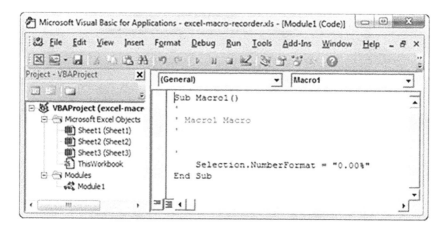

The macro, called Module 1, is placed in a module. The code that is placed in the module is always available to the full workbook. This means you can change the format for the numbers in all the sheets in the workbook. If you assign a macro to the command button, you should remember that the macro would only be available for that specific sheet.

Macro Storage and Security

The developers at Microsoft changed the security settings that help to prevent macros from running. This development was only made when macros were used to deliver some high-profile viruses. We covered some information about the security of macros in the first part of the book. Let us now look at how you can adjust the default settings in a macro.

You can either control the settings for a macro in some workbooks by saving the workbook in trusted locations or by adjusting the security settings globally. If you store a workbook with a macro in a folder that you label a trusted location, the macros will automatically be enabled when you open the workbook.

You can check the security of your macro in the Developer tab under the Macro Security icon. If you click this icon, a dialog box with the settings category will be displayed. You can access the folders that you trust by scrolling down the left navigation bar.

How to Add a Trusted Location

As mentioned earlier, you can save the workbooks with macros in a folder that you mark as a trusted location. If you save a workbook in that folder, the macros will always be enabled. The developers suggest that you should always have a trusted location in your hard drive. Remember that you can never trust the location on a network drive.

If you want to specify a trusted location, you should follow the steps given below:

1. Go to the Developer Tab and click on Macro Security.

2. Move to the left navigation pane in the Trust Center and choose the Trusted Location.

3. If you want to save the file on a network drive, you should add that location into the trusted locations.

4. Go to 'My Networks' in the Trusted Location dialog box and click the 'Add New Location' button.

5. You will see the list of Trusted Locations in a dialog box.

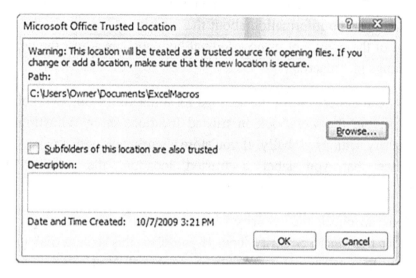

6. Now click the Browse button and go to the parent folder of the folder that you want to make a trusted location. Now click on the Trusted Folder. You will not find the name of the Folder in the text box, but click OK. The correct name will come in the Browse dialog box.

7. If you want to include the subfolders in the selected folder, you should select the radio button against the 'Subfolders of this location are also trusted' option.

8. Now, click OK to add the folder to the list.

How to Enable Macros outside a Trusted Location

When you do not save an Excel workbook in a trusted location, Excel will always rely on the macro settings. In Excel 2003, a macro could have a low, medium, high or very high security. These settings were later renamed by the developers in Microsoft. If you want to access the macro settings, you should go to the Developers Tab and choose Macro Security. Excel will then display the Macro

Settings dialog box. You should select the 'Disable All Macros with Notification' option. Let us look at the description of the options in the dialog box.

Disable All Macros without Notification

This setting will not allow any macro to run. If you do not always want to run the macro when you open the workbook, you should choose this setting. Since you are still learning how to use macros and work with them, you should not use this setting. This setting is equivalent to the Very High Security that is found in Excel 2003. If you choose this setting, you can only run macros if they are saved in a Trusted Location.

Disable All Macros with Notification

This setting is like the Medium security setting in Excel 2003. This is the recommended setting that you should use. If you use this setting, Excel will ask you if you want to Enable or Disable a macro when you open a workbook. You may often choose this option if you are a beginner. In Excel 2010, you will see a message in the message area, which states that the macros have been disabled. You can either choose to enable or disable the content in the workbook by choosing that option.

Disable All Macros except Digitally Signed Macros

If you wish to use this setting, you should always use a digital signing tool like VeriSign or any other provider to sign your macro. If you are going to sell your macros to other parties, you should use this security option. This is a hassle if you want to write macros only for your use.

Enable All Macros

Experts suggest that you do not use this option since dangerous codes can also run on your system. This setting is equivalent to the Low security option in Excel 2003, and is the easiest option to use. This option will open your system up to attacks from malicious viruses.

Disabling All Macros with Notification

Experts suggest that you set your macro to disable all content after it gives you a notification. If you save a workbook with a macro using this setting, you will see a security warning right above the formula bar when you open the workbook. If you know that there are macros in the workbook, all you need to do is click 'Enable Content.' You can click on the X on the far right of the bar if you do not want to enable any of the macros in the workbook.

If you do forget to enable the macro and then attempt to run that macro, Excel will indicate that the macro will not run since you have disabled all macros in the workbook. If this happens, you should reopen the workbook to enable the macros again.

Exercises

1. Write a program to protect all worksheets in a workbook.

2. Write a program to lock or protect cells in a worksheet.

Chapter Three

How to Manipulate Data in Excel

A macro processes code written in the Visual Basic Editor to manage and manipulate huge volumes of data. The previous chapter provides information on how you can use a macro to format certain fields or cells in Excel to meet your criteria.

The following is an example of a VBA script:

```
Sub ConfigureLogic()

    Dim qstEntries

    Dim dqstEntries

    Dim qstCnt, dqstCnt

    qstEntries = Range("QualifiedEntry").Count

    qst = qstEntries -
    WorksheetFunction.CountIf(Range("QualifiedEntry"),
    "")

    ReDim QualifiedEntryText(qst)

    'MsgBox (qst)

    dqstEntries = Range("DisQualifiedEntry").Count

    dqst = dqstEntries -
    WorksheetFunction.CountIf(Range("DisQualifiedEntry"
    ), "")

    ReDim DisqualifiedEntryText(dqst)

    'MsgBox (dqst)
```

```
For qstCnt = 1 To qst

QualifiedEntryText(qstCnt) =
ThisWorkbook.Worksheets("Qualifiers").Range("J" & 8
+ qstCnt).value

'MsgBox (QualifiedEntryText(qstCnt))

logging ("Configured Qualified Entry entry #" & qstCnt
& " as {" & QualifiedEntryText(qstCnt) & "}")

Next

For dqstCnt = 1 To dqst

DisqualifiedEntryText(dqstCnt) =
ThisWorkbook.Worksheets("Qualifiers").Range("M" &
8 + dqstCnt).value

'MsgBox (DisqualifiedEntryText(dqstCnt))

logging ("Configured DisQualified Entry entry #" &
qstCnt & " as {" & DisqualifiedEntryText(dqstCnt) &
"}")

Next

includeEntry =
ThisWorkbook.Worksheets("Qualifiers").Range("Includ
eSibling").value

'MsgBox (includeEntry)

logging ("Entrys included in search - " & includeEntry)

End Sub
```

How to Analyze and Manipulate Data in a Spreadsheet

If you want to use VBA to analyze data, you should check the macro settings in Excel. Ensure that the settings as per your requirements. You should also make sure that the macro settings are activated in Excel. Now, create a worksheet and call it 'Qualifiers.'

We will be using this worksheet to check the data and ensure that the data qualifies all the selections that you require. You must then set up the qualifiers based on the code you have written. You cannot cut and paste these qualifiers, but will need to enter them manually.

ThisWorkbook.Worksheets("Qualifiers").Range("J" & 8 + qstCnt).value

How to Construct an Array and Locate The Range

In the above function, the range will start from Cell J9. The function notes 8, but the range is 9 since we have declared the qstCnt to be 1 using the following code:

For qstCnt = 1 To qst

It is because of this statement that the list will start at 9.

If you want to construct an array using the entries in the Qualifiers worksheet, you should add random words or numbers between cells J9 and J13, including those cells. When the rows are complete, you can find and manipulate the data in Excel.

```
Private Sub CountSheets()

    Dim sheetcount

    Dim WS As Worksheet

    sheetcount = 0

    logging ("*****Starting Scrub*********")

    For Each WS In ThisWorkbook.Worksheets

    sheetcount = sheetcount + 1

    If WS.Name = "Selected" Then

    'need to log the date and time into sheet named
    "Logging"
```

```
ActionCnt = ActionCnt + 1

logging ("Calling sheet: " & WS.Name)

scrubsheet (sheetcount)

Else

ActionCnt = ActionCnt + 1

logging ("Skipped over sheet: " & WS.Name)

End If

Next WS

'MsgBox ("ending")

ActionCnt = ActionCnt + 1

logging ("****Scrub DONE!")

Application.ScreenUpdating = True

End Sub
```

The following example will show you how you can write a macro for a working tab counter:

```
Dim sheetcount

Dim WS As Worksheet

sheetcount = 0

logging ("*****Starting Scrub*********")

For Each WS In ThisWorkbook.Worksheets

sheetcount = sheetcount + 1
```

When you initialize the sheet count variable, you should first set it to zero before you restart the counter. You can also use the logging() subroutine to keep track of all the actions in the qualifiers tab to make the correct selections. The For loop in the above example will set up the counting variable in the Active Workbook.

Once you initialize WS, it will make the worksheet that you are currently in the active worksheet. Since this module is unnamed, it will run in any workbook. If you have many workbooks open, this module may run in an incorrect workbook. If you want to avoid any errors, you should name the workbook that you want the module to run in.

When the loop runs, it will add another variable to the sheet count and keep a track of the tabs. We will then move to

```
If WS.Name = "Selected" Then
'need to log the date and time into sheet named "Logging"
ActionCnt = ActionCnt + 1
logging ("Calling sheet: " & WS.Name)
scrubsheet (sheetcount)
Else
ActionCnt = ActionCnt + 1
logging ("Skipped over sheet: " & WS.Name)
End If
```

In this section of the code, we are looking for the Selected tab. If the variable WS is the same as the Selected worksheet, you can fire up the Scrub sheet subroutine. If the variable WS is not the same as the Selected worksheet, then the sheet will be skipped and the action will be counted. The code above is an example of how you can write a macro to count the number of tabs and locate a specific tab.

The next parts of this chapter talk about the different ways you can manipulate data in Excel.

Different Ways to Manipulate Data

Count the Number of Sheets in a Workbook

```
Dim TAB

For Each TAB In ThisWorkbook.Worksheets

'some routine here

Next
```

Filter by using Advanced Criteria

```
Range("A2:Z99").Sort key1:=Range("A5"),
order1:=xlAscending, Header:=xlNo
```

Find The Last Column, Cell Or Row On A Worksheet

```
Dim cellcount

cellcount =
Cells(ThisWorkbook.Worksheets("worksheet").Rows.Count
, 1).End(xlUp).Row
```

Getting Values from another Worksheet

```
dim newvalue

newvalue =
ThisWorkbook.Worksheets("worksheet").Range("F1").valu
e
```

Apply Auto-Fit To A Column

```
Columns("A:A").EntireColumn.AutoFit
```

Adding Named Ranges to Specific Sheets

```
ThisWorkbook.Worksheets("worksheet").Names.Add
Name:="Status", RefersToR1C1:="=worksheet!C2"
```

Insert Rows Into A Worksheet

```
Dim Row, Column

Cells(Row, Column).EntireRow.Select

Selection.Insert
```

Copy an Entire Row for Pasting

```
ActiveSheet.Range("A1").EntireRow.Select

Selection.Copy

Delete An Entire Row

ActiveSheet.Range("A1").EntireRow.Select

Selection.Delete
```

Inserting a Column into a Worksheet

```
Dim Row, Column

Cells(Row, Column).EntireColumn.Select

Selection.Insert
```

Insert Multiple Columns into a Worksheet

```
Dim insertCnt

Dim Row, Column

For insertCnt = 1 To N

ThisWorkbook.Worksheets("worksheet").Select

Cells(Row, Column).EntireColumn.Select

Selection.Insert

Next
```

Select a Specific Sheet

ThisWorkbook.Worksheets("worksheet").Select

Compare Values In A Range

Dim firstrange

Dim Logictest

Logictest = "some word or value"

If (Range(firstrange).value = Logictest) then

'some routine here

End If

Chapter Four

Fundamentals of VBA

VBA is a visual programming environment. That is, you see how your program will look before you run it. Its editor is very visual, using various windows to make your programming experience easy and manageable. You will notice slight differences in the appearance of the editor when you use it with Vista as compared to older versions of Windows. Regardless of which version of Windows you use or which Office Product you use, the Visual Basic Editor has the same appearance, same functionality and same items.

The IDE is like a word processor, database form or a spreadsheet. The IDE, like every other application editor has special features which makes it easy to work with data. Apart from that, the IDE can also be used to write special instructions which help with data manipulation and analysis. VBA will follow the instructions in the program. The figure below shows you the IDE Window in Excel:

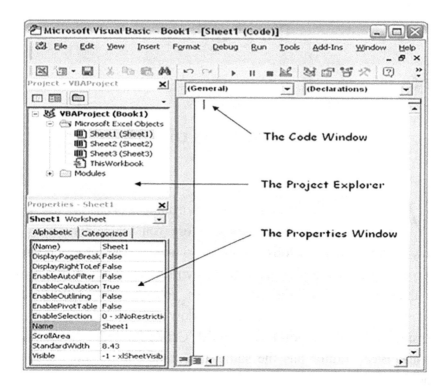

The Code Window

The Project Explorer

The Properties Window

The IDE in VBA consists of a toolbar, menu system, a Properties window, a Project Explorer window and a Code window. Below is a summary of what each Window contains.

Project Explorer

This window provides a list of the items or objects that are in your project. These items contain the document elements that are present in a single file. This application exists within a file which you will see in the Project Explorer window.

Properties

When you select an object, the Properties window will give you all the information you need about that object. For instance, this window will tell you whether the object is empty or whether there are some words in it.

Code

Eventually, you will need to write some code which will make the application work. This window will contain the special words which will tell the editor what it needs to do. This space is analogous to a to-do list or an algorithm.

Looking at the VBA Toolbox

You will not have to write a program for every task that you want Excel to perform. The IDE also allows you to use forms, which are similar to the forms that you use to perform different tasks. In case of VBA, you will decide what should appear on the forms and also decide how the forms should act when a user enters some data into the forms. VBA allows you to use the toolbox to create a form. This toolbox contains controls used to create forms.

Each Toolbox button performs a unique task. For example, when you click one button, a text box may appear on the screen. If you click another button, a mathematical operation may take place.

Starting the Visual Basic Editor

One can start the Visual Basic Editor in different ways depending on the application you are using. The newer versions of the Office Product use a different approach when compared to the older versions.

Step 1: Go to Option "View" on the toolbar.

Step 2: In the drop-down list, select "Record Macro."

Step 3: The interface will open and you can begin typing the code for the worksheet you are in.

Using Project Explorer

The Project Explorer will appear in the Project Explorer Window, and you can use this to interact with different objects that make up the project. Every project is an individual file that you can use to hold your program or at least some pieces of it. This project will reside in the Office document which you are using. Therefore, when you open the document, you also open the project. We will look at how programs and projects interact with each other in later chapters. The Project Explorer works like the left pane in Windows Explorer.

The Project Explorer lists the different objects you are using in the project. These objects depend on the type of application you are working with. For example, if you are working with Word, you see documents and document templates. Likewise, if you are working with Excel, you will come across different workbooks and worksheets. Regardless of the type of application you work with, the Project Explorer will be used in the same way.

A project can contain modules, class modules and forms. Let us look at the description of these objects:

- Forms: These contain some user interface elements that allow you to interact with a user and collect necessary information.

- Modules: These contain the nonvisual parts of your code or application. For instance, you can use a module to store some calculations.

- Class modules: These contain objects that you want to develop, and you can use a class module to create new data types.

Working with special entries

You can sometimes see some special entries in the Project Explorer. For instance, when you work on a Word document, you will see a References folder which will contain the references that the Word document makes. This contains a list of templates which the document uses to format the data in the document.

194

In many cases, you cannot modify or manipulate the objects in the folders. This is the case when Word document objects use a Reference folder. This folder is only available to provide information. If you want to modify or develop a referenced template, you should look for the object in the Project Explorer window. We will not discuss these concepts in the book since you do not work with these often.

Using the Properties window

Most objects that you select in the IDE in VBA always have properties that describe the objects in a specific way. The "Property values are up" section talks about the properties that you have not worked with before. The following section will provide more information about the Properties Window.

Understanding property types

A property will always describe the object. When you look at an object, you will assume something about the product depending on whether the object is red, yellow or green. In the same way, every

VBA object has a specific type. One of the most common types is text. The property of every form is text, and this text appears at the top or bottom of the form when a user opens it. Another common property type is a Boolean value.

Getting help with properties

Do not expect to memorize every property for every object that VBA applications can create. Not even the gurus can do that. To determine what a property will do for your application, just highlight the property and press F1, and, in most cases, VBA displays a Help window like the image below.

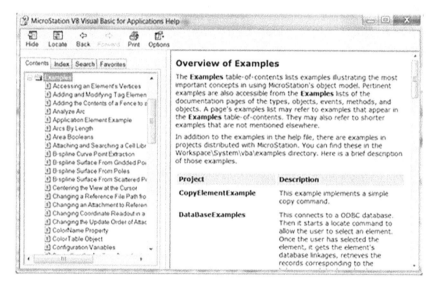

Using the Code window

The Code Window is the space where you will write the code for your application. This window works like every other text editor that you have used, except that you type according to the syntax.

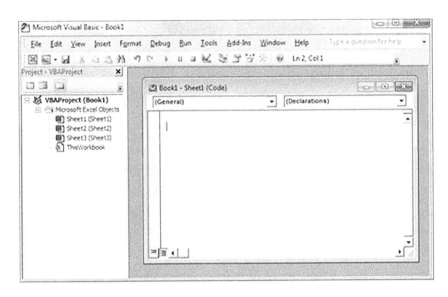

The Project Explorer window and Property window are no longer present in the image above. You can display these again by following the path: View -> Project Explorer and View ->Properties Window commands.

Opening an existing Code window

Sometimes you will not have the time to complete the code for an application and will need to work on it later. If you want to open an existing code window, you should find the module you want to work on in the Project Explorer. Double-click the name of the module that you want to enter. You will see the code in the IDE window. This Code window will also appear when you want to perform a variety of tasks.

Creating a new Code window

When you want to develop a new module in an existing document or template, you should open a new code window by using the following path: Insert -> Module or Insert -> Class Module command. Once you save this class module or module, it will always be in the Project Explorer with every other module that is in your project.

197

It is easier to execute one line of code at a time to understand where you may have made an error. You can do this by using the Immediate Window. You will always find this window at the bottom of the IDE, and it will not contain any information until you type something in it.

A developer spends a lot of time using the Immediate Window to check if there are any errors in the applications they are developing. You can use the immediate window to check with VBA if the function you have written produces the required value. To try this feature, type String1 = "Hello World" in the Immediate window and then press Enter. Now type '? String1' and then press Enter. Here, you have asked the editor to create a variable called String1 and assign it a value of Hello World. You can use the '?' operator to check the value assigned to the variable String1.

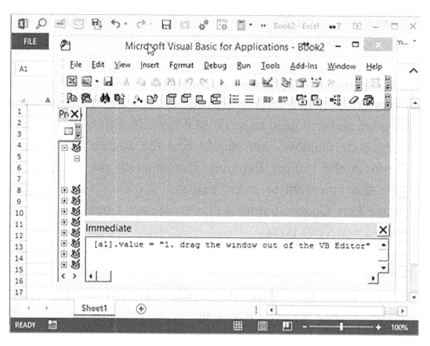

Chapter Five

Working With Loops and Conditional Statements

In the first part of the book, we looked at the different types of loops that one can use in Excel VBA. This chapter covers some examples and exercises that you can use to practice.

For Loop

Most people use the For Loop in VBA. There are two forms of the For Loop – For Next and For Each In Next. The For Loop will move through a series or data in a sequence. You can use the Exit statement to end the For Loop at any point. The loop will continue to run until the condition is met. When the final condition is met, the editor will move to the next statement in the program, which is the natural direction.

Let us look at the syntax of the loop:

The For ... Next loop has the following syntax:

    For counter = start_counter To end_counter

    'Do something here (your code)

    Next counter

In the syntax above, we are initializing the counter variable, which will maintain the loop. This counter variable will be set to a value that is equal to the start counter, which will be the beginning of the loop. This variable will increase in number until it meets the end condition which is the end counter variable. The loop will continue to run until the value of the counter is equal to the value of the end counter variable. This loop will execute once until the values match, after which the loop will stop.

The explanation above can be slightly confusing, therefore let us look at a few examples that you can use to understand the For Loop better. Before we look at the examples, follow the steps given below:

- Open a new workbook and save it using the .xlsm extension.

- Now, press Alt+F11 to launch the Visual Basic Editor screen.

- Now, insert a new module.

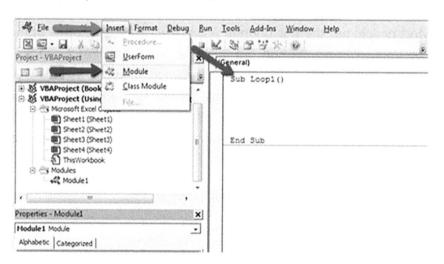

Example 1

In this example, we will display a number using a message box.

Sub Loop1()

Dim StartNumber As Integer

Dim EndNumber As Integer

200

EndNumber = 5

For StartNumber = 1 To EndNumber

MsgBox StartNumber & " is " & "Your StartNumber"

Next StartNumber

End Sub

```
(General)                              ▼   Loop1                              ▼
Sub Loop1()                                                                   ▲
Dim StartNumber As Integer
Dim EndNumber As Integer
EndNumber = 5

    For StartNumber = 1 To EndNumber
        MsgBox StartNumber & " is " & "Your StartNumber"
    Next StartNumber

End Sub                                                                       ▼
```

In the above code, the StartNumber and EndNumber variables are declared as integers, and the StartNumber is the start of your loop. The values that you enter in the loop can be anywhere in between the StartNumber and EndNumber. The code will start from StartNumber, which is 1, and end at EndNumber which is 5. Once the code runs, the following message will be displayed on the screen.

Example 2

In this example, we will fill values in the Active worksheet.

> Sub Loop2()
>
> 'Fills cells A1:A56 with values of X by looping' --- Comment
>
> 'Increase value of X by 1 in each loop' --- Comment
>
> Dim X As Integer
>
>   For X = 1 To 56
>
>   Range("A" & X).Value = X
>
>   Next X
>
> End Sub

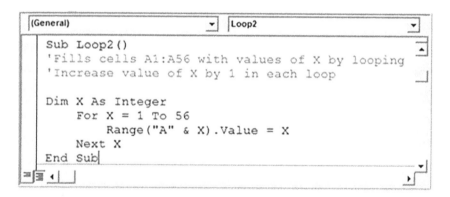

You will see the following output.

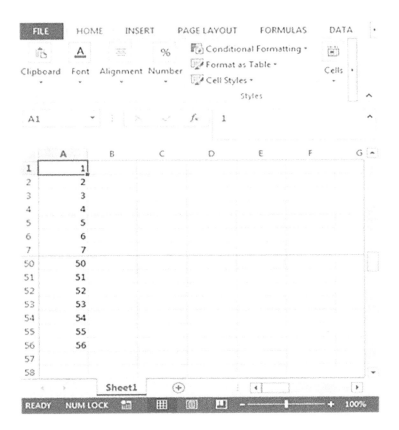

Example 3

In this example, we will fill the cells in the active worksheet with a background color.

```
Sub Loop3()

' Fills cells B1:B56 with the 56 background colors'---
Comment

Dim X As Integer

  For X = 1 To 56

    Range("B" & X).Select

    With Selection.Interior

      .ColorIndex = X
```

.Pattern = xlSolid

End With

Next X

End Sub

```
(General)                                    ▼    Loop3                          ▼

Sub Loop3()
' Fills cells B1:B56 with the 56 background colours
Dim X As Integer
    For X = 1 To 56
        Range("B" & X).Select
        With Selection.Interior
            .ColorIndex = X
            .Pattern = xlSolid
        End With
    Next X
End Sub
```

You will see the following output.

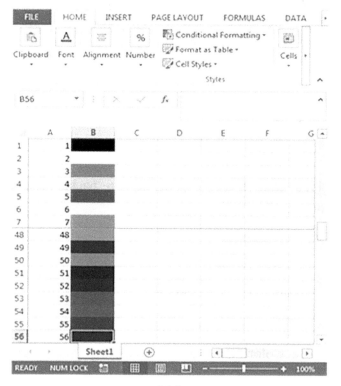

Example 4

It is important to remember that a loop does not necessarily have to move from a low value to a higher value. You can use the For Loop to move from higher values to lower values using the STEP function. This example will show you how you can perform the same function.

Sub Loop5()

'Fills cells from D1:D50 with values of X' --- Comment

'In this case X decreases by 1' --- Comment

Dim X As Integer, Row As Integer

Row = 1

For X = 50 To 0 Step -1

Range("D" & Row).Value = X

Row = Row + 1

Next X

End Sub

```
(General)                          ▼   Loop5                        ▼
Sub Loop5 ()
    ' Fills cells from D1:D50 with values of X
    ' In this case X decreases by 1
Dim X As Integer, Row As Integer

Row = 1

    For X = 50 To 0 Step -1
        Range ("D" & Row).Value = X
        Row = Row + 1
    Next X

End Sub
```

The output of the program is below:

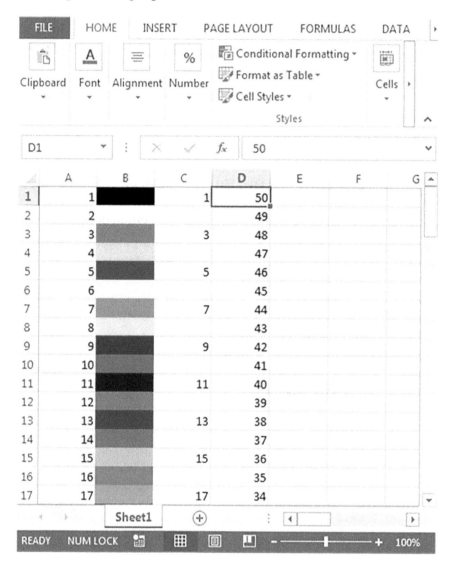

Exercises

1. Write a program to fill the values in the cells in the active worksheet with an increment of 2.

2. Using example 4, write a program to fill values in cells in the reverse order using the STEP function.

3. Write a program to fill in values in a spreadsheet from a specific cell.

The solutions to the exercises above are in the last chapter of the book. If you can write these programs, you will know how to write any kind of program using the for loop.

Do...Loop Statement

In the first part of the book, we looked at what the Do...Loop statement is and how you can use it in Excel VBA. In this section, we will look at the syntax and understand every part of the syntax. There are some examples and exercises in this section that will help you master the Do...Loop statement.

Syntax

Type 1

Do { While | Until } condition

    [statements]

    [Continue Do]

    [statements]

    [Exit Do]

    [statements]

Loop

Type 2

Do

    [statements]

    [Continue Do]

    [statements]

    [Exit Do]

    [statements]

Loop { While | Until } condition

Understanding The Parts

Term	Definition
Do	This term is necessary to include since this starts the Do Loop.
While	This is required unless you use UNTIL in the loop. This keyword will ensure that the editor runs the loop until the condition is false.
Until	This keyword is necessary unless you are using the WHILE keyword. This will ensure that the editor will run the loop until the condition holds true.
Condition	This is optional, but it should always be a Boolean expression. If the condition is nothing, the editor will treat it as false.
Statements	These are optional. You can add one or more statements that you want the editor to repeat until the condition holds true.
Continue Do	This is also an optional statement. If you use this statement in the loop, the editor will move to the next iteration of the loop.
Exit Do	This is optional, and if you use it, the editor will move out of the Do Loop.
Loop	This keyword is necessary since it terminates the loop.

You should use the Do...Loop structure if you want to repeat a set of statements infinitely until the condition holds true. If you want to repeat the statements in the loop for a specific number of times, you should use the For...Next statements. You can either use the Until or While keywords when you specify a condition, but you should never use both.

You can test the condition either at the start or the end of the loop. The first book mentions which structure you should use depending on when you want to test the condition. If you want to test the condition at the beginning the loop does not have to run even once. If you test the condition at the end of the loop, the statements in the body of the loop will run at least once. This condition is a Boolean value and is often a comparison of two values. These values can be of any data type that the editor can convert to Boolean.

You can nest a Do loop by adding another loop in it. You can also nest different control structures within the Do Loop. These concepts have been covered in the first book of the series.

You should remember that the Do...Loop structure is more flexible than the While...End While statement. This is because the former allows you to decide if you want to end the loop when the condition first becomes true or when it stops being true. You also have the ability to test the condition either at the start or the end of the loop.

Exit Do

You can use the Exit Do statement as an alternative way to exit the Do...Loop. This statement will transfer the control to the statements that follow the Loop statement. The Exit Do is used if you nest conditional statements within the loop. If you know that there is some condition that is unnecessary or makes it impossible for the editor to evaluate the statements within the loop. You can use this statement if you want to check for a condition that can lead to an endless loop. This statement will help you exit the loop immediately. You can use any number of Exit Do statements in the Do…Loop structure.

When you use the Exit Do statement in a nest Do loop, the editor will move from the statements within the innermost loop to the next level of nesting statements.

Example 1

In the example below, the editor will run the statements in the loop only when the index variable is greater than 10. The Until keyword will end the loop.

```
Dim index As Integer = 0

Do

    Debug.Write(index.ToString & " ")

    index += 1

Loop Until index > 10

Debug.WriteLine("")
```

The output will be,

0 1 2 3 4 5 6 7 8 9 10

Example 2

In the example below, we will use a While clause instead of the Until clause. The editor will test the condition at the start of the loop.

```
Dim index As Integer = 0

Do While index <= 10

    Debug.Write(index.ToString & " ")
```

```
        index += 1

    Loop

    Debug.WriteLine("")
```

The output will be,

0 1 2 3 4 5 6 7 8 9 10

Example 3

In the example below, the condition will ensure that the editor stops running the statements in the loop if the index variable is larger than 100. This example uses conditional statements within the loop, and the Exit Do statement in the program will cause the statement to stop if the value of index is greater than 10.

```
    Dim index As Integer = 0

    Do While index <= 100

        If index > 10 Then

            Exit Do

        End If

        Debug.Write(index.ToString & " ")

        index += 1

    Loop

    Debug.WriteLine("")
```

The output will be,

0 1 2 3 4 5 6 7 8 9 10

Example 4

In the example below, the editor will read every line in a text file. The OpenText method will open the text file and returns the StreamReader which will read the characters in the text. In the example below, the Peek method in the Do...Loop condition will determine whether there are additional characters present in the text.

```
Private Sub ShowText(ByVal textFilePath As String)

    If System.IO.File.Exists(textFilePath) = False Then

        Debug.WriteLine("File Not Found: " & textFilePath)

    Else

        Dim sr As System.IO.StreamReader =
System.IO.File.OpenText(textFilePath)

        Do While sr.Peek() >= 0

            Debug.WriteLine(sr.ReadLine())

        Loop

        sr.Close()

    End If

End Sub
```

Conditional Statements

Example 1

```
Module Nested

    Public Sub Main()

        ' Run the function as part of the WriteLine output.
```
213

```vbnet
        Console.WriteLine("Time Check is " & CheckIfTime()
& ".")

    End Sub


    Private Function CheckIfTime() As Boolean

        ' Determine the current day of week and hour of day.

        Dim dayW As DayOfWeek =
DateTime.Now.DayOfWeek

        Dim hour As Integer = DateTime.Now.Hour


        ' Return True if Wednesday from 2 to 3:59 P.M.,

        ' or if Thursday from noon to 12:59 P.M.

        If dayW = DayOfWeek.Wednesday Then

            If hour = 14 Or hour = 15 Then

                Return True

            Else

                Return False

            End If

        ElseIf dayW = DayOfWeek.Thursday Then

            If hour = 12 Then

                Return True

            Else
```

```
            Return False

         End If

      Else

         Return False

      End If

   End Function

End Module

'This example displays output like the following:

'Time Check is False.
```

Example 2

```
Module SingleLine

   Public Sub Main()

      'Create a Random object to seed our starting values

      Dim randomizer As New Random()

      Dim A As Integer = randomizer.Next(10, 20)

      Dim B As Integer = randomizer.Next(0, 20)

      Dim C As Integer = randomizer.Next(0, 5)

      'Let's display the initial values for comparison

      Console.WriteLine($"A value before If: {A}")

      Console.WriteLine($"B value before If: {B}")

      Console.WriteLine($"C value before If: {C}")
```

' If A > 10, execute the three colon-separated statements in the order

' that they appear

If A > 10 Then A = A + 1 : B = B + A : C = C + B

'If the condition is true, the values will be different

Console.WriteLine($"A value after If: {A}")

Console.WriteLine($"B value after If: {B}")

Console.WriteLine($"C value after If: {C}")

End Sub

End Module

'This example displays output like the following:

'A value before If: 11

'B value before If: 6

'C value before If: 3

'A value after If: 12

'B value after If: 18

'C value after If: 21

Chapter Six

Data Types in VBA

Data types are a way to define the different variables you use in the program to make it easier for the editor to perform the necessary calculations. The computer will always look at the data as a series of bits, but there are different types of data types that you can use in VBA. A computer can see only the binary value, 1000001b, but it does not do anything with that value. VBA will see the binary value as a letter or a number depending on the data type that you use to assign the value. The data type is important in understanding the value and working with it. Using a data type also ensures that the program follows certain rules. Otherwise, the data could become corrupted because the program could mishandle it.

Although a variable, in general, is simply a box for storing data, you can think of these data types as special boxes for storing specific kinds of data. Just as you would use a hatbox to store a hat and not a car engine, you use these special box types to store kinds of data. For example, you use a string to hold text, not logical (true/false) values. VBA supports several standard data types, including Boolean, Byte, Long, Currency, Integer, Single, Decimal, Double, String, Variant, Date and Object. In addition to using the defined data types, you can create user-defined data types so that you can mark the information as needed for your program. A user-defined data type gives you the power to extend the VBA interpretation of data. (The computer still looks at the data as binary information.) Each of the data type descriptions that follows has a different purpose, and you can work with the data type in a variety of ways.

Using strings for text

In the first book, we discussed the data type string, and you should have a clear idea of what a string is. If you do not remember it, go back to the first few chapters where we used a message box to give the user an output. When you create the message box, you will use the string as an input. The string is the most useful data type in VBA. This chapter only introduces strings. The next chapter provides information on how you can manipulate strings in VBA.

Understanding strings

A programmer uses fancy terms to describe objects that an average person will recognize. A string is a sequence of characters. The characters cannot always be printed, but they can always include some control characters that will determine what type of text will appear on the screen. A string will also include special characters like commas and other types of punctuation, or some special features like an umlaut or circumflex. A string can contain each of these elements, but the main part of a string is always text.

Adding strings together with + or &

Sometimes you will need to combine two or more strings to make a longer string. The process of adding two or more strings together is concatenation. For instance, you may want to combine the first name and last name of a person to create their full name. You may need to take this information from more than one source and combine it together to obtain new information.

Using character codes

Strings can contain several elements. In the earlier examples, we used a control character like vbCrLF. This constant is made up of two control characters: a line feed and a carriage return. The latter will send the cursor to the beginning of the sentence while the former moves the cursor to the next line. The result of using these control characters together is like pressing the Enter key on your keyboard. You can also use special functions like Chr, which will allow you to create a special character. You can combine this function with the Character Map utility to produce any character that you need for your program

Using numbers for calculations

Numbers form the basis for a lot of the information computers store. You use numbers to perform tasks in a spreadsheet, to express quantities in a database, and to show the current page in a document. Programs also use numbers to count things such as loops, to determine the position of items such as characters in a string and to check the truth value of a statement. Finally, VBA uses numbers in myriad ways, such as determining which character to display onscreen or how to interact with your code.

Understanding the numeric types

The numbers are always looked at as a single entity. Every number is simply just that, a number. The computer will view these numbers in different ways, and the reason for this diversity is that a processor works differently with numbers. Processors will either work with integer values - that is numbers without a decimal point - or with floating-point values, which are numbers with decimal points. The four basic number types include:

Integer

The integer data type does not have any decimal point in it. Integers can hold any whole numbers like 5 but never a number with a decimal, like 5.0. Essentially these numbers are the same, bu the first is an integer and the second is not.

219

Real

Unlike an integer, a real number contains a decimal point. The decimal section of the number does not necessarily have to contain a value, and the number 5.0 is a valid real number. VBA stores a read number in a different format when compared to the format of an integer.

Currency

A financial calculation always needs special accuracy, and a small error can cause larger problems. This numeric type always stores numbers with great precision, but it uses a lot of memory and takes a lot of time to process.

Decimal

A computer often stores information using the binary or base 2 format. Human beings use the base 10 or decimal system to store numbers when you need to work with them. Simple errors are often made when you convert numbers from one numbering system to another. These simple errors will create larger errors. The decimal numeric system will always store the number in a base 10 format which will eliminate many computing errors. This system requires more processing time and more memory than any other numeric type.

Using Boolean values to make decisions

The Boolean type is the easiest to use and understand. This type is used to indicate yes or no, true or false and on or off. You can use this type to work with any two-state information. It has commonly used to represent data values that are diametrically opposed.

Working with Operators

Operators determine how VBA works with two variables and what result it produces. The examples in this chapter use operators to add numbers and concatenate (add) strings. In both cases, your code uses the + operator to perform the task. The result differs. When you are using numbers, the result is a summation, such as $1 + 2 = 3$. When you are using strings, the result is a concatenation, such as Hello + World = Hello World.

VBA groups operators into four areas:

- Arithmetic: Operators that perform math operations, such as addition (+), subtraction (-), division (/) and multiplication (*)

- Comparison: Operators such as less than (<), greater than (>) and equal (=) that compare two values and produce a Boolean result

- Concatenation: Operators such as & and + that are used to add two strings together

- Logical: Operators such as Not, And, Or and Xor that are used to perform Boolean operations on two variables

Exercises

1. Write a program to change the case of a letter in a cell.

2. Write a program to highlight misspelled words in a worksheet.

3. Write a program to obtain the numeric part of the string from a cell.

Chapter Seven

Parts of the Program

You should follow a syntax and a structure when you want to write a code in VBA to help the debugger understand what the point of your code is. This chapter formalizes the meaning for each structural element.

Defining the parts of a program

A program is the highest level of physical structure. It contains everything needed to perform a given task. A program can cross module, class module and form boundaries. The concept of a program comes from the earliest use of computers. A program acts as a container for the code used to implement a set of features required by the operating system or the user. Some people have a hard time understanding what a program is because modern software packages often define the term incorrectly. You are not creating a new program when you create a new project. A VBA project can actually contain a number of VBA programs."

Programming Blocks

A VBA program consists of building blocks. In fact, because programming is abstract, people tend to use physical examples to explain how things work. You still need to know about the abstract elements of VBA programming, or else you cannot write a program. This section explains the basic constructs of VBA programming. Every VBA code has the following elements:

Project

The project acts as a container for the modules, class modules and forms for a file. Excel users normally see just one project for the file that they have open.

Module, class module and forms

The three elements will always contain the main programming elements like procedures and class descriptions. A single project can have multiple class modules, forms and modules in it, but each of these must have a different name.

Function and Sub

The sub and function elements hold the statements or individual lines of code. A function will always return the value that the user requires while a sub does not. You can access the code using the Sub, but never through the function. Therefore, you must always provide the VBA editor access to the program through a Sub.

Statement

Experts and other developers often call an individual line of code as a statement.

Using the Macro Recorder

The Macro Recorder will allow you to record all the actions and keystrokes that you perform when you work on Excel. You can use this to record some tasks like setting up a document or anything as simple as highlighting text.

The Macro Recorder can help you perform the following tasks:

- Create a macro based on your actions.
- Discover how Word performs certain tasks.
- Decide how to break your program into tasks.
- Help you create the basis for a more complex program.

The Macro Recorder is not a complete solution for your VBA needs. For example, you cannot use the Macro Recorder to create interactive programs without extra coding. The same holds true for programs that must change based on user input, the environment or the data you are manipulating. All these tasks require you to add more code. It is a good starting point for many structured programming tasks. You can get the basics down quickly using the Macro Recorder and then make changes as needed.

- Start the Macro Recorder.

- Perform all the steps that you normally perform to accomplish a task.

- Stop the Macro Recorder.

- Save the macro when the Office application prompts you.

- Optionally, open the resulting macro and make any required changes.

Using Subs

A sub is the simplest way to reduce the size of the code, packaging method that appears in the Macro dialog box. Consequently, the one place where you always use a Sub is the main entry point for a program unless the program is a utility that you use only for programming purposes. A second way to use a Sub is to perform a task and not receive a direct return value. You can use a Sub to display an informational message. A Sub can modify information in several ways; it just cannot return a value. Only a function can return a value. You can, however, use arguments as a way to modify the information in a function by using a Sub. A second method relies on global variables. You can use the Sub as a way to break up large volumes of code. You can avoid creating a code that is written on many pages, and use Subs to break the code into smaller segments. This makes it easier for you and for another viewer to read the code.

Using Functions

You might not see a use for the Function after spending some time working with the Sub. Not every problem is a screw requiring the use of a screwdriver or a nail in search of a hammer. You use a Function for different problems than a Sub can answer. In most cases, there is a correct answer to using a Function or a Sub. For example, you always use a Sub when you want to access program code from within the host application, and you always use a Function when you want to perform a calculation with a return result.

A Function always returns a value, which makes it different from a Sub. For this reason, you can write functions that contain code that you plan to repeat a lot within a program. To process a list of names, you might create a Function to process each name individually and then call that Function once for each name. The Function can provide the processed information as a return value. In Chapter 5, I describe how to create repeating code using structures such as Do...Until.

You can also use a Function for public code that you do not want to list in the Macro dialog box. You normally do not see a Function listed in the Macro dialog box — this dialog box usually lists only Subs.

Comments

It is important to write comments in your code to help other users understand the purpose of the code.

Writing basic comments

Comments can take several forms. One always writes a pseudo-comment in the program since this is the most natural one to use. A developer will always add comments to the program he or she is writing. They will also provide information about who wrote the program or when it was written. These comments will also provide information on the list of updates made to the code. Some developers begin to write better comments at this point.

An important comment that you should add to your code is why you would want to write the original program. You should also explain why you chose to write it in a specific way. You cannot simply say that the program will perform a specific task. This is not enough since you can perform the same task in different ways. When you talk about why you chose that specific way to write the code, you can avoid making any errors when you update the code. You will also know when you need to update the code.

As a good programmer, you should include the mistakes made as a part of the comments if you want to help another programmer avoid making the same mistakes. These comments will always help a beginner or an expert. That way they can avoid the mistakes that one may usually make.

Knowing when to use comments

You should always use comments whenever and wherever you think you need them. You may believe that comments are difficult to include and type, but you can include one or two lines of comments to explain the program that you are writing. You are correct — writing good comments can be time-consuming and can be difficult because writing these makes you think yet again about the code. When you do not have enough comments in your code, you will find it difficult to update that program. You may also have to start writing the code from scratch because you do not know what your code is all about.

Writing Good Comments

A comment is always good if you can understand what it says. Do not use fancy terms — write everything in plain terms that you can understand. If you think you want to explain a certain line of code, feel free to do it. You can also write comments against every line of code since that will help an amateur understand your train of thought.

Chapter Eight

Arrays

Arrays will allow you to store more than one item in a single variable or container that you can use in your program. You should think of an array as a large box with a finite number of smaller boxes within it. Every small box will store some value depending on the data type of the array. You can choose the number of small boxes that you want to store in your array when you create it. You should use the array when you must store several related items of the same data type.

Structured Storage

Arrays are a list of items. A classic example of an array is a to-do list that you prepare for yourself. The piece of paper where you write your tasks form a single container. This single container will hold several strings, and each of these strings will contain a task that you need to perform. Similarly, you can create a paper in your VBA program in the form of an array. You can define an array using a variety of techniques, but each of these techniques will use similar approaches.

Example

```
' Tell VBA to start all arrays at 0.

Option Base 0

Public Sub SingleDimension()

' Define an output string.
```

```
Dim Output As String
' Define a variant to hold individual strings.
Dim IndividualString As Variant
' Define the array of strings.
Dim StringArray(5) As String
' Fill each array element with information.
StringArray(0) = "This"
StringArray(1) = "Is"
StringArray(2) = "An"
StringArray(3) = "Array"
StringArray(4) = "Of"
StringArray(5) = "Strings"
' Use the For Each...Next statement to get each array
' element and place it in a string.
For Each IndividualString In StringArray
' Create a single output string with the array
' array elements.
Output = Output + IndividualString + " "
Next
' Display the result.
MsgBox Trim(Output), _
vbInformation Or vbOKOnly, _
"Array Content"
End Sub
```

If you look at the above code, you will notice that the code starts with the Option Base 0 statement. This statement will tell VBA if it needs to start counting the elements in the array from 0 or 1. The default setting in VBA is that it will count the elements in the array from 0. Most programming languages will use 0 as the starting point, and it is for this reason that the developers at Microsoft made the default 0 for VBA. Older versions of VBA do use 1 as the starting point.

If you want your program to work in every environment, you should include the Option Base statement. Since the array will begin at 0 and not at 1, you can only store six items in the array, although you have defined that the array has five elements. The number you include in the declaration is always at the top, but this is not one of the numbers in the element.

Array Types

One can classify an array in several ways, and the first method is the type of data that the array will hold. A string array is very different from an integer array, but the array will always ensure that the elements are unique. If you use a Variant data type, you can mix the data types in an array. You should always be careful when you use this technique since it can lead to errors which are difficult to debug.

Another method is to define the dimensions in an array. The dimension will define the number of directions in which the array will hold the information. A simple list, like the one in the earlier "Understanding array usage" section, gives an example of a single-dimensional array. A table which consists of columns and rows is a two-dimensional array. One can create an array using any number of dimensions.

Example: Adding an Element to an Array

    Dim a As Range

229

```
Dim arr As Variant  'Just a Variant variable (i.e., don't pre-
define it as an array)

For Each a In Range.Cells

    If IsEmpty(arr) Then

        arr = Array(a.value) 'Make the Variant an array with a
single element

    Else

        ReDim Preserve arr(UBound(arr) + 1) 'Add next array
element

        arr(UBound(arr)) = a.value          'Assign the array
element

    End If

Next
```

VBA Array

In this section, we will look at the steps you need to follow to create an array.

Step 1 – Create a New Workbook

1. Open Microsoft Excel.

2. Save the excel workbook with the extension .xlsm

Step 2 – Add a Command Button

Now that you are familiar with creating an interface in a workbook. The previous chapters in the book will help you gather more information about the subroutines or subs and functions in VBA.

1. Add a command button to the active worksheet.

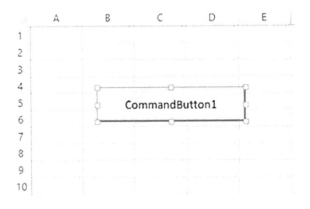

2. Set the property name to cmdLoadBeverages.

3. Now, set the Caption Property as Load Beverages.

The interface should now display the following:

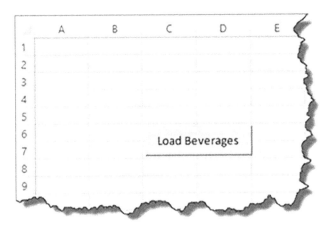

Step 3 – Save the File

1. You should now click the save as button in the macro-enabled form.

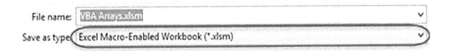

Step 4 – Write the Code

Let us now write the code for the application.

1. Right click on the button and choose to view the code.

2. Add the code in the code window.

```
Private Sub cmdLoadBeverages_Click()

    Dim Drinks(1 To 4) As String

    Drinks(1) = "Pepsi"

    Drinks(2) = "Coke"

    Drinks(3) = "Fanta"

    Drinks(4) = "Juice"

    Sheet1.Cells(1, 1).Value = "My Favorite Beverages"

    Sheet1.Cells(2, 1).Value = Drinks(1)

    Sheet1.Cells(3, 1).Value = Drinks(2)

    Sheet1.Cells(4, 1).Value = Drinks(3)

    Sheet1.Cells(5, 1).Value = Drinks(4)

End Sub
```

Example to Enter Student's Marks

Without An Array

In the example below, we will look at how you can enter the marks for every student without using an array.

```
Public Sub StudentMarks()

    With ThisWorkbook.Worksheets("Sheet1")
```

```vb
' Declare variable for each student

Dim Student1 As Integer

Dim Student2 As Integer

Dim Student3 As Integer

Dim Student4 As Integer

Dim Student5 As Integer

' Read student marks from cell

Student1 = .Range("C2").Offset(1)

Student2 = .Range("C2").Offset(2)

Student3 = .Range("C2").Offset(3)

Student4 = .Range("C2").Offset(4)

Student5 = .Range("C2").Offset(5)

' Print student marks

Debug.Print "Students Marks"

Debug.Print Student1

Debug.Print Student2

Debug.Print Student3

Debug.Print Student4

Debug.Print Student5

   End With

End Sub
```

The output will be the following,

```
Immediate                                              x
  Students Marks                                       ▲
     89
     67
     77
     42
     70
                                                       ▼
◄|      |                                            ►
```

Using an Array

Public Sub StudentMarksArr()

  With ThisWorkbook.Worksheets("Sheet1")

    ' Declare an array to hold marks for 5 students

    Dim Students(1 To 5) As Integer

    ' Read student marks from cells C3:C7 into array

    Dim i As Integer

    For i = 1 To 5

      Students(i) = .Range("C2").Offset(i)

    Next i

    ' Print student marks from the array

    Debug.Print "Students Marks"

    For i = LBound(Students) To UBound(Students)

      Debug.Print Students(i)

    Next i

  End With

End Sub

Notice the difference in the variables used in the two programs, and also notice the length of the program.

Example with Loops

```
Public Sub ArrayLoops()

  ' Declare  array

  Dim arrMarks(0 To 5) As Long

  ' Fill the array with random numbers

  Dim i As Long

  For i = LBound(arrMarks) To UBound(arrMarks)

    arrMarks(i) = 5 * Rnd

  Next i

  ' Print out the values in the array

  Debug.Print "Location", "Value"

  For i = LBound(arrMarks) To UBound(arrMarks)

    Debug.Print i, arrMarks(i)

  Next i

End Sub
```

Sorting an Array

```
Sub QuickSort(arr As Variant, first As Long, last As Long)
  Dim vCentreVal As Variant, vTemp As Variant
  Dim lTempLow As Long
  Dim lTempHi As Long
  lTempLow = first
  lTempHi = last
```

```
vCentreVal = arr((first + last) \ 2)
 Do While lTempLow <= lTempHi

    Do While arr(lTempLow) < vCentreVal And lTempLow
< last

      lTempLow = lTempLow + 1

    Loop

    Do While vCentreVal < arr(lTempHi) And lTempHi >
first

      lTempHi = lTempHi - 1

    Loop

    If lTempLow <= lTempHi Then

      ' Swap values

      vTemp = arr(lTempLow)

      arr(lTempLow) = arr(lTempHi)

      arr(lTempHi) = vTemp

      ' Move to next positions

      lTempLow = lTempLow + 1

      lTempHi = lTempHi - 1

    End If

  Loop

  If first < lTempHi Then QuickSort arr, first, lTempHi
  If lTempLow < last Then QuickSort arr, lTempLow, last
End Sub
```

Example for Creating a Two-Dimensional Array

```
Public Sub TwoDimArray()

    ' Declare a two dimensional array

    Dim arrMarks(0 To 3, 0 To 2) As String

    ' Fill the array with text made up of i and j values

    Dim i As Long, j As Long

    For i = LBound(arrMarks) To UBound(arrMarks)

        For j = LBound(arrMarks, 2) To UBound(arrMarks, 2)

            arrMarks(i, j) = CStr(i) & ":" & CStr(j)

        Next j

    Next i

    ' Print the values in the array to the Immediate Window

    Debug.Print "i", "j", "Value"

    For i = LBound(arrMarks) To UBound(arrMarks)

        For j = LBound(arrMarks, 2) To UBound(arrMarks, 2)

            Debug.Print i, j, arrMarks(i, j)

        Next j

    Next i

End Sub
```

Exercise

1. Write a program to sort an array using the bubble sort method.

Chapter Nine

Working with Excel Workbooks and Worksheets

The Workbook Collection

The Workbooks collection provides a list of all workbooks that you have open at a given time. You can select a single workbook from this list that you want to use in your program. The Workbook object that you select will provide general information about the file, including its name and location. You can also use this object to access other major objects in the document. These objects include standalone Chart objects and Worksheet objects.

Example:

```
Public Sub WorkbookDemo()
' Holds the output data.
Dim Output As String
' Get the test workbook.
Dim ActiveWorkbook As Workbook
Set ActiveWorkbook =
Application.Workbooks("ExcelObjects.xls")
' Get the workbook name and location.
Output = "Name: " + ActiveWorkbook.Name + vbCrLf + _
"Full Name: " + ActiveWorkbook.FullName + vbCrLf + _
"Path: " + ActiveWorkbook.Path + vbCrLf + vbCrLf
```

```vba
' Holds the current sheet.

Dim CurrSheet As Worksheet

' Look for every sheet.

Output = "Worksheet List:" + vbCrLf

For Each CurrSheet In ActiveWorkbook.Worksheets

Output = Output + CurrSheet.Name + vbCrLf

Next

' Holds the current chart.

Dim CurrChart As Chart

' Look for every chart.

Output = Output + vbCrLf + "Chart List:" + vbCrLf

For Each CurrChart In ActiveWorkbook.Charts

Output = Output + CurrChart.Name + vbCrLf

Next

' Display the output.

MsgBox Output, vbInformation Or vbOKOnly, "Object List"

End Sub
```

The code starts by using the Application Workbooks collection which will allow you to retrieve a single Workbook object. You should always use the full name of the Excel file as the index in the collection. You should also include the extension of the file. The resulting workbook object will contain information about the document. This object will also provide the summary information of the document, and you can use this object to control and maintain the windows, and also add new elements like worksheets.

Once the code accesses the workbook, it will use the ActiveWorkbook object to access the worksheets in the list. The code will rely on the For Each...Next statement to access these worksheets. Alternatively, you can use an index to access the individual worksheets in the code. The Worksheet, ActiveWorksheet, contains properties and methods for manipulating any data that the Worksheet contains, including embedded objects, such as charts or even pictures. Every worksheet appears in the ActiveWorkbook object list by its object name (not the friendly name that you give it), so you can access them without using the Worksheets collection.

Only independent charts will appear when you use the ActiveWorkbook object. The same technique can be used to access any Chart object in the worksheet as a Worksheet object. The difference is that you should use Charts Collection instead of the Worksheets Collection. You should note that the Chart names will appear in the list of objects that are present in the ActiveWorkbook. This means that you can access the chart directly without having to use the Charts collection.

The Worksheet Collection

One of the easiest methods to access a worksheet in many situations is to use the Sheets collection. You do not follow the Excel object hierarchy when you want to identify the worksheet you want tot work with. If you access the worksheet at the top of the hierarchy, it means that there are no objects that exist at lower levels available either, so this technique is a tradeoff.

You can access any type of sheet, and not just a worksheet if you use the Sheets collection. A standalone Chart object that you use in any of the sheets can also come into this collection. Look at the example in the previous section, "Using the Workbooks collection," and you will notice that the charts and worksheets are treated as different objects.

240

Example:

```
Public Sub ListSheets()

' An individual entry.

Dim ThisEntry As Variant

' Holds the output data.

Dim Output As String

' Get the current number of worksheets.

Output = "Sheet Count: " + _

CStr(Application.Sheets.Count)

' List each worksheet in turn.

For Each ThisEntry In Application.Sheets

' Verify there is a sheet to work with.

If ThisEntry.Type = XlSheetType.xlWorksheet Then

Output = Output + vbCrLf + ThisEntry.Name

End If

Next

' Display the result.

MsgBox Output, _

vbInformation or vbOKOnly, _

"Worksheet List"

End Sub
```

In the example above, we will create a Variant, which will hold the different sheet types. If you use a Chart or Worksheet object, the code will fail since the Sheets enumeration will return a valid type, but not the type you need. The issue with using this Variant is that the editor in VBA cannot provide automatic completion or balloon help. You have to ensure that you type the method in correctly and use the correct property names without any help.

Once the code creates the necessary variables, it will provide the number of sheets in the workbook. This number will include all the worksheets and charts in the workbook, and not just the sheets.

A For Each...Next loop will retrieve each sheet in turn. You should notice how we use the If...Then statement to compare the values of the Variant type and the XlSheetType.xlWorksheet constant. When you use this technique, you can separate the worksheet you are using from other Sheets collection types whenever necessary.

Charts Collection

The Charts collection is a way to build a custom chart whenever necessary. An advantage of creating charts by using a code is that they do not use too much space, and you can create a variety of different charts without spending too much time on the theme.

Example:

```
Public Sub BuildChart()

' Create a new chart.

Dim NewChart As Chart

Set NewChart = Charts.Add(After:=Charts(Charts.Count))

' Change the name.

NewChart.Name = "Added Chart"

' Create a series for the chart.

Dim TheSeries As Series

NewChart.SeriesCollection.Add _
```

```
Source:=Worksheets("My Data Sheet").Range("A$3:B$8")

Set TheSeries = NewChart.SeriesCollection(1)

' Change the chart type.

TheSeries.ChartType = xl3DPie

' Change the series title.

TheSeries.Name = "Data from My Data Sheet"

' Perform some data formatting.

With TheSeries

.HasDataLabels = True

.DataLabels.ShowValue = True

.DataLabels.Font.Italic = True

.DataLabels.Font.Size = 14

End With

' Modify the chart's legend.

With NewChart

.HasLegend = True

.Legend.Font.Size = 14

End With

' Modify the 3-D view.

With NewChart

.Pie3DGroup.FirstSliceAngle = 90
```

```
.Elevation = 45

End With

' Format the chart title.

NewChart.ChartTitle.Font.Bold = True

NewChart.ChartTitle.Font.Size = 18

NewChart.ChartTitle.Format.Line.DashStyle _

= msoLineSolid

NewChart.ChartTitle.Format.Line.Style = msoLineSingle

NewChart.ChartTitle.Format.Line.Weight = 2

' Compute the optimal plot area size.

Dim Size As Integer

If NewChart.PlotArea.Height > NewChart.PlotArea.Width

Then

Size = NewChart.PlotArea.Width

Else

Size = NewChart.PlotArea.Height

End If

' Reduce the plot area by 10%.

Size = Size - (Size * 0.1)

' Format the plot area.

With NewChart.PlotArea
```

```
.Interior.Color = RGB(255, 255, 255)

.Border.LineStyle = XlLineStyle.xlLineStyleNone

.Height = Size

.Width = Size

.Top = 75

.Left = 100

End With

' Format the labels.

Dim ChartLabels As DataLabel

Set ChartLabels = TheSeries.DataLabels(0)

ChartLabels.Position = xlLabelPositionOutsideEnd

End Sub
```

In the above example, the code will create a new chart. This chart will appear in the workbook as the last chart, but will not appear as the last item in the workbook. A worksheet which appears after the last chart will also appear after the new chart that is created. The NewChart.Name property will change the name that appears at the bottom of the chart. This property does not change the name of the chart.

At this point, the chart is blank, and you must add a clear one series to the chart if you want to display some data on it. A pie chart will use only one series at a time, but there are other charts that allow you to use multiple data series. For instance, you can use a bubble chart to show multiple series of data. The next task of the code will create a data series based on the worksheet named My Data Sheet. You will notice that the code cannot set TheSeries variable equal to the output of the method Add in this example. Therefore, it uses an additional step to obtain the new series from the SeriesCollection collection.

You should also notice that the Range property has two columns of information. When you are working with Excel 2007, the first column defines the XValues property for the chart. The XValues property determines the entries in the legend for a pie chart. On the other hand, these values appear at the bottom of the display for a bar chart. In both cases, you want to display the labels onscreen so that you can see their effect on the overall display area.

Exercises

1. Write a program to unhide all worksheets in a workbook.

2. Write a program to hide all worksheets in the workbook except for the active worksheet.

3. Write a program to sort worksheets alphabetically using VBA.

Chapter Ten

How to Redirect the Flow

You might run into situations where the existing program flow does not work, and you must disrupt it to move somewhere else in the code. The GoTo statement provides a means of redirecting program flow. Used carefully, the GoTo statement can help you overcome specific programming problems. Unfortunately, the GoTo statement has caused more problems (such as creating hard-to-understand code and hiding programming errors) than any other programming statement because it has a great potential for misuse. Novice programmers find it easier to use the GoTo statement to overcome programming errors rather than to fix these problems. Always use the GoTo statement with extreme care. Designing your code to flow well before you write it and fixing errors when you find them are both easier than reading code with misused GoTo statements.

Using the GoTo statement correctly

The GoTo statement allows you to redirect the flow of your program. The first book of the series also provides information on this statement. Before you use the GoTo statement, you should always think of a different way to perform the redirection, like using a loop. If there is not any other way to perform the programming task efficiently, using a GoTo statement is acceptable.

You might run into situations where the existing program flow does not work, and you must disrupt it to move somewhere else in the code. The GoTo statement provides a means of redirecting program flow. Used carefully, the GoTo statement can help you overcome specific programming problems. Unfortunately, the GoTo statement has caused more problems than any other programming statement because it has a great potential for misuse. Novice programmers find it easier to use the GoTo statement to overcome programming errors rather than to fix these problems. Always use the GoTo statement with extreme care. Designing your code to flow well before you write it and fixing errors when you find them are both easier than reading code with misused GoTo statements.

Loops

You should never use the GoTo statement to replace the end statement in a loop. The statements in your loop will always give the user Never use a GoTo statement as a loop replacement. The statements used for loops signal others about your intent. In addition, standard loop statements contain features that keep bugs, such as endless loops, to a minimum.

Exits

You should avoid using the GoTo statement when you want to exit a program. You can, however, use the End statement for the same task.

Program flow problems

If you detect any problems in the flow of your program, you should check the pseudo-code and then design the documents again. You have to ensure that you always implement the design correctly. The design might require change as well. Do not assume that the design is correct, especially if this is the first attempt.

Chapter Eleven

Error Handling

The easiest errors that you can avoid are the syntax errors, but these are some of the hardest errors to spot. The error can be because of the misuse of a punctuation, misuse of a language element or a spelling mistake. If you forget to include the End If statement in an If...Then statement, you have made a syntax error.

Typos are common syntax errors. These are especially hard to find if you make those errors in variable names. For example, the editor in VBA will view the MySpecialVariable and MySpecialVaraible as different variables, but there is a possibility that you will miss it when you begin to write the code. When you include the Adding Option Explicit at the beginning of the module, form or class module that you create, you can remove this problem. VBA can help you find a variety of typos if you add this statement to the start of your code. It is important that you use this statement in every part of your program when you write it.

There are times when you miss some of the subtle aids in locating the errors in syntax if you do not understand or view the tasks that the IDE or Integrated Development Environment performs. VBA will only display the balloon help feature when the editor in VBA can recognize the function name that you need to enter. If you do not see a balloon help button, you should understand that VBA does not know what function name you are referring to. This means that you will need to look at your code to identify the error. Unfortunately, this feature will only work where the editor in VBA

249

will display the balloon help option. This does not work when you use property names.

Understanding compile errors

VBA uses a compiler to look for any errors that will prevent the program from functioning properly. You can create an If...Then statement and not include the End If statement in the program. The compiler will continue to run continuously and will allow you to find the mistakes in the code immediately once you make them.

VBA will use a compiler to find the syntax error in your code and then display an error message. Try the following when you write a new program. Open a new project, create a Sub using a specific name and type MsgBox(). Now, press Enter. VBA will display a message box, which will state that it was expecting the equal to sign. If you use the parentheses after the keyword MsgBox, VBA will expect that you should include a result variable, which will hold the required result. For example, MyResult = MsgBox("My Prompt"). As mentioned earlier, the debugger highlights the error in red.

Understanding run-time errors

A run-time error often occurs when there is an issue with something outside of your program. There are times when you type in the incorrect information and other times when the system rejects your access to the memory or disk. Your VBA code is completely correct, but the code will fail to function since there is an external error. Most companies, like Microsoft, always run a beta program to avoid any run-time errors. A beta program is a one that programmers develop to test their vendor-sponsored program before they release it into the market.

Understanding semantic errors

This is a particularly difficult error to understand and find since it is a semantic error. This error occurs when the VBA code and logic are both correct, but the meaning behind the code is incorrect. For instance, you can use the Do...Until loop in place of the Do...While loop. It may the case that the code is correct and the logic behind the code is also correct, but the result is not what you expected since the meaning of a Do...Until loop is different from the meaning of a Do...While loop.

When you write a code, the words you use in the code should match your intent. Since a good book always relies on precise terms, a good program also relies only on the precise statements that you use in VBA. These statements will help VBA understand what you want it to do. One of the best ways to avoid making any semantic errors in the application is to always plan your program in advance. You should use a pseudo-code to "pre-write" the design, and then convert that code into the actual VBA code.

Chapter Twelve

Solutions and Additional Programs

Sheet Protection

Example 1

'This code will protect all sheets in the workbook

```
Sub ProtectAllSheets()

Dim ws As Worksheet

For Each ws In Worksheets

ws.Protect

Next ws

End Sub
```

Example 2

'This macro code will lock all the cells with formulas

```
Sub LockCellsWithFormulas()

With ActiveSheet

  .Unprotect

  .Cells.Locked = False
```

.Cells.SpecialCells(xlCellTypeFormulas).Locked = True

.Protect AllowDeletingRows:=True

End With

End Sub

For Loop

Exercise 1

Sub Loop4()

' Fills every second cell from C1:C50 with values of X' --- Comment

Dim X As Integer

For X = 1 To 50 Step 2

Range("C" & X).Value = X

Next X

End Sub

```
(General)                              ▼  Loop4                        ▼
Sub Loop4 ()
' Fills every second cell from C1:C50 with values of X
Dim X As Integer
    For X = 1 To 50 Step 2
        Range("C" & X).Value = X
    Next X
End Sub
```

The output will be:

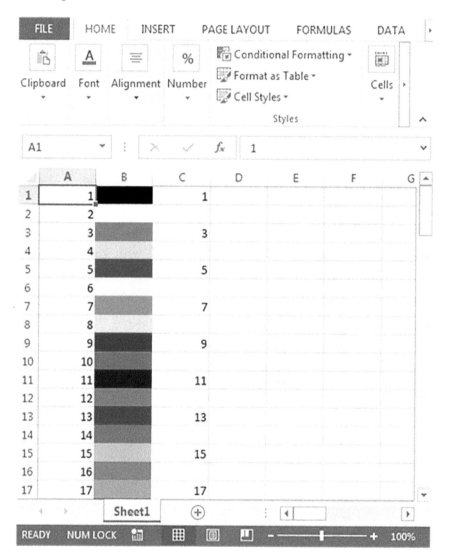

Exercise 2

Sub Loop6()

' Fills every second cell from E1:E100 with values of X' --- Comment

' In this case X decreases by 2' --- Comment

Dim X As Integer, Row As Integer

Row = 1

   For X = 100 To 0 Step -2

      Range("E" & Row).Value = X

      Row = Row + 2

   Next X

End Sub

```
(General)                              ▼   Loop6                    ▼
Sub Loop6()
 ' Fills every second cell from E1:E100 with values of X
 ' In this case X decreases by 2
Dim X As Integer, Row As Integer
Row = 1
    For X = 100 To 0 Step -2
         Range("E" & Row).Value = X
         Row = Row + 2
    Next X
End Sub
```

The output will be,

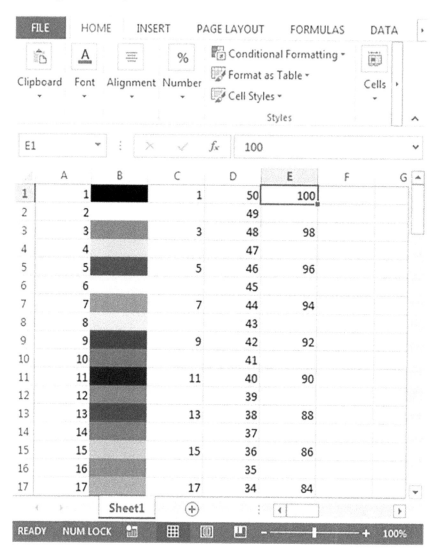

Exercise 3

```
Sub Loop7()

' Starts to fill cells F11:F100 with values of X' --- Comment

' This will exit from the loop after 50' --- Comment

Dim X As Integer

  For X = 11 To 100

    Range("F" & X).Value = X

    If X = 50 Then

      MsgBox ("Bye Bye")

      Exit For

    End If

  Next X

End Sub
```

```
(General)                              ▼   Loop7                          ▼

Sub Loop7()                                                              ▲
' Starts to fill cells F11:F100 with values of X
' This will exit from the loop after 50

Dim X As Integer

For X = 11 To 100
Range("F" & X).Value = X
    If X = 50 Then
        MsgBox ("Bye Bye")
        Exit For
    End If
Next X

End Sub
```

The output will be,

257

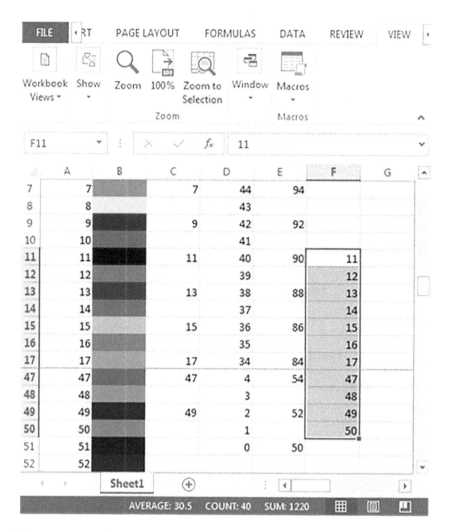

If you enter 50 in the cell F50, the editor will display the following message box on your screen.

Strings

Example 1

'This code will change the Selection to Upper Case

```vba
Sub ChangeCase()

    Dim Rng As Range

    For Each Rng In Selection.Cells

    If Rng.HasFormula = False Then

    Rng.Value = UCase(Rng.Value)

    End If

    Next Rng

End Sub
```

Example 2

'This code will highlight the cells that have misspelled words

```vba
Sub HighlightMisspelledCells()

    Dim cl As Range

    For Each cl In ActiveSheet.UsedRange

    If Not Application.CheckSpelling(word:=cl.Text) Then

    cl.Interior.Color = vbRed

    End If

    Next cl

End Sub
```

Example 3

'This VBA code will create a function to get the numeric part from a string

```
Function GetNumeric(CellRef As String)

    Dim StringLength As Integer

    StringLength = Len(CellRef)

    For i = 1 To StringLength

    If IsNumeric(Mid(CellRef, i, 1)) Then Result = Result & Mid(CellRef, i, 1)

    Next i

    GetNumeric = Result

End Function
```

Arrays

Exercise 1

```
Sub BubbleSort(list())

'   Sorts an array using bubble sort algorithm

    Dim First As Integer, Last As Long

    Dim i As Long, j As Long

    Dim Temp As Long

        First = LBound(list)

    Last = UBound(list)

    For i = First To Last - 1
```

```
For j = i + 1 To Last

    If list(i) > list(j) Then

        Temp = list(j)

        list(j) = list(i)

        list(i) = Temp

    End If

Next j

Next i

End Sub
```

Worksheet and Workbook Methods

Exercise 1

'This code will unhide all sheets in the workbook

```
Sub UnhideAllWoksheets()

    Dim ws As Worksheet

    For Each ws In ActiveWorkbook.Worksheets

    ws.Visible = xlSheetVisible

    Next ws

End Sub
```

Exercise 2

'This macro will hide all the worksheet except the active sheet

```
Sub HideAllExceptActiveSheet()

    Dim ws As Worksheet

    For Each ws In ThisWorkbook.Worksheets

    If ws.Name <> ActiveSheet.Name Then ws.Visible = xlSheetHidden

    Next ws

End Sub
```

Exercise 3

'This code will sort the worksheets alphabetically

```
Sub SortSheetsTabName()

    Application.ScreenUpdating = False

    Dim ShCount As Integer, i As Integer, j As Integer

    ShCount = Sheets.Count

    For i = 1 To ShCount - 1

    For j = i + 1 To ShCount

    If Sheets(j).Name < Sheets(i).Name Then

    Sheets(j).Move before:=Sheets(i)

    End If

    Next j

    Next i

    Application.ScreenUpdating = True

End Sub
```

Additional Programs

Sum of Two numbers

```
Private Sub Calculate_Click()
    Dim a As Integer
    Dim b As Integer
    Dim c As Integer
    a = Val(`TextBox1.Text`)
    b = Val(`TextBox2.Text`)
    c = a + b
    MsgBox (c)
End Sub
```

Concatenate Two Strings

```
Sub ConcatenateStrings()
    Dim str1 As String, str2 As String
    str1 = "Captain"
    str2 = "America"
    'returns "Captain America":
    MsgBox str1 & str2
    MsgBox str1 & " " & str2
    'returns "Captain America":
    MsgBox str1 & " " & str2 & " in Australia"
    'returns "Captain America in Australia":
End Sub
```

Prime Number

```
Function IsPrime(Num As Double) As Boolean
    Dim i As Double
    If Int(Num / 2) = (Num / 2) Then
        Exit Function
    Else
        For i = 3 To Sqr(Num) Step 2
            If Int(Num / i) = (Num / i) Then
                Exit Function
            End If
        Next i
    End If
    IsPrime = True
End Function
```

IIf function

```
' Test if a Supplied Integer is Positive or Negative.
Dim testVal As Integer
Dim sign1 As String
Dim sign2 As String
' First call to IIf function. The test value is negative:
testVal = -2
sign1 = IIf( testVal < 0, "negative", "positive" )
' sign1 is now equal to "negative".
```

' Second call to IIf function. The test value is positive:

testVal = 8

sign2 = IIf(testVal < 0, "negative", "positive")

' sign2 is now equal to "positive".

Fibonacci Series

```
Private Sub Command1_Click()
    Dim x, g, n, i, sum As Integer
    n = Val(Text1.Text)
    x = 0
    y = 1
    Print x
    Print y
    For i = 3 To n
    sum = x + y
    Print sum
    x = y
    y = sum
    y = sum
    Next i
End Sub
```

For Each…Next Statement

```vba
Sub Unhide_First_Sheet_Exit_For()
'Unhides the first sheet that contain a specific phrase
'in the sheet name, then exits the loop.
Dim ws As Worksheet
  For Each ws In ActiveWorkbook.Worksheets
    'Find the sheet that starts with the word "Report"
    If Left(ws.Name, 6) = "Report" Then
      ws.Visible = xlSheetVisible
      'Exit the loop after the first sheet is found
      Exit For
    End If
  Next ws
End Sub
```

Conclusion

Thank you for purchasing the book. Most organizations have begun to use VBA to automate some of their processes in Excel. You can copy and paste information or create a pivot in Excel using VBA. If you want to improve some processes and gather more information about the different tools you can use in Excel, you have come to the right place. This is the third series of the book which provides more information on how you can use VBA to improve processes.

You must remember that experts also make many errors when they build applications and programs. Therefore, you should never beat yourself up if you make any mistakes. You should take some time to understand what the error is and identify a way to fix it. You have to always practice to improve your skills at programming in VBA.

I hope you gather all the information you are looking for. I believe you can automate some or all processes that you work on and impress your bosses and colleagues!

Thank you again for buying the book and if you're finding the information valuable so far, please be sure to leave **5-star feedback on Amazon.**

Sources

https://www.google.co.in/url?sa=i&rct=j&q=&esrc=s&source=ima
ges&cd=&cad=rja&uact=8&ved=2ahUKEwjDrZTG0frdAh
UIEnIKHWGVCVMQjRx6BAgBEAU&url=http%3A%2F
%2Fwww.databison.com%2Fhow-to-write-a-macro-in-
excel%2F&psig=AOvVaw0XYs9S9qRneDdPgmz6Bmld&
ust=153921https://docs.microsoft.com/en-us/dotnet/visual-
basic/language-reference/statements/do-loop-
statement8405542672

https://docs.microsoft.com/en-us/dotnet/visual-basic/language-
reference/statements/do-loop-statement

https://www.google.co.in/url?sa=i&rct=j&q=&esrc=s&source=ima
ges&cd=&cad=rja&uact=8&ved=2ahUKEwjDrZTG0frdAh
UIEnIKHWGVCVMQjRx6BAgBEAU&url=http%3A%2F
%2Fwww.databison.com%2Fhow-to-write-a-macro-in-
excel%2F&psig=AOvVaw0XYs9S9qRneDdPgmz6Bmld&
ust=1539218405542672

https://www.exceltip.com/vba/for-loops-with-7-examples.html

https://www.excel-easy.com/vba/examples/macro-recorder.html

https://docs.microsoft.com/en-
us/office/vba/api/excel.application.automationsecurity

http://www.informit.com/articles/article.aspx?p=1610813&seqNum
=4

https://chartio.com/resources/tutorials/how-to-get-values-from-
another-sheet-in-excel-using-vba/

https://ccm.net/faq/53497-how-to-manipulate-data-in-excel-using-vba

http://www.databison.com/how-to-write-a-macro-in-excel/

http://www.la-solutions.co.uk/content/V8/MVBA/MVBA-Tips.htm

http://www.homeandlearn.org/the_excel_vba_editor.html

https://www.excelcampus.com/vba/vba-immediate-window-excel/

https://www.guru99.com/vba-arrays.html

https://www.excel-easy.com/vba/array.html

https://excelmacromastery.com/excel-vba-array/

https://www.excel-easy.com/vba/if-then-statement.html

https://docs.microsoft.com/en-us/dotnet/visual-basic/language-reference/statements/if-then-else-statement

https://bettersolutions.com/vba/arrays/sorting-bubble-sort.htm

https://trumpexcel.com/excel-macro-examples/#tab-con-20

Excel VBA

A Comprehensive, Step-By-Step Guide On Excel VBA Finance For Data Reporting And Business Analysis

Introduction

VBA is an amazing tool that many organizations have begun to use to perform some tasks in a few minutes or a few seconds. For instance, you can use VBA to analyze some information or extract some information from a given data set. You can also perform some special types of data analysis. When you write a macro in VBA, you can be certain that you have mastered your work.

If you want to learn how you can use VBA for finance and data analysis, you have come to the right place. Over the course of the book you will gather information on what VBA is, and what different parts of VBA you need to be aware of. You will learn more about the data types, the modules and other functions you can use to automate tasks.

Thank you for purchasing the book. I hope you gather all the information you are looking for.

If you enjoyed this title, please visit my author profile in Amazon and consider leaving a review.

Chapter One

Introduction to VBA

Visual Basic for Applications or VBA is a programming language, which is compatible with most Microsoft Office Products, including Excel. In other words, you can use VBA to develop programs in Excel. These programs will make Excel operate accurately and very fast.

What can you do with VBA?

Most people use Excel for a million different reasons. Here are a few examples:

- Forecasting and Budgeting

- Analyzing data

- Developing diagrams and charts using data

- Creating lists

- Creating forms and invoices

This list is endless, but I am sure you get the idea. In other words, you can use Excel to perform a variety of tasks, and I am sure you are reading this book because you have a set of expectations. If you want to automate the functions of Excel, you should use VBA.

For example, you may want to create a program that will help you import some data or numbers and then format that data to print a report. Once you develop the code, you can execute the macro

274

using a command or a button. This will ensure that Excel performs the task in a few seconds or minutes.

Common Uses of VBA

You must understand why you want to use VBA. You must ensure that you can take some time out of your busy schedule to sit down and write a VBA code. You must understand the different tasks you can use VBA for. You cannot use VBA to perform your chores, but you can use it to make some tasks easier for you. This section covers some tasks that you can perform with VBA.

Automating Documents

Most people do not like to prepare documents, and if these documents contain the same information, they will not want to work on that document. You can use the Excel Ad-in called Mail Merge to automate letters, but this is not an option to use when you want to write individual letters or documents. In such situations, you can use a VBA code to create a form that will include the common information. You can include check boxes that VBA will use to write the document for you.

Word processing is not the only task you can automate using VBA. You can also automate the spreadsheet and there are numerous programs you can create for the same. For example, you can extract information or data from the Internet into a spreadsheet by clicking a button. Therefore, you can limit the time you spend on simply copying the data from the web and pasting it according to the required format in your Excel worksheet.

Customizing Application Interfaces

There are times when the features of an application will bug you, and you can turn off those features. But, that is not an option if you want to use that feature in your work. Instead of disabling that feature, you can use VBA to create a new feature that has all the functions that you need. For instance, instead of using conditional formatting every time you need to make changes in a worksheet, you can write a VBA code to do that for you.

It is easy to change the interface of an application, so it works better for you. You can customize toolbars or menu systems, and can also move some elements around in the interface to make it look presentable. Additionally, you can use multiple interfaces and use a VBA code to shift between those interfaces.

One of the most common applications of VBA is to perform a variety of calculations. You can create different equations and graphs using the data you obtain. There are times when you will need to make changes to the data so you can perform some calculations on it. If you find that an equation is complicated, you can use VBA to simplify the process. You can also use iterative functions to perform a calculation.

Sometimes the number that you create using a calculation does not mean much — it is just a number until someone makes a decision. Some decisions are easy to make yet repetitive. Smart applications save you more time for playing that game of Solitaire.

Adding new application features

Most vendors or developers never use the applications they build. Therefore, they never update the code for their application. You can add new features to the application using VBA codes and work on developing an application. When you develop applications that complete some of your work in a few minutes, you will impress your boss and colleagues. This is an added advantage

Chapter Two

The IDE

VBA is a visual programming environment. That is, you see how your program will look before you run it. Its editor is very visual, using various windows to make your programming experience easy and manageable. You will notice slight differences in the appearance of the editor when you use it with Vista as compared to older versions of Windows. No matter which Office product and version of Windows you use, the editor has essentially the same appearance (and some small differences), the same menu items, and the same functionality.

An IDE is an editor, just like your word processor, spreadsheet, or database form. Just as application editors have special features that make them especially useful for working with data, an IDE is a programming editor with special features that make it useful for writing instructions that the application should follow. These instructions are procedural code — a set of steps. The figure below shows you the IDE Window in Excel:

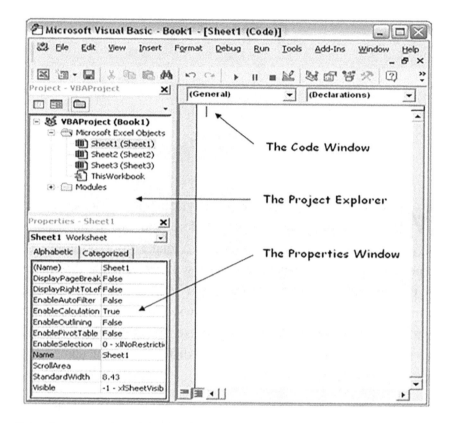

(https://www.google.co.in/url?sa=i&rct=j&q=&esrc=s&source=images&cd=&ca
d=rja&uact=8&ved=2ahUKEwjDrZTG0frdAhUIEnIKHWGVCVMQjRx6BAgB
EAU&url=http%3A%2F%2Fwww.databison.com%2Fhow-to-write-a-macro-in-
excel%2F&psig=AOvVaw0XYs9S9qRneDdPgmz6Bmld&ust=15392184055426
72)

The VBA IDE consists of a menu system, toolbars, a Project
Explorer window, a Properties window, and a Code window. Below
is a summary of what each Window contains.

Project Explorer

This window contains a list of the items in your project, which
contains all the document elements in a single file. Your application
exists within a file that appears in the Project Explorer window.

Properties

Whenever you select an object, the Properties window tells you about it. For example, this window tells you whether the object is blue or whether it has words on it.

Code

Eventually, you must write some code to make your application work. This window contains the special words that tell your application what to do. Think of it as a place to write a specialized to-do list.

Looking at the VBA Toolbox

You will not have to write code for every task in VBA. The IDE also supports forms, just like the forms that you use to perform other tasks. In this case, you decide what appears on the form and how the form acts when the user works with it. To make it easier to create forms, VBA provides the Toolbox, which contains controls used to create forms.

Each Toolbox button performs a unique task. For example, when you click one button, a text box may appear on the screen. But, if you click another button, a mathematical operation may take place.

Starting the Visual Basic Editor

How you start the Visual Basic Editor depends on the application that you are using. Newer versions of Office use a different approach than older versions.

Step 1: Go to Option "View" on the toolbar.

Step 2: In the drop-down list, select "Record Macro."

Step 3: The interface will open, and you can begin typing the code for the worksheet you are in.

Using Project Explorer

Project Explorer appears in the Project Explorer window. You use it to interact with the objects that make up a project. A project is an individual file used to hold your program, or at least pieces of it. The project resides within the Office document that you are using, so when you open the Office document, you also open the project. See Chapter 3 for a description of how projects and programs interact. Project Explorer works much like how the left pane of Windows Explorer does.

The objects listed in Project Explorer depend on the kind of application that you are working with. For example, if you are working with Word, you see documents and document templates. Likewise, if you are working with Excel, you see worksheets and workbooks. However, no matter what kind of application you work with, the way that you use Project Explorer is the same.

A project can contain forms, modules, and class modules. Here is a description of these special objects:

- **Forms**: Contain user interface elements and help you interact with the user.

- **Modules**: Contain the nonvisual code for your application. For example, you can use a module to store a special calculation.

- **Class modules**: Contain new objects that you want to build. You can use a class module to create a new data type.

Working with special entries

Sometimes you see a special entry in Project Explorer. For example, when you work with a Word document, you might see a References folder, which contains any references that the Word document makes. Normally, it contains a list of templates that the document relies upon for formatting.

In many cases, you cannot modify the objects in the special folders. This is the case with the References folder used by Word document objects. The References folder is there for information only. To modify the referenced template, you need to find its object in Project Explorer. We will not discuss these concepts in the book since you do not work with these often.

Using the Properties window

Most of the objects that you click in the VBA IDE have properties that describe the object in some way. The earlier "Property values are up" section of this chapter tells about properties if you have not worked with them before. The following sections provide details about the Properties window.

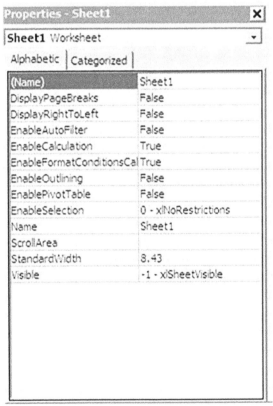

(http://www.affordsol.be/vba-prog-1-3-editor-properties.htm)

Understanding property types

A property needs to describe the object. When you look at an object, you naturally assume something about the information provided by a use red, yellow, or green. Likewise, VBA object properties have specific types. One of the most common property types is text. The Caption property of a form is text. The text appears at the top of the form when the user opens it. Another common property type is a logic, or Boolean, value.

Getting help with properties

Do not expect to memorize every property for every object that VBA applications can create. Not even the gurus can do that. To determine what a property will do for your application, just highlight the property and press F1, and, in most cases, VBA displays a Help window like the image below.

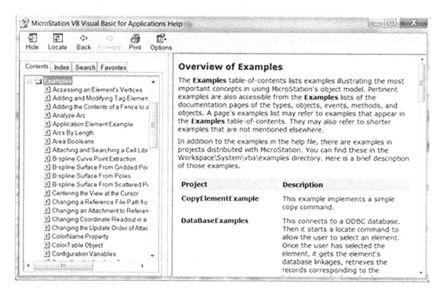

(http://www.la-solutions.co.uk/content/V8/MVBA/MVBA-Tips.htm)

Using the Code Window

The Code window is where you write your application code. It works like any other editor that you have used, except that you type according to the syntax.

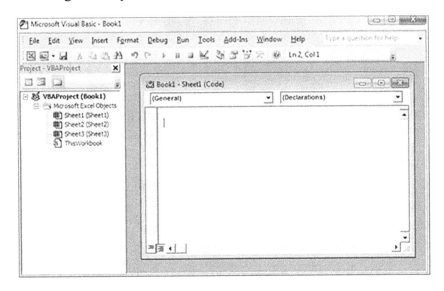

(http://www.homeandlearn.org/the_excel_vba_editor.html)

Notice that the Project Explorer window and the Properties window are gone — you can display them again by using the View -> Project Explorer and View ->Properties Window commands.

Opening an existing Code window

Sometimes you will not be able to complete an application and need to work on it later. To open an existing Code window, find the module that you want to open in Project Explorer. Double-click the module entry, and the IDE displays the code within it with your code loaded. The Code window also appears when you perform different tasks.

Creating a new Code window

When you start a new module within an existing document or template, open a new Code window by using either the Insert -> Module or Insert -> Class Module command. After you save this module or class module, it appears in Project Explorer with the other modules in your project.

It is easier to execute one line of code at a time to understand where you may have made an error. You can do this by using the Immediate Window. This window normally appears at the bottom of the IDE, and it will not contain any information until you type something in it.

Most developers spend their days using the Immediate window to check their applications for errors. You can use the Immediate window to ask VBA about the value of a variable, for example. To try this feature, type String1 = "Hello World" in the Immediate window and then press Enter. Now type '? String1' and then press Enter. You asked VBA to create a variable named String1 and assign it a value of Hello World. You can use the '?' operator to check the value assigned to the variable String1.

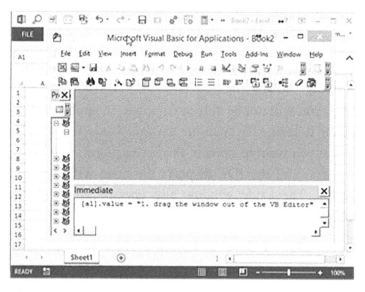

(https://www.excelcampus.com/vba/vba-immediate-window-excel/)

Chapter Three

VBA, A Primer

Macro Recorder

As mentioned in the previous book, the macro recorder is an important and useful tool in Excel. This tool will record every action that you perform in Excel. You only need to record a task once using the macro recorder, and you can execute that same task a million times by clicking a button. If you do not know how to program a specific task in Excel, you can use the Macro Recorder to help you understand what you need to do. You can then open the Visual Basic Editor once you have recorded the task to see how you can program it.

You cannot perform many tasks when you use the Macro Recorder. For instance, you cannot use the macro recorder to loop through data. The macro recorder also uses more code than you need, which will slow the process down.

Record a Macro

- Go to the Menu Bar and move the Developer Tab, and click the button to Record the Macro.

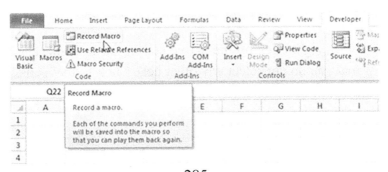

- Enter the name of the macro.

- Choose the workbook where you want to use the macro. This means that the macro can only be used in the current workbook.

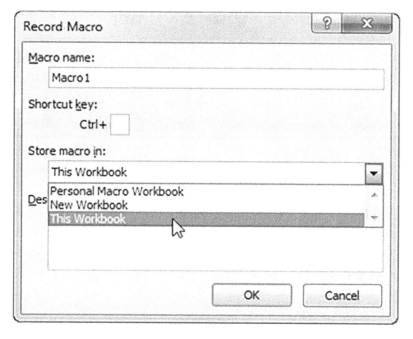

4. If you store the macro in a personal macro workbook, you can access the macro in all your workbooks. This is only because Excel stores the macro in a hidden workbook, which will open automatically when it starts. If you store the macro in a new workbook, you can use the macro only in the opened workbook.

5. Click OK.

6. Now, right click on the active cell in the worksheet. Ensure that you do not select any other cell. Click format cells.

7. Select the percentage.

8. Click OK.

9. Now, select the stop recording.

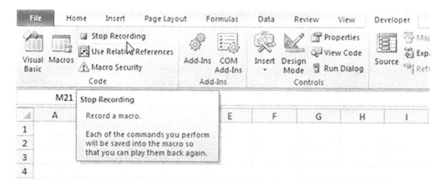

You have successfully recorded your macro using the macro recorder.

Run the Recorded Macro

You will now need to test the macro and see if you can change the format of the numbers to percentage.

10. Enter any numbers between 0 and 1 in the spreadsheet.

11. Select the numbers.

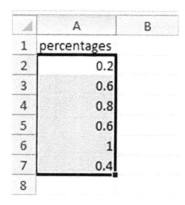

	A	B
1	percentages	
2	0.2	
3	0.6	
4	0.8	
5	0.6	
6	1	
7	0.4	
8		

12. Move to the Developer tab, and click macros.

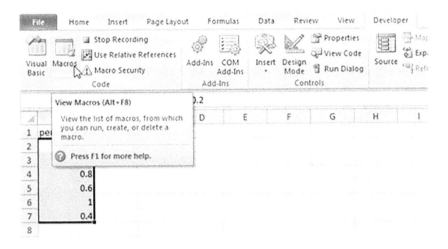

13. Now click run.

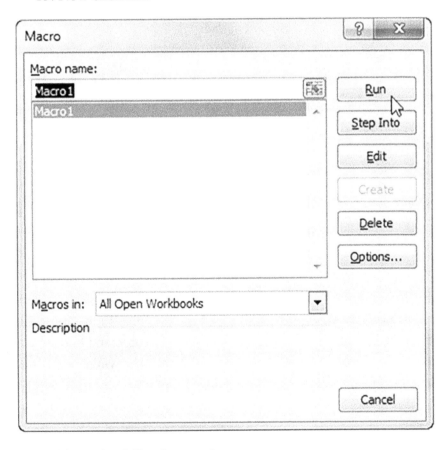

You will see the following result.

	A	B
1	percentages	
2	20.00%	
3	60.00%	
4	80.00%	
5	60.00%	
6	100.00%	
7	40.00%	
8		

See the Macro

If you want to look at the macro, you should open the Visual Basic Editor.

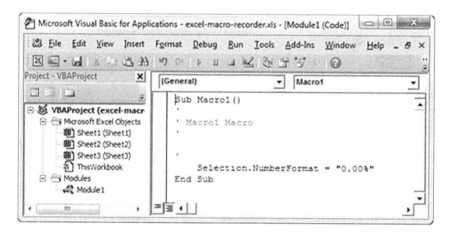

The macro, called Module 1, is placed in a module. The code that is placed in the module is always available to the full workbook. This means you can change the format for the numbers in all the sheets in the workbook. If you assign a macro to the command button, you should remember that the macro would only be available for that specific sheet.

Macro Storage and Security

The developers at Microsoft changed the security settings that help to prevent macros from running. This development was only made when macros were used to deliver some high-profile viruses. We covered some information about the security of macros in the first part of the book. Let us now look at how you can adjust the default settings in a macro.

You can either control the settings for a macro in some workbooks by saving the workbook in trusted locations or by adjusting the security settings globally. If you store a workbook with a macro in a folder that you label a trusted location, the macros will automatically be enabled when you open the workbook.

You can check the security of your macro in the Developer tab under the Macro Security icon. If you click this icon, a dialog box with the settings category will be displayed. You can access the folders that you trust by scrolling down the left navigation bar.

How to Add a Trusted Location

As mentioned earlier, you can save the workbooks with macros in a folder that you mark as a trusted location. If you save a workbook in that folder, the macros will always be enabled. The developers suggest that you should always have a trusted location in your hard drive. Remember that you can never trust the location on a network drive.

If you want to specify a trusted location, you should follow the steps given below:

1. Go to the Developer Tab and click on Macro Security.

2. Move to the left navigation pane in the Trust Center and choose the Trusted Location.

3. If you want to save the file on a network drive, you should add that location into the trusted locations.

4. Go to 'My Networks' in the Trusted Location dialog box and click the 'Add New Location' button.

5. You will see the list of Trusted Locations in a dialog box.

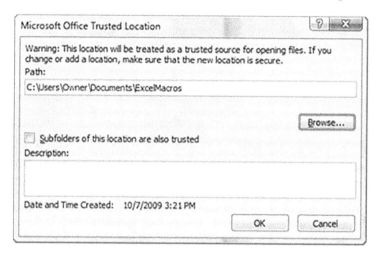

6. Now click the Browse button and go to the parent folder of the folder that you want to make a trusted location. Now click on the Trusted Folder. You will not find the name of the Folder in the text box, but click OK. The correct name will come in the Browse dialog box.

7. If you want to include the subfolders in the selected folder, you should select the radio button against the 'Subfolders of this location are also trusted' option.

8. Now, click OK to add the folder to the list.

How to Enable Macros Outside a Trusted Location

When you do not save an excel workbook in a trusted location, excel will always rely on the macro settings. In Excel 2003, a macro could have a low, medium, high or very high security. The developers of Microsoft later renamed these settings. If you want to access the macro settings, you should go to the Developers Tab and choose Macro Security. Excel will then display the Macro Settings dialog box. You should select the 'Disable All Macros with

Notification' option. Let us look at the description of the options in the dialog box.

Disable All Macros Without Notification

This setting will not allow any macro to run. If you do not always want to run the macro when you open the workbook, you should choose this setting. Since you are still learning how to use macros and work with them, you should not use this setting. This setting is equivalent to the Very High Security that is found in Excel 2003. If you choose this setting, you can only run macros if they are saved in a Trusted Location.

Disable All Macros With Notification

This setting is like the Medium security setting in Excel 2003. This is the recommended setting that you should use. If you use this setting, Excel will ask you if you want to Enable to Disable a macro when you open a workbook. You may often choose this option if you are a beginner. In Excel 2010, you will see a message in the message area, which states that the macros have been disabled. You can either choose to enable or disable the content in the workbook by choosing that option.

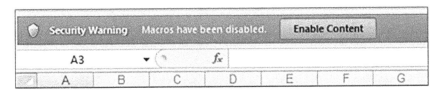

Disable All Macros Except Digitally Signed Macros

If you wish to use this setting, you should always use a digital signing tool like VeriSign or any other provider to sign your macro. If you are going to sell your macros to other parties, you should use this security option. This is a hassle if you want to write macros only for your use.

Enable All Macros

Experts suggest that you do not use this option since dangerous codes can also run on your system. This setting is equivalent to the Low security option in Excel 2003, and is the easiest option to use. This option will open your system up to attacks from malicious viruses.

Disabling All Macros With Notification

Experts suggest that you set your macro to disable all content after it gives you a notification. If you save a workbook with a macro using this setting, you will see a security warning right above the formula bar when you open the workbook. If you know that there are macros in the workbook, all you need to do is click 'Enable Content.' You can click on the X on the far right of the bar if you do not want to enable any of the macros in the workbook.

If you do forget to enable the macro and then attempt to run that macro, Excel will indicate that the macro will not run since you have disabled all macros in the workbook. If this happens, you should reopen the workbook to enable the macros again.

Hi there! If you found the topic or information useful, it would be a great help if you can leave a quick review on Amazon. Thanks a lot!

Chapter Four

Data Types

Data types are a way to define the data to make it easier for the user to assign values to a variable within the program. The computer will still compute the data in the form of bits, and VBA uses different data types in different ways. The computer will see that binary value 1000001b, but it will not do anything with that value. The compiler in VBA will view this specific value as a letter or number depending on the data type that you assign to that value. It is important to understand what a data type is, and how you should use data types. You should adhere to some rules when you use data types. The data can be corrupted by another program or procedure.

Although a variable, in general, is simply a box for storing data, you can think of these data types as special boxes for storing specific kinds of data. Just as you would use a hatbox to store a hat and not a car engine, you use these special box types to store kinds of data. For example, you use a string to hold text, not logical (true/false) values. VBA supports several standard data types, including Boolean, Byte, Long, Currency, Integer, Single, Decimal, Double, Date, Object, String and Variant. Apart from these defined data types, you can also create some user-defined data types so you can mark the necessary information for your program. A user-defined data type gives you the power to extend the VBA interpretation of data. (The computer still looks at the data as binary information.) Each of the data type descriptions that follow has a

295

different purpose, and you can work with the data type in a variety of ways.

Using strings for text

The first data type that I discuss in this chapter is one that you have already seen in the message box examples: the string. When you create a message box, you use a string as input. The string is the most useful data type in VBA. This chapter only introduces strings. The next chapter provides information on how you can manipulate strings in VBA.

Understanding strings

Programmers often use fancy terms for things that the average person easily recognizes. A string is a sequence of characters. The characters are not always printable but can include control characters that determine how the text appears on-screen. A string can also include special characters, such as punctuation, or even special features, such as a circumflex or an umlaut. Although a string can contain all these elements, the main content of a string is always text.

Adding strings together with + or &

Sometimes you will want to concatenate two or more strings to make a longer string. Concatenation is the process of adding strings together. For example, you might want to add a person's first name to their last name to create their full name. Often, you need to take information from more than one place and join it together to create a new kind of information.

Using character codes

Strings can contain several elements. In previous examples, I show you strings that contain control character constants such as vbCrLf. This constant contains two control characters: a carriage return and a line feed. The carriage return sends the cursor back to the beginning of the line; the line feed places the cursor on the next line. The result of using both control characters together is the same as pressing Enter on the keyboard. Strings can also use a special function, Chr, to create special characters. You can combine this function with the Character Map utility to produce any character that you need for your program

Using numbers for calculations

Most computers store information in the form of numbers. You can use a number to express some values in a database, perform a few tasks in spreadsheets or show the reader or user the current page in a document or webpage. In procedures, numbers are used to count iterations in loops, determine the position of values in arrays or check a specific condition. You can use numbers in VBA in different ways, like interacting with your code or determining which character you want to view on screen.

Understanding the numeric types

Numbers are always looked at as a single entity, and a number is simply just that – a number. A computer can view the number in different ways since the processor works differently with numbers. For example, you have a data type for an integer value, which is a value that does not have a decimal point and a data type for a decimal point. The four types of numeric data types are:

1. **Integer**: As mentioned earlier, these numbers do not have a decimal point. Integers can only hold whole numbers like 5, but cannot hold numbers like 5.6.

2. **Real**: A real number can contain a decimal point, and the number after the decimal point does not necessarily have to contain a value. This means the number 5.0 is accepted as a real number. The compiler will store a real number in a different format when compared to an integer.

3. **Currency**: A financial calculation will require some accuracy since you will be using small currency values. Even the smallest issue with the program can cause an error.

297

The currency numeric allows you to store numbers with extreme precision, but the compiler takes a lot of time to process or store this data type.

4. **Decimal**: A computer stores information in the binary or base 2 format. When you use a base 10 or decimal value when you work with numbers, the compiler will need to convert the number into binary before it can use it.

Using Boolean values to make decisions

The Boolean type is the easiest to use and understand. This type is used to indicate yes or no, true or false and on or off. You can use this type to work with any two-state information. It is commonly used to represent data values that are diametrically opposed.

Working with Operators

Operators determine how VBA works with two variables and what result it produces. The examples in this chapter use operators to add numbers and concatenate (add) strings. In both cases, your code uses the + operator to perform the task. However, the result differs. When you are using numbers, the result is a summation, such as 1 + 2 = 3. When you are using strings, the result is a concatenation, such as Hello + World = Hello World.

VBA groups operators into four areas:

1. **Arithmetic**: Operators that perform math operations, such as addition (+), subtraction (-), division (/), and multiplication (*)
2. **Comparison**: Operators such as less than (<), greater than (>), and equal (=) that compare two values and produce a Boolean result
3. **Concatenation**: Operators such as & and + that are used to add two strings together
4. **Logical**: Operators such as Not, And, Or, and Xor that are used to perform Boolean operations on two variables

Chapter Five

Decision Making Statements

Few programs use all the statements in the program file all the time. You might want the program to perform one task when you click Yes and another task when you click No. The statements for both tasks appear in the code, but the program executes only one set of statements. To control program execution, the developer adds special statements — such as the If...Then statement — that shows the beginning and end of each task and decide which task to execute. You might think that letting the computer decide which task to execute would cause the developer to lose control of the program. However, the developer has not lost control of the program, because the decision-making process is predefined as part of the program design.

If...Then Statement

Most programs require decision-making code. When you need to make the same decision every time that you perform a task and the outcome of the decision is always the same, then making the decision is something that you can tell VBA to do for you by using the If...Then statement. Decision-making code has several benefits:

1. **Consistency**: The decision is made by using the same criteria and in the same manner every time.

2. **Speed**: A computer can make static decisions faster than humans can. However, the decision must be the same every

time, and the decision must have the same answer set every time.

3. **Complexity**: Requesting that the computer make static decisions can reduce program complexity. Fewer decisions translate into ease of use for most people.

Example:

Public Sub IfThenTest()

> *' Create a variable for the selected text.*

> *Dim TestText As String*

> *' Get the current selection.*

> *TestText = ActiveWindow.Selection.Text*

> *' Test the selection for "Hello."*

> *If TestText = "Hello" Then*

>> *' Modify the selected text to show it's correct.*

>> *TestText = "Correct!" + vbCrLf + "Hello"*

> *End If*

If...Then...Else statement

The If...Then...Else statement makes one of two choices. If the expression controlling the statement is true, VBA executes the first set of statements. On the other hand, if the expression is false, VBA executes the second set of statements.

If...Then...ElseIf statement

When making multiple comparisons, you can use the If...Then...ElseIf statement to make the code easier to read. Using this format can also reduce the number of decisions that VBA must make, which ensures that your code runs as quickly as possible.

Using the IIf function

You might need to decide in a single line of code instead of the three lines (minimum) that other decision-making techniques require. The IIf function is a good choice when you need to make simple and concise decisions in your program. It has the advantage of providing decision-making capability in a single line of code.

Chapter Six

Loops

Many tasks that you perform require more than one check, change, or data manipulation. You do not change just one entry in a worksheet; you change all the affected entries. Likewise, you do not change just one word in a document; you might change all occurrences based on certain criteria. Databases require multiple changes for almost any task.

Loops provide a method for performing tasks for more than one time. You can use loops to save code-writing time. Simply write the code to perform the repetitive task once and then tell VBA to perform the task multiple times. When using loops, you decide how the code determines when to stop. You can tell the loop to execute a specific number of times or to continue executing until the program meets a certain condition.

Do While...Loop statement

A Do While...Loop statement keeps performing a task until a certain condition is true. The loop checks the expression first and then executes the code within the structure if the expression is true. You use this loop to perform processing zero or more times. A Do While...Loop works especially well if you cannot determine the number of times that the loop should execute when you design your program.

Do...Loop While statement

The Do...Loop While statement works the same as the Do While...Loop statement. The difference is that this statement always executes once because the expression used to verify a need to loop appears at the end of the structure. Even if the expression is false, this statement still executes at least one time. You can use this statement when you want to ensure that a task is always completed at least one time.

Do Until...Loop statement

The Do Until...Loop statement continues processing information until the expression is false. You can view the Do While...Loop statement as a loop that continues while a task is incomplete. The Do Until...Loop statement continues until the task is finished. The subtle difference between the two statements points out something interesting: They rely on your perspective of the task to complete. These two statement types are completely interchangeable. The big difference is how you define the expression used to signal the end of the looping sequence.

Do...Loop Until statement

The Do...Loop Until statement is the counterpart of the Do Until...Loop statement. This statement examines the expression at the end of the loop, so it always executes at least once even if the expression is false.

For...Next statement

The For...Next statement is very handy for performing a task a specific number of times. If you can determine how many times to do something in advance, this is the best looping option to use because there is less chance of creating an infinite loop. You can create absurdly large loops, but they eventually end.

For Each...Next statement

The For Each...Next statement is like the For...Next statement in operation. However, this statement does not rely on an external counter. The statement uses an object index as a counter. The advantage of using this statement is that you do not have to figure out how many times to perform the loop — the object provides this information. The disadvantage of using this statement is that you lose a little control over how the loop executes because the counter is no longer under your control.

Chapter Seven

Arrays

Arrays provide a way for your programs to store more than one item in a single container. Think of the array as a large box with a bunch of small boxes inside. Each small box can store a single value. You decide how many small boxes the array can hold when you create the array. Use arrays when you need to store several related items of the same data type.

Structured Storage

An array is a list of items. When you write a list of tasks to perform for the day, you create an array. The piece of paper is a single container that holds several strings, each of which is a task that you must perform. Likewise, you can create a single piece of paper in your VBA program — an array — and use that array to hold multiple items. You can define arrays by using several techniques. However, all these techniques use the same basic approach.

Example:

> *' Tell VBA to start all arrays at 0.*
>
> *Option Base 0*
>
> *Public Sub SingleDimension()*
>
> *' Define an output string.*
>
> *Dim Output As String*
>
> *' Define a variant to hold individual strings.*

```
Dim IndividualString As Variant
' Define the array of strings.
Dim StringArray(5) As String
' Fill each array element with information.
StringArray(0) = "This"
StringArray(1) = "Is"
StringArray(2) = "An"
StringArray(3) = "Array"
StringArray(4) = "Of"
StringArray(5) = "Strings"
' Use the For Each...Next statement to get each array
' element and place it in a string.
For Each IndividualString In StringArray
' Create a single output string with the array
' array elements.
Output = Output + IndividualString + " "
Next
' Display the result.
MsgBox Trim(Output), _
vbInformation Or vbOKOnly, _
"Array Content"
End Sub
```

Notice that the code begins with an Option Base 0 statement. This statement tells VBA whether you want to start counting array elements at 0 or 1. The default setting is 0. Most programming languages use 0 as the starting point, which is why Microsoft made

0 the default for VBA. However, older versions of Visual Basic (including VBA) use 1 as the starting point. When you want to ensure that your program works in every environment, include the Option Base statement.

Because the array begins at 0 and not at 1, you can store six items in an array that is defined as having five elements. The number that you include in the declaration is always the top element number of the array and not the actual number of elements.

Array Types

One can classify an array in several ways, and the first method is the type of data that the array will hold. A string array is very different from an integer array, but the array will always ensure that the elements are unique. If you use a Variant data type, you can mix the data types in an array. You should always be careful when you use this technique since it can lead to errors which are difficult to debug.

Another method is to define the dimensions in an array. The dimension will define the number of directions in which the array will hold the information. A simple list, like the one in the earlier "Understanding array usage" section gives an example of a single-dimensional array. A table which consists of columns and rows is a two-dimensional array. One can create an array using any number of dimensions.

Example: Adding an Element to an Array

Dim a As Range

Dim arr As Variant 'Just a Variant variable (i.e. don't pre-define it as an array)

For Each a In Range.Cells

        If IsEmpty(arr) Then

arr = Array(a.value) 'Make the Variant an array with a single element

Else

ReDim Preserve arr(UBound(arr) + 1) 'Add next array element

arr(UBound(arr)) = a.value   'Assign the array element

End If

Next

VBA Array

In this section, we will look at the steps you need to follow to create an array.

Step 1 – Create A New Workbook

1. Open Microsoft Excel.

2. Save the excel workbook with the extension .xlsm

Step 2 – Add A Command Button

Now that you are familiar with creating an interface in a workbook. The previous chapters in the book will help you gather more information about the subroutines or subs and functions in VBA.

1. Add a command button to the active worksheet.

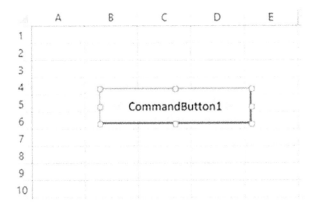

2. Set the property name to cmdLoadBeverages.

3. Now, set the Caption Property as Load Beverages.

The interface should now display the following:

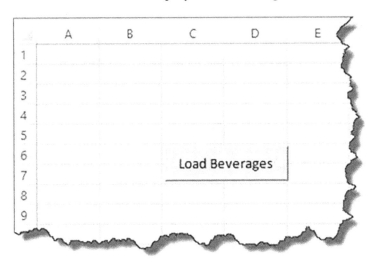

Step 3 – Save the File

1. You should now click the save as button in the macro-enabled form.

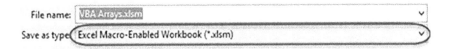

File name: VBA Arrays.xlsm

Save as type Excel Macro-Enabled Workbook (*.xlsm)

309

Step 4 – Write the Code

Let us now write the code for the application.

1. Right click on the button and choose to view the code.

2. Add the code in the code window.

```
Private Sub cmdLoadBeverages_Click()

    Dim Drinks(1 To 4) As String

    Drinks(1) = "Pepsi"

    Drinks(2) = "Coke"

    Drinks(3) = "Fanta"

    Drinks(4) = "Juice"

    Sheet1.Cells(1, 1).Value = "My Favorite Beverages"

    Sheet1.Cells(2, 1).Value = Drinks(1)

    Sheet1.Cells(3, 1).Value = Drinks(2)

    Sheet1.Cells(4, 1).Value = Drinks(3)

    Sheet1.Cells(5, 1).Value = Drinks(4)

End Sub
```

Example to Enter Student's Marks

Without An Array

In the example below, we will look at how you can enter the marks for every student without using an array.

```
Public Sub StudentMarks()

    With ThisWorkbook.Worksheets("Sheet1")
```

```vba
' Declare variable for each student
Dim Student1 As Integer
Dim Student2 As Integer
Dim Student3 As Integer
Dim Student4 As Integer
Dim Student5 As Integer
' Read student marks from cell
Student1 = .Range("C2").Offset(1)
Student2 = .Range("C2").Offset(2)
Student3 = .Range("C2").Offset(3)
Student4 = .Range("C2").Offset(4)
Student5 = .Range("C2").Offset(5)
' Print student marks
Debug.Print "Students Marks"
Debug.Print Student1
Debug.Print Student2
Debug.Print Student3
Debug.Print Student4
Debug.Print Student5
End With
End Sub
```

The output will be the following,

Using an Array

```
Public Sub StudentMarksArr()

  With ThisWorkbook.Worksheets("Sheet1")

    ' Declare an array to hold marks for 5 students

    Dim Students(1 To 5) As Integer

    ' Read student marks from cells C3:C7 into array

    Dim i As Integer

    For i = 1 To 5

       Students(i) = .Range("C2").Offset(i)

    Next i

    ' Print student marks from the array

    Debug.Print "Students Marks"

    For i = LBound(Students) To UBound(Students)

       Debug.Print Students(i)

    Next i

  End With

End Sub
```

Notice the difference in the variables used in the two programs, and also notice the length of the program.

Example with Loops

```vba
Public Sub ArrayLoops()

   ' Declare  array

   Dim arrMarks(0 To 5) As Long

   ' Fill the array with random numbers

   Dim i As Long

   For i = LBound(arrMarks) To UBound(arrMarks)

      arrMarks(i) = 5 * Rnd

   Next i

   ' Print out the values in the array

   Debug.Print "Location", "Value"

   For i = LBound(arrMarks) To UBound(arrMarks)

      Debug.Print i, arrMarks(i)

   Next i

End Sub
```

Sorting an Array

```vba
Sub QuickSort(arr As Variant, first As Long, last As Long)

  Dim vCentreVal As Variant, vTemp As Variant

  Dim lTempLow As Long

  Dim lTempHi As Long

  lTempLow = first
```

```
lTempHi = last
vCentreVal = arr((first + last) \ 2)
Do While lTempLow <= lTempHi
  Do While arr(lTempLow) < vCentreVal And lTempLow < last
   lTempLow = lTempLow + 1
  Loop
  Do While vCentreVal < arr(lTempHi) And lTempHi > first
   lTempHi = lTempHi - 1
  Loop
  If lTempLow <= lTempHi Then
     ' Swap values
     vTemp = arr(lTempLow)
     arr(lTempLow) = arr(lTempHi)
     arr(lTempHi) = vTemp
      ' Move to next positions
     lTempLow = lTempLow + 1
     lTempHi = lTempHi - 1
   End If
  Loop
  If first < lTempHi Then QuickSort arr, first, lTempHi
  If lTempLow < last Then QuickSort arr, lTempLow, last
```

End Sub

Example for Creating a Two-Dimensional Array

```
Public Sub TwoDimArray()

    ' Declare a two dimensional array

    Dim arrMarks(0 To 3, 0 To 2) As String

    ' Fill the array with text made up of i and j values

    Dim i As Long, j As Long

    For i = LBound(arrMarks) To UBound(arrMarks)

        For j = LBound(arrMarks, 2) To UBound(arrMarks, 2)

            arrMarks(i, j) = CStr(i) & ":" & CStr(j)

        Next j

    Next i

    ' Print the values in the array to the Immediate Window

    Debug.Print "i", "j", "Value"

    For i = LBound(arrMarks) To UBound(arrMarks)

        For j = LBound(arrMarks, 2) To UBound(arrMarks, 2)

            Debug.Print i, j, arrMarks(i, j)

        Next j

    Next i

End Sub
```

Chapter Eight

How to Manipulate Data in Excel

A macro processes code written in the Visual Basic Editor to manage and manipulate huge volumes of data. The previous chapter provides information on how you can use a macro to format certain fields or cells in Excel to meet your criteria.

The following is an example of a VBA script:

```
Sub ConfigureLogic()

    Dim qstEntries

    Dim dqstEntries

    Dim qstCnt, dqstCnt

    qstEntries = Range("QualifiedEntry").Count

    qst = qstEntries -
    WorksheetFunction.CountIf(Range("QualifiedEntry"), "")

    ReDim QualifiedEntryText(qst)

    'MsgBox (qst)

    dqstEntries = Range("DisQualifiedEntry").Count

    dqst = dqstEntries -
    WorksheetFunction.CountIf(Range("DisQualifiedEntry"),
    "")

    ReDim DisqualifiedEntryText(dqst)

    'MsgBox (dqst)
```

```
For qstCnt = 1 To qst

QualifiedEntryText(qstCnt) =
ThisWorkbook.Worksheets("Qualifiers").Range("J" & 8 +
qstCnt).value

'MsgBox (QualifiedEntryText(qstCnt))

logging ("Configured Qualified Entry entry #" & qstCnt & "
as {" & QualifiedEntryText(qstCnt) & "}")

Next

For dqstCnt = 1 To dqst

DisqualifiedEntryText(dqstCnt) =
ThisWorkbook.Worksheets("Qualifiers").Range("M" & 8 +
dqstCnt).value

'MsgBox (DisqualifiedEntryText(dqstCnt))

logging ("Configured DisQualified Entry entry #" & qstCnt
& " as {" & DisqualifiedEntryText(dqstCnt) & "}")

Next

includeEntry =
ThisWorkbook.Worksheets("Qualifiers").Range("IncludeSi
bling").value

'MsgBox (includeEntry)

logging ("Entrys included in search - " & includeEntry)

End Sub
```

How to Analyze and Manipulate Data on a Spreadsheet

If you want to use VBA to analyze data, you should check the macro settings in Excel. Ensure that the settings as per your requirements. You should also make sure that the macro settings are activated in Excel. Now, create a worksheet and call it 'Qualifiers.' We will be using this worksheet to check the data and ensure that the data qualifies all the selections that you require. You must then set up the qualifiers based on the code you have written. You cannot cut and paste these qualifiers but will need to enter them manually.

ThisWorkbook.Worksheets("Qualifiers").Range("J" & 8 + qstCnt).value

How to Construct an Array and Locate the Range

In the above function, the range will start from Cell J9. The function notes 8, but the range is 9 since we have declared the qstCnt to be 1 using the following code:

For qstCnt = 1 To qst

It is because of this statement that the list will start at 9.

If you want to construct an array using the entries in the Qualifiers worksheet, you should add random words or numbers between cells J9 and J13, including those cells. When the rows are complete, you can find and manipulate the data in Excel.

```
Private Sub CountSheets()

    Dim sheetcount

    Dim WS As Worksheet

    sheetcount = 0

    logging ("*****Starting Scrub*********")

    For Each WS In ThisWorkbook.Worksheets

    sheetcount = sheetcount + 1

    If WS.Name = "Selected" Then

    'need to log the date and time into sheet named
    "Logging"
```

318

```
        ActionCnt = ActionCnt + 1

        logging ("Calling sheet: " & WS.Name)

        scrubsheet (sheetcount)

        Else

        ActionCnt = ActionCnt + 1

        logging ("Skipped over sheet: " & WS.Name)

        End If

        Next WS

        'MsgBox ("ending")

        ActionCnt = ActionCnt + 1

        logging ("****Scrub DONE!")

        Application.ScreenUpdating = True

    End Sub
```

The following example will show you how you can write a macro for a working tab counter.

```
        Dim sheetcount

        Dim WS As Worksheet

        sheetcount = 0

        logging ("*****Starting Scrub********")

        For Each WS In ThisWorkbook.Worksheets

        sheetcount = sheetcount + 1
```

When you initialize the sheet count variable, you should first set it to zero before you restart the counter. You can also use the logging() subroutine to keep track of all the actions in the qualifiers tab to make the correct selections. The For loop in the above example will set up the counting variable in the Active Workbook. Once you initialize WS, it will make the worksheet that you are currently in the active worksheet. Since this module is unnamed, it will run in any workbook. If you have many workbooks open, this module may run in an incorrect workbook. If you want to avoid any errors, you should name the workbook that you want the module to run in.

When the loop runs, it will add another variable to the sheet count and keep a track of the tabs. We will then move to

```
If WS.Name = "Selected" Then

'need to log the date and time into sheet named "Logging"

ActionCnt = ActionCnt + 1

logging ("Calling sheet: " & WS.Name)

scrubsheet (sheetcount)

Else

ActionCnt = ActionCnt + 1

logging ("Skipped over sheet: " & WS.Name)

End If
```

In this section of the code, we are looking for the Selected tab. If the variable WS is the same as the Selected worksheet, you can fire the Scrub sheet subroutine. If the variable WS is not the same as the Selected worksheet, then the sheet will be skipped, and the action will be counted. The code above is an example of how you can write a macro to count the number of tabs and locate a specific tab.

The next parts of this chapter talk about the different ways you can manipulate data in Excel.

Different Ways to Manipulate Data

Count the Number of Sheets in a Workbook

```
Dim TAB

For Each TAB In ThisWorkbook.Worksheets

'some routine here

Next
```

Filter by Using Advanced Criteria

```
Range("A2:Z99").Sort key1:=Range("A5"),
order1:=xlAscending, Header:=xlNo

Find The Last Column, Cell Or Row On A Worksheet

Dim cellcount

cellcount =
Cells(ThisWorkbook.Worksheets("worksheet").Rows.Count
, 1).End(xlUp).Row
```

Getting Values from Another Worksheet

```
dim newvalue

newvalue =
ThisWorkbook.Worksheets("worksheet").Range("F1").valu
e

Apply Auto-Fit To A Column

Columns("A:A").EntireColumn.AutoFit
```

Adding Named Ranges to Specific Sheets

```
ThisWorkbook.Worksheets("worksheet").Names.Add
Name:="Status", RefersToR1C1:="=worksheet!C2"
```

Insert Rows Into A Worksheet

```
Dim Row, Column
Cells(Row, Column).EntireRow.Select
Selection.Insert
```

Copy an Entire Row for Pasting

```
ActiveSheet.Range("A1").EntireRow.Select
Selection.Copy
```

Delete An Entire Row

```
ActiveSheet.Range("A1").EntireRow.Select
Selection.Delete
```

Inserting a Column into a Worksheet

```
Dim Row, Column
Cells(Row, Column).EntireColumn.Select
Selection.Insert
```

Insert Multiple Columns into a Worksheet

```
Dim insertCnt
Dim Row, Column
For insertCnt = 1 To N
ThisWorkbook.Worksheets("worksheet").Select
Cells(Row, Column).EntireColumn.Select
Selection.Insert
Next
```

Select a Specific Sheet

ThisWorkbook.Worksheets("worksheet").Select

Compare Values In A Range

```
Dim firstrange

Dim Logictest

Logictest = "some word or value"

If (Range(firstrange).value = Logictest) then

'some routine here

End If
```

Chapter Nine

Working with Excel Workbooks and Worksheets

The Workbook Collection

The Workbooks collection provides a list of all workbooks that you have open at a given time. You can select a single workbook from this list that you want to use in your program. The Workbook object that you select will provide general information about the file, including its name and location. You can also use this object to access other major objects in the document. These objects include standalone Chart objects and Worksheet objects.

Example:

```
Public Sub WorkbookDemo()

' Holds the output data.

Dim Output As String

' Get the test workbook.

Dim ActiveWorkbook As Workbook

Set ActiveWorkbook =

Application.Workbooks("ExcelObjects.xls")

' Get the workbook name and location.

Output = "Name: " + ActiveWorkbook.Name + vbCrLf + _

"Full Name: " + ActiveWorkbook.FullName + vbCrLf + _
```

```vba
"Path: " + ActiveWorkbook.Path + vbCrLf + vbCrLf

' Holds the current sheet.

Dim CurrSheet As Worksheet

' Look for every sheet.

Output = "Worksheet List:" + vbCrLf

For Each CurrSheet In ActiveWorkbook.Worksheets

Output = Output + CurrSheet.Name + vbCrLf

Next

' Holds the current chart.

Dim CurrChart As Chart

' Look for every chart.

Output = Output + vbCrLf + "Chart List:" + vbCrLf

For Each CurrChart In ActiveWorkbook.Charts

Output = Output + CurrChart.Name + vbCrLf

Next

' Display the output.

MsgBox Output, vbInformation Or vbOKOnly, "Object List"

End Sub
```

The code starts by using the Application.Workbooks collection which will allow you to retrieve a single Workbook object. You should always use the full name of the Excel file as the index in the collection. You should also include the extension of the file. The resulting workbook object will contain information about the document. This object will also provide the summary information of the document, and you can use this object to control and maintain the windows, and also add new elements like worksheets.

Once the code accesses the workbook, it will use the ActiveWorkbook object to access the worksheets in the list. The code will rely on the For Each...Next statement to access these worksheets. Alternatively, you can use an index to access the individual worksheets in the code. The Worksheet, ActiveWorksheet, contains properties and methods for manipulating any data that the Worksheet contains, including embedded objects, such as charts or even pictures. Every worksheet appears in the ActiveWorkbook object list by its object name (not the friendly name that you give it), so you can access them without using the Worksheets collection.

Only independent charts will appear when you use the ActiveWorkbook object. The same technique can be used to access any Chart object in the worksheet as a Worksheet object. The difference is that you should use Charts Collection instead of the Worksheets Collection. You should note that the Chart names will appear in the list of objects that are present in the ActiveWorkbook. This means that you can access the chart directly without having to use the Charts collection.

The Worksheet Collection

One of the easiest methods to access a worksheet in many situations is to use the Sheets collection. You do not follow the Excel object hierarchy when you want to identify the worksheet you want tot work with. If you access the worksheet at the top of the hierarchy, it means that there are no objects that exist at lower levels available either, so this technique is a tradeoff.

You can access any type of sheet, and not just a worksheet if you use the Sheets collection. A standalone Chart object that you use in any of the sheets can also come into this collection. Look at the example in the previous section, "Using the Workbooks collection," and you will notice that the charts and worksheets are treated as different objects.

Example:

```
Public Sub ListSheets()

' An individual entry.

Dim ThisEntry As Variant

' Holds the output data.

Dim Output As String

' Get the current number of worksheets.

Output = "Sheet Count: " + _

CStr(Application.Sheets.Count)

' List each worksheet in turn.

For Each ThisEntry In Application.Sheets

' Verify there is a sheet to work with.

If ThisEntry.Type = XlSheetType.xlWorksheet Then

Output = Output + vbCrLf + ThisEntry.Name

End If

Next

' Display the result.

MsgBox Output, _

vbInformation or vbOKOnly, _

"Worksheet List"

End Sub
```

In the example above, we will create a Variant which will hold the different sheet types. If you use a Chart or Worksheet object, the code will fail since the Sheets enumeration will return a valid type, but not the type you need. The issue with using this Variant is that the editor in VBA cannot provide automatic completion or balloon help. You have to ensure that you type the method in correctly and use the correct property names without any help.

Once the code creates the necessary variables, it will provide the number of sheets in the workbook. This number will include all the worksheets and charts in the workbook, and not just the sheets.

A For Each...Next loop will retrieve each sheet in turn. You should notice how we use the If...Then statement to compare the values of the Variant type and the XlSheetType.xlWorksheet constant. When you use this technique, you can separate the worksheet you are using from other Sheets collection types whenever necessary.

Charts Collection

The Charts collection is a way to build a custom chart whenever necessary. An advantage of creating charts by using a code is that they do not use too much space, and you can create a variety of different charts without spending too much time on the theme.

Example:

```
Public Sub BuildChart()

' Create a new chart.

Dim NewChart As Chart

Set NewChart = Charts.Add(After:=Charts(Charts.Count))

' Change the name.

NewChart.Name = "Added Chart"

' Create a series for the chart.

Dim TheSeries As Series

NewChart.SeriesCollection.Add _
```

```
Source:=Worksheets("My Data Sheet").Range("A$3:B$8")

Set TheSeries = NewChart.SeriesCollection(1)

' Change the chart type.

TheSeries.ChartType = xl3DPie

' Change the series title.

TheSeries.Name = "Data from My Data Sheet"

' Perform some data formatting.

With TheSeries

.HasDataLabels = True

.DataLabels.ShowValue = True

.DataLabels.Font.Italic = True

.DataLabels.Font.Size = 14

End With

' Modify the chart's legend.

With NewChart

.HasLegend = True

.Legend.Font.Size = 14

End With

' Modify the 3-D view.

With NewChart

.Pie3DGroup.FirstSliceAngle = 90
```

.Elevation = 45

End With

' Format the chart title.

NewChart.ChartTitle.Font.Bold = True

NewChart.ChartTitle.Font.Size = 18

NewChart.ChartTitle.Format.Line.DashStyle _

= msoLineSolid

NewChart.ChartTitle.Format.Line.Style = msoLineSingle

NewChart.ChartTitle.Format.Line.Weight = 2

' Compute the optimal plot area size.

Dim Size As Integer

If NewChart.PlotArea.Height > NewChart.PlotArea.Width

Then

Size = NewChart.PlotArea.Width

Else

Size = NewChart.PlotArea.Height

End If

' Reduce the plot area by 10%.

Size = Size - (Size * 0.1)

' Format the plot area.

With NewChart.PlotArea

```
.Interior.Color = RGB(255, 255, 255)

.Border.LineStyle = XlLineStyle.xlLineStyleNone

.Height = Size

.Width = Size

.Top = 75

.Left = 100

End With

' Format the labels.

Dim ChartLabels As DataLabel

Set ChartLabels = TheSeries.DataLabels(0)

ChartLabels.Position = xlLabelPositionOutsideEnd

End Sub
```

In the above example, the code will create a new chart. This chart will appear in the workbook as the last chart but will not appear as the last item in the workbook. A worksheet which appears after the last chart will also appear after the new chart that is created. The NewChart.Name property will change the name that appears at the bottom of the chart. This property does not change the name of the chart.

At this point, the chart is blank, and you must add at lear one series to the chart if you want to display some data on it. A pie chart will use only one series at a time, but there are other charts that allow you to use multiple data series. For instance, you can use a bubble chart to show multiple series of data. The next task of the code will create a data series based on the worksheet named My Data Sheet. You will notice that the code cannot set TheSeries variable equal to the output of the method Add in this example. Therefore, it uses an additional step to obtain the new series from the SeriesCollection collection.

You should also notice that the Range property has two columns of information. When you are working with Excel 2007, the first column defines the XValues property for the chart. The XValues property determines the entries in the legend for a pie chart. On the other hand, these values appear at the bottom of the display for a bar chart. In both cases, you want to display the labels onscreen so that you can see their effect on the overall display area.

Chapter Ten

Automating Processes
Using VBA

You can use a visual basic application (VBA) to automate any process that you want to in any MS Office product. All you need to ensure is that you have a basic understanding of what VBA is. This chapter will provide some real examples of how you can use VBA to automate processes in Excel. You can see how you can transform an entire business process into the click of a button.

We will look at how you can create a composite key and identify all the records in a file that will match the master source file that you are using. We will also see how you can analyze the records that do not match the source data by using a pivot table to recognize or identify patterns.

Before we delve into learning how to write the code, we will need to ensure that you develop the right mindset to ensure that VBA works for you. You can save enough time when you use VBA to automate the processes. This will also make you a hero at work, but you must ensure that you do use it wisely. There is a fundamental shift that will happen when you begin to work with VBA, and you need to learn how to make that shift work for you and for the company.

The Macro Mindset

When you have automated most or all the processes that are related to your job, you will have adopted a new outlook on how you can use the different MS Office products, especially Excel. You will develop this mindset once you have a good understanding of the object hierarchy of the applications. You will also gain this mindset when you learn how to use the macro recorder effectively.

When you understand how a macro works, you will look for different ways to automate other processes and potentially save yourself a lot of time. A macro is like any other program – you will need to map some input parameters to output parameters. This is often done to automate work. When you do this, you can say that your mindset has shifted from the fundamental mindset to the macro mindset.

This mindset will cause problems if you do not know how you should use it, or in what context you should use it in. You certainly can automate every process that your firm does, but what is the cost of doing that?

You need to keep two points in mind:

1. How much time will I take to automate the process?

2. Will I ever have an issue with any overlapping in the functionality of other processes or applications?

Let us now look at how you should decide on when you should use VBA to automate processes.

Understand the Context of your Automation Project

As with every project, you should first understand the parts of the process that you want to automate. You should define the timeline and define your deadlines and the life expectancy of every solution that you develop.

You should also try to understand what the risks are of using VBA are, and also look at other alternatives. For instance, if the department you are in is investing in some new business intelligence tool which will solve the issue, you should focus on testing the tool before you write any VBA code.

You should always look at the timeline and understand how long it will take you to finish writing the code. You should compare that with the time it will take you to finish that task manually. Also try to understand how long you will need to perform this task for. If you know that your process will change in a few months, you should see whether it is required for you to automate the process.

Changes made to the decisions in resource allocation and IT procurement will reduce the life expectancy or use of the code that you write. This means that you must understand that there is a probability that you may be wasting your time developing a solution using VBA which can be replaced by any other tool. The code you write can also become obsolete because of some changes in the business. For example, you may have developed the process for a client who your company no longer works with.

That being said, a business intelligence tool will cost a company thousands of dollars, and there are many companies that use Microsoft Office tools by default. Therefore, there is very little risk in starting the VBA project, identifying that the project is no longer useful and then removing the process altogether. You can instead investigate the tool and see how it can be used to improve the process. You can then spend some hours training yourself on the tool, and then identify that the tool cannot be used in the company because of some issues with the compatibility.

You can use VBA to automate processes in small companies, small departments in large companies and companies that are downsizing. This is because they operate on a small budget and would use any tool that they have access to. In other words, departments and companies that are trying to save a lot of money will find it easier to use VBA to automate processes when compared to business intelligence tools.

You should keep the following rules in mind when you choose to use VBA:

- If you want to save money, and that is a high priority, you should use VBA.

- A VBA solution is highly flexible.

- A VBA solution is best when it is maintained, and there are only some users who use the process.

- Most VBA solutions are written in Excel.

- A small company can use VBA more when compared to larger companies.

- A VBA solution is robust if you know how to word the program correctly.

One of the main objectives of VBA and macros is to save you some time. This will also add to the functionality, but the focus here is always time. When you know you are saving yourself some time, the macro mindset will work best for you.

Let us now look at some actual code.

Product Code Lookup Procedure

If you are new to VBA, you should understand that a procedure is a block of code that can be executed independently. The idea behind this procedure is to understand whether the products in the ProductReport file do contain the product specification codes for new item catalogue categories. This means that the product specifications do not exist in the master database. If this is the case, the code will identify the items and also give you a count of the number of items. In this example, we will be using a text file called ProductReport, which you can download from GitHub. This report is a third-party report, and the base file is an Excel workbook which stores the historical information. It would be a good idea to scan the "ProdCodeLookup2" in GitHub in full. This chapter will break it down into smaller sections.

```vba
Sub ProdCodeLookup2()

'Reformats the Product Report (ProdReport), creates the ProdCombo for all items, _

and then uses VLookup to find matches

Application.ScreenUpdating = False




Dim rngX As Range, rngY As Range, rngZ As Range

Dim ICC As String

Dim ItemNum As Variant

Dim Prod1 As String, Prod2 As String, Prod3 As String, Prod4 As String, Prod5 As String

Dim ProdCombo As Variant

Dim FinalRow As Long, StartTime As Long

Dim SecondsElapsed As Double

Dim PRwb As Workbook, BLwb As Workbook

Dim PRsht As Worksheet, BLsht As Worksheet

Dim LVal As Range, VLtable As Range

Dim VLOutput As Variant

Dim Count As Integer
```

```
Dim ProdMatchTotal As Variant


Set PRwb = Application.Workbooks("ProductReport")

Set BLwb = Application.Workbooks("Baseline")

Set PRsht = PRwb.Worksheets("Export Worksheet")

Set BLsht = BLwb.Worksheets("Static Table")



StartTime = Timer

'Abbreviate two important header names:

ICC = "Item Catalog Category"

PC = "ProdCombo"



PRsht.Activate
```

'Hide all columns except those that comprise the ProdCombo, _

format the headers, and add the headers for ProdCombo and ProdCode:

```
        Columns("C:D").EntireColumn.Hidden = True

        Columns("G:N").EntireColumn.Hidden = True

        Columns("Q:AK").EntireColumn.Hidden = True
```

```vba
Columns("AM").EntireColumn.Hidden = True

Columns("AO:AU").EntireColumn.Hidden = True

Columns("AW:BM").EntireColumn.Hidden = True

Range("BN1").Value = "ProdCombo"

Range("BO1").Value = "ProdCode"

Range("1:1").Select

    Selection.Font.Bold = True




'Filter by Label:

    ActiveSheet.Range("1:1").AutoFilter

'Find the correct header to filter by:

    Set rngX = ActiveSheet.Range("1:1").Find(ICC,
LookAt:=xlWhole)

        If Not rngX Is Nothing Then

        End If




'Filter Item Catalog Category by "Labels":

    ActiveSheet.Range(rngX.Address,
Selection.End(xlDown)).AutoFilter Field:=rngX.Column,
Criteria1:="Label"

    'Create the ProdCombo:
```

```
FinalRow = Cells(Rows.Count, 2).End(xlUp).Row

For Count = 0 To FinalRow - 2
```

'List the first cell here in the primary key column and ensure that there are no blanks:

```
ItemNum = Range("B2").Offset(Count, 0).Value
```

'Now define the products to ensure they're aligned with the first Item Number:

```
Prod1 = Cells(Count + 2, 48).Value

Prod2 = Cells(Count + 2, 40).Value

Prod3 = Cells(Count + 2, 15).Value

Prod4 = Cells(Count + 2, 16).Value

Prod5 = Cells(Count + 2, 38).Value
```

'Now concatenate them in the correct order with spaces:

```
ProdCombo = Prod1 & " " & Prod2 & " " & Prod3 & " " & Prod4 & " " _

& Prod5
```

'Now specify where you want the ProdCombo to appear:

```
Range("BN2").Offset(Count, 0) = ProdCombo

Next Count
```

'Delete blanks from ProdCombo:

```
Set rngY = ActiveSheet.Range("1:1").Find(PC, LookAt:=xlWhole)

If Not rngY Is Nothing Then
```

```
            End If

        ActiveSheet.Range(rngY.Address,
Selection.End(xlDown)).AutoFilter Field:=rngY.Column,
Criteria1:="="

        ActiveCell.Offset(1, 0).Rows("1:1").EntireRow.Select

        Range(Selection, Selection.End(xlDown)).Delete

        ActiveSheet.ShowAllData

        ActiveSheet.Range(rngX.Address,
Selection.End(xlDown)).AutoFilter Field:=rngX.Column,
Criteria1:="Label"




        'Now run the ProdCodeLookup2 sub procedure

        FinalRow = Cells(Rows.Count, 1).End(xlUp).Row

        Set VLtable = BLsht.Range("$AY$1:$BA$29741")

        On Error Resume Next

        For Count = 0 To FinalRow


            Set LVal = SRsht.Range("BN2").Offset(Count, 0)


            VLOutput = Application.VLookup(LVal, VLtable, 3,
False)
```

```
        If IsError(VLOutput) Then

            VLOutput = 0

        Else

            PRsht.Range("BO2").Offset(Count, 0) = VLOutput

        End If

    Next Count

    On Error GoTo 0




    Set rngZ = ActiveSheet.Range("1:1").Find("ProdCode",
LookAt:=xlPart)

        If Not rngZ Is Nothing Then

        End If

    ActiveSheet.Range(rngZ.Address,
Selection.End(xlDown)).AutoFilter Field:=rngZ.Column,
Criteria1:="<>"

    ProdMatchTotal =
Application.Count(Range(rngZ.Offset(1), rngZ.Offset(FinalRow)))

    MsgBox ("There are " & ProdMatchTotal & " baseline
product matches")
```

Application.ScreenUpdating = True

SecondsElapsed = Round(Timer - StartTime, 2)

MsgBox "This code ran successfully in " & SecondsElapsed & " seconds", vbInformation

End Sub

ProdCodeLookup2 Breakdown

The most important part of every process is to break the problem down into smaller bits and tackle each of those individually. One of the best ways to do this is to write every block of code in the order in which you will perform your task as if you were doing it manually. You can then refine the process once you have a better understanding of the process. You can also rewrite the code to improve readability and performance.

Let us look at the first piece of code that is manageable:

Sub ProdCodeLookup2()

'Reformats the Product Report (ProdReport), creates the ProdCombo for all items, _

and then uses VLookup to find matches

Application.ScreenUpdating = False

You should also notice that the name of every procedure follows the Pascal Code. We also end the name with a number which is a good way to write code. It is painful when you realize that you are troubleshooting the incorrect procedure. You should always look for a way to update your code and create some working copies of the procedure.

The first statement in line 5 has been written to increase or improve the performance of the macro. ScreenUpdating is a property that controls whether the compiler needs to update the screen when the macro runs. When you turn off this property, you will see that the changes are only made once the full code has run. It is always a good idea to set this property to true at the end of the code.

Dim rngX As Range, rngY As Range, rngZ As Range

Dim ICC As String

Dim ItemNum As Variant

Dim Prod1 As String, Prod2 As String, Prod3 As String, Prod4 As String, Prod5 As String

Dim ProdCombo As Variant

Dim FinalRow As Long, StartTime As Long

Dim SecondsElapsed As Double

Dim PRwb As Workbook, BLwb As Workbook

Dim PRsht As Worksheet, BLsht As Worksheet

Dim LVal As Range, VLtable As Range

Dim VLOutput As Variant

Dim Count As Integer

Dim ProdMatchTotal As Variant

The names used in the block of code above are not creative, and you do not want to get creative with the names since it becomes harder to debug the code. If there is something wrong with the code, a simple name will help you identify where the issue is.

It is easier to work with variables and manage them by grouping them based on their function and data type. For instance, you may use the keyword rng to describe the range variables. You can then use them to find the columns or the parts of the table that you will need to work with.

You should also notice that the lookup variables are all defined in the same space. When you write a longer procedure, it will be easier to add comments to these lines, and also declare a variable in a new line using the "Dim" keyword.

If you make this a habit, it will make it easier for you to update the code or troubleshoot any errors. For instance, the above code has been rewritten in the style described above.

```
Dim rngX As Range 'Range X, ICC header

Dim rngY As Range 'Range Y, Product Combo

Dim rngZ As Range 'Range Z, Product Code

Dim ICC As String 'Item Catalogue Category

Dim ItemNum As Variant 'Item Number; used to eliminate
blanks

Dim Prod1 As String 'Product 1, the first attribute in the
composite key

Dim Prod2 As String 'Product 2, the second attribute in the
key

Dim Prod3 As String 'Product 3

Dim Prod4 As String 'Product 4
```

```vba
Dim Prod5 As String 'Product 5

Dim ProdCombo As Variant 'Product Combo

Dim FinalRow As Long 'FinalRow formula variable

Dim StartTime As Long 'Used to calculate total runtime

Dim SecondsElapsed As Double 'Used to calculate total
runtime

Dim PRwb As Workbook 'ProductReport workbook

Dim BLwb As Workbook 'Baseline workbook

Dim PRsht As Worksheet 'ProductReport worksheet

Dim BLsht As Worksheet 'Baseline worksheet
```

I am sure you get the idea now. All you need to do is write the name of the variable using a short phrase and describe how you will use it. This is a straightforward method, and it is important that you understand it.

You should now assign the workbooks and worksheets to different object variables. You can benefit in many ways through this action. You will also improve readability and performance. When you master writing code in VBA, you can always avoid doing this. The goal is to ensure that your code is easy for you to understand, thereby making it easy for you to troubleshoot any errors.

You should now assign the worksheet and workbook variables to different objects. You should first assign workbook variables since they are the parent objects.

```vba
Set PRwb = Application.Workbooks("WorkbookName1")

Set BLwb = Application.Workbooks("WorkbookName2")

Set PRsht = PRwb.Worksheets("Export Worksheet")
```

```vba
Set BLsht = BLwb.Worksheets("Static Table")
```

Let's check out the next part (lines 25-30):

```vba
StartTime = Timer

'Abbreviate two important header names:

ICC = "Item Catalog Category"

PC = "ProdCombo"


PRsht.Activate
```

We will use the StartTime variable to hold the initial value of the timer and use the variable to calculate the time it takes to run the application. You can also create shorter variables if you want to refer to those variables multiple times in the code. You can ensure that you do not make any mistakes.

The last line in this section will define the scope for the block of code below. You should never expect that the compiler will guess which worksheet or workbook it needs to refer to. Therefore, you must ensure that you specify this.

You will need to prepare the data and format it before you can create the "ProdCombo" composite key. You will first need to hide all the columns in the baseline workbook and remove any columns that are irrelevant for us. You should then create the new columns using the headers that we are going to use. To ensure that the labels are readable, you can make them bold.

```vba
'Hide all columns except those that comprise the
ProdCombo, _
```

```vba
format the headers, and add the headers for ProdCombo and
ProdCode:
```

```
Columns("C:D").EntireColumn.Hidden = True

Columns("G:N").EntireColumn.Hidden = True

Columns("Q:AK").EntireColumn.Hidden = True

Columns("AM").EntireColumn.Hidden = True

Columns("AO:AU").EntireColumn.Hidden = True

Columns("AW:BM").EntireColumn.Hidden = True

Range("BN1").Value = "ProdCombo"

Range("BO1").Value = "ProdCode"

Range("1:1").Select

Selection.Font.Bold = True
```

In the lines 44 through 52, we are turning the filters on for every header, and are removing all the values except for the labels. Let us make the assumption that we are only looking at the product specifications.

We are creating a ProdCombo in the lines 50 through 69 using a loop. We are also concatenating or combining the values in the columns using a space delimiter.

It is always a good idea to delete a blank product, and this is what the lines 70 to 78 do. In this example, we only want to look at those products that have some value in one of the five fields. We do not need to look at any values that have blanks in all the labels.

You must always look at the comments. You will notice that the comment in line 80 talks about running the ProdCodeLookup2 procedure.

If you are using VLOOKUP for the first time in a macro, you should write two different procedures – one for every other process and one just to execute the lookup. Experts recommend this method since it is easier to develop the code. The ProdCodeLookup2 will perform a lookup in every cell that is in a specified column and will loop all the records in the table until it reaches the end.

Before we look at the next section where we perform some analyses, let us look at some ways to deal with issues that crop up with using VBA.

Tips to Deal with VLookups in VBA

Errors and blanks will often return an error statement when you use a vlookup function. This may cause the entire procedure to crash. If you do choose to use vlookup in your code, you will need to include an error handling option to ensure that the code does not crash. We cover this in the next chapter.

There are many examples for the same on Stack Overflow. You can learn more about how to handle errors with VLOOKUP through those examples. You can solve the problem by wrapping the loop up in the lines 83 and 96 in the code above. This should help to solve the problem in a simple manner.

You should then perform the following tasks in the last lines of the code:

1. Use the column name to define the location of the ProdCode column header.

2. Count the values under the ProdCode column header and assign the number to a variable using the workbook function "Count."

3. You can then return the result using a message box.

4. Turn the ScreenUpdating on.

5. You can also return the time it took for the application to run. Display this in a message box.

This will conclude the first VBA script. You may probably be wondering where the data analysis is. Let us look at the next section to understand more about how to analyze data.

Data Analysis

This information is certainly useful, but what should you do about the remaining products? How will the results of those compare to the remaining categories or the labels that you use? What types of comparison should you investigate or analyze? What about those items or products that do not match your requirement? What is it that you can learn about those products? Let us now add a status flag to every product. This will make things interesting and slightly complicated. This status will represent whether the product specification code that you are looking at is active.

To recap quickly, the dimensions of the analysis can be summarized into "active/inactive status," "product category" and "match/no match status." Now that we have these details in mind, you can use a pivot table to help you visualize the different user cases. The data analysis is in the procedure written below:

Sub ProdFlag_v3()

'Run this on a ProductReport to find records without any specs and copy all of the records _

without specs onto a separate worksheet (only copy columns A-G). Analysis tab added with pivot tables.

Application.ScreenUpdating = False

Dim PRtable As Range, rngX As Range, SpecHeader As Variant

```vba
Dim PRTableRows As Long, PRTableColumns As Long

Dim PRsht As Worksheet, nsPRsht As Worksheet

Dim FinalRow As Long, i As Long

Dim IstatActive As Variant, IstatInactive As Variant

Istat = "Item Status"



Set PRsht = Worksheets("Export Worksheet")



PRTableRows = PRsht.Cells.Find("*", _
searchorder:=xlByRows, searchdirection:=xlPrevious).Row

PRTableColumns = PRsht.Cells.Find("*", _
searchorder:=xlByColumns, searchdirection:=xlPrevious).Column



Set PRtable = PRsht.Range("A1", Cells(PRTableRows, _
PRTableColumns))



Sheets.Add After:=ActiveSheet

Sheets("Sheet1").Name = "NoSpecs"
```

```
Set nsPRsht = Worksheets("NoSpecs")

FinalRow = Cells(Rows.Count, 2).End(xlUp).Row

PRsht.Range("1:1").AutoFilter


For Each SpecHeader In PRsht.Range("H1:BM1").Cells
    Range(SpecHeader.Offset(1), _
SpecHeader.Offset(FinalRow)) _
        .AutoFilter Field:=SpecHeader.Column, Criteria1:="="
    Next SpecHeader



PRtable.Resize(PRTableRows, 7).Copy _

nsPRsht.Range("A1")

Application.CutCopyMode = False

PRsht.ShowAllData

nsPRsht.Range("A1").Select



FinalRow = Cells(Rows.Count, 2).End(xlUp).Row

For i = 2 To FinalRow

    If Cells(i, 1) = "Active" Then

        Cells(i, 1).Resize(, 5).Font.ColorIndex = 25
```

```vba
    ElseIf Cells(i, 1) = "Inactive" Then

        Cells(i, 1).Resize(, 5).Font.ColorIndex = 3

    Else

        With Cells(i, 1).Resize(, 5).Font

            .Name = "TimesNewRoman"

            .Bold = True

        End With

    End If

Next i



ActiveSheet.Range("1:1").AutoFilter

Set rngX = ActiveSheet.Range("1:1").Find(Istat, LookAt:=xlPart)

        If Not rngX Is Nothing Then

        End If



IstatActive = Application.CountIf(Range(rngX.Offset(1), rngX.Offset(FinalRow)), "Active")

IstatInactive = Application.CountIf(Range(rngX.Offset(1), rngX.Offset(FinalRow)), "Inactive")

FinalRow = Cells(Rows.Count, 2).End(xlUp).Row
```

```vba
'Create the NoSpecs_CategoryAnalysis tab with pivot tables

Sheets.Add

ActiveSheet.Name = "NoSpecs_Analysis"


ActiveWorkbook.PivotCaches.Create(SourceType:=xlDatabase, SourceData:= _

        "NoSpecs!R1C1:R23405C7",
Version:=6).CreatePivotTable TableDestination:= _

        "NoSpecs_Analysis!R3C1",
TableName:="PivotTable1", DefaultVersion:=6

        With
ActiveSheet.PivotTables("PivotTable1").PivotFields("Item Catalog
Category" _

        )

        .Orientation = xlRowField

        .Position = 1

    End With

        ActiveSheet.PivotTables("PivotTable1").AddDataField
ActiveSheet.PivotTables( _

        "PivotTable1").PivotFields("Item"), "Item Count",
xlCount

    With
ActiveSheet.PivotTables("PivotTable1").PivotFields("Item Status")

        .Orientation = xlColumnField

        .Position = 1
```

End With

ActiveSheet.PivotTables("PivotTable1").PivotFields("Item Catalog Category"). _

AutoSort xlDescending, "Item Count"

ActiveSheet.PivotTables("PivotTable1").AddDataField ActiveSheet.PivotTables(_

"PivotTable1").PivotFields("Item"), "Percent", xlCount

With ActiveSheet.PivotTables("PivotTable1").PivotFields("Percent")

.Calculation = xlPercentOfTotal

.NumberFormat = "0.00%"

End With

ActiveWorkbook.Worksheets("NoSpecs_Analysis").PivotTables("PivotTable1"). _

PivotCache.CreatePivotTable TableDestination:="NoSpecs_Analysis!R13C1", _

TableName:="PivotTable2", DefaultVersion:=6

With ActiveSheet.PivotTables("PivotTable2").PivotFields("Item Status")

.Orientation = xlRowField

.Position = 1

```
        End With

            ActiveSheet.PivotTables("PivotTable2").AddDataField
ActiveSheet.PivotTables( _

            "PivotTable2").PivotFields("Item"), "Item Count",
xlCount

            ActiveSheet.PivotTables("PivotTable2").AddDataField
ActiveSheet.PivotTables( _

            "PivotTable2").PivotFields("Item"), "Percent", xlCount

        Range("C13").Select

        With
ActiveSheet.PivotTables("PivotTable2").PivotFields("Percent")

            .Calculation = xlPercentOfTotal

            .NumberFormat = "0.00%"

        End With



        Sheets.Add

        ActiveSheet.Name = "SpecAnalysis"



ActiveWorkbook.PivotCaches.Create(SourceType:=xlDatabase,
SourceData:= _

            "Export Worksheet!R1C1:R26363C65",
Version:=6).CreatePivotTable TableDestination:= _
```

```
            "SpecAnalysis!R3C1", TableName:="PivotTable3",
DefaultVersion:=6
        With
ActiveSheet.PivotTables("PivotTable3").PivotFields("Item Catalog
Category" _
            )
            .Orientation = xlRowField
            .Position = 1
        End With

            ActiveSheet.PivotTables("PivotTable3").AddDataField
ActiveSheet.PivotTables( _
            "PivotTable3").PivotFields("Item"), "Item Count",
xlCount
        With
ActiveSheet.PivotTables("PivotTable3").PivotFields("Item Status")
            .Orientation = xlColumnField
            .Position = 1
        End With


ActiveSheet.PivotTables("PivotTable3").PivotFields("Item Catalog
Category"). _
            AutoSort xlDescending, "Item Count"


            ActiveSheet.PivotTables("PivotTable3").AddDataField
ActiveSheet.PivotTables( _
```

```
"PivotTable3").PivotFields("Item"), "Percent", xlCount

    With
ActiveSheet.PivotTables("PivotTable3").PivotFields("Percent")

        .Calculation = xlPercentOfTotal

        .NumberFormat = "0.00%"

    End With




    Sheets.Add

        ActiveSheet.Name = "Label_Material"

        ActiveWorkbook.Worksheets("SpecAnalysis").PivotTables(
"PivotTable3").PivotCache _

        .CreatePivotTable
TableDestination:="Label_Material!R3C1",
TableName:="PivotTable1" _

        , DefaultVersion:=6

        ActiveSheet.PivotTables("PivotTable1").AddDataField
ActiveSheet.PivotTables( _

        "PivotTable1").PivotFields("Item"), "Item Count",
xlCount

        ActiveSheet.PivotTables("PivotTable1").AddDataField
ActiveSheet.PivotTables( _

        "PivotTable1").PivotFields("Item"), "Percent", xlCount
```

```
    With
ActiveSheet.PivotTables("PivotTable1").PivotFields("Item Catalog
Category" _

        )

            .Orientation = xlPageField

            .Position = 1

        End With

    With
ActiveSheet.PivotTables("PivotTable1").PivotFields("Label
Material")

            .Orientation = xlRowField

            .Position = 1

        End With


ActiveSheet.PivotTables("PivotTable1").PivotFields("Item Catalog
Category"). _

            CurrentPage = "(All)"

    With
ActiveSheet.PivotTables("PivotTable1").PivotFields("Item Catalog
Category")

            .PivotItems("Bar Wrapper").Visible = False

            .PivotItems("IFC & Inner Tray").Visible = False

            .PivotItems("Printed Pouches & Packets").Visible =
False

            .PivotItems("Shrink Sleeve").Visible = False
```

```vba
        End With

        With
ActiveSheet.PivotTables("PivotTable1").PivotFields("Percent")

            .Calculation = xlPercentOfTotal

            .NumberFormat = "0.00%"

        End With


ActiveSheet.PivotTables("PivotTable1").PivotFields("Label
Material").AutoSort _

            xlDescending, "Percent"

        With
ActiveSheet.PivotTables("PivotTable1").PivotFields("Label
Material")

            .PivotItems("(blank)").Visible = False

        End With



        Sheets.Add

            ActiveSheet.Name = "COATING"

            ActiveWorkbook.Worksheets("SpecAnalysis").PivotTables(
"PivotTable3").PivotCache _

            .CreatePivotTable
TableDestination:="COATING!R3C1",
TableName:="PivotTable1" _

            , DefaultVersion:=6
```

```
        ActiveSheet.PivotTables("PivotTable1").AddDataField
ActiveSheet.PivotTables( _

        "PivotTable1").PivotFields("Item"), "Item Count",
xlCount

        ActiveSheet.PivotTables("PivotTable1").AddDataField
ActiveSheet.PivotTables( _

        "PivotTable1").PivotFields("Item"), "Percent", xlCount

    With
ActiveSheet.PivotTables("PivotTable1").PivotFields("Item Catalog
Category" _

        )

        .Orientation = xlPageField

        .Position = 1

    End With

    With
ActiveSheet.PivotTables("PivotTable1").PivotFields("COATING")

        .Orientation = xlRowField

        .Position = 1

    End With


ActiveSheet.PivotTables("PivotTable1").PivotFields("Item Catalog
Category"). _

        CurrentPage = "(All)"
```

```vba
    With
ActiveSheet.PivotTables("PivotTable1").PivotFields("Item Catalog
Category")

        .PivotItems("Bar Wrapper").Visible = False

        .PivotItems("IFC & Inner Tray").Visible = False

        .PivotItems("Printed Pouches & Packets").Visible =
False

        .PivotItems("Shrink Sleeve").Visible = False

    End With

    With
ActiveSheet.PivotTables("PivotTable1").PivotFields("Percent")

        .Calculation = xlPercentOfTotal

        .NumberFormat = "0.00%"

    End With


ActiveSheet.PivotTables("PivotTable1").PivotFields("COATING")
.AutoSort _

        xlDescending, "Percent"

    With
ActiveSheet.PivotTables("PivotTable1").PivotFields("COATING")

        .PivotItems("(blank)").Visible = False

    End With



        MsgBox ("There are " & FinalRow & " records with no
specifications" & vbNewLine & _
```

vbNewLine & "Number of Active records without specs: "
& IstatActive & vbNewLine _

& "Number of Inactive records without specs: " &
IstatInactive)

Application.ScreenUpdating = True

End Sub

This procedure does not use any pivot tables. You should keep the following points in mind when you write your own procedure:

Using Pivot Tables in VBA

There are some prerequisites to using a pivot table in VBA. You must ensure that the data source that you use has valid, high-quality and normalized data. The same holds true in the example above. You should create the test data for any product, its specifications and categories. In this section, you will learn how you should automate one of the most used and advanced features in Excel.

4. Copy the lines that were used in the lines 63 and 64 in the code above.

5. Now, navigate to the workbook and choose the option "Record Macro" in the Developer Tab.

6. Choose the cell you want to use to as the data for the pivot and click on "Ctrl + A" to select the cells.

7. Now, press "Alt + N + V + Enter."

8. You should now create the pivot table manually. Drag the columns that you want to use, filter, group, and format the values as necessary.

9. Now, press the "Record Macro" button.

10. You now need to click on "Alt + F11" to get back to the editor window. Find the code that Excel recorded.

11. Paste this code into the project in the worksheet that you have created. Read the code and see how you can shorten it.

12. You can write the same code for any number of pivots in different worksheets. You will need to be careful about the filters you will be using.

Learn to Use Cell Referencing

Most people are not used to using the R1C1 style of cell referencing, but this is what the macro recorder will use. It is important that you familiarize yourself with this type of referencing to ensure that you save time when you work with pivot tables. This way you will have very little to do when you are editing the code that is generated by the macro recorder.

You can now decide which pivot table object or feature you want to use when you are learning to use VBA. You can always automate a file that has more than 20 pivot tables in a few minutes. You can only do this once you understand the keyboard shortcuts, set up the tables in your file properly and know how you should prepare the code.

Efficiently Allocating Your Time

If you want to automate the processes that you use to analyze information in Excel effectively, you must keep the following points in mind:

- You should spend most of your time in preparing and cleaning the data. You must ensure that the quality of the information you are using is top-notch, and you should think about any keys, flags, reconciliation, validation and any other simple calculation that you may want to use.

- You should always visualize the end result when you are building and refining the table.

You may be surprised that we focused very little on writing the code to automate a pivot table or any function in Excel. You should remember to always prepare the data set well and ensure that there are no issues with the data. This will make it easier to automate the process. You can save enough time and effort if you know how to use VBA efficiently.

Chapter Eleven

Error Handling

The easiest errors that you can avoid are the syntax errors, but these are some of the hardest errors to spot. The error can be because of the misuse of a punctuation, misuse of a language element or a spelling mistake. If you forget to include the End If statement in an If...Then statement, you have made a syntax error.

Typos are common syntax errors. These are especially hard to find if you make those errors in variable names. For example, the editor in VBA will view the MySpecialVariable and MySpecialVaraible as different variables, but there is a possibility that you will miss it when you begin to write the code. When you include the Adding Option Explicit at the beginning of the module, form or class module that you create, you can remove this problem. VBA can help you find a variety of typos if you add this statement to the start of your code. It is important that you use this statement in every part of your program when you write it.

There are times when you miss some of the subtle aids in locating the errors in syntax if you do not understand or view the tasks that the IDE or Integrated Development Environment performs. VBA will only display the balloon help feature when the editor in VBA can recognize the function name that you need to enter. If you do not see a balloon help button, you should understand that VBA does not know what function name you are referring to. This means that you will need to look at your code to identify the error. Unfortunately, this feature will only work where the editor in VBA will display the balloon help option. This does not work when you use property names.

Understanding compile errors

VBA uses a compiler to look for any errors that will prevent the program from functioning properly. You can create an If...Then statement and not include the End If statement in the program. The compiler will continue to run continuously and will allow you to find the mistakes in the code immediately once you make them.

VBA will use a compiler to find the syntax error in your code and then display an error message. Try the following when you write a new program. Open a new project, create a Sub using a specific name and type MsgBox(). Now, press Enter. VBA will display a message box, which will state that it was expecting the equal to sign. If you use the parentheses after the keyword MsgBox, VBA will expect that you should include a result variable, which will hold the required result. For example, MyResult = MsgBox("My Prompt"). As mentioned earlier, the debugger highlights the error in red.

Understanding run-time errors

A run-time error often occurs when there is an issue with something outside of your program. There are times when you type in the incorrect information and other times when the system rejects your access to the memory or disk. Your VBA code is completely correct, but the code will fail to function since there is an external error. Most companies, like Microsoft, always run a beta program to avoid any run-time errors. A beta program is a one that programmers develop to test their vendor-sponsored program before they release it into the market.

367

Understanding semantic errors

This is a particularly difficult error to understand and find since it is a semantic error. This error occurs when the VBA code and logic are both correct, but the meaning behind the code is incorrect. For instance, you can use the Do...Until loop in place of the Do...While loop. It may be the case that the code is correct and the logic behind the code is also correct, but the result is not what you expected since the meaning of a Do...Until loop is different from the meaning of a Do...While loop.

When you write a code, the words you use in the code should match your intent. Since a good book always relies on precise terms, a good program also relies only on the precise statements that you use in VBA. These statements will help VBA understand what you want it to do. One of the best ways to avoid making any semantic errors in the application is to always plan your program in advance. You should use a pseudo-code to "pre-write" the design, and then convert that code into the actual VBA code.

Conclusion

Thank you for purchasing the book. Most organizations have begun to use VBA to automate some of their processes in Excel. You can copy and paste information or create a pivot in Excel using VBA. If you want to learn VBA coding to improve processes at your workplace, you can use this book as your guide.

I hope you gather all the information you are looking for. I hope you can use the information in the book to perform data analysis.

Will You Help Me?

H i there, avid reader! If you have extra time on your hands, I would really, really appreciate it if you could take a moment to click my author profile in Amazon. In there, you will find all the titles I authored and who knows, you might find more interesting topics to read and learn!

If it's not too much to ask, you can also leave and write a review for all the titles that you have read – whether it's a positive or negative review. An honest and constructive review of my titles is always welcome and appreciated since it will only help me moving forward in creating these books. There will always be room to add or improve, or sometimes even subtract certain topics, that is why these reviews are always important for us. They will also assist other avid readers, professionals who are looking to sharpen their knowledge, or even newbies to any topic, in their search for the book that caters to their needs the most.

If you don't want to leave a review yourself, you can also vote on the existing reviews by voting Helpful (Thumbs Up) or Unhelpful (Thumbs Down), especially on the top 10 or so reviews.

If you want to go directly to the vote or review process for my titles, just visit on any of the below titles:

> Excel VBA: A Step-By-Step Tutorial For Beginners To Learn Excel VBA Programming From Scratch. Audiobook format is now available in Audible US and Audible UK.

> Excel VBA : Intermediate Lessons in Excel VBA Programming for Professional Advancement . Audiobook format is now available in Audible US and Audible UK

> Excel VBA: A Step-By-Step Comprehensive Guide on Advanced Excel VBA Programming Techniques and

Strategies . Audiobook format is now available in Audible US and Audible UK.

Again, I truly appreciate the time and effort that you will be putting in leaving a review for my titles or even just for voting. This will only inspire me to create more quality content and titles in the future.

Thank you and have a great day!

Peter Bradley

Sources

https://www.excel-pratique.com/en/vba/introduction.php

http://www.easyexcelvba.com/introduction.html

https://www.tutorialspoint.com/excel_vba_online_training/excel_vba_introduction.asp

https://www.thespreadsheetguru.com/getting-started-with-vba/

https://www.tutorialspoint.com/vba/vba_strings.htm

https://www.excel-easy.com/vba/string-manipulation.html

https://www.guru99.com/vba-data-types-variables-constant.html

https://corporatefinanceinstitute.com/resources/excel/study/vba-variables-dim/

https://powerspreadsheets.com/vba-data-types/

https://www.tutorialspoint.com/vba/vba_loops.htm

https://www.excel-easy.com/vba/loop.html

https://www.excelfunctions.net/vba-loops.html

https://powerspreadsheets.com/excel-vba-loops/

https://www.excelfunctions.net/vba-conditional-statements.html

https://analysistabs.com/excel-vba/conditional-statements/

https://www.techonthenet.com/excel/formulas/if_then.php

http://www.cpearson.com/excel/errorhandling.htm

https://excelmacromastery.com/vba-error-handling/

https://docs.microsoft.com/en-us/dotnet/visual-basic/language-reference/statements/on-error-statement

https://simpleprogrammer.com/vba-data-analysis-automation/

Excel VBA

A Step-by-Step Comprehensive Guide on Excel VBA Programming Tips and Tricks for Effective Strategies

Introduction

I want to thank you for choosing this book, *Excel VBA - A Step-by-Step Comprehensive Guide on Excel VBA Programming Tips and Tricks for Effective Strategies'* and hope you find the book informative to learn Excel VBA.

It is difficult for a person to become an expert in VBA within a matter of days. It takes patience, time and practice to master coding in VBA. The first few books of the series provided information on different parts of Excel VBA. You learnt about the different data types, functions and methods you can use in Excel VBA. You also covered information on how you can handle errors and exceptions in VBA using the compiler and the visual basic environment.

There are still some topics that you will need to familiarize yourself with if you want to master coding in VBA. This book covers some of those topics. As a programmer, you will use the words procedures and sub procedures numerous times. This is because you will only be working on building and writing code for sub procedures. This book will provide information on what a sub procedure is, and how you can develop one for your project. You will also gather information on some tips and tricks that you can use to improve the project that you develop.

There are times when your system will slow down because of the volume of data, or code. In such situations, you can use some of the tips mentioned in this book to improve the performance of your project.

Thank you for purchasing the book. I hope you gathered all the information you were looking for.

Chapter One

Facts about VBA

Unlike the usual programming languages with only take code to build a program, we can record actions in VBA using the macro recorder. This has been covered extensively in the previous books. This chapter covers some important facts about macros and VBA.

Making macros available on every MS Excel Worksheet

When you begin to record a macro in VBA, Excel will prompt you to save the macro in a specific location. You can choose from the following locations: the workbook you are writing the macro in or the common workbook. If you save the macro in the current workbook, it will not be available for any other user to use in a different workbook. If you want to use a single macro or procedure across different workbooks, you should save it in personal.xlsb.

The personal.xlsb workbook is a hidden file, and cannot be seen or edited unless you unhide the file. You can view the file when you choose to look at all files in an Excel window.

Types Of Codes Found Across The Internet

You will come across three types of macros across the internet. The first type is the sub() macro. This is a macro that will run and execute a block of code or statements. This is the most common macro type available on the internet.

The second type is a function. This function is like the function that you use in excel, but unlike Excel functions, it is a user defined function. This function will also use VBA code.

The third type of macro is an event procedure that will work only when a certain event occurs. A macro which runs the moment you open your workbook is a classic example of this this type of macro.

You can choose a macro depending on what you want to another. For example, you can record a macro and use a shortcut key to call it when you want to format some cells. Alternatively, you can define a formula within a macro and store it in your files.

Where To Use The Code You Find On The Internet

You must remember to place the coffee write or source in the right place. If you do not save it correctly, it will not work. You can add functions and subs to the modules in your workbook. If you want to insert a module, go to Insert -> Module. Select the module that you want to insert, click it to open it and paste the code. You can include multiple codes in the same module. For some events, you will need to place a macro in the same sheet.

Saving A Workbook

You should always remember to save a workbook as a macro enabled workbook. A sheet that contains a macro will have different properties when compared to a sheet that does not have a macro. If you need to save the workbook as a macro enabled workbook, you should choose to save the workbook in the xlsm format.

Chapter Two

Resources for VBA Help

You cannot expect to become a VBA expert in a day. It is a journey and you will need to practice a lot before you become an expert. The best part about coding in Excel VBA is that there are many resources that you can use to improve your knowledge in Excel. This chapter covers some of the best places you can visit and some of the best resources you can use if you need a push in the right direction.

Allow Excel to Write the Code for You

If you have read the previous books, you know that you can use the macro recorder to help you with understanding your code. When you record any macro or the steps you want to automate using a record macro, Excel will write the underlying code for you. Once you record the code, you can review it and see what the recorder has done. You can then convert the code that the recorder has written into something that will suit your needs.

For instance, if you need to write a macro to refresh a pivot table or all pivot tables in your workbook and clear all the filters in the pivot table, it will get difficult to write the code from scratch. You can instead start recording the macro, and refresh every pivot table and remove all the filters yourself. When you stop recording the macro, you can review it and make the necessary changes to the code.

For a new Excel user, it would seem that the Help system is an add-in that always returns a list of topics that do not have anything to do with the topic you are looking for. The truth is that when you learn how to use the Help System correctly, it is the easiest and the fastest way to obtain more information about a topic. There are two basic tenets that you must keep in mind:

The Location Matters When You Ask For Help

There are two Help Systems in Excel – one that provides help on the different features in Excel and the other that provides information on some VBA programming topics. Excel will not perform a global search but will throw the criteria against the Help system, which is in your current location. This means that you will receive the help that you need depending on which area of Excel you are working in. If you want help on VBA and macros, you need to be in the Visual Basic Environment (VBE) when you look for information. This will ensure that the keyword search is performed on the correct help system.

Choose Online Help over Offline Help

When you look for some information on a topic, Excel will see if you are connected to the internet. If your system is connected to the internet, Excel will return results using some online content on Microsoft's website. Otherwise, Excel will use the help files that are stored offline in Microsoft office. It is always good to choose online help since the content is more detailed. It also includes updated information and the links to other resources that you can use.

Using Code for Excel VBA from the Internet

The secret about coding or programming is that there is no necessity to build original code. The macro syntax that you need to use is always available on the internet. This proves that there is no need to create or develop code from scratch. You can use some existing code on the internet and then apply the code to a specific scenario.

If you are stuck with creating or writing a macro for a specific task, all you need to do is describe the task you want to accomplish using Google Search. All you need to do is add the words "Excel VBA" before you describe your requirement.

For instance, if you want to write a macro to delete every blank row in a worksheet, you should look for, "How to delete blank rows in a worksheet in Excel VBA?" You can bet a whole years' worth of salary that a programmer has already developed code for the same problem. There is probably an example that is available on the internet, which will give you an idea of what you need to do. This way you can simply build your own macro.

Making Use of Excel VBA Forums

If you find yourself in a spot, and are unsure of what to do, you should post a question on a forum. The experts on these forums will guide you based on your requirement. A user forum is an online community that revolves around specific topics. You can ask numerous questions in these forums and get advice from experts on how you should solve some problems. The people answering your questions are volunteers who are passionate about helping the Excel community solve some real-world problems.

Many forums were built or developed to helping people with Excel. If you want to find such a forum, you should type "Excel Forum" in Google Search. Let us look at some tips you can use to get the most out of the user form.

You should always read the forum and follow all the rules before you begin. These rules will often include some advice on how you should post your questions and also the etiquette you should follow.

Always check if the question you want to ask has already been answered. You should try to save some time by looking at the archives. Now, take a moment to look at the forum and verify if any of the questions you want answers to have already been asked.

You should use accurate and concise titles for any of your questions. You should never create a forum question using an abstract title like "Please Help" or "Need advice."

You should always ensure that the scope of your question is narrow. You should never ask vague questions like "Can I build an accounting tool in Excel?"

You should always be patient, and remember that the people who are trying to answer your question also have a day job. You should always give the experts time to answer the questions.

You should always check often when you post your questions. You will probably receive some information when they will ask you to provide some information about your question. Therefore, you should always return to your post to either respond to some questions or review the answer.

You should always thank the person who has answered your question. If the answer helps you, you should let the expert know the same.

Visiting Excel VBA Expert Blogs

Some Excel Gurus have shared their knowledge about VBA on their blogs. These blogs have a large number of tips and tricks that you can use to improve your VBA skills. They have some information that you can use to build your skills. The best part of using these blogs is that they are free to use.

These blogs do not necessarily answer your specific questions, but they offer many articles that you can use to advance your knowledge of VBA and Excel. These blogs can also provide some general guidance on how you can apply Excel in different situations. Let us look at a few popular Excel blogs:

ExcelGuru

ExcelGuru is a blog that was set up by Ken Puls. He is an Excel expert who shares all his knowledge on his blog. Apart from the blog, Ken also offers many learning resources you can use to improve your knowledge in Excel.

Org

Org is a blog that was set up by Purna Chandoo Duggirala. He is an Excel expert from India who joined the scene in 2007. His blog offers innovative solutions and some free templates that will make you an Excel expert.

Contextures

Debra Dalgleish is the owner of a popular Excel website and is great with Microsoft Excel. Se has included close to 350 topics on her website, and there will definitely be something that you can read.

DailyDose

The DailyDose is a blog that is owned by Dick Kusleika. It is the longest running Excel blog, and Dick is an expert at Excel VBA. He has written articles and blogs for over ten years.

MrExcel

Bill Jelen always uses Excel to solve any problems he has at work. He offers a large archive of training resources and over thousands of free videos.

Mining YouTube for Some Excel VBA Training Videos

If you know that there are some training videos that are available on the internet, and these sessions are better than articles, you should look for those videos. There are many channels that are run by amazing experts that are passionate for sharing knowledge. You will be pleasantly surprised to see the quality of those videos.

Attending a Live Online Excel VBA Training Class

Live training sessions are a great way to absorb good Excel knowledge form a diverse set of people. The instructor is providing some information on different techniques, but the discussions held after the class will leave you with a wealth of ideas and tips. You may have never thought of these ideas ever before. If you can survive these classes, you should always consider attending more of these sessions. Here are some websites that you can use for such sessions:

1. Org

2. ExcelHero

3. ExcelJet

4. Learning From The Microsoft Office Developer Center For Help With VBA

You should use the Microsoft Office Dev Center to get some help on how to start programming in Office products. The website is slightly difficult to navigate, but it is worth it to look at the sample code, free resources, step-by-step instructions, tools and much more.

Dissecting Other Excel Files in Your Organization

Previous employees or current employees may have created files that already answer some of your questions. You should try to open different Excel files that contain the right macros, and also look at how these macros function. Then see how other employees in the organization develop macros for different applications. You should try not to go through the macro line-by-line but should look for some new techniques that may have been used.

You can also try to identify new tricks that you may have never thought of. You will probably also stumble upon some large chunks of code that you can implement or copy into your workbooks.

Ask the Local Excel Guru

Is there an excel genius in your department, company, community or organization? If yes, you should become friends with that person now. That person will become your own personal guru. Excel experts love to share their knowledge, so you should never be afraid to approach an expert if you have any questions or want to seek advice on how you can solve some problems.

Chapter Three

How to Improve
the Performance of Macros

There are times when VBA will run very slowly, and this is certainly frustrating. The good news is that there are some steps that you can take to improve the performance of the macro. This chapter will provide some information on the different steps you should take to improve the speed and performance of a macro. Regardless of whether you are an IT administrator, end user or a developer, you can use these tips to your benefit.

Close Everything Except for the VBA Essentials

The first thing to do to improve the performance of VBA is to turn off all the unnecessary features like screen updating, animation, automatic events and calculations when the macro runs. All these features will always add an extra overhead, which will slow the macro down. This always happens when the macro needs to modify or change many cells and trigger a lot of recalculations or screen updates.

The code below will show you how you can enable or disable the following:

1. Animations

2. Screen updates

3. Manual Calculations

```vba
Option Explicit

Dim lCalcSave As Long

Dim bScreenUpdate As Boolean

Sub SwitchOff(bSwitchOff As Boolean)

 Dim ws As Worksheet

 With Application

  If bSwitchOff Then

   ' OFF

   lCalcSave = .Calculation

  bScreenUpdate = .ScreenUpdating

   .Calculation = xlCalculationManual

   .ScreenUpdating = False

   .EnableAnimations = False

   '

   ' switch off display pagebreaks for all worksheets

   '

   For Each ws In ActiveWorkbook.Worksheets

    ws.DisplayPageBreaks = False

   Next ws

  Else
```

```
        ' ON

    If .Calculation <> lCalcSave And lCalcSave <> 0 Then
.Calculation = lCalcSave

    .ScreenUpdating = bScreenUpdate

    .EnableAnimations = True

  End If

  End With

End Sub

Sub Main()

  SwitchOff(True) ' turn off these features

  MyFunction() ' do your processing here

  SwitchOff(False) ' turn these features back on

End Sub
```

Disabling All The Animations Using System Settings

You can disable animations through the Ease of Access center in Windows. You can use this center to disable some specific features in Excel by going to the Ease of Access or Advanced Tabs on the menu. For more information, please use the following link: https://support.office.com/en-us/article/turn-off-office-animations-9ee5c4d2-d144-4fd2-b670-22cef9fa

Disabling Office Animations Using Registry Settings

You can always disable office animations on different computers by changing the appropriate registry key using a group policy setting.

HIVE: HKEY_CURRENT_USER

Key Path: Software\Microsoft\Office\16.0\Common\Graphics

Key Name: DisableAnimations

Value type: REG_DWORD

Value data: 0x00000001 (1)

If you use the Registry Editor incorrectly, you can cause some serious problems across the system. You may need to re-install Windows to use the editor correctly. Microsoft will help you solve the problems of a Registry Editor, but you should use this tool if you are willing to take the risk.

Removing Unnecessary Selects

Most people use the select method in the VBA code, but they add it in places where it is not necessary to use them. This keyword will trigger some cell events like conditional formatting and animations, which will hinder the performance of the macro. If you remove all the unnecessary selects, you can improve the performance of the macro. The following example will show you the code before and after you make a change to remove all the extra selects.

Before

```
Sheets("Order Details").Select

Columns("AC:AH").Select

Selection.ClearContents
```

After

```
Sheets("Order Details").Columns("AC:AH").ClearContents
```

Using the With Statement to Read Object Properties

When you work with objects, you should the With statement to decrease the number of times that the compiler reads the properties of the object. In the example below, see how the code changes when you use the With statement.

Before

```
Range("A1").Value = "Hello"

Range("A1").Font.Name = "Calibri"

Range("A1").Font.Bold = True

Range("A1").HorizontalAlignment = xlCenter
```

After

```
With Range("A1")

  .Value2 = "Hello"

  .HorizontalAlignment = xlCenter

    With .Font

      .Name = "Calibri"

      .Bold = True

    End With

  End With
```

Using Arrays And Ranges

It is expensive to read and write to cells every time in Excel using VBA. You incur an overhead every time there is some movement of data between Excel and VBA. This means that you should always reduce the number of times the data moves between Excel and VBA. It is at such a time that ranges are useful. Instead of writing or reading the data individually to every cell within a loop, you can simply read the entire range into an array, and use that array in the loop. The example below will show you how you can use a range to read and write the values at once without having to read each cell individually.

```
Dim vArray As Variant

Dim iRow As Integer

Dim iCol As Integer

Dim dValue As Double

vArray = Range("A1:C10000").Value2 ' read all the values at once from the Excel cells, put into an array

For iRow = LBound(vArray, 1) To UBound(vArray, 1)

  For iCol = LBound(vArray, 2) To UBound(vArray, 2)

    dValue = vArray (iRow, iCol)

    If dValue > 0 Then

      dValue=dValue*dValue ' Change the values in the array, not the cells

    vArray(iRow, iCol) = dValue

  End If

Next iCol

Next iRow

Range("A1:C10000").Value2 = vArray ' writes all the results back to the range at once
```

Use .Value2 Instead Of .Text or .Value

You can retrieve your values in different ways from a cell. The property you use to retrieve that information will have an impact on the performance of your code.

.Text

Most programmers use the .Text value to retrieve only the information from a cell. The property will return the formatted value of the cell. It takes a lot of processing time to retrieve a cell value along with its format, and it is for this reason that this property is slow.

.Value

The .Value keyword is a slight improvement over the previous keyword since it does not return a value with its format. Regardless of whether a cell has been formatted with a date or currency, this keyword will only return the VBA date and VBA currency, and the values for these outputs are truncated at decimal places.

.Value2

The .Value2 keyword only returns the underlying value of the cell. This keyword does not take any formatting into account and works faster than the .Text and .Value keywords. This keyword works faster if you use a variant array.

If you want to learn more about how these keywords work, please read the following post: https://fastexcel.wordpress.com/2011/11/30/text-vs-value-vs-value2-slow-text-and-how-to-avoid-it/

Avoid Using Copy and Paste

When you use the macro recorder to record any operations, including copy and paste that you perform in Excel, the code that the recorder writes will use these methods as default operations. It

393

is always a good idea to avoid using the copy and paste operations, and use some in-built VBA functions to perform these operations. You can also use the in-built functions to copy formulae or formatting across a block of cells. The following example will give you an idea about how you should use the in-built VBA operations and functions as opposed to manual copy and paste operations.

Before

```
Range("A1").Select

Selection.Copy

Range("A2").Select

ActiveSheet.Paste
```

After

```
' Approach 1: copy everything (formulas, values and formatting

Range("A1").Copy Destination:=Range("A2")

' Approach 2: copy values only

Range("A2").Value2 = Range("A1").Value2

' Approach 3: copy formulas only

Range("A2").Formula = Range("A1").Formula
```

If you think that the code is still functioning slowly, you can use the following fix: https://support.microsoft.com/en-in/help/2817672/macro-takes-longer-than-expected-to-execute-many-in

Use The Option Explicit Keyword To Catch Undeclared Variables

Option Explicit is one of the many Module directives that you can use in VBA. This directive will instruct VBA about how it should treat a code within a specific module. If you use Option Explicit, you should ensure that all the variables in the code are declared. If there is any variable that is not declared, it will throw a compile error. This will help you catch any variables that have been named incorrectly. It will also help to improve the performance of the macro where variables are defined at different times. You can set this by typing "Option Explicit" at the top of every module you write. Alternatively, you can check the "Require Variable Declaration" in the VBA editor under "Tools -> Options."

Chapter Four

Some Problems with Spreadsheets and How to Overcome Them

Most people use Excel to make a repository. This is because it is easy to make a list of small items for yourself or your colleagues in Excel. You may perhaps want to use some formulae to create something sophisticated. You may also want to use macros to automate the process of collecting and processing data. You can do this by typing an equal to sign in the cell before you write the formula. Excel will be your guide. There are some problems that everybody will face when it comes to using Excel, and that is its simplicity. You may start with a small project in Excel, and this project will grow until it becomes a daunting task. At this point, you may also face some issues with stability and speed, or some development problem that you cannot solve.

This chapter examines some of the common issues that people come across when they use spreadsheets, and also provides some solutions to tackle those problems. It will also tell you when you should switch to a database instead of sticking to Excel.

Multi-User Editing

When an Excel system begins to grow, you will quickly run into a problem where only one user can open the workbook at a time and make changes to it. Any other person who wants to open the workbook will be notified that someone already has the book open and that they can view the workbook as a read-only version or wait until the file is closed by the first user. Excel does promise to let you know when the first user has closed the file, but this is a hollow promise since Excel does not always check the status, and there are times when it may never give you an update. Even if it does give you an update, someone may already have opened the file before you.

You can get around this in the following ways:

1. You should use Excel Online. This application is a web-based and abridged version of Microsoft Excel.

2. Turn on the feature that will allow you to share the workbook.

3. Split the workbook into smaller workbooks. This will allow different users to access different workbooks without causing any hindrances in the work.

Shared Workbooks

If you use Excel online, you can allow multiple users to edit the workbook at the same time. There is so much functionality that goes missing, which makes it a contender only for simple tasks. The shared workbook features in Excel will allow you to share the workbook between multiple users, but there are many restrictions. For instance, you cannot delete a group of cells or create a table in a shared workbook.

It is easy to walk around some restrictions, but for others, it is a matter of changing the structure of the entire workbook instead of using a workbook that has already been set up. These workarounds can, however, get in the way. As a result of this, it is impossible to use a workbook that is shared in the same way that you may use a single user workbook.

Any changes made in a shared workbook will be synchronized between the users every time the workbook is saved. These changes can be saved on a time schedule, meaning that a workbook can be saved or force saved every few minutes. The overhead of regular checking and savings every share user change is quite large. The size of the workbook can increase which will put a strain on your network thereby slowing down every other system.

A shared workbook is prone to corruption. Microsoft office knows that this is the problem, but there is nothing much you can do about the issue. The alternative to this situation is to use Excel online since you can have multiple users working on the same workbook. Not many users will switch to excel online until Microsoft will remove all the restrictions on a shared workbook, and extend a multi-authoring tool to the Excel offline application.

Linked Workbooks

If you want to overcome the issue of multi-user editing, you should try to split the data across multiple workbooks. It is likely that these workbooks must be linked so that any value entered in one can be used in another. The links between workbooks also help to separate data using a logical method instead of using separate worksheets in one workbook.

Unfortunately, these links lead to instability and frustration. This is because the links need to be absolute or relative. In the case of absolute links, you will need to include the full path resource workbook while in the case of relative links, you only need to include the difference between the destination and source paths. This may sound sensible until you come across the rules the Excel decides to employ on when you can use each type of link, and when you can change them.

These rules are governed by numerous options. Some of these rules are dependent on whether the workbook was saved and whether it was saved before every link was inserted. There are times when Excel will automatically change the link when you open a workbook and use the save as option to copy the file. Excel may also change the links when you simply save the workbook down. One of the main disadvantages of using this option is that the links can break easily, and it is difficult to recover all the broken links. This is also a time-consuming affair since you cannot use the files that are affected by the broken links.

The linked data will only be updated when all the underlying files are open unless you edit links and update values. It is because of this that you may need to open 3 or 4 workbooks to ensure that all the information is flowing through in the right order. If you made it changed it the value in the first workbook but open only 3rd workbook, you will not see any changes because this is a second workbook still does not have the updated values.

It is logical to create a change a data, but this will increase the likelihood that the data is incorrect or and when you open a workbook somebody else is already editing the underlying work. You can avoid the use of link workbooks, but there is a chance that you will end up entering the same data in more than one workbook. The danger with this is that you may type the data differently each time.

Data Validation

You must remember that any user can enter data on any computer system. People can transpose digits in numbers or mistype words with monotonous regularity. You must ensure that you check the data when it is entered or you will have a problem in the end.

Excel will always accept whatever any user types. Therefore, it is possible to set up a validation using lists, but it is impossible to maintain this list especially if that field is used in multiple places. For example, if a user should enter a customer reference number or a document ID they can enter the wrong record. To avoid this, it is always good to have some checks across the workbook. If there is no Data integrity, the system will be fatally compromised, which will affect the analysis.

You may already be suffering from this problem without having realized what the root cause is. Let us consider a situation where there is a list of invoices that you have entered in Excel Find the user has typed the name of every customer differently on every invoice. You got invoices to John limited, John Ltd and John. You are aware that these invoices point to the same company or customer, but Excel is not aware of this. This means that any analysis that you made using this data will always give you multiple results when they should only be one.

Navigation Issues

It is difficult to navigate through large workbooks. The number of sheet tabs in the bottom of the window is difficult to use and is a terrible way to find your way around the workbook. If there are many sheets in the workbook, and you cannot see all of them on the screen, it will be difficult for you to find what you are looking for. You can always click on the arrow to the left of your active sheet, but you will only see the first twenty sheets in that window. You cannot sort or group the list of sheets in any order.

Security Issues

You can add a lot of security features to an Excel workbook, but it is still going to have many problems. It is more important to work toward protecting the structure of the workbook, instead of worrying about the data. You can always lock some sheets and cells in the workbook to prevent some users from making any changes to the data or formulae. Regardless of whether you protect the sheet or not, if someone can see the data, they can make changes to it. You can avoid this by using some clever macro skills.

Speed Issues

You must remember that Excel is not the fastest application there is, and the programming language we use in Excel, VBA is slow and slightly sluggish when compared to the more professional languages like C and C#. This is because of the intended use of Excel and its flexibility. You should remember that Excel is a spreadsheet engine alone, and it can only be used to manage large volumes of data. This does not mean that you must always use Excel for this type of work. There are many other applications that you can use to perform such tasks since those applications were designed to perform these functions.

Enter the database

If you are facing any of the issues that have been listed above, you should not ignore them. The answer or solution to these problems is to store the data in a structured manner. This means that we will need to start saving data in a database. This will allow you to think about your data in a logical manner. You have the ability to see how the data welding together and how you will need to interact with it to analyze the information.

You must, however, take heed. If you move from spreadsheets to databases, you should not duplicate the design of a spreadsheet. Instead, you should find a way to make the design better. There are some general database applications, listed below with which you can construct a simple solution. Alternatively, you can also use specialist database applications that allow you to switch from spreadsheet to databases within a few minutes point these applications are a better fit to big data.

For example, if you have a list of customers, their details and any interaction you have had with these customers you should consider using a customer relationship management system. Customer relationship management system is a specialized database. Similarly, you can save accounts on packages like Sage and

QuickBooks. The may be times when you cannot find an existing application to suit your needs. As such times you may need to build a database by yourself or request see IT department or any consultant to build the database for you.

The relational database is the most common type of database used in today's world. This database stores information or data in the form of tables, which consists of columns and rows of data. Every row data will hold a separate item and every column will describe a different attribute of that item. For example, if the rows hold customer information, the columns can describe attributes like customer name and customer ID. All you need to do is enter the data once, and then you can use the same data to print on every invoice.

Every table in a relational database has a relationship between them. You can take the relationship between an invoice and the customer ID. Here you can always find an invoice that is related to a specific customer using the customer ID. Alternatively, you can also retrieve customer information from the invoice if necessary. All you need to do is enter the customer data of one in the database to create a record, and you can use that information across different invoices without having to type the data again. To use or create a database, you must define the tables and the relationships between those tables, and then define the type of layout you want to use to edit or list the data.

There are over a dozen applications that you can choose from. Some of the applications are easy to use and do the job for you. These applications will allow you to define the table, the data screen, and the reports. There are other applications that are more useful in specific areas but will require other tools to perform the job.

For example, some applications may be very powerful when comes defining a table and the relationship that table shares with the database and other tables, and it may also have some excellent analysis and reporting features. This application can, however, lack a tool, which will allow you to define the data entry screen. An obvious example of such an application is Microsoft SQL. As is the case with large database systems, the SQL server will only take care of the back-end annual expect you to use, and other tools like visual studio to develop or maintain the front-end.

Choosing the Right Database

Access

Microsoft Access is one of the oldest databases available. This is easy to use and is extremely easy to abuse. You can design screens, reports, and tables from scratch or use an existing template. Some of the templates in Access do not teach you some good practices, but they will help you get started quickly. The programming and screen features and options are sophisticated, and you can deploy the application on the intranet without having to rely on sharing the files with users.

SharePoint

SharePoint is a document storage application and a database. This application can be used to compile and link simple lists. You can use the form designer to customize your dashboard, but it is important to remember that it is not a sophisticated application to use. SharePoint has the ability to suck the information from Excel and put it into a custom list. This makes it a useful application since everybody in your network will have access to the list. You can choose to add some security features, which will restrict the access for some people. SharePoint can also send you an alert email when someone makes a change – adds, deletes or edits – to a record. You can also synchronize the information with Outlook if you have some data that concerns a person, calendar or task.

403

There is a database application that you can use in the Zoho office services available on the internet. You can drag and drop the required layout in an easy way. This will also help you decide how the work should flow and what the interaction can be like. Since this is a web application, the data you use and the applications you develop can be found anywhere. Therefore, you should use the simple security features that this application provides to keep your data private. Zoho charges you per month but will allow you to store only some records depending on the price you choose to pay. If you want to use advanced features like email integration, you will need to pay an additional amount of money.

Hi there! If you found the topic or information useful, it would be a great help if you can leave a quick review on Amazon. Thanks a lot!

Chapter Five

Sub Procedures

If you have read Excel tutorials that talk about VBA and macros, you would have come across the term procedure at least a hundred times. If you are unsure of what these are, you should learn this now. There are many good reasons why this is important.

If you want to become an expert at writing macros and using VBA, you should understand what a procedure is, the different types of procedures and how you should work with them. This is one of the most essential tools to learn if you want to become a VBA expert. This chapter will provide all the information you need about procedures and will dig deeper into the concepts of sub procedures. Let us first begin with an introduction to sub procedures.

What Is A Sub Procedure?

If you have written programs or code in VBA, you will know that a procedure is a block of code or statements that are enclosed between a declaration statement and an End statement. The purpose of the procedure is to perform a specific action or task. All the instructions that you want to give the compiler are within a procedure. If you want to master coding in VBA, you should fully understand this concept. There are two types of procedures in VBA – Function procedures and sub procedures. This chapter will focus only on Sub procedures.

The following are the differences between a VBA sub procedure and a function procedure:

1. A VBA sub procedure will perform some function or action with Excel. This means that when you execute a sub procedure, Excel will do something. The changes or functions that happen in Excel depend on what the code says.

2. A function procedure will perform some calculations and return a value. The value returned can either be an array, number or string. If you have worked regularly with functions in Excel, you already know how the function procedure will work. This is because they work in the same way as Excel functions. These procedures will perform some function on the data in Excel and return a value.

Experts say that most macros that people write are sub procedures. If you always use the macro recorder to create your macro, you are creating a sub procedure. From the above comments, it is clear that you will work a lot with Excel VBA Sub procedures.

How Does The VBA Sub Procedure Look?

The image below will show you how a VBA sub procedure looks. You should notice that this procedure has the following features:

1. It begins with the statement "Sub." This is the declaration statement.

2. There is an End declaration statement.

3. There is a block of code that is enclosed between the declaration statements.

```
Sub Delete_Blank_Rows_3()

'
' Delete_Blank_Rows_3 Macro
' Deletes rows when cells within the row are blank.
'
' Keyboard Shortcut: Ctrl+Shift+B
'

On Error Resume Next
Selection.EntireRow.SpecialCells(xlBlanks).EntireRow.Delete
On Error GoTo 0

End Sub
```

(https://powerspreadsheets.com/vba-sub-procedures/)

The purpose of this VBA sub procedure is to delete some rows in the worksheet where there are blank cells. Before we move on, let us take a look at the first statement in the sub procedure. There are three sections to look at:

1. The sub keyword, also the declaration statement, which tells the compiler that the sub procedure has started.

2. The name of the sub procedure. We will cover the rules that must be followed when working with sub procedures in the following sections.

3. The parentheses in the sub procedure are where you will need to add the arguments that you will be using from other procedures. You should separate these by using a comma. You can always create a VBA sub procedure that does not use any arguments. You should, however, include an empty set of parentheses when you name the sub procedure.

The following are the four elements that you should include in a VBA sub procedure:

- Sub statement

- Name

- Parentheses

407

- End Sub keyword

You can include two optional elements in a sub procedure:

1. A list of arguments that you will need to include in the parentheses.

2. Valid instructions that are included in the declaration statements in the code.

Apart from these, you can include three optional items in a VBA sub procedure. These items are optional, but they are important to consider. Before we look at them, let us look at how this procedure will be structured.

[Private/Public] [Static] Sub name ([Argument list])

[Instructions]

[Exit Sub]

[Instructions]

End Sub

To learn more about the Sub statement, you should read the articles found in the Microsoft Dev Center. Let us take a look at the optional elements that are present in the above structure. These items are written in square brackets to indicate that they are optional.

Element #1: [Private/Public]

The keywords private and public are called access modifiers. If you type private before the declaration statement in a sub procedure, it implies that only the procedures or codes written within the same module can access that sub procedure.

If you choose to use the keyword public, the sub procedure will not have any access restrictions. Despite this, if you were to use the keywords option private statement at the beginning of the sub procedure, any procedure outside the relevant project cannot refer to or use the sub procedure. We will talk a little more about the scope of the project in the sections below.

Element #2: [Static]

If you use the keyword static at the beginning of the sub procedure, any variable, which is the part of the sub procedure will be preserved even when the module ends.

Element #3: [Exit Sub]

The exit sub statement is the final declaration statement, which is used to immediately exit A sub procedure. This means that any statements within the sub procedure not run once the compiler reaches this decoration statement.

How to Name A VBA Sub Procedure

You must always name a procedure. The rules that you need to follow when naming A sub procedure are given below:

1. You should always use a letter as the first character.

2. The remaining characters in the name can be numbers, letters or some punctuation characters. For example, the following characters can't be used: #, $, %, &, @, ^, * and !

3. You should avoid using spaces and periods.

4. Since VBA is not a case sensitive language, cannot distinguish between lowercase and uppercase letters.

5. Any sub procedure can have a name, which has a maximum of 255 characters.

Experts suggest that we be a procedure name should always:

6. Describe what the purpose of the sub procedure is or what it is supposed to do.

7. Have some meaning.

8. Be a combination of a noun and a verb.

There are some programmers who choose useful sentences to name the sub procedures. There is one advantage and disadvantage of doing this:

1. A sentence will definitely let any other user of programmer know what the purpose of the sub procedure is. This is because a sentence is very unambiguous and descriptive.

2. When you type of full sentence you will use more time. This means that you will take longer to finish your macro.

I believe that you should always use a name that is descriptive, unambiguous and meaningful. It is at this point that you should choose what your style is, and always stick to something that is comfortable and will help you achieve your goals.

How to Determine the Scope of A VBA Sub Procedure

The scope will define how you are when you should call upon a VBA sub procedure. When you create a BBA procedure you have the option to determine which other procedure can call it. You can do this by using the keywords public and private which were introduced in the above section as an optional element of a procedure.

Let us now take a look at what the meaning of these keywords is and how you can determine whether a specific VBA procedure is public or private.

Public VBA Sub Procedures

Every sub procedure is public by default. If a specific procedure is public there is no access restriction. Since the default option is that a procedure is public, you do not have to include the public keyword at the beginning of the name. For instance, the following procedure delete_blank_rows_3 is a public procedure although we did not use the keyword public.

```
Sub Delete_Blank_Rows_3()

    ' Delete_Blank_Rows_3 Macro
    ' Deletes rows when cells within the row are blank.
    '
    ' Keyboard Shortcut: Ctrl+Shift+B
    '

    On Error Resume Next
    Selection.EntireRow.SpecialCells(xlBlanks).EntireRow.Delete
    On Error GoTo 0

End Sub
```

no "Public"

(https://powerspreadsheets.com/vba-sub-procedures/)

If you want to make the courts near, you should try to include the public keyword in the procedure. Most programmers do follow this practice. In the image below, you will see that the keyword public has been included in the delete_blank_rows_3 macro.

```
Public Sub Delete_Blank_Rows_3()

    '
    ' Delete_Blank_Rows_3 Macro
    ' Deletes rows when cells within the row are blank.
    '
    ' Keyboard Shortcut: Ctrl+Shift+B
    '

    On Error Resume Next
    Selection.EntireRow.SpecialCells(xlBlanks).EntireRow.Delete
    On Error GoTo 0

End Sub
```

(https://powerspreadsheets.com/vba-sub-procedures/)

In both cases, the sub procedure is public. In simple words both the macros, with and without the public keyword are the same.

Private VBA Sub Procedures

When you use the private keyword ahead of the sub procedure, the content of the statements within the sub procedure can only be accessed by other procedures within the same module. If there is any other procedure or module that wants to access this sir procedure it cannot, even if the module is in the same Excel workbook. For instance, if you need the delete_blank_rows_3 macro a private macro you will need to follow the syntax given in the image below.

```
Private Sub Delete_Blank_Rows_3()

'
' Delete_Blank_Rows_3 Macro
' Deletes rows when cells within the row are blank.
'
' Keyboard Shortcut: Ctrl+Shift+B
'

On Error Resume Next
Selection.EntireRow.SpecialCells(xlBlanks).EntireRow.Delete
On Error GoTo 0

End Sub
```

(https://powerspreadsheets.com/vba-sub-procedures/)

How to Make All VBA Sub Procedures in a Module Private to A VBA Project

A person using the public in the private keywords, you can also make a sub procedure accessible to other modules in different BBA project by using the option private statement. To use the option private statement, you must include the keywords "option private module" before the sub procedure. If you are certain that you want to use this statement ensure that the keywords are ahead of the declaration statement in the sub procedure.

412

The image below shows how VBA uses three different methods to delete a row based on whether the row has an empty cell or not. The third macro or sub procedure in the image below is the Delete_Blank_Rows_3 macro. This macro does not appear fully in the image.

```
Option Private Module

Sub Delete_Blank_Rows()

'
' Delete_Blank_Rows Macro
' Deletes rows with blank cells in selected range.
'
' Keyboard Shortcut: Ctrl+Shift+D
'
    On Error Resume Next
        Range("E6:E257").Select
        Selection.SpecialCells(xlCellTypeBlanks).EntireRow.Delete
End Sub
Sub Delete_Blank_Rows_2()

'
' Delete_Blank_Rows_2 Macro
' Deletes rows with blank cells in selected range.
'
' Keyboard Shortcut: Ctrl+Shift+E
'
    On Error Resume Next
    With Range("E6:E257")
        .Value = .Value
        .SpecialCells(xlCellTypeBlanks).EntireRow.Delete
    End With

End Sub
Sub Delete_Blank_Rows_3()

'
' Delete_Blank_Rows_3 Macro
' Deletes rows when cells within the row are blank.
```

(https://powerspreadsheets.com/vba-sub-procedures/)

Found this title interesting or useful? Then a review on Amazon will be highly appreciated!

All the sub procedure is in the above image can only be accessed referenced by module or the procedures in the VBA project that contains them.

When to Make VBA Sub Procedures Private: An Example

You can always execute A sub procedure by using another procedure to call it. Most programmers use this method to run or execute a procedure. In some cases, you may also have procedures that are designed to be called by other sub procedures. If you have any procedures in a specific workbook, it is always good to make them private. When you do this the sub procedure will no longer be listed in the macro dialog box. The macro dialog box is one of the easiest and fastest ways to execute A sub procedure.

If you do not understand how this works, do not worry. I will explain how you can call VBA sub procedure from other procedure or by using the macro dialogue box in the section below.

How to Execute / Run / Call a VBA Sub Procedure

When you work with macros you will often use the terms run execute or call interchangeably. These words refer to the action of executing the statements in the sub procedure. You can use these words interchangeably.

You can execute run a call A sub procedure in many ways. This section provides 9 different ways in which you can execute or run the statements in a procedure. There is a 10th option, which you can use but this is out of the scope of this book. This in this option you will need to execute the macro or the statement using a customized context menu. This section does not talk about using a context menu customization to run a block of code since it is a separate topic that we need to be covered extensively.

We will use the delete_blank_rows_3 macro as an example in all the options in this section.

Option One: How to Execute A VBA Sub Procedure Directly From the Visual Basic Editor

Experts state that this is the best and the fastest way to execute the block of code in a sub procedure. In this method, you will run the procedure directly in the visual basic editor using the module in which it is written.

Describe the factor this is one of the fastest methods, most people do not use it often. In practice, people often execute the macro only when they are in excel and not in the visual basic editor. There are some other options that are listed in this section, which will allow you to do this.

This method will only work when a specific sub procedure that you want to run does not require any arguments from other procedures and macros. The reason is that this option does not allow you to use any arguments are inputs from other procedures.

If you ever want to run a sub procedure, which contains arguments, you can only do it by calling it from another procedure. The procedure used to call the sub procedure will need to pass the arguments that the sub procedure required to execute the block of code.

If you do choose to use this method to call or run the code in the sub procedure, you should follow the following steps:

Step One: Open the Visual Basic Editor
You can open the visual basic editor using the keyboard shortcut Alt + F11. Alternatively, you can go to the developer tab in the ribbon and choose the visual basic icon.

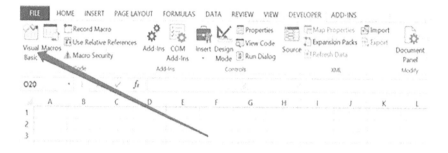

(https://powerspreadsheets.com/vba-sub-procedures/)

Step Two: Open The VBA Module That Contains The VBA Sub Procedure You Want To Execute.

You now want the visual basic editor to give you the code that is in the sub procedure that you are calling. This can be done in several ways. One of the easiest methods is to double click on the relevant module or procedure. For instance, if the sub procedure that you want to call is within module 1, you will simply need to click module 1 in the project explorer in the visual basic editor.

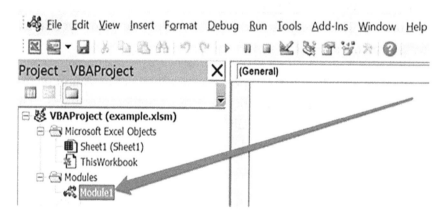

(https://powerspreadsheets.com/vba-sub-procedures/)

As a result of this, the visual basic editor will display the relevant code in the programming window in the visual basic environment.

(https://powerspreadsheets.com/vba-sub-procedures/)

Step Three: Run The VBA Sub Procedure.

If you want to call A sub procedure directly using the relevant module in the visual basic editor, you must use the following methods:

1. Go to the run menu and click on the option "Run Sub/UserForm."

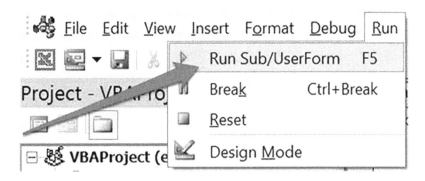

(https://powerspreadsheets.com/vba-sub-procedures/)

2. Click on F5, which is the keyboard shortcut.

Option Two: How to Execute A VBA Sub Procedure Using the Macro Dialog

This method, as the first method, will only work when the sub procedure does not require any arguments. It is because of the same reason mentioned earlier - you cannot specify the arguments.

Regardless of what the arguments are, this is an option that most programmers used to execute sub procedures. When you use this method you can run the sub procedure in two steps. Let us look at them.

Step One: Open the Macro dialog.
You should first instruct Excel to open the macro dialog box using the following methods:

1. Click on Alt + F8, which is the shortcut key.

2. Go to the developer tab in the ribbon, and click on the macros option.

(https://powerspreadsheets.com/vba-sub-procedures/)

Excel window display the macro dialog box which will look as follows:

(https://powerspreadsheets.com/vba-sub-procedures/)

Step Two: Select The Macro You Want To Execute And Execute It.

In the above image, you will notice that there is only one macro open in every Excel workbook. This macro is the Delete_Blank_Rows_3 macro. Since this is the only method that is listed, we will only be running or executing the code within that macro.

You are already aware that when you use this method you cannot use any arguments in the sub procedure. Therefore any sab procedure that requires arguments will not appear in the macro dialog box.

It is also important to remember that the macro dialog box will only show procedures that are public. You can still execute A sub procedure, which is private. For this, you should fill the relevant sub procedure name in the macro name field, which appears in the image below. The macro dialogue box does not show any sub

419

procedure, which contains and adding. In this case, you can execute a macro by typing in the relevant macro in the name field.

The rule to select and run or execute macro is the same regardless of whether you have one or multiple macros in the open or active Excel workbook. You can always select the matter that you want to run in the following ways:

Double click the name of the matter that you want to execute. For example, we want to run the Delete_Blank_Rows_3 macro. For this, we will need to double click on the name of the macro.

(https://powerspreadsheets.com/vba-sub-procedures/)

Click on the name of the macro you want to run, and hit run button on the top right corner.

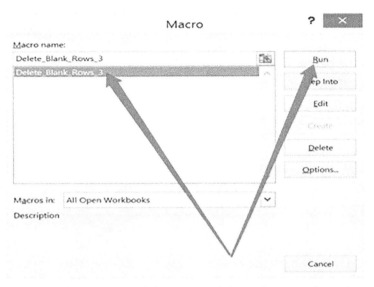

(https://powerspreadsheets.com/vba-sub-procedures/)

Option Three: How to Execute A VBA Sub Procedure Using a Keyboard Shortcut

You can also execute or run a sub procedure using keyboard shortcuts. If you want to run a sub procedure using this method you have to select a press the relevant key combination. It is important to remember that this does not work for macros that require arguments for the same reason as mentioned above.

You may now be wondering how you can assign keyboard shortcuts to a macro. This can be done in two ways:

In this method, you will need to assign a keyboard shortcut to the macro when you are in the macro recorder. When you use the macro recorder to record the process, you will encounter a record macro dialog box. In this dialog box, you can determine whether you want to call a macro using a keyboard shortcut and also determine which keys will compose that shortcut.

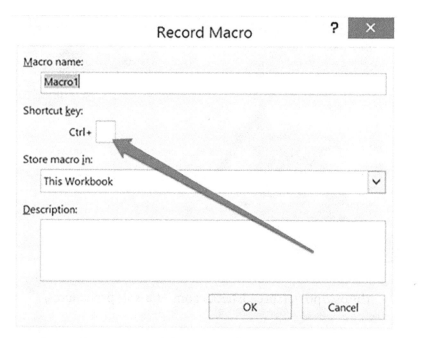

(https://powerspreadsheets.com/vba-sub-procedures/)

This method is more interesting when compared to the previous method. In this method you can assign or edit a keyboard shortcut to any macro in the following method:

Step One: Open The Macro Dialog.

You can use the shortcut Alt + F8 to access the microbe dialogue box. Alternatively, you can go to the developer tab in the ribbon and click on the icon of the macro.

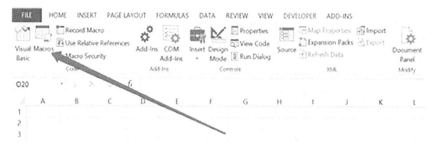

(https://powerspreadsheets.com/vba-sub-procedures/)

Step Two: Select The Macro You Want To Assign A Keyboard Shortcut To.

Now you should select the sub procedure you want to assign a macro to all shortcuts to and click on the options button on the bottom right corner of the dialog box. For example, we have selected the Delete_Blank_Rows_3 macro in the image below.

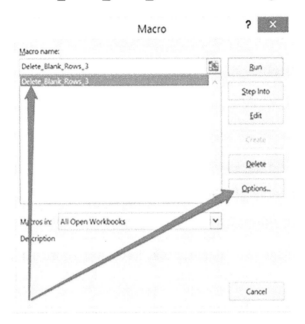

(https://powerspreadsheets.com/vba-sub-procedures/)

Step Three: Assign A Keyboard Shortcut.

When you see the macro option dialog box open, you can assign a keyboard shortcut and click the ok button at the bottom of the box.

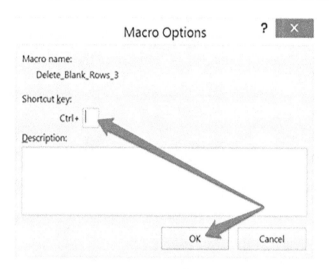

(https://powerspreadsheets.com/vba-sub-procedures/)

It is important to remember that keyboard shortcuts will always take the form of control + letter or control + shift + letter.

When you select the keyboard shortcut, you have to be careful that you are not assigning a combination all shortcuts that already exist in VBA. If you choose as an existing of built-in shortcut, you will be disabling the latter.

For instance, the control + B shortcut is a built-in shortcut for bold. If you assign the same shortcuts to any other Microsoft procedure, you cannot use it to make text bold.

It is always a better idea to use the control + shift + letter form of a shortcut since it reduces the risk of disabling a pre-existing shortcut. Regardless of what the situation is, you have to be careful about what combination you assign a sub procedure.

Option Four: How to Execute A VBA Sub Procedure Using a Button or Other Object

The idea behind using this method is that you can always attach a macro to a specific object. Here I am not referring to a specific object in the macro, but I am referring to the type of object that Excel will allow you to use in a worksheet. Experts have classified these objects into the following classes:

1. ActiveX controls

2. Form controls

3. Inserted objects, like as shapes, text boxes, clip art, SmartArt, WordArt, charts and pictures.

In this section, we will see how you can attach a macro to a button using the form controls option or to any other inserted object in the workbook.

How to Assign a Macro to a Form Control Button

You can attach any macro sub procedure to a form control button using the following four steps:

Step One: Insert a Button

You should first go to the ribbon and navigate to the developer tab. now move to the insert and choose the button form of control. The image below will show you exactly what needs to be done in the step.

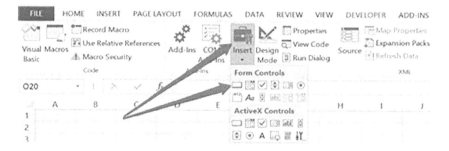

(https://powerspreadsheets.com/vba-sub-procedures/)

Step Two: Create the Button

Now that you have created the button form control, you will need to create the button in the Excel worksheet point you can create the Spartan of places button in any section of the worksheet where you want it to appear.

For example, if I want the button to be in Cell B5, I will click on the top left corner of that cell.

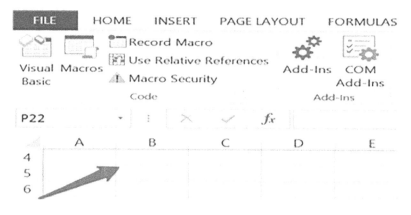

(https://powerspreadsheets.com/vba-sub-procedures/)

Step Three: Assign a Macro to the Button

Once you have selected the location where you want the button to be, Excel will display the assign macro dialog box.

(https://powerspreadsheets.com/vba-sub-procedures/)

Based on what the buttons name is, excel will suggest a macro that you can assign to that button. In the example below, we have named the button "Button1_Click."

(https://powerspreadsheets.com/vba-sub-procedures/)

In most cases, the suggestion excel gives will not match what you want. Therefore, you have to select a method that you want to assign to the button and then click on ok at the bottom right corner of the dialog box. In the example below, we will be using the Delete_Blank_Rows_3 macro and assign a button to that macro.

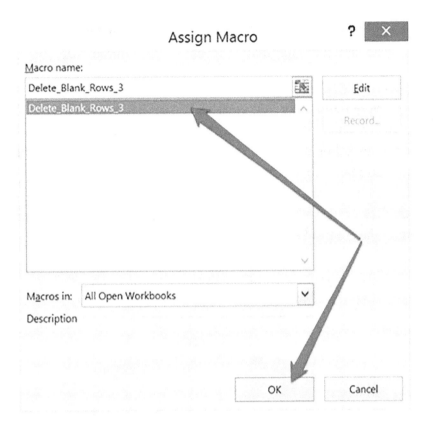

(https://powerspreadsheets.com/vba-sub-procedures/)

Step Four: Edit Button (Optional)

When you have completed the steps described above, Excel will create the button. Now, you only need to execute the relevant sub procedure by clicking on that button.

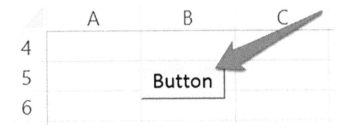

(https://powerspreadsheets.com/vba-sub-procedures/)

Once the button is in place, you can edit it in some ways. You the following are the four main aspects of the button that you can change:

<u>Size</u>: Every button that you create an Excel has a default size. You can always adjust the size by joining the handles of the button with your mouse. For example, if you want to increase the size of a button so that it covers at least four cells, you can drag the bottom right handle as required. If you cannot find the handles, you can right click on the button or press the left mouse button at the same time as the control key to view the handles.

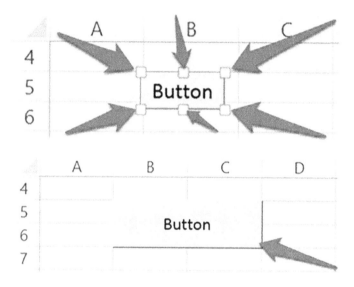

(https://powerspreadsheets.com/vba-sub-procedures/)

<u>Location</u>: You can always modify the location of a button by dragging it with your mouth. You can only track the button using the left button of your mouth is the handles are visible. If they are not visible, you will need to right click on the button and then attempt to drag it to a different location. Alternatively, you can simply change the position of the button by dragging it using the right mouse button. For example, if you want to move the button to cover a couple of cells down, that is it should cover the cells B8, B9, C8 and C9, you should drag the button until the desired point.

When you drive the button excel will show you a Shadow in the new location but will leave the button and its original spot. When you let go or remove your hand from the right now button, accessories display the contextual menu. You should choose the option to move the button by selecting "move here."

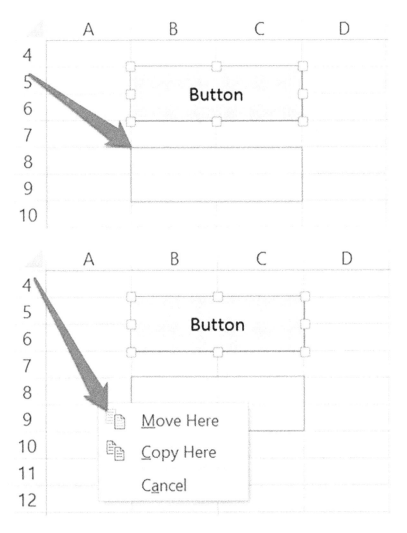

(https://powerspreadsheets.com/vba-sub-procedures/)

Text: If you want to edit the text on the button, you should I click on the button. Excel will then display a contextual menu where you can choose to edit text. Excel word and place the cursor inside the button, so you can modify the text. When you are done click outside of the button to confirm the changes made. Since we are using the Delete_Blank_Rows_3 macro as an example, we will rename the button to delete blank rows in that is more appropriate.

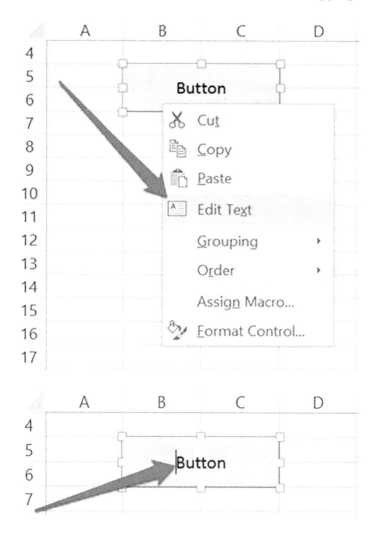

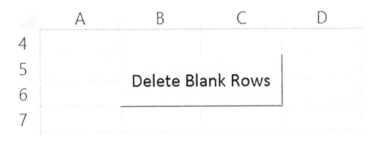

(https://powerspreadsheets.com/vba-sub-procedures/)

Assigned macro: If there is a necessity, you can always change the VBA sub procedure, and assign it to a different macro by right-clicking on the button. In this case, Excel will take you back to the macro dialogue box where you can select which sub procedure you want to assign to the button. You are already familiar with this process since it has been described above. In addition to this, you can also edit many other aspects of the button by right-clicking on the button and choosing the option to format control. Excel will now display the format control dialogue box. By using the options in this box, you can determine or make changes to many settings of the macro button.

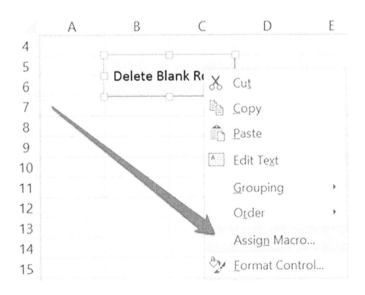

433

(https://powerspreadsheets.com/vba-sub-procedures/)

Some of the settings that you can change during the format control dialog box are:

1. Font, including typeface, style, size, underline, color and effects

2. Text alignment and orientation

3. Internal margins

4. Size

5. Whether the button moves and/or sizes with cells

How to Assign a Macro to another Object

In addition to assigning macros to form control buttons, x I will also allow you to assign a macro to other objects. As explain the bug these objects can include text boxes, shapes, SmartArt, WordArt, text boxes, pictures or charts. It is extremely easy to attach a sub procedure to an object in excel. Let us see how you can do this in the case of a word art object which reads delete blank rows.

Step One: Open the Assign Macro Dialog

Right click on the object, and select the assign macro option. This will open the assigned macro dialog box.

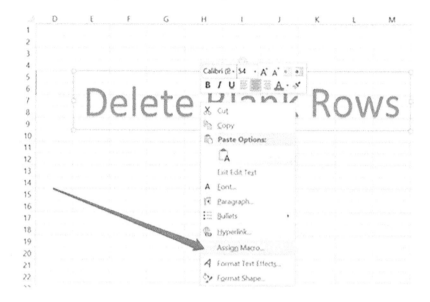

(https://powerspreadsheets.com/vba-sub-procedures/)

Step Two: Select Macro to Assign

Once you complete the step above, Excel will display the macro dialogue box. You are already familiar with this box. To assign a sub procedure to the object in the image above, you should select the matter you want to assign and click ok. In the example below, we will be using the Delete_Blank_Rows_3 macro.

(https://powerspreadsheets.com/vba-sub-procedures/)

When you have finished the steps above, you can always execute the procedure by clicking on the relevant object.

Delete Blank Rows

(https://powerspreadsheets.com/vba-sub-procedures/)

Option Five: How to Execute A VBA Sub Procedure from another Procedure

Experts mention that most programmers use an existing procedure to execute a sub procedure. This process is called calling code since you are running a procedure to run an existing sub procedure point it is only when you call this procedure that the cold within the sub procedure is invoked. The calling code will always specify the correct irrelevant sub procedure and will transfer the control to that procedure. When the sub procedure has run the control will go back to the calling code or the main procedure.

Experts also say that there are many reasons why one should not call other procedures when running a sub procedure including the following:

This will help to reduce the size of the code and will also ensure that the code is crisp and clear for any other user to understand. It is also easier for you to debug, maintain or modify the code. Generally, it is a good idea to use this method to maintain several different procedures. You can use to create long procedures, but experts suggest that you avoid this. You should instead follow the suggestions of expert and create several small procedures, and write the main procedure to call all the small procedures. In the diagram below, you will see how it is easy to call upon several sub procedures using the main procedure. The main procedure is on the left side of the image while the sub procedures are on the right.

438

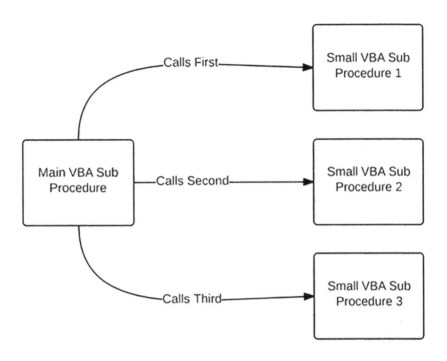

(https://powerspreadsheets.com/vba-sub-procedures/)

This will also help you avoid redundancies and repetition in the data. There are times when you will need to create a macro, which will carry out the same action in multiple places. In such cases, you can either create a sub procedure, which you will call in all those instances, or create a piece of code every time you need to call upon it. I am sure you know that it is easier and faster to use the same sub procedure across different applications of parts of the workbook.

If there are some procedures that you use often, you can store them in a module that you frequently used. When you do this you can import that sub procedure into every VBA project. When the module is imported you can call on the macros whenever required. The alternative to this is to copy and paste the code into a new VBA sub procedure point you will probably want to use the first option since it is easier and faster to implement in your work.

You can use any of the methods mentioned below to call A sub procedure from any other procedure or module letters look at these three methods in detail.

Method One: Use VBA Sub Procedure's Name

When you use this method, you will need to enter the following two things in the BBA cold where you are calling the sub procedure:

6. The name of the procedure that you will be calling in the sub procedure.

7. The argument that you will be using in the procedure will it be separated by commas.

In other words, the syntax that you will need to apply when I use this method is "Procedure_Name Arguments".

Latest assume that you will create a VBS the procedure, which will only call the Delete_Blank_Rows_3 macro.

The macro that we have written does not make sense because you can execute the Delete_Blank_Rows_3 macro directly. Since the structure is simple, we will use it as an example to see how the method works.

We have not developed a new sub procedure call calling Delete_Blank_Rows_3. This macro will only contain the following statements:

Sub Calling_Delete_Blank_Rows()

Delete_Blank_Rows_3

End Sub

The image below will show you have the BBA code will appear in the visual basic editor environment.

```
Sub Calling_Delete_Blank_Rows()

    '
    ' Calling_Delete_Blank_Rows Macro
    ' Calls the Delete_Blank_Rows_3 macro.
    '
    ' Keyboard Shortcut: Ctrl+Shift+C
    '

    Delete_Blank_Rows_3

End Sub
```

(https://powerspreadsheets.com/vba-sub-procedures/)

You can always as a statement to the sub procedure to make it more useful and realistic.

Method Two: Use Call Statement

If you want to apply this method, you should proceed in the same fashion as method 1. In this case, you will also enter the name and the arguments of the procedure, which you will be calling within the VBA sub procedure.

There are two main differences between the methods 1 and 2:

3. In this method, you will need to use the call statement. This keyword will always be written ahead of the procedure you want to call.

4. In this method, arguments will always be enclosed in the parentheses.

In other words, if you use the second method you will need to apply the syntax "Call Procedure_Name (Arguments)".

Latest now locate how this will look in practice. We will create a simple VB A sub procedure and the sole purpose of this procedure is to call the Delete_Blank_Rows_3 macro. Latest call this new macro Delete_Blank_Rows_2. The syntax for this matter is given below:

Sub Calling_Delete_Blank_Rows_2()

Call Delete_Blank_Rows_3

End Sub

The sub procedure will look as follows in the visual basic editor environment.

```
Sub Calling_Delete_Blank_Rows_2()

    '
    ' Calling_Delete_Blank_Rows_2 Macro
    ' Calls the Delete_Blank_Rows_3 macro.
    '
    ' Keyboard Shortcut: Ctrl+Shift+D
    '

    Call Delete_Blank_Rows_3

End Sub
```

(https://powerspreadsheets.com/vba-sub-procedures/)

You may wonder why you would need to use a method where you should use the call keyword when you can use the previous method, which does not require the use of any keyword. One of the main reasons for using this method is that it provides clarity. Experts say that some programmers used the call keyword although it is optional to ensure that another procedure is being called whenever necessary.

Describe the above reasons expert suggest that you do not use the call keyword when running a sub procedure. According to the information found at the Microsoft development center, call statement is often used when a sub procedure does not begin with a specific identifier.

Method Three: Use The Application.Run Method

You should use the application.run method to execute the VBA sub procedure.

Experts suggest that you use this method if you want to call A sub procedure which has a name assigned to another variable. When you use the application.run method you can run the block of code in the sub procedure because you are passing the variable as an argument in the run method.

An example of this can be found in the book titled Excel 2013 power programming with VBA.

How to Call A VBA Sub Procedure from a Different Module

If you want to refer to A VBA sub procedure from other procedures, you will need to follow the process given below:

The search will first be carried out in the same module. If you do not find the VBA sub procedure in a module, you should look at the accessible procedures in different modules in the same workbook. If you want to call a procedure, which is private, both the procedures should be within the same module.

There will be cases where you have different procedures with the same name but in different modules. When you try to call one of the sub procedures by stating its name you will see that an error message is displayed.

This does not mean that you can always ask Excel to execute a procedure, which you want. To be more precise, you call a procedure, which is in a different module you have to clarify the following:

4. You should always state the name of the relevant module before you name the procedure.

5. You should always use a dot to separate the name of the sub procedure from the module.

You must use the following syntax in these cases: "Module_Name.Procedure_Name".

Now that you know how you should handle the cases where you have to call A sub procedure in a different module, you can choose to run the module in a different Excel workbook. Therefore we should now take a look at how to call a VBA sub procedure that is present in a different workbook.

How to Call A VBA Sub Procedure from a Different Excel Workbook

Experts say that there are two different ways in which excel will execute or run a sub procedure, which is stored in a different Excel workbook.

Build or establish a reference to different workbooks.

Specify the name of the workbook you explicitly want to refer to when you run the method.

Let us now look at how you can use either method for this purpose:

Method One: Establish A Reference To Another Excel Workbook.

You can create a reference to an Excel workbook using the following steps:

Step One: Open The References Dialog.

You should now go to the tools menu in the visual basic editor and select references.

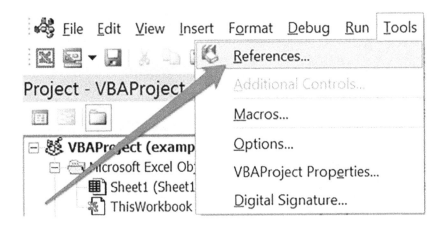

(https://powerspreadsheets.com/vba-sub-procedures/)

Step Two: Select The Excel Workbook To Add As Reference.

When you have completed the first step, Excel will display the reference dialog box.

This dialog box and provide all the references that you can use. The workbooks that are currently open are listed in that box. For example, look at the image below to see which Excel workbooks appear on the list.

In this case, every Excel workbook is not listed using its regular name. Instead, they will appear under the visual basic editor as their project names. Since every project name is VBAProject by default, the situation below is not very uncommon.

If you want to identify which VBA project you want to use as a reference, you can use the location data, which appears, at the bottom of the dialog box. Alternatively, you can always go back to the visual basic editor and change the name of the relevant project. If you want to add in Excel workbook, which is currently open, you should double click the name and select it. Then click on the ok button.

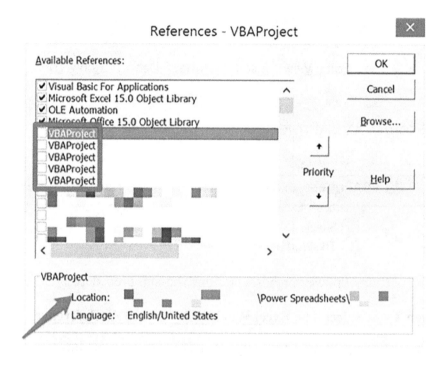

(https://powerspreadsheets.com/vba-sub-procedures/)

The references dialogue box only lists the Excel workbooks, which are open currently. You can also create a list of the references to workbooks, which are not currently open. To do this you will first need to click on the browse button on the right side in the references dialog box.

You see that the add reference dialog box is displayed. This box looks like every other dialogue box that you have used before. You should use the add reference dialog box to move to the folder where you have the relevant Excel workbook, selected workbook and then open it.

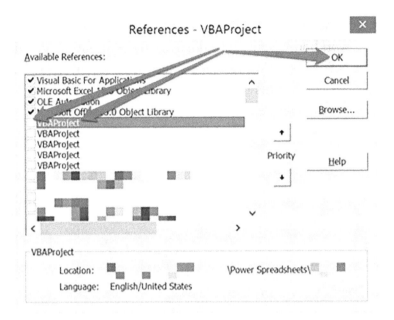

(https://powerspreadsheets.com/vba-sub-procedures/)

In this example below, we will add one sample Excel workbook for the purpose of this section.

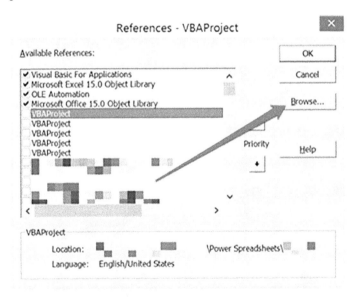

(https://powerspreadsheets.com/vba-sub-procedures/)

When you have completed the above step you will see that the relevant workbook is now I added to the bottom of the list of available references. You can then select the relevant reference and click ok. The references dialogue box will allow you to use this as the reference.

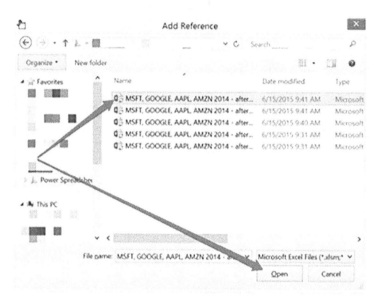

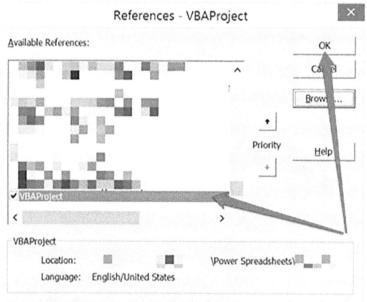

(https://powerspreadsheets.com/vba-sub-procedures/)

You are officially done. When you carry the steps mentioned above, the new reference that you have included will be listed in the project window in the visual basic editor. You can find this information in the references node. You can now prefer a call any procedures in a reference workbook as a divided the same workbook where you have written the sub procedure. This can be done by using a call keyword or the sub procedure's name.

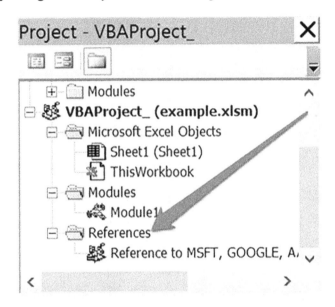

(https://powerspreadsheets.com/vba-sub-procedures/)

In the book titled Excel 2013 power programming with VB a, the author says that you should use the following syntax if you want to identify a procedure within another Excel workbook:

Project_Name.Module_Name.Procedure_Name

In simple words, experts suggest that you should first specify the name of your project, the name of the module and then the name of the actual sub procedure you want to use.

You will notice that when you open an Excel workbook, it will reference another workbook, which will be open automatically. Additional e you cannot close the referenced workbook without closing the originally opened workbook. If you try to do this excel will send you a warning message that this workbook is being referenced by another workbook and therefore cannot be closed.

(https://powerspreadsheets.com/vba-sub-procedures/)

Method Two: Use The Application.Run Method.

You can use the application.run method to execute any VBA sub procedure. If you want to use this method, you do not have to create a reference as explained in the previous section. You must, however, have the Excel workbook, which contains a sub procedure open. To see an example of how you can use this method, please refer to the book titled 'Excel 2013 Power Programming with VBA'.

Option Six: How to Execute A VBA Sub Procedure Using the Ribbon

If you want to include a button to the ribbon which points to a relevant sub procedure, you should follow the steps below. You can execute the macro by clicking on the button in the Ribbon.

In this section, we will look at how you can add a button to the ribbon, and what you should do to run the macro or the block of code within that sub procedure. We will continue to use the Delete_Blank_Rows_3 macro for our example. This is the most appropriate method that one can use for a macro that is present in the personal workbook.

450

The personal workbook is where you will store the relevant macros that you can use in an Excel workbook. In simple words, the macros that are stored in the personal workbook can be called upon or used regardless of which excel workbook you are working on. Let us look at five simple steps that you will need to follow to add the button to the Ribbon.

Step One: Access The Excel Options Dialog.

Right click on the ribbon and choose the option "Customize the Ribbon" to display the context menu.

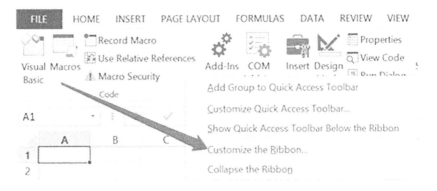

(https://powerspreadsheets.com/vba-sub-procedures/)

Step Two: Choose To Work With Macros.

In the Excel Options dialog box, you can choose the commands you want to include to the ribbon from the drop-down menu in the customize ribbon tab.

(https://powerspreadsheets.com/vba-sub-procedures/)

You can browse through different commands before you add them to the Ribbon. All you need to do is click the command, and then select "Macros."

(https://powerspreadsheets.com/vba-sub-procedures/)

When you have done this, you will see a list of all the macros that you can include in the Ribbon. This list will be found in the Choose commands list, and will appear below the choose commands drop down menu. Please see the image below for a better understanding.

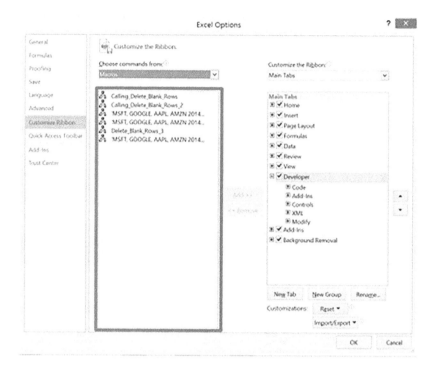

(https://powerspreadsheets.com/vba-sub-procedures/)

Step Three: Select The Tab And Group Of Commands To Which You Want To Add The Macro.

You can find the Customize the Ribbon list on the right side in the Excel Options dialog box. This is where you will find the list of all the commands that can be found in the Ribbon. You will notice that these commands are organized by groups of commands and tabs.

The image below will show you how there are five groups of commands, namely Add-Ins, Code, XML, Modify and Controls in the Developer Tab. You can choose where to add the macro button to the ribbon in the "Customize the Ribbon" List. You can also expand or contract a tab in Excel or any group of commands using the plus and minus signs that appear in the list on the left side. You can now include new command groups or tabs to the Excel workbook using the buttons in the Customize Ribbon list dialog box.

(https://powerspreadsheets.com/vba-sub-procedures/)

You can now choose to create a new command group or choose an existing command group when you want to add a macro to the Ribbon. In the section below, we will talk about how you can add a new group of commands and tab to the ribbon.

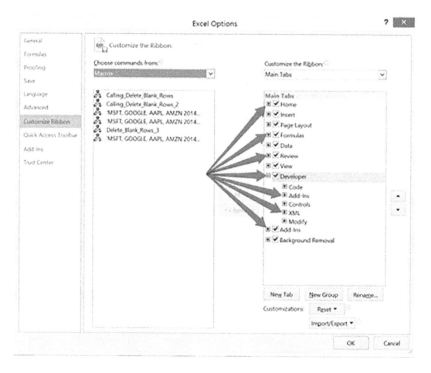

(https://powerspreadsheets.com/vba-sub-procedures/)

In the example below, we will add a new tab immediately after the Developer tab in Excel. To do this, you should go to the "Developer" Tab and click the "New Tab" button.

You can choose to rename the newly included tab by clicking the Rename button. Excel will now display the Rename dialog box. You should enter the name of the collection and click OK. You must repeat this process for the command group. You should first select the "New Group (Custom)" option and then rename the button.

(https://powerspreadsheets.com/vba-sub-procedures/)

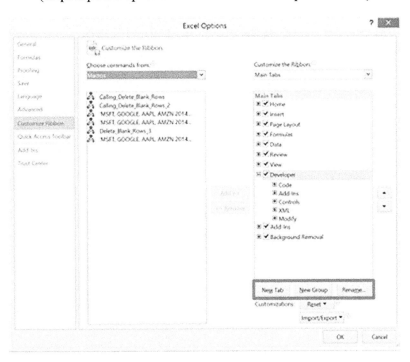

(https://powerspreadsheets.com/vba-sub-procedures/)

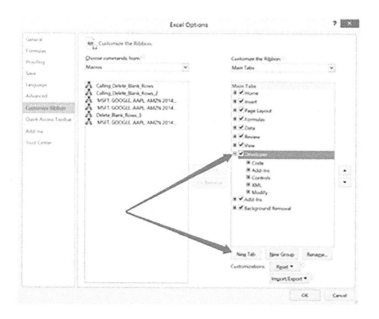

(https://powerspreadsheets.com/vba-sub-procedures/)

Excel will display a different rename box, which will allow you to choose the name or a symbol that will represent the group of command.

(https://powerspreadsheets.com/vba-sub-procedures/)

You can choose an icon if you want. In this example, we will choose an icon and then enter the name for the command group. Click OK once you are sure of the changes.

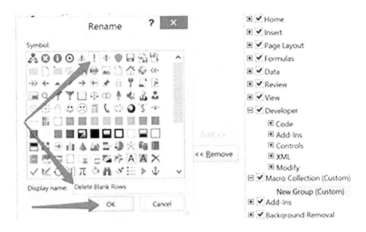

(https://powerspreadsheets.com/vba-sub-procedures/)

When all the steps are in order, you should choose the group of commands that you wish to include in the macro. In the example below, the Delete Blank Rows group is the command group that has just been created.

(https://powerspreadsheets.com/vba-sub-procedures/)
459

Step Four: Add VBA Sub Procedure To The Ribbon.

When you want to add a macro button to the ribbon, you should select the relevant macro from choose commands list and hit the Add button, which is present in the center of the dialog box. The image below will show you how you can add the Delete_Blank_Rows_3 macro to the ribbon.

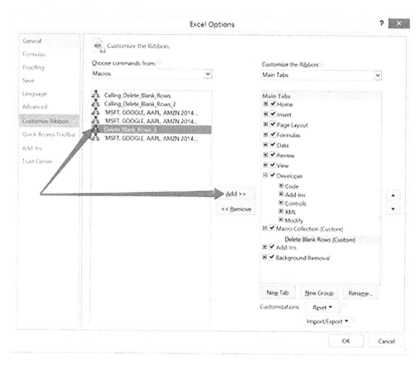

(https://powerspreadsheets.com/vba-sub-procedures/)

Step Five: Finish The Process.

To complete the process, you should click OK which is found at the bottom right corner of the dialog box.

(https://powerspreadsheets.com/vba-sub-procedures/)

Excel will now close the Excel Options dialog box and make the necessary changes. You will notice that in the case of this example, there is already a new tab, called Macro Collections that has been included. You will also see that a group of commands and a button have been included to the ribbon.

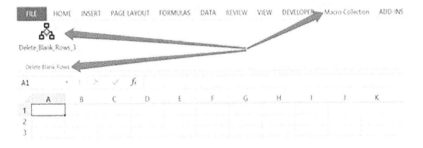

(https://powerspreadsheets.com/vba-sub-procedures/)

When you complete this process, you can execute the macro or the sub procedure by simply clicking on the correct button in the Ribbon. Excel will enable this icon even if the workbook that has the macro in it is closed. If the relevant workbook is closed, Excel will open that workbook with the macro in it, before it executes the code.

Option Seven: How to Execute A VBA Sub Procedure Using the Quick Access Toolbar

You can find the Quick Access Toolbar on the upper left corner in your Excel workbook.

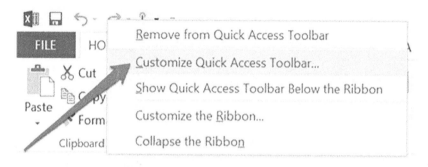

(https://powerspreadsheets.com/vba-sub-procedures/)

Just like we did with Ribbon, you can make some changes to the Quick Access Toolbar to include a button that is assigned to the sub procedure. This means that you can execute the code in the procedure by simply clicking that button.

You should use this method only when the macro you are including to the quick access toolbar is found in your personal workbook. It is the same as the method of using the ribbon to execute the sub procedure. You should also remember that if you include the macro to the Quick Access toolbar, you can also ensure that this button only appears in the Excel workbook that has the macro written in it.

We will look at how you can use the quick access toolbar and how you can customize it for this purpose. Let us first look at how you can add a macro button to the toolbar in five simple steps.

Step One: Access the Excel Options Dialog

In the previous sections, you have learned how you can access the Options dialog box, and this section provides some additional information that you can use. For this specific example, it is always a good idea to access the Quick Access Toolbar tab using the Excel Options dialog box. All you need to do is right-click on the Quick Access toolbar and select the option to "Customize Quick Access Toolbar." When you complete this step, you will see the Options Dialog box open in front of you.

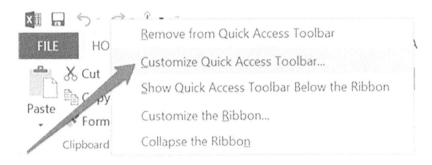

(https://powerspreadsheets.com/vba-sub-procedures/)

Step Two: Choose For Which Excel Workbooks The Customized Quick Access Toolbar Applies.

You will see a drop-down menu in the top right corner of the excel options dialog box. This drop-down menu is for the Quick Access toolbar. You should navigate to the section where you can make some changes to which workbooks should reflect the change you make. Choose your preferred option from the drop-down menu in the Customize Quick Access dialog box.

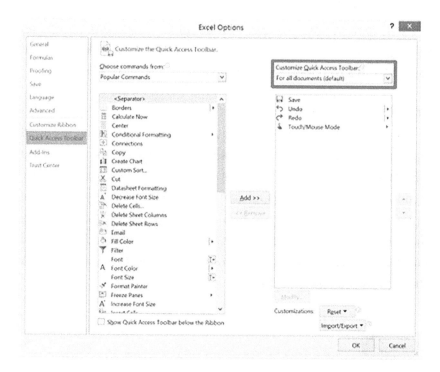

(https://powerspreadsheets.com/vba-sub-procedures/)

If you want this button to appear in every Excel workbook, you should choose the option "For all documents (default). This is the default setting that will be applied to every workbook.

If you want the button to appear only in one workbook, you should choose the name of the workbook. The image below shows a section of the options that you can find in the drop-down menu in the Customize Quick Access Toolbar section.

(https://powerspreadsheets.com/vba-sub-procedures/)

In this example, we only have the workbook named "Book 1" open on the system. In this example, we will use the default option. This customization will apply to ever workbook that you open.

(https://powerspreadsheets.com/vba-sub-procedures/)

Step Three: Choose To Work With Macros.

In the Excel Options dialog box, you should navigate to the top left corner in the Quick Access toolbar. Here, you will find the choose commands option in the drop-down menu. Select "Macros" from the drop-down list.

Step Four: Add Macro To Quick Access Toolbar.

Once you complete the step above, you will see a list of all the macros in your Excel workbook in the options dialog box. These are the macros that you can include to the Quick Access Toolbar. These macros will be in the choose Commands list on the left side of the Quick Acess toolbar tab in the dialog box.

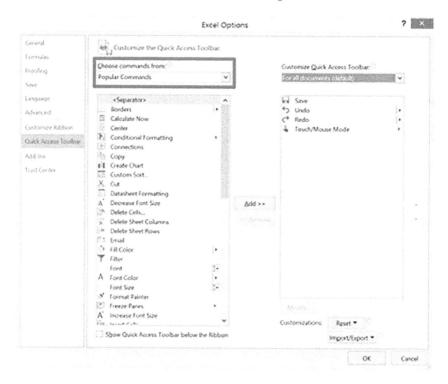

(https://powerspreadsheets.com/vba-sub-procedures/)

You should now choose the macro that you want to include from the Choose Commands option in the list box. Click on Add button, which will appear in the center of the Options dialog box. The

466

image below will show you how you should include the Delete_Blank_Rows_3 macro.

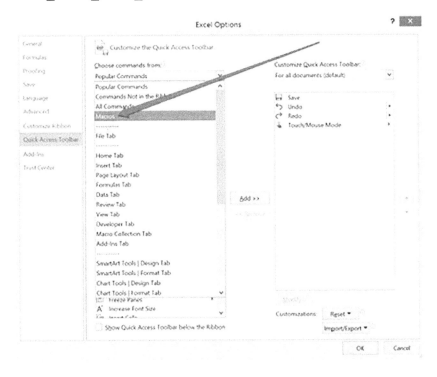

(https://powerspreadsheets.com/vba-sub-procedures/)

Step Five: Click The OK Button.

Once you run the first four steps, you will see the macro button in the Quick Access Toolbar. You will see that this button is found in the Customize Quick Access Toolbar list. This list is found on the right side of the options dialog box. You should now press the OK button at the bottom right corner of the options dialog box to complete the process. This will implement the necessary changes.

(https://powerspreadsheets.com/vba-sub-procedures/)

(https://powerspreadsheets.com/vba-sub-procedures/)

When you move back to Excel, you will see that the necessary macro button has been included in the Quick Access Toolbar. To run or execute the sub procedure, you can click on the button that you added to the Quick Access toolbar.

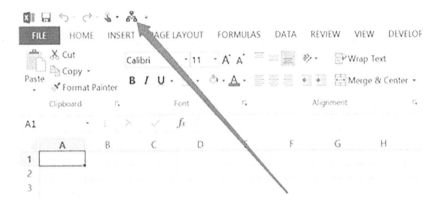

(https://powerspreadsheets.com/vba-sub-procedures/)

Option Eight: How to Execute A VBA Sub Procedure When a Particular Event Occurs

You can run a specific VBA Sub procedure in Excel even when an event occurs. Excel will check with you if the sub procedure should run, and you can either choose to ignore the procedure or ignore the event. In the book titled, 'Excel 2013 Power Programming With VBA,' the author talks about several events where you may come across this issue:

1. Entering information in a worksheet

2. Opening a workbook

3. Clicking a command button

4. Saving a file

A VBA Sub procedure that is executed even when an event occurs is called an event handler procedure. This type of procedure has

469

two characteristics that separate it from the other Sub procedures in VBA.

The name of this sub procedure will always have a different structure. Their name will need to stick to the following syntax – "object_EventName." The names of such procedures will have three elements:

1. Objects

2. Underscore

3. Name of the event

The module for the object in the name is the VBA module in which this sub procedure is written or stored. It is important to learn more about event handler procedures, and this is an extensive topic to cover. To learn more about this topic, you should refer to chapter seventeen in the book titled 'Excel 2013 Power Programming With VBA.'

Option Nine: Executing the VBA Sub Procedure Using the Immediate Window

It is a good idea to execute a sub procedure in VBA using the immediate window in the environment. It is always a good idea to do this if you are building an application in the visual basic environment. The Immediate Window can be found at the bottom section of the Visual Basic Editor.

*If you're finding the information valuable so far, please be sure to leave **5-star feedback on Amazon***

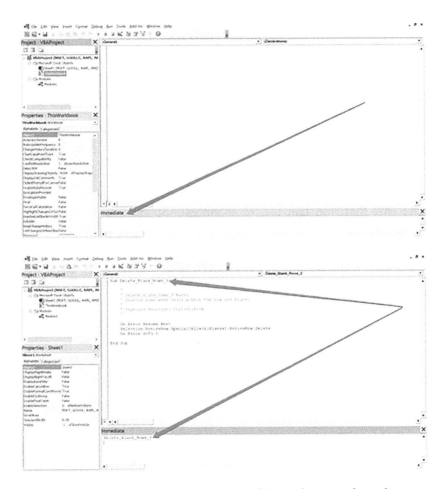

(https://powerspreadsheets.com/vba-sub-procedures/)

To learn more about the Immediate Window, please read the first few books of the series. You can also learn more about the IDE in VBA in those books. If you want to run a sub procedure in VBA in the Immediate Window, you should type the name of that procedure in the window and click Enter. To conclude, the concept of procedures and sub procedures is used frequently in most blogs and books that cover VBA and macros. It is important for you to understand what these terms mean if you want to become an expert in VBA.

471

Conclusion

Thank you for purchasing the book. If you want to master VBA, there are some concepts that you should know well. You should also have some tricks and tips up your sleeve to help you overcome any problems you may have with VBA. This book will help you master some of the concepts, and also leave you with some tips that you can use to troubleshoot and handle any errors and exceptions.

I hope the information in the book will help you improve your VBA programming skills.

P.S. If you don't mind, please drop a short review of my title on Amazon and feel free to tell me what you think! Thanks a lot!

Will You Help Me?

Hi there, avid reader! If you have extra time on your hands, I would really, really appreciate it if you could take a moment to click my author profile in Amazon. In there, you will find all the titles I authored and who knows, you might find more interesting topics to read and learn!

If it's not too much to ask, you can also leave and write a review for all the titles that you have read – whether it's a positive or negative review. An honest and constructive review of my titles is always welcome and appreciated since it will only help me moving forward in creating these books. There will always be room to add or improve, or sometimes even subtract certain topics, that is why these reviews are always important for us. They will also assist other avid readers, professionals who are looking to sharpen their knowledge, or even newbies to any topic, in their search for the book that caters to their needs the most.

If you don't want to leave a review yourself, you can also vote on the existing reviews by voting Helpful (Thumbs Up) or Unhelpful (Thumbs Down), especially on the top 10 or so reviews.

If you want to go directly to the vote or review process, please visit my author file page in Amazon for my below titles:

> Machine Learning For Beginners : A Comprehensive, Step-by-Step Guide to Learning and Understanding Machine Learning Concepts, Technology and Principles for Beginners . Audiobook format is also available at www.audible.com

> Machine Learning : A Comprehensive, Step-by-Step Guide to Intermediate Concepts and Techniques in Machine Learning

Machine Learning : A Comprehensive, Step-by-Step Guide to Learning and Applying Advanced Concepts and Techniques in Machine Learning

Excel VBA : A Step-By-Step Tutorial For Beginners To Learn Excel VBA Programming From Scratch . Audiobook format is also available at www.audible.com

Excel VBA : Intermediate Lessons in Excel VBA Programming for Professional Advancement . Audiobook format is also available at www.audible.com

Excel VBA: A Step-By-Step Comprehensive Guide on Advanced Excel VBA Programming Techniques and Strategies

Again, I truly appreciate the time and effort that you will be putting in leaving a review for my titles or even just for voting. This will only inspire me to create more quality content and titles in the future.

Thank you and have a great day!

Peter Bradley

Sources

https://www.dummies.com/software/microsoft-office/excel/10-resources-for-excel-vba-help/

https://techcommunity.microsoft.com/t5/Excel/9-quick-tips-to-improve-your-VBA-macro-performance/td-p/173687

http://what-when-how.com/excel-vba/ten-vba-tips-and-tricks/

https://www.tutorialspoint.com/vba/vba_sub_procedure.htm

https://powerspreadsheets.com/vba-sub-procedures/

https://docs.microsoft.com/en-us/office/vba/language/concepts/getting-started/calling-sub-and-function-procedures

https://www.excelfunctions.net/vba-functions-and-subroutines.html

https://powerspreadsheets.com/vba-sub-procedures/

Machine Learning

A Comprehensive, Step-by-Step Guide to Learning and Understanding Machine Learning Concepts, Technology and Principles for Beginners

Introduction

I want to thank you for choosing this book '*Machine learning - A Comprehensive, Step-by-Step Guide to Learning and Understanding Machine Learning Concepts, Technology and Principles for Beginners.*'

Machines are used in most households and their capabilities have evolved beyond performing manual tasks. There are some countries that use machines in their armies and some companies are using machines to perform some menial tasks. Now, machines can also work on tasks that require some cognition. Human beings were the only ones who had the ability to perform these tasks in the past. Predicting the outcome of tournaments, playing chess, driving cars, diagnosing diseases are some examples of the complex tasks that machines can perform.

However, the remarkable capabilities of machines have instilled fear in some people. They are wary of how powerful machines are and how they can change the world. For example, if you have watched Doctor Who, there are some robots, called Daleks, who wanted to take over the Earth because they were smarter than human beings. Skeptics fear that they may lose their jobs and some fear that the world may be taken over by robots and machines because they are smarter than human beings. The former is a valid fear since there is a possibility that machines can perform your job better than you. The BBC conducted the "Will robots take over my job?" survey and concluded that jobs like taxi drivers, actuaries, accountants, bar workers and receptionists will be automated soon.

The latter fear is not valid since it is difficult to teach a machine. Learning is a process that includes many smaller processes. In this book, we will look at the different ways a machine can learn. You

479

will notice that the processes used to teach machines are similar to how human beings learn.

Research on automation must be read with a slight level of skepticism since the future of machines and artificial intelligence is unknown. Technology is moving fast, but its adoption is an unchartered path with unforeseen challenges. Machine learning is not simple since it does not only involve turning switches on and off. Machine learning is also not an out–of–the–box solution. Machines operate in parallel to the statistical algorithms, which machine learning engineers and data scientists often oversee. Industry experts believe that there could be a time when there will be an inadequate supply of people to operate machines.

Your path to becoming an expert in machine learning probably starts from here. But, you can also satisfy your thirst for knowledge with a base understanding of what machine learning is for now. You do not need to make hasty decisions. Let us proceed with the assumption that you want to train to become a machine learning engineer or data scientist. This book will help you achieve either goal.

If you are a beginner, this book will act as a guide. It covers all the information needed to understand machine learning better. In the first few chapters of the book, you will gather information on what machine learning is and types of machine learning. It also covers information on different algorithms that engineers developed to improve machine learning. Experts recommend that you practice and build projects to understand machine learning better. This book leaves you with some projects and ideas that you can use to enhance your learning.

Thank you for purchasing the book. I hope you gather all the information you are looking for.

Chapter One

What is Machine Learning?

Machines with artificial intelligence often learn processes and identify problems and solutions through machine learning. Some uses of such machines are data analysis, recognition, predictions, projections and diagnosis. They learn from training data, a sample dataset that resembles the complete population, to identify different patterns within the data and use those patterns to find a solution to a variety of problems. There are different learning mechanisms used to help a machine learn, of which supervised learning, unsupervised learning and reinforcement learning are the most common. We will cover these concepts in the following chapters.

In simpler words, a change made to the structure of the machine to enhance the performance of the machine is a type of machine learning. It is important to remember that not every change made to a machine helps the machine learn. For example, if a machine must predict which team will win the Barclays Premier League, the programmer will train the machine with historical information about the team's performance and the players' performances. Using this information, the machine can identify the patterns and correlations within the dataset. It can then use those patterns and predict which team will win the Barclay's Premier League.

Skeptics often wonder why machines must learn since they are wary of what these machines are capable of. Facebook had used machine learning and artificial intelligence to develop a machine trained with a specific vocabulary dataset. However, this machine began to develop its own language using the alphabet in the dataset. If multiple machines learned that language they can communicate with each other thereby making it difficult for us to understand what they are saying. Regardless of what the outcome was, Facebook and Google are trying to help machines learn through training datasets.

There are many reasons why machine learning is important. Psychologists are using some concepts of machine learning to help them understand human learning better. Machine learning also helps to improve the accuracy and efficiency of machines. It also helps to reduce the volume of code that a programmer writes to help the machine learn. There are times when a programmer may forget a small part of the code, which can lead to constant errors. It takes time for the programmer to identify this error in the lengthy code. Machine learning reduces the volume of code that a programmer writes thereby reducing the effects of human error.

Subjects involved in machine learning

Machine learning uses concepts from different subjects. The subjects mentioned in this section are not an exhaustive list since the field of machine learning is developing as you read this book. However, the concepts in the subjects mentioned below, especially those in statistics, are the foundation of machine learning.

Statistics

The concepts in statistics like regression, clustering, data analysis and hypothesis testing are the foundation of machine learning. Most machine learning algorithms use these concepts to train the machine. Training is a common problem in both statistics and machine learning. Training is the process where different sample datasets help the machine draw information about the population. The machine stores the information and uses it to predict or project futuristic values. The machine can also identify a problem and a solution to that problem using the training dataset. Another problem that is common to both statistics and machine learning is the identification of the values of a function at a given point. Solutions to such problems are instances of machine learning since problems that involve the estimation of future events often use data about past events.

Brain modeling

A concept of brain modeling called neural networks is closely related to machine learning. Scientists believe that one can replicate the model of the neurons in the human brain and build a non-linear neural network. The layers in this network have nodes and the engineer can assign weights to those nodes to calculate the output. Psychologists and scientists are now using neural networks to understand human learning better. Sub-symbolic processing, connectionism and brain style computations are a few spheres that they are exploring to understand human and machine learning better.

Adaptive control theory

Control theory studies how systems control their efficiency by adapting to a change in the system. A problem that most systems face is the change in the environment. A system uses different methods to adapt to the changes in the environment and continue to perform effectively. The idea is to make the system capable enough to anticipate any changes in the environment and adapt to maintain the efficiency and accuracy of the machine.

Evolutionary models

Evolutionary studies conclude that human beings and animals both learn to not only adapt to a change in their environment but also learn to perform better. The concepts of learning and evolution can are the same for machine learning and human learning. The methods that psychologists use to understand human learning help scientists improve how a machine learns.

483

Varieties of Machine Learning

So far, this book has introduced machine learning and has answered the question about the subjects that constitute it. Now, we come to the more important question of what can be learned about machine learning. The following are a few topics on which knowledge can be gained through the study of machine learning:

- Programs and logic rule sets

- Terminology and grammars

- Finite state machines

- Problem - solving systems

- Functions

- Artificial Intelligence

- Statistics

Out of the above, the two most focused on topics are those of statistics and artificial intelligence. These two subjects are used extensively in machine learning. We now move on to chapters that describe the two broad categories of machine learning techniques: supervised machine learning and unsupervised machine learning.

Uses of Machine Learning

Most organizations and enterprises use machines to complete manual tasks that were once impossible to complete in a short time, especially if large volumes of data were used. Over the last few decades, the volume of data available has rapidly increased making it impossible for human beings to analyze that data. This increase in data paved the way for automated processes and machines to work on tasks that are difficult for human beings to complete.

One can derive useful information from data analysis and this information can help us drive our businesses and lives. We have set foot in the world of Business Analytics, Big Data, Data Science and Artificial Intelligence. Predictive analytics and Business Intelligence are no longer just for the elite but also for small companies and businesses. This has given these small businesses a chance to participate in the process of collecting and utilizing information effectively.

Let us now look at some technical uses of machine learning and see how these uses can be applied to real-world problems.

Data replication

Machine learning allows the model or the algorithm to develop data that looks like the training dataset. For example, if you run the manuscript of a book through a machine, the machine identifies the density of the words in every page of the manuscript. The output is text that is similar to the information in the manuscript.

Clustering variables

Machines use the clustering algorithm, covered in a later chapter, to group variables that may be related to one another. This tool is useful when you are unaware of the how a change in the variables affects the machine. You can also gather information on how a change in one variable affects the other variables in the group. When the dataset is large, the machine can look for latent variables and use them to understand the obtained data.

Reduction of Dimensionality

Data always has variables and dimensions. It is difficult for human beings to analyze data that has more than three dimensions. Machine learning helps to reduce the dimensions of the data by clustering similar variables together. This process helps a human being understand and identify relationships within and between the variable clusters.

Visualization

There are times when the user may want to visualize the relationship that exists between variables or obtain the summary of the data in a visual form. Machine learning assists in both these processes by summarizing the data for the user using specified or non – specified parameters.

Chapter Two

Facts about Machine Learning

Machine learning is permeating numerous aspects of our everyday lives, right from optimizing Netflix recommendations to Google searches. Machine learning has contributed to improving different facets of building mechanics in smart building space and the experiences of the occupant. You do not have to have a Ph.D. to understand the different facets and functions of machine learning. This section covers some facts about machine learning that are very basic and important to know.

Bifurcation of Machine Learning

Supervised and unsupervised machine learning are two techniques that programmers and scientists use to help machines learn. Smart buildings incorporate both types. Here is a simple example of how these types of machine learning look like: Let us assume that you want to teach a computer to recognize an ant. When you use a supervised approach, you will tell the computer that an ant is an insect that could either be small or big. You will also need to tell the computer that the ant could either be red or black. When you use an unsupervised approach, you will need to show the computer different animal groups and then tell the computer what an ant looks like and then show the computer another set of pictures and ask the computer to identify the ant until the computer learns the features specific to an ant.

Smart building spaces use both supervised and unsupervised machine learning techniques. The applications in these smart buildings allow the users to provide feedback to the building to improve the efficiency of the building.

Machines are not fully automatic

Machine learning helps computers automate, anticipate and evolve but that does not mean that they can take over the world. Machine learning uses algorithms that human beings develop. Therefore, machine learning still needs human beings since they will need to set parameters and train the machine with different training datasets.

Machine learning helps a computer discover patterns that are not possible for human beings to see. The computer will then make an adjustment to the system. However, it is not good to identify and understand why those patterns exist. For instance, smart buildings human beings created smart buildings to ensure that the people inside the building help to improve the living conditions of the people. However, one cannot expect that a machine will learn to become more productive. A human must set up the definitions and rules that the building will need to follow.

It is important to note that the data cannot always explain why any anomalies or outliers occur. Consider a scenario where the people in the building constantly request that the temperature of the building must reduce by 20 degrees when compared to the external environment. The machine-learning algorithm will take this request into account and notify the operator about the request. Therefore, it is important for skilled people to operate machines to ensure that the conclusions obtained are accurate.

Anyone can use machine learning

Writing a machine-learning algorithm is very different from learning how to use that algorithm. After all, you do not need to learn how to program when you use an app on your phone. The best platforms always create an abstract of the program to present the users with an interface, which need minimal training to use. If you do know the basic concepts of machine learning, you are ready to go! Data scientists must edit or change the algorithms.

Machine learning has come of this age and is growing quickly. Buildings are using machine learning in different ways to make the existing infrastructure efficient and help to enhance the experience of the occupants residing in the building. Right from an energy usage standpoint, buildings are always learning and analyzing the needs of the occupants.

How does this affect us going forward? This advance in machine learning goes to say that most things will happen without the need for us to ask. Machine learning engineering could go beyond managing lighting and temperature. Machine learning implies that there will be some future state of multiple layers and levels of automation adjusting based on the current activity.

Data Transformation is where the work lies

When you read through the different techniques of machine learning, you will probably assume that machine learning is mostly about selecting the right algorithm and tuning that algorithm to function accurately. The reality is prosaic – a large chunk of your time goes into cleansing the data and then transforming that data into raw features that will define the relationship between your data.

Revolution of Machine Learning has begun

During the 1980s there was a rapid development and advancement in computing power and computers. This gave rise to enormous amount of fear and excitement around artificial intelligence, computers and machine learning which could help the world solves a variety of ailments – right from household drudgery to diseases. As artificial intelligence and machine learning developed as formal fields of study, turning these ideas and hopes into reality was more difficult to achieve and artificial intelligence retreated into the world of theory and fantasy. However, in the last decade, the advances in data storage and computing have changed the game again. Machines are now able to work on tasks that once were difficult for them to learn.

Machine Learning and Artificial Intelligence are interrelated

Machine learning is a subset of artificial intelligence that drives the process of data mining. What is the difference between these terms? Experts spend hours debating on where they must draw the line between machine learning and artificial intelligence.

Artificial intelligence allows machines to think like human beings. At any given minute, human beings can capture thousands of data points using the five different senses. The brain can recall memories from the past, draw conclusions based on causes and effects and make decisions. Human beings learn to recognize patterns, but every being has a limit.

One can think of machine learning as a continuous and automated version of data mining. Machines use data mining to detect certain patterns in data sets that human beings will not be able to find. Machine learning is a process that can reduce the size of the data to detect and extrapolate patterns that will allow us to apply that information to identify new actions and solutions.

In smart building spaces, machine learning enables any building to run efficiently while also responding to occupants' changing needs. For instance, you can look at how a machine learning application can do more when compared to how a smart building may handle a recurring board meeting. However, any machine-learning algorithm can make sense of more than a thousand variables at any given time of the year to create an ideal thermal environment during the business meeting.

Chapter Three

Types of Machine Learning

Unsupervised and Reinforcement Machine Learning

Reinforcement learning is a technique that allows the machine to interact with the ambient environment through actions. The machine receives a reward if the environment reacts positively to the action. However, the machine will receive punishment if it receives a negative response. The machine learns from these responses and improves its performance to maximize a positive response from the environment. If you pay close attention to the description, you will relate reinforcement learning to human learning. For example, you feed a baby when she cries. The baby is aware that she can get food if she cries. She also knows that she can gather attention from people around her if she reacts positively.

Reinforcement learning is a technique that is related to decision theory in statistics and management sciences and control theory in engineering. The problems studied in these subjects are like the subjects that one studies in under machine learning. However, the subjects focus on different parts of the problem.

Unsupervised machine learning is another technique that uses some concepts from both reinforcement learning and game theory. However, in unsupervised machine learning, the environment is dynamic and can include many machines. These machines produce actions and receive rewards and the objective of every machine is to maximize the rewards. They must also assess how the other machines work. The application of game theory to such a situation with multiple, dynamic systems is a popular area of research.

Unlike reinforcement learning, a machine receives a training dataset if the engineer uses unsupervised machine learning to train the machine. However, the dataset does not contain information about the required output. This begs the question - how can the machine possibly learn anything without receiving any feedback from the environment or having information about target outputs? The idea is to allow the machine to develop input vectors that the machine can use to predict the output for different types of input datasets. Dimensionality reduction and clustering both use unsupervised machine learning techniques. The technique of unsupervised learning is closely related to the fields of information theory and statistics.

Supervised Machine Learning

Supervised machine learning uses training datasets to help machines learn. These datasets contain various examples that consist of the input and the desired output, commonly known as supervisory signals. Machines use supervisory learning algorithms that help to generate inferred functions that forecast or predict events. These functions are called classifiers if the output is discrete and regression functions if the outputs are continuous. The supervisory algorithm must conceive a generalized method that helps the machine reach the desired output. Human beings and animals learn in a similar way through concepts. For example, if you are in a trigonometry class, you will learn a set of functions that you should use to solve specific problems. Let us look at how the supervised machine algorithm works.

Step 1

The engineer must determine what types of example should be a part of the training dataset. The engineer must be careful with the training dataset since the machine learns from the examples in the set. He must ensure that the examples have the right input and output. For example, if the machine must learn to recognize speech, the engineer must provide examples of words, sentences, paragraphs or phonemes. If the engineer provides the machine with numbers or images, the machine is not going to produce the desired output.

Step 2

The engineer must collect the data and clean it before she uses it as the training dataset. The dataset must represent all the possible outcomes and functions that the machine can develop for some input. The engineer must ensure that she maps the input examples with their correct outputs.

Step 3

The engineer must now decide how the input examples she should provide to the machine. This is an important step since the accuracy of the machine is solely dependent on the representation of the input. Vectors represent the data and this vector contains information about the attributes and characteristics of the data. For example, if one of the inputs contains information on the products available at the store, the input vector can contain the following

- Product Name

- Brand

- Product Type

- Manufacturer

- Distributor and so on.

However, the machine must learn to only include some attributes to avoid a long training period. Many features may also lead to failure since the machine cannot identify or predict the output.

Step 4

The engineer must decide on the structure of the function that the machine should develop or use. She must also identify the algorithm that the machine should use to obtain the desired output. Common algorithms used are regression, clustering and decision trees.

Step 5

The engineer must then complete the design. She should run the algorithm on the dataset. There are some control parameters that the engineer must enter to ensure that the algorithm works well. Cross-validation methods help to estimate the parameters. If the dataset is large, it is best to break the set into smaller subsets and use the cross-validation method to estimate the parameters.

Step 6

Once the algorithms run and the machine generates the function, the engineer should measure the accuracy of the function. The engineer must use a testing dataset instead of the training dataset to check the accuracy of the function.

There are many supervised machine-learning algorithms in use and each of these algorithms has its strengths and weaknesses. The selection of the learning algorithm is an important step in the process since the engineer cannot use a definitive algorithm to train the machine.

Issues to consider in Supervised Learning

With the usage of supervised learning algorithms, there arise a few issues associated with it. Given below are four major issues:

Bias-variance tradeoff

The bias-variance tradeoff is an issue that every engineer should be wary of while working with machine learning. Consider a situation where we have various but equally good training sets. If the engineer uses different datasets to train the machine, the learning algorithm may form a bias to the input. Machines often give systematically incorrect outputs if the machine forms a bias to the input. Learning algorithms have a high input variance, which occurs when the algorithm causes the machine to predict different outputs for that input in each training set. The sum of the bias and variance of the learning algorithm is known as the prediction error for the classifier function. There exists a tradeoff between bias and variance. A requirement for learning algorithms with low bias is that they need to be flexible enough to accommodate all the data sets. However, if they are too flexible, the learning algorithms might end up giving varying outputs for each training set and increases the variance. Supervised learning methods need to be able to adjust this tradeoff that happens automatically. The alternative is to use an adjustable parameter.

Function complexity and amount of training data

The second issue is concerned with the training data. The training dataset must be prepared depending on what time of function the machine should generate, a classifier or a regressor. If the function must be simple, a simple learning algorithm, with a low variance and high bias, can help the machine learn. However, on many occasions, the function will be complex if there are many input variables or factors. The machine must act differently for different parts of the input vector. In such cases, the machine can only learn through a large training dataset. These cases also require the algorithms used to be flexible with low bias and high variance. Therefore, efficient learning algorithms automatically arrive at a tradeoff for the bias and variance depending on the complexity of the function and the amount of training data required.

Dimensionality of the input space

Dimensionality of the vector space is another issue that the engineer must deal with. If the input vector includes many features, the learning problem will become difficult even if the function only considers a few of these features as valuable inputs. Since there are many input variables, the input vector will have many dimensions, which can lead to confusion. This situation ultimately leads to the first issue that we discussed. So, when the input dimensions are large, the engineer should make an adjustment to the classifier to offset the effects of low variance and high bias. In practice, the engineer could manually remove the irrelevant features to improve the accuracy and efficiency of the learning algorithm. However, this might not always be a practical solution. In recent times, some algorithms can remove unnecessary features and retaining only the relevant ones. This concept is known as dimensionality reduction, which helps in mapping input data into lower dimensions to improve the performance of the learning algorithm.

Noise in the output values

The final issue on this list is concerned with the interference of noise in the desired output values. The output values are wrong in some situations since there is some noise associated with the sensors. There is a possibility that these values are wrong because of human error. In such cases, the learning algorithm should not look to match the training inputs with their exact outputs. For such cases, algorithms with high bias and low variance are desirable.

Other factors to consider

- The engineer must always consider the heterogeneity of data. She must choose an algorithm that considers the level of heterogeneity of the data. Some algorithms work better on datasets with a limit on the number of inputs used. Some examples are support vector machines, logistic regression, neural networks, linear regression and nearest neighbor methods. Nearest neighbor methods and support vector machines with Gaussian kernels work especially better with inputs limited to small ranges. On the other hand, there exist algorithms like decision trees that work very well with heterogeneous data sets.

- There is a possibility that the dataset is redundant. A few algorithms perform poorly in the presence of high redundancy. This happens due to numerical instabilities. Examples of these types of algorithms are logistic regression, linear regression and distance-based methods. The engineer must include regularization to ensure that the algorithm performs better.

- While choosing algorithms, engineers need to consider the amount of non - linearities in the inputs and the interactions within different features of the input vector. If there is little to no interaction and each feature contributes independently to the output, algorithms based on distance functions and linear functions perform very efficiently. However, when there are some interactions within the input features, it is best to use the decision trees and neural network algorithms. These algorithms detect the interactions between the input vectors. If the engineer decides to use linear algorithms, he must specify the interactions that exist.

The engineer can compare various algorithms before she chooses the one to address a specific application. However, she must spend some time and collect training data and tune the algorithm to ensure it works for the application. If provided with many resources, it is advisable to spend more time collecting data than spending time on tuning the algorithm because the latter is extremely tedious. The most commonly used learning algorithms are neural networks, nearest neighbor algorithms, linear and logistic regressions, support vector machines and decision trees.

Chapter Four

Top Six Real Life Applications
of Machine Learning

We use many applications regularly that involve machine learning.

Image Recognition

The most common application of machine learning is image recognition. Most laptops and phones use the algorithm for image recognition. There are many situations when you can classify a certain object as an image. The measurements of every digital image always give the user an idea about the output of each pixel in the image.

If you were to look at a black and white image, the intensity of every pixel in the image serves as a measurement. If the image has M*M pixels, the measurement is M^2.

The machine splits the pixels into three measurements that give the intensity of the three primary colors (RBG). So, if there was an M*M image, there will be three M^2 measurements.

Face Detection

The most common category is the presence of a face versus the presence of no face. There can also be a separate category for every person in a database with multiple individuals.

Character Recognition

You can segment pieces of writing into images of small sizes where each image contains one character. These categories may comprise the 26 letters of the English alphabet, the first ten numbers and some special characters.

Speech Recognition

Speech recognition application is the translation of spoken words into actual text. Experts refer to it as Automatic Speech Recognition (ASR), Speech to text (STT) or Computer Speech Recognition (CSR).

The programmer uses spoken words to train the machine to recognize speech and convert the words into text. Facebook and Google are both using this method to train their machines. Machines use measurements to represent the signal of speech. These signals are further split into distinct words and phonemes. The algorithm uses different energies to represent the speech signals.

The details of the representation of signals are outside the scope of this book, but it is important to know that real values represent these signals. Applications on speech recognition often include voice user interfaces. These interfaces are call routing, voice dialing and other similar applications. These applications can also use data entry and other simple methods of processing information.

Prediction

Let us assume that a bank is trying to calculate the probability of a loan applicant defaulting on a repayment. To calculate this probability, the system will first have to identify, clean and classify the data that is available in groups. Analysts classify the data based on certain criteria. Prediction is one of the sought-after machine learning algorithms. If you were to look at a retailer, you can get reports on the sales that happened in the past. Now, you can predict what the sales may be soon. This will help the business make the right decision in the future.

Medical Diagnosis

Machine learning (ML) provides techniques; tools and methods that help a doctor solve prognostic and diagnostic problems in many medical domains. Doctors and patients can both use these techniques to enhance their medical knowledge and analyze the symptoms to obtain the prognosis. The result of this analysis will help to enhance the medical knowledge most doctors have. Doctors can also use machine learning to identify the irregularities in unstructured data, the interpretation of continuous data and to monitor results efficiently.

The successful use of different methods helps to integrate computer-based systems with the healthcare environment thereby providing the medical world with opportunities to enhance and improve treatments.

In medical diagnosis, the interest is to establish the existence of a disease and then identify the disease accurately. There are different categories for each disease that are under consideration and one category where the disease may not be present. Machine learning helps to improve the accuracy of a diagnosis and analyzes the data of the patients. The measurements used are the results of the many medical tests conducted on the patient. The doctors identify the disease using these measurements.

Statistical Arbitrage

Statistical Arbitrage, a term often used in finance, refers to the science of using trading strategies to identify the short-term securities one can invest in. In these strategies, the user can implement an algorithm on an array of securities based on the general economic variables and historical correlation of the data.

500

The measurements used help to resolve the classification and estimation problems. The assumption is that the stock price will always lie close to a historical average.

Index arbitrage is a strategy that uses machine-learning methods. The linear regression and support vector regression algorithms help a user to calculate the different prices of funds and stocks. Using the principal component analysis, the algorithm breaks the data into dimensions to identify the trading signals as a mean reverting process.

Buy, hold, sold, put, call or do nothing are some categories under which the algorithm places these securities under. It then calculates the expected return for each security for the future. These estimates help the user decide which security to buy or sell securities.

Learning Associations

Learning association is the process of developing an insight into the association between groups of products. There are several products that reveal an association with one another although they seem unrelated. The algorithm uses the buying habits of customers to establish an association.

Basket learning analysis, which deals with studying about the association between products purchased by different customers, is an application of machine learning. If we assume that Amy has bought a product X, we can try to identify if she will buy product Y based on an association between the two products. Let us use the example of fish and chips to understand this concept. If a new product enters the market, the association between the existing products will change. If one knows these relationships, they can identify the right products to give their customers. To increase purchasing power, a company can choose to introduce products in pairs.

Big Data analysts use machine-learning algorithms to identify if there is a relationship between different products. Algorithms use probabilities to establish a relationship between products.

Chapter Five

Machine Learning Algorithms

The many subjects that have laid the foundation of machine learning are discussed in the first chapter. This chapter covers some of the machine learning algorithms that engineers use to train the machine.

Dimension Reduction Methods

There are millions or billions of records and variables in the databases that engineers use to derive the training dataset. It is impossible to conclude that these variables are not dependent on one another with absolutely any correlation between them. It is important for the engineer to remember that there are multiple collinearities that exist between the variables. In this situation, the predictor variables are correlated in some way that can affect the output.

A lot of instability arises in the solution set when there is multicollinearity between variables leading to incoherent results. For instance, if you look at multiple regressions, there are multiple correlations between the predictor variables that have a significant impact on the output set. However, individual predictor variables may not have a significant impact on the solution set. Even if the engineer identifies a way to remove such instability, there are times when the users may include variables with a high level of correlation between them. In this case, the algorithm will focus on some parts of the input vector more than the others.

When the dataset has many predictor variables, an unnecessary complication arises where the algorithm must identify a model between the predictor and response variables. This situation complicates the analysis and its interpretation and violates the principle of parsimony. The principle of parsimony states that an analyst should always stick to a certain number of predictor variables, which makes it easy for human beings and now machines to interpret the results. If the engineer retains too many variables, there is a possibility that there could be over fitting, which will hinder the analysis. The new dataset that the engineer uses will not behave in the same way as the training dataset or the predictor data.

There is also the question of how the analysis performed at the variable level will miss the relationships that lie between the predictors. For instance, there can be numerous single predictor variables that fall into a single group or component that will address only one aspect of the data. If you look at a person's account, you will need to group the account balance and any deposits or savings made from that account into one category alone.

There are certain applications, such as image analysis, where the full dimensionality of the variable is retained which makes the problem intractable. For instance, a face classification system based on 256×256-pixel images could potentially require vectors of dimension 65,536. Human beings can discern and understand certain patterns in an image at a glance. These patterns can elude the human eye if the output represents them as an algebraic equation or graph. However, the most advanced visualization techniques also do not go beyond five dimensions. How do you think we can identify the relationships that could exist between a massive data set that has thousands of variables?

The goal of dimension reduction methods is to use the structure of correlation among the different predictor variables to accomplish the following goals:

- Reduce the number of predictor components in the data set

- Ensure that these predictor components are independent of one another

- Provide a dynamic framework which will help in the interpretation of the analysis

The most common dimension reduction methods are Principal Component Analysis (PCA), User Defined Composites and Factor Analysis.

Clustering

Clustering is a machine learning technique that groups different data points in the dataset that are similar. An engineer often uses this algorithm to classify and categorize the data points into specific groups. Data points or variables in the same group should bear some similarities, while variables in different groups should bear no similarities. Clustering is an unsupervised machine-learning algorithm that an engineer commonly uses for statistical data analysis.

Data scientists use clustering analysis to derive insights from the data by identifying the groups that the data points or variables fall into when the algorithm runs. This section covers some clustering algorithms that an engineer uses to train the machine.

K Means

The K-Means clustering algorithm a well-known clustering algorithm. This is a concept that every engineer and data scientist must know the algorithm well since it is easy to implement in a code.

- The algorithm must first select the number of groups or classes and initialize the center points of these classes. If you are unsure of how many classes to use, look at the data and identify the different categories and classes within the data. The center points of these classes are the lengths of the vectors.

- The algorithm classifies the data points by calculating the distance between the point and all the center points. The engineer then uses this distance to categorize that data point in the class whose center is the closest to that point.

- Using the classified points, the algorithm computes the center of the data points or variables in the class using the mean.

- The engineer must repeat these steps multiple times until the center of the groups does not change between the iterations. You can also initialize centers in the groups at random and then select an iteration that represents the best results.

This clustering algorithm has an advantage that it is simple and fast to use since you are only computing the distance between the variables and the center of the groups. On the other hand, it also has a few disadvantages. You must select the number of classes by looking at the data and this is not an ideal method to use since you want some insight from the dataset. There is also the point where you should select the center points of groups at random, which can lead to different results in different iterations. Thus, you may not obtain a consistent output that makes it difficult to select the center points of the group.

Mean Shift Clustering

An engineer uses the mean shift-clustering algorithm to find dense areas in the dataset. This algorithm also uses the center points of every group. However, the goal of the algorithm is to update the possible center points of the class within the sliding-window to locate the actual center point. The algorithm removes the center points after the processing stage to remove duplicates and form the final set of cluster points and place them in their groups.

- Let us consider a set of points in a two-dimensional space. The first step is to define the point around which the circular sliding window is positioned. The circular window should have a radius r called the kernel. This algorithm is a hill-climbing algorithm and it constantly moves the kernel to denser regions until the values converge.

- The sliding window moves to denser regions at every iteration. The algorithm does this by shifting the center point of the group to the mean point. The density of the points in the sliding window is directly proportional to the number of data points in it. Therefore, when the algorithm shifts the mean of the points in the window, it moves towards areas in the data with a higher density.

- The sliding window moves according to the change in the mean and there is no specific direction in which the window moves.

- The algorithm repeats the first three steps using different sliding windows until it can categorize all the data points in the set into different sliding windows.

In this method, you do not have to select the number of classes or clusters, which is a great advantage. It is also good that the center points converge to the mean of the highly dense data region. This algorithm understands data and fits any application that is data-driven. The selection of the kernel is trivial, which is the only drawback of this method.

It is best to use the K-Means algorithm if you are a beginner. Once you understand this algorithm, you can use other clustering algorithms in your analysis.

Regression Modeling

Regression modeling is an algorithm that an engineer uses frequently to estimate the values of continuous target variables. There are many regression models that you can choose from. However, the simplest form of the regression algorithm is the simple linear regression model. In this model, the algorithm defines the relationship between a continuous predictor variable and continuous response variable using a straight line. There are models that use multiple predictor variables to define the response variable.

Apart from the models mentioned above, engineers use two algorithms called the least squared regression and logistic regression methods to train machines. However, the assumptions of the regression model have created a disparity. It is imperative that the engineer validates these assumptions before writing the algorithm and building the model. If the engineer builds a model and uses it without verifying the assumptions, there is a possibility that the engineer cannot use the output since the model may have failed without the knowledge of the engineer.

When the engineer obtains the result, she must ensure that there is no linear relationship between the variables of the model. There are times when the dataset has variables that have a hidden linear relationship. However, there is a systematic approach, called inference, which the engineer can use to determine the linear relationship. The inference methods that an engineer can use to determine the relationship are:

- The t-test for the relationship between the response variable and the predictor variable

- The confidence interval for the slope, $\beta 1$

- The confidence interval for the mean of the response variable given a value of the predictor

- The prediction interval for a random value of the response variable given a value of the predictor

The inferential methods described above depend on the assumptions that the engineer makes at the beginning of the process. It is easy for the engineer to assess whether the data adheres to the assumptions using two graphical methods - a plot of the normal probability and a plot of the standardized residuals against the predicted or fitted values.

A normal probability plot is a quantile-quantile plot of the quantiles of a distribution against the quantiles of the standard normal distribution for the purposes of determining whether the specified distribution deviates from normality. In a normality plot, the engineer makes a comparison between the values observed for the distribution of interest and the expected number of values from the normal distribution. If the distribution is normal, the bulk of the points in the plot should fall on a straight line; systematic deviations from linearity in this plot indicate non-normality. An engineer can evaluate the validity of the regression assumptions by verifying if some patterns exist in the residual plot. If there is a pattern, the engineer must identify which assumption does not hold true. However, if no patterns exist, the assumptions remain intact.

If these graphs indicate violations of the assumptions, we may apply a transformation to the response variable y, such as the ln (natural log, log to the base e) transformation. If the relationship between the response variables and the predictor variables is not linear, the algorithm can use transformations. We may use either "Mosteller and Tukey's ladder of re-expression" or a "Box-Cox transformation."

Regression with Categorical Predictors

Thus far, our predictors have all been continuous. However, the engineer can choose to give categorical predictor variables as inputs to regression models using dummy or indicator variables.

509

For use in regression, the algorithm transforms categorical variables with k categories to a set of (k-1) indicator variables. An indicator variable is a binary 0/1 variable, which takes the value 1 if the observation belongs to the given category and takes the value 0 otherwise.

Logistic Regression

The engineer uses the logistic regression algorithm to approximate the relationship between a set of continuous predictor variables and a categorical response variable. It is difficult to use linear regression in such instances. The logistic regression algorithm is like the linear regression algorithm except that the former uses methods to estimate the relationship between the predictor and response variables. In other words, the engineer uses the linear regression method to approximate the relationship between a set of continuous predictor variables and a continuous response variable. Logistic regression, on the other hand, refers to methods for describing the relationship between a categorical response variable and a set of predictor variables.

An attractive attribute of the linear regression algorithm is that the engineer can obtain closed-form solutions for the optimal values of the coefficients through the least-squares method. However, in logistic regression, the engineer must use the likelihood functions to estimate the parameters of the model. This method obtains parameters by maximizing the likelihood of the observing data.

The engineer can find the value of the maximum likelihood estimators by differentiating the likelihood function, $L (\beta|x)$, with respect to each parameter and then setting the resulting forms to be equal to zero. Unfortunately, unlike linear regression, closed-form solutions for these differentiations are not available. Therefore, the engineer must apply other methods like iterative weighted least squares.

Logistic regression assumes that the relationship between the predictor and the response is nonlinear. In linear regression, the response variable is a random variable $Y = \beta 0 + \beta 1x + \varepsilon$ with conditional mean $\pi(x) = E(Y|x) = \beta 0 + \beta 1x$. The conditional mean for logistic regression takes on a different form from that of linear regression.

Variable Selection Methods

Different variable selection methods are available for the engineer to use to determine which variable must be a part of the dataset, including forward selection, backward elimination, stepwise selection and best subsets. These variable selection methods are essentially algorithms that construct the model with the optimal set of predictors.

Forward Selection Procedure

The forward selection procedure does not use any variables.

Step 1: For the first variable to enter the model, select the predictor most highly correlated with the target. (Without loss of generality, denote this variable x1.) If the resulting model is not significant, stop and report that no variables are significant predictors; otherwise, proceed to step 2.

Step 2: For each remaining variable, compute the sequential F-statistic for that variable given the variables already in the model. For example, in this first pass through the algorithm, these sequential F-statistics will be $F(x2|x1)$, $F(x3|x1)$ and $F(x4|x1)$. On the second pass through the algorithm, these might be $F(x3|x1, x2)$ and $F(x4|x1, x2)$. Select the variable with the largest sequential F-statistic.

Step 3: For the variable selected in step 2, test for the significance of the sequential F-statistic. If the resulting model is not significant, stop and report the current model without adding the variable from step 2. Otherwise, add the variable from step 2 into the model and return to step 2.

Backward Elimination Procedure

The backward elimination procedure begins with all the variables or all a user-specified set of variables in the model.

Step 1: Perform the regression on the full model; that is using all available variables. For example, perhaps the full model has four variables, namely, $x1$, $x2$, $x3$ and $x4$.

Step 2: For each variable in the current model, compute the partial F-statistic. In the first pass through the algorithm, there will be F $(x1|x2, x3, x4)$, F $(x2|x1, x3, x4)$, F $(x3|x1, x2, x4)$ and F $(x4|x1, x2, x3)$. Select the variable with the smallest partial F-statistic. Denote this value as F-min.

Step 3: Test for the significance of F-min. If F-min is not significant, remove the variable associated with F-min from the model and return to step 2. If F-min is significant, stop the algorithm and report the current model. If this is the first pass through the algorithm, the current model is the full model. The algorithm reduces the number of variables if this is not the first pass.

Stepwise Procedure

The stepwise procedure represents a modification of the forward selection procedure. A variable that is present in the forward selection algorithm may become insignificant once other variables are present in the model. The stepwise procedure checks on this possibility by performing at each step a partial F-test using the partial sum of squares for each variable currently in the model. If there is a variable in the model that is no longer significant, the algorithm eliminates the variable with the smallest partial F-statistic from the model. The procedure terminates when the algorithm cannot enter or remove any variable.

Best Subsets Procedure

For data sets where the number of predictors is not too large, the best subsets procedure represents an attractive variable selection method. However, if there are more than 30 or so predictors, the best subsets method encounters a combinatorial explosion and becomes intractably slow. The best subsets procedure works as follows:

Step 1: The analyst specifies how many (k) models of each size he or she will like to report, as well as the maximum number of predictors (p) the analyst wants in the model.

Step 2: In this step, the algorithm builds all models of one predictor: for example, $y = \beta 0 + \beta 1$ (sugars) $+\varepsilon$, $y = \beta 0 + \beta 2$ (fiber) $+\varepsilon$ and so on. The algorithm calculates their R2, R2adj, Mallows' Cp and reports the best k models based on these measures.

Step 3: The algorithm builds all models of the two predictor variables: for example, $y = \beta 0 + \beta 1$ (sugars) $+ \beta 2$ (fiber) $+\varepsilon$, $y = \beta 0 + \beta 1$ (sugars) $+\beta 4$ (shelf2) $+\varepsilon$ and so on. The algorithm calculates their R2, R2adj, Mallows' Cp and reports the best k models based on these measures.

The procedure continues in this way until the algorithm reaches the maximum number of predictors (p). The analyst then has a listing of the best models of each size 1, 2... etc. to assist in the selection of the best overall model.

513

Chapter Six

Machine learning Projects

In this chapter, we will cover some simple and easy machine learning projects that a beginner can use. It is always good to work on projects since they are a great investment of your time and make learning fun. You will notice that you are making faster progress when you work on the projects.

You can read volumes of theory, but that can never help you build confidence in the subject when compared to hands-on practice. Most people believe that they become masters when they read textbooks and articles. But, when they try to apply the theory, they notice that it is harder than it looks.

When you work on projects, you improve your skills and have the chance to explore interesting topics. You can also add these projects to your portfolio, which will make it easier for you to land a job. You can complete the projects in this chapter over the weekend. However, you can expand them to build longer projects if you want.

Data Analysis

The data analysis project is one that most people begin with since it helps to hone some statistical skills. By working on this project, you can build your practical intuition around machine learning. The goal of this exercise is to help you use different models and apply those models to a variety of datasets. There are three reasons why you should begin with this project.

- You will learn to identify which model will fit your problem. For example, some datasets may have missing information. When you work on this project, you will know which model you should use for such datasets. You can always dig through texts and articles to learn which model is better, but it is better to see it in action.

- You will develop the art of creating prototypes of models. It is often difficult to identify if a model will work best for the problem without trying it.

- You must keep the process flow or workflow of the machine in mind when you build a model. You will master this technique when you work on this project. For example, you can practice:

  o How to import data

  o Which tools should you use to clean data

  o How to split the data into training sets

  o Pre-processing of data

  o What transformations must you make to the data

Since you use different models, you can focus on the development of the skills mentioned above. For instructions, you can look at the Python (sklearn) and R (caret) documentation pages. You must also practice classification, clustering and regression algorithms.

Social Media

Social media is synonymous with big data because of the volumes of content that users generate. You can mine this data and keep tabs on trends, public sentiments and opinions. Facebook, YouTube, WhatsApp, Instagram and many other platforms have data that you can use to achieve your objective.

Social media data is important for branding, marketing and for a business since every generation spends more time on social media when compared to its preceding generation. Twitter is one of the platforms you should start with when you begin to practice machine learning. You have interesting data sets and metadata that can open an endless path for analysis.

Fantasy Leagues or Sports Betting

If you have read the book Moneyball, you know how the Oakland A's changed the face of baseball through their analytical scouting. Based on the analysis, the team built a highly competitive squad and bought the players for almost a third of the price when compared to the Yankees players. If you have not read the book yet, you must grab a copy and read it now.

There are large volumes of data in the sports world that you can play with. You can use data for games, teams, players and scores to analyze patterns. These data are available online. For instance, you can try the following projects and see where they lead you.

- You can bet on specific box scores in different games based on the data available on the Internet right before a game begins. You can analyze the data and identify where you should place your bets to increase your chances of winning.

- You can scout for talent in schools and colleges using the statistics for different players. This analysis can help college scouts identify the players they want on their team.

- You can become a manager for a fantasy team and use your analysis to win games and leagues.

The sports domain is especially useful since it helps a beginner practice exploratory analysis and data visualization. These skills will help you identify what types of data you should include in your analysis.

Stock Market

An aspiring data scientist will always base his projects on the stock market since that is like Disneyland for them. The stock market is an interesting area to work on since you have different types of data available. You can find data on fundamentals, prices, stocks, economic scenarios, macroeconomic and microeconomic indicators, volatilities and many more.

The data available is granular which makes it easier for people to obtain historical data, also called time series data, for every company. Using this data, you can build creative trading strategies. Since financial markets have small cycles, you can validate any prediction you make immediately.

- You can analyze the data and assess the movement of prices for different stocks for a period of 6 months. You should use the quarterly reports provided by the company to make this prediction.

- You can use a time series models and recurrent neural network models to forecast the correlation between the stock prices. You can also assess the volatility of the prices.

It is simple to build a financial trading model to improve your skills in machine learning. However, it is difficult to profit from these models here. Experts recommend that you do not use real money to trade until you have perfected the model.

Writing Machine Learning Algorithms

It is important for a beginner to learn how to write machine-learning algorithms from scratch for two reasons:

- There is no better way to understand the mechanics of the algorithms since you must think about the process flow of the algorithm thereby helping you master algorithms.

- You can translate statistical and mathematical instructions into working code, which allows you to apply algorithms in your academic research.

It is best to start off with simpler algorithms since you must make hundreds of decisions. Once you are comfortable with simple algorithms, you can extend the functionality of those algorithms to complex algorithms like regression and clustering.

Your packages may be slow and may not be as fancy as the algorithms in existing packages. It took the developers years to build these packages.

Chapter Seven

Artificial Intelligence

An amazing development has taken place over the last few years. You may have watched how robots in Star Wars were able to perform so many actions and maybe, just maybe, you would wondered how wonderful it would be if it were to happen in this decade. You may not have seen it coming, but this was an inevitable turn of events – the emergence of Artificial Intelligence (AI). Everywhere we look today; we come across some intelligent systems that talk to us – Siri, Google Assistant – offering us advice and offering us recommendations. These systems improve almost every year to improve its interpretation of images, voice recognition and to drive cars based on different techniques used by Facebook and Google's Deep Learning Efforts. Other work always aims to understand and generate machines that can understand our language and communicate with us.

The reemergence of AI has caused a lot of confusion since there are so many companies that have begun to explore the scene. How do we make sense of any of it?

Let us start with a simple definition of AI. Artificial Intelligence or AI is a field of computer science that aims to develop computers that can perform tasks that human beings can perform.

AI has had some excellent runs. In the early sixties, experts made promises about the abilities of machines and what they can do. In the eighties, artificial intelligence revolutionized businesses. But in those eras, the promises made were too difficult to deliver. So, what makes the latest developments in AI any different? What makes the systems developed now any different from the diagnostic programs and neural nets of the past? There are some reasons why the developments in this era are different from the last.

Increased Computational Resources

The computers we have in this era are faster and can think harder thereby increasing the computational power. The techniques used earlier worked well only in the past, but now there is a necessity to improve the computational grid and expand it.

Deeper Focus

AI has shifted away from looking at smaller aspects of data to look at specific problems. The systems now are capable of thinking about a problem as opposed to daydreaming without any problem. Systems like Cortana and Siri work well within limited domains that focus on speech and image recognition (covered in chapter four). These platforms use words and sentences to understand what you need and provide you with the required output.

Alternative Reasoning Models

Experts use alternative reasoning models, which assume that the systems do not have to reason like human beings to be smart. The machine can think like a machine.

It is these factors put together that have given the world the first renaissance of intelligent machines that have become a part of our lives. We are now using different machines to ease our work and lives.

Knowledge Engineering

Different types of learning study the problem and issues with knowledge engineering. The systems developed these days use their ways to learn. The bottleneck in the systems in the past helped us add more rules to avoid such bottlenecks in the further processing of data. Most approaches in the modern times focus on learning these rules automatically.

Growth of Data

Over the years, the data collected has increased by a vast amount and the engineer feeds the machine with this data to enhance the machine's computational abilities. This goes to say that learning systems get better at understanding more data and would now be able to look at thousand examples as opposed to only a few hundred.

Exploring AI

As mentioned earlier, some engineers allow machines to think like machines. The key word here is most. Some developers still look to create machines that are capable of thinking like human beings. The only opposition to this is the doubt about the intentions of the machine. Some people are worried about what machines could be capable of if they could think exactly like human beings.

There are two types of artificial intelligence – strong AI and weak AI.

Strong AI

The sphere of strong AI deals with the development of machines and systems that are capable of thinking like humans. This entails that the machines should be able to reason out and solve problems the way humans do. They should be capable of explaining their solutions as well. Basically, these machines need to have abilities like those of human cognition.

Weak AI

As mentioned earlier, people have qualms about designing machines capable of human thinking. So, weak AI deals with the development of machines that work but not at the level of human thinking. Essentially, it deals with the creation of systems and machines that can behave like humans and perform tasks that we can but are devoid of any thinking capabilities that rival human cognition. A great example of such a machine is the Deep Blue made by IBM. The machine became a brilliant chess player, but it was unable to explain its moves or show any cognitive abilities.

Anything in Between

In addition to the two types of AI mentioned above, engineers and scientists are developing machines that are in between the above types. These types of systems are capable of learning and can also understand the human reasoning. However, they are not subservient to it. The trend in recent times has shifted to these types of machines. The essence of this type of development is to use human cognitive skills and emotions to train the machines but not use them as the models for the machines.

The main conclusion of the previous few paragraphs is that, as opposed to the consensus from previous times, machines do not have to think like humans to be smart. However, a machine that thinks like a machine can learn using training datasets.

Assessing Data using AI and Machine Learning

All the major consumer systems around the world are constantly trying to estimate human beings. For instance, online shopping websites such as eBay and Amazon are constantly using machine learning and AI to figure out your likes and dislikes so that they can put forth a list of recommendations for you. As mentioned earlier, the machines learn from the data that you provide them with when you browse and look for products (transactional information). Even web pages like Facebook use this concept to recommend pages that you might want to follow.

Using profile data is only a small step in this process. The machines also use information from different categories for training purposes. Most machines also recommend some products using information like your budget, your likes and your buying history. These systems also look at the customers who live around you to further refine the list of recommendations it presents you with.

The results of these processes are almost always a group of characteristics:

For instance, if you were someone who just purchased a garden and is looking to grow plants on it, you would probably go online to look for gardening tools. The next time that you would visit that website, you would see recommendations related to gardening. This is how the machine develops that list - it cross-references the products you looked for with products that people have already bought and then looks at what else they purchased. It accesses this list and presents it to you as a recommendations list.

Chapter Eight

Glossary

This chapter provides a list of words and their definitions when we talk about machine learning.

Data Science

Data science, in its truest form, represents the resource and process optimization of the data analysis. Through data science, you can produce data insights and use those insights to improve your investments, business, health, lifestyle and social life. For any pursuit or goal, you can use data science methods to help you understand and predict the path you must take to meet your goals and objectives. You will also be able to anticipate any obstacles or hurdles that come your way.

Data Mining

Many businesses use the process of data mining to convert the collected raw data into information that it can use. There are specialized tools that the business can use to detect patterns in large-scale information. These patterns help the business learn more about its consumers and respond to their concerns while developing strategies that will help to increase your revenue. The objective of data mining is to increase profits. Data mining is effective only when the process of collecting and storing data is done the right way.

Artificial Intelligence

Artificial Intelligence or AI is a field of computer science that aims at developing computers that can perform tasks that human beings perform.

Additive Property

The next axiom that is important to note can only be true when both events A and B are mutually exclusive.

$$P(A+B) = P(A) + P(B)$$

This axiom states that the probability of both events A and B occurring is the same as the sum of the individual probabilities of the events occurring if and only if both events exclude each other. For example, if A is the event that we get a six on rolling a die and B is the event that we get a five rolling a die, then this axiom hold. But, if B is the event where we get an even number, this set will include the number six making the axiom false.

Regression

Regression is closely related to classification. Classification is directly concerned with the prediction of discrete classes. When the class has continuous variables, the engineer uses machine learning to obtain the output. Linear regression is an example of regression techniques. To learn more about regression, please read the previous chapter.

Joint Probability

This property can be expressed as follows:

$$P(a, b) = P(A=a, B=b)$$

This property can be read as the probability of a and b is the same as the probability that event A turns out in state 'a' and event B turns out in state 'b.'

Bayes' Rule

This rule is used to identify the conditional probability when P (A, B) is not known. The equation used is as follows:

$$P (A|B) = [P (B|A)*P (A)]/P (B)$$

These various axioms are a great way to understand the logic behind Markov Models. Let us now look at the mathematical aspects of the Markov Model. As mentioned above, Markov Models is a concept that was discovered in the year 1916 by Andreevich Markov, a scientist who was studying and analyzing the frequency of different types of words in Pushkin's poems. These models have now become an integral model to use while working with data science, artificial intelligence and machine learning.

Classification

Classification is concerned with separating data into unique classes using models. The engineer builds these models using a training dataset that is named to help the algorithm learn. Users input real-time data with the classes that are present in the model. This will help the model predict the relationship that exists within the data based on what the model has learned from the training dataset. Well – known classification schemes are support vector machines and decision trees. Since these algorithms will need an explicit definition of classes, classification is a form of supervised machine learning.

Support Vector Machines

Support Vector Machines (SVMs) allow the user to classify linear and nonlinear data. They work by transforming the training dataset into higher dimensions. The model inspects these dimensions to calculate the optimal boundary separation between classes. In SVMs, these boundaries are called hyperplanes. The algorithm identifies hyperplanes using support vectors or the instances that define the classes and their margins, which are lines that are parallel to the hyperplanes. These are defined by the shortest distance between the hyperplane and the support vector associated with it.

The goal behind using an SVM is to identify the hyperplane that separates two classes if there are many dimensions. This process helps to delineate the member classes in the dataset. When the algorithm repeats the process several times, it generates enough hyperplanes that can help to separate dimensions in an n – dimension space.

Clustering

Clustering is a technique that an engineer or data scientist uses to analyze data that does not include pre-labeled classes or any class attribute at all. The instances in the data are grouped using the concept of maximizing the similarity within classes and minimize the similarity between classes. This loosely translates into the clustering algorithm that identifies and groups the instances that are like each other. The best – known clustering algorithm is k – means clustering. Clustering does not require the pre-labeling of instance classes; therefore, it is a form of unsupervised machine learning meaning that the algorithm learns more from observation as opposed to learning by example.

Association

Association can be explained easily by introducing a market basket analysis, which is a task that it is well–known for. This type of analysis always tries to identify the association that exists between different data instances that are chosen by any shopper and placed in their basket. This could either be real or virtual and the algorithm always assigns confidence and support measures for comparison. The value of this always lies in customer behavior analysis and cross marketing. Association algorithms are generalizations of market-based analyses and are like classification algorithms in the sense that any attribute can be predicted when using association. Apriori is one the best – known association algorithms. If you have deduced that association is an example of unsupervised machine learning, then you are right.

Machine Learning

Although this book covers machine learning in detail, we will just look at it one more time. Machine learning is concerned with how a computer can be constructed to automatically improve the experience of the user. Machine learning is an interdisciplinary science that employs techniques from different fields like computer science, artificial intelligence, mathematics and statistics and so on. The main aspects of machine learning research include algorithms that help to facilitate this improvement from experience. Artificial intelligence, data mining and computer vision are some fields that use these algorithms.

Decision Trees

Decision trees are recursive, divide – and – conquer and top-down classifiers. These trees are composed of two main tasks: tree pruning and tree induction. The latter is the task where a set of pre-classified instances are taken as inputs after which decisions are made based on which attributes are split on thereby splitting the dataset and recursing on the resulting split datasets until every training instance is categorized. While building the tree, the main goal is to split all the attributes to create the child nodes that are pure. This ensures that the number of splits needed to classify the instances in the dataset is small. The purity of the child nodes is measured using information that relates to the volume of information that the machine must know about a previous instance and how it should categorize it.

A complete decision tree model can always be complicated and may contain some unnecessary structure, which make it difficult for human beings to interpret the output. Unnecessary structure or branches are removed through tree pruning, which makes the decision tree easily readable, more efficient and accurate for human beings to comprehend. This increased accuracy due to tree pruning helps to reduce over fitting.

Fundamental Axioms

Let us look at the various axioms that are used in machine learning to understand the math that supports the model. One of the most fundamental axioms can be expressed as follows:

$$0 < P(A) < 1$$

This states that the probability of any event occurring is always going to be greater than zero but less than one, both inclusive. This implies that the probability of the occurrence of any event can never be negative. This makes sense since the probabilities can never be more certain than a hundred percent and least certain than zero percent.

Deep Learning

Deep learning is a method that uses neural networks to identify solutions. This type of learning uses different layers and nodes of input that send signals to the hidden layers in the network to identify the solution to any input. The work in deep learning is defined by how the human mind learns and how the mind learns. It also considers how calculations and computations take place in the cerebral cortex of the human brain.

Generative Model

In statistics and probability, a generative model is used to generate data sets when some parameters are hidden. These models are used in machine learning to either model the data directly or used as an intermediate step to form a conditional probability density function.

Conclusion

The Industrial Revolution led to the development of machines. This development started small, where a machine was used to perform laborious tasks. Since then, machines have entered the lives of every human being and they are here to stay. This increased dependency on machines led to the development of artificial intelligence. Scientists and engineers are looking for different ways to train machines into performing difficult and intelligent tasks. Experts from different fields of study are now using machines to enhance the processes. Therefore, it is of utmost importance to understand what machine learning is and how it improves life.

This book provides information on what machine learning is and types of machine learning. It also gives you information on the subjects that laid the foundation for machine learning. You will gather information on different algorithms used in machine learning. As a beginner, it is always good to practice some algorithms used in machine learning to enhance your understanding. There are some projects in the book that you can complete over the weekend or extend them if you want to. It is important to practice as much as you can to improve your knowledge on machine learning. It is difficult to remember the many words that are used in machine learning. There is a glossary of words in the last chapter of the book that you can go through.

Thank you for purchasing the book. I hope you have gathered all the information necessary for machine learning.

Finally, if you enjoyed this book, then I'd like to ask you for a favor, would you be kind enough to leave a review for this book on Amazon? It'd be greatly appreciated!

Resources

https://www.kdnuggets.com/2016/08/10-algorithms-machine-learning-engineers.html

https://towardsdatascience.com/linear-regression-detailed-view-ea73175f6e86

http://www.statisticssolutions.com/what-is-linear-regression/

https://towardsdatascience.com/logistic-regression-detailed-overview-46c4da4303bc

https://www.statisticssolutions.com/what-is-logistic-regression/

https://medium.com/app-affairs/9-applications-of-machine-learning-from-day-to-day-life-112a47a429d0

https://machinelearningmastery.com/supervised-and-unsupervised-machine-learning-algorithms/

https://searchenterpriseai.techtarget.com/definition/supervised-learning

https://towardsdatascience.com/supervised-vs-unsupervised-learning-14f68e32ea8d

https://www.datarobot.com/wiki/unsupervised-machine-learning/

https://home.deib.polimi.it/matteucc/Clustering/tutorial_html/

https://towardsdatascience.com/the-5-clustering-algorithms-data-scientists-need-to-know-a36d136ef68

http://blog.aylien.com/10-machine-learning-terms-explained-in-simple/

https://www.forbes.com/sites/bernardmarr/2016/12/06/what-is-the-difference-between-artificial-intelligence-and-machine-learning/#2769c962742b

Machine Learning

A Comprehensive, Step-by-Step Guide to Intermediate Concepts and Techniques in Machine Learning

Introduction

I want to thank you for choosing this book, '*Machine Learning - A Comprehensive, Step-by-Step Guide to Intermediate Concepts and Techniques in Machine Learning.*'

In the first part of the book, I covered the basics of machine learning. This book is an intermediate level and will help you gather a deeper understanding of what machine learning is. You will also learn about how you can build a machine learning algorithm or model in Python. It can be difficult to build an algorithm from scratch, but this book will help you every step of the way. This book provides a step-by-step process that you need to follow to build the algorithm from scratch.

This book also provides some information about deep learning and artificial neural networks. It also provides information about the different types of neural networks that you can use to train machines. You will also learn how to build an algorithm for a deep learning model.

Thank you for purchasing the book. I hope you gather all the information you were looking for.

Chapter One

Practical Examples of Machine Learning

One can use machine learning and artificial intelligence in many ways, and there are many applications and tools that use the concepts of machine learning to improve our lives. These tools also help businesses make informed decisions and optimize their operations. In the first part of the book, we have covered the different uses of machine learning, and some applications of machine learning. This chapter provides a deeper understanding of how machine learning can be used in different industries.

Consumer Goods

The Hello Barbie doll uses machine learning, advanced analytics and natural language processing to listen and respond to a child. The microphone in the doll's necklace records what the child says and transmits that information to the servers in ToyTalk. The machine analyzes the recording and determine what the response should be using 8,000 lines of responses. The servers will then transmit the response back to the doll in less than a second to respond to the child. The answers to some questions like what the doll's favorite food is are stored in the database. These answers are used in later conversations.

Coca-Cola's extensive product list and global market make it one of the largest beverage companies in the world. The company creates large volumes of data, and it has embraced a lot of new technology that helps it put the data to good use. The company uses the data to

536

develop new products and also uses augmenting reality an artificial learning in the bottling plants.

Heineken, the Dutch company, is a worldwide leader and has been a leader for over 150 years. The company wants to use the large volumes of data that it collects to catapult its success in the United States. Right from improving the operations using data analytics to the Internet of Things to the data-driven marketing, Heineken uses data and artificial intelligence augmentation to improve its advertising, marketing, customer service and operations.

Creative Arts

It is true that culinary arts require a human touch. The AI-enabled Chef Watson developed by IBM shows the world how one can use artificial intelligence to become a chef in the kitchen. It can also advise its human counterparts on what combinations of food they should use to develop unique flavors. This way the chef can develop unique flavors through artificial intelligence. Human beings and artificial intelligence can always create something new together.

You can also use big data and artificial intelligence in the world of design and art. A classic example would be IBM's machine, Watson. This machine was fed with thousands of images of the artist Gaudi's work. The machine was also fed with complementary material that allowed the machine to learn how Barcelona, its biographies, cultures, song lyrics and historical articles influenced his work. The machine then analyzed the information and then derived the appropriate results to human artists. These artists used the information provided by Watson to sculpt in Gaudi's style.

Some algorithms are also being used to inspire new songs. If you give these algorithms enough input, it will look at different insights and develop new lyrics. These inputs come from newspaper headlines, speeches and millions of conversations. Machines like the Watson BEAT identify different musical elements that one can use to inspire some composers. Artificial intelligence also helps a musician understand what its audience wants to hear. It will then help the musician understand what songs will ultimately reach the top 50s.

Energy

BP, which is a global energy leader, has realized that it can use artificial intelligence and big data to create more opportunities. This company now uses technology to improve performance levels, optimize the use of resources and also improve the production of oil and gas. There are sensors that have been included in the system which provide the management with information about the site. BP allows scientists, decision-makers and engineers to use the data to improve performance.

GE Power also uses machine learning, the Internet of Things and big data to deliver energy to the 21st century. It is using these tools to build an "Internet of energy." Machine learning and advanced analytics help the company enable predictive power and maintenance. It also helps the business optimize its work and work towards developing a digital power plant.

Financial Services

Credit reference agencies like Experian obtain large volumes of data from transactional records, public information records and marketing databases. The volume of business continues to increase since the number of individuals increases around the world. Experian is incorporating machine-learning algorithms into its products to allow for effective and quick decision-making. The machines can learn to distinguish between the data points and identify those points that are important. Experian can then use this information to optimize its processes.

American Express relies only on machine learning algorithms and data analytics to detect fraud using real-time data. This allows the company to save millions of dollars in losses. AmEx processes close to one trillion dollars every day and has over 100 million cards in operation. The company is also using data flow to develop an application, which will connect a cardholder with services and products, and other special offers. The company also gives merchants the chance to look at how their peers are performing.

Healthcare

Deep learning and artificial intelligence are being used by Infervision to save lives. Due to the population in China, it becomes impossible for radiologists to review the CT scans of over 1.5 billion people to look for some early signs of lung cancer. A radiologist needs to review thousands of scans every day, and this is a tedious process. This will also lead to errors. Infervision built and trained many algorithms to perform the work of a radiologist, and allow the algorithm to diagnose cancer efficiently and accurately.

Google's DeepMind uses neuroscience as its foundation and inspiration. DeepMind is a machine that can mimic the emotions and thoughts of the human brain. DeepMind has beaten human beings at games, but what is intriguing about this system is that it can be used in healthcare to reduce the time it takes for doctors to diagnose the issue and plan the treatments.

Manufacturing

One can use the data generated by cars in many ways. Volvo has collected large volumes of data which it uses to predict when a part in the car will fail or when a vehicle needs to be serviced. Through artificial intelligence and machine learning, Volvo upholds impressive records of safety. It also helps to improve the passenger and driver convenience using this data. Volvo has started to conduct some research on autonomous vehicles.

At the heart of its business model, BMW has some machine learning and big-data technology. It uses the data to make informed decisions about the business right from engineering and design to aftercare and sales. The company has also improved its driverless technology. This means that BMW cars can drive themselves without any human intervention.

The artificial intelligence technology revolution has also hit farming. John Deere is doing his best to develop automation and data-driven analytical tools that a farmer can use. They also acquired Blue River Technology to use the advanced machine learning algorithms to give robots a chance to make informed decisions based on some visual data. It can also assess whether a plant is a pest or not. It will also tell the farmer how it can treat the plant without the need to use a pesticide. The company has already developed a vehicle that will automatically plow and sow and helps the farmer making informed decisions.

Media

Talking with Machines, the BBC project is a drama that allows listeners to have a conversation using their smart speakers. The listeners can be a part of the story, and the machine prompts the listeners to answer some questions. It also allows a listener to insert his or her own lines into the script. This project was developed only for smart speakers like Google Home and Amazon Echo. BBC also plans to expand to other devices in the near future.

Press Association, a news agency in the UK, is hoping artificial intelligence and robots will save newspapers and local news. They have partnered with Urbs Media, a news automation specialist. They want to develop robots that write at least 30,000 articles and stories every month. This project is known as Reporters and Data and Robots (RADAR). The machine is fed with different information from public services, local authorities and government. It uses natural language generation technology to develop content.

These robots fill in a gap in the coverage that human beings cannot fill.

Netflix uses Big Data Analytics to predict what a customer may want to watch. Netflix also creates content and uses the data it collects to identify the type of content it wants to invest in. This is because of the confidence they have on the predictions of data. It is for this reason that Netflix is willing to commission multiple seasons of new shows instead of leaving it at a pilot episode.

Retail

When you look at Burberry, you will only think about handbags and perfume. You will never believe that the company is a digital business. What most people do not know is that Burberry has been reinventing itself. It uses artificial intelligence and big data to improve sales, customer relationships and to combat counterfeit products. The company wants to nurture personal and deep connections with the customers to increase sales. It is for this reason that they have developed a reward and loyalty program that will help them create a personalized shopping experience for its customers. They are also trying to improve the shopping experience in retail stores.

Walmart is the second-largest retailer and is always looking for a way to transform the retail business and also provide better service. Walmart uses the Internet of Things, Machine learning, big data and artificial intelligence to ensure that both its online and retail customers have a great experience. This is something that Amazon is still unable to do.

Social Media

Twitter uses machine learning and artificial intelligence to recommend tweets, fight inappropriate content (content that is racist or sexist) and to enhance the user experience. The use of machine learning and artificial intelligence algorithms has improved the product. Twitter can now process a lot of data using deep neural networks that learn user preferences over time.

Facebook uses deep learning to draw some value from the unstructured data-sets. This data-set is through the clicks and cursor movements of over two billion people. These people update their statuses at least 300,000 times in a minute. Most deep learning technology is built on a Torch platform that focuses on neural networks and deep learning technologies.

Instagram also uses artificial intelligence and big data to prevent cyber bullying, remove any offensive comments and also target advertising. When the volume of content grows, the application uses artificial intelligence concepts to show users some information that they may like to see.

Chapter Two

Advantages and Disadvantages
of Machine Learning

The previous chapter covered some of the applications of machine learning in different industries. Before we delve into the intermediate machine learning techniques, let us look at a few advantages and disadvantages of machine learning.

Advantages of Machine Learning

Due to sheer volume and magnitude of the tasks, there are some instances where an engineer or developer cannot succeed no matter how hard they try; in those cases, the advantages of machines over humans are clearly stark.

Improves efficiency

Human beings have designed machines in a specific way without appreciating the many capabilities. This is because they are unaware of the various situations in which a computer can work. Through machine learning and artificial intelligence, a machine will learn to adapt to environmental changes and improves its own efficiency regardless of its surroundings.

Helps machines handle large datasets

Machine learning brings with it the capability to handle multiple dimensions and varieties of data simultaneously and in uncertain conditions. Therefore, a system that has artificial intelligence and uses machine learning algorithm can function in a dynamic environment. This emphasizes the efficient use of resources.

Through machine learning one can build tools that will improve the quality in small and large process environments.

Completes specific tasks

Programmers develop machines to complete some tasks that are tedious or repetitive. These tasks are often an elaborate and arduous program where there is scope for the programmer to make errors of omission. This means that he or she may forget to include some details in the program. If you use machine-learning algorithms, you can be certain that the system will learn the processes and tasks on its own.

Identifying patterns

When the engineer gives a machine with artificial intelligence a training dataset, the machine will learn to identify patterns within the data and produce results for any other similar inputs that the engineers provide the machine with. This is efficiency far beyond that of a normal analyst. Due to the strong connection between machine learning and data science (which is the process of crunching large volumes of data and unearthing relationships between the underlying variables), through machine learning one can derive important insights into large volumes of data.

Helps Machines Adapt to the Changing Environment

With ever-changing technology and the development of new programming languages to communicate these technological advancements, it is nearly impossible to convert all existing programs and systems into these new syntaxes. Redesigning every program from its coding stage to adapt to technological advancements is counter-productive. In such times it is highly efficient to use machine learning so that the very machines can upgrade and adapt themselves to the changing technological climate.

Disadvantages of Machine Learning

1. It is difficult to interpret the results accurately to determine the effectiveness of the machine-learning algorithm.

2. The engineer must experiment with different algorithms before he or she chooses one to train the machine with.

3. There is some improvement made to technology regularly. This means that every machine needs to constantly learn. Machines should also know how to adapt to the changes in technology.

4. It is difficult to acquire data to train the machine. An engineer should know what type of data he needs, and which algorithm he will use to train the machine. There can be a significant impact on the results obtained if the engineer does not make the right decision.

Hi there! If you found the topic or information useful, it would be a great help if you can leave a quick review on Amazon. Thanks a lot!

Chapter Three

How to Create and Train
Machine Learning Models

This chapter will provide information on how an engineer can train a machine learning or deep learning model.

Training from Scratch

When you build a model from scratch, you need to collate large volumes of information and labeled data. You will then need to design the model or algorithm and ensure that it can learn all the features present in the data-set. You should do this if you are building a model for the first time or are building a model that has many output categories. Most engineers do not use this approach since the network will take a few days or weeks to learn the process due to the large volume of training data.

Transfer learning

Engineers prefer to train their models by using the transfer learning approach. In this approach, a pre-trained or pre-existing model is fine-tuned. You can start with networks like GoogleNet and AlexNet, and feed these networks with new data containing some unknown classes. A few tweaks made to the model will make it function differently. This means that you do not need to procure volumes of data to train the network. This reduces computation time to a few seconds, minutes or hours.

If you want to use transfer learning to train a model, you will need an interface that will allow you to connect to the pre-existing network. You can use this interface to modify and enhance the network to complete a task. Software like MATLAB has functions and tools that you can use for this purpose.

Feature Extraction

This is a slightly less common and specialized approach that an engineer uses to train a machine-learning model. The model must first identify the different instances and attributes in the data-set. You can then extract these features from the model whenever you need to during the training process. You can then use these features to train support vector machines or a machine-learning model.

Chapter Four

An Introduction to Deep Learning

Most engineers and developers help machines learn using different machine learning techniques. You can make a machine learn by example using deep learning techniques. This is one of the key technologies that engineers used to help a car navigate through the streets driverless. Cars can now identify lampposts, stop signs and pedestrians. Deep learning is also used in voice control devices like phones, tablets, televisions and other hands-free devices like Alexa. The technology industry will reach new heights through deep learning.

Computer models using deep learning techniques learn to perform classification tasks from text, sound or images. Machines that have a deep learning model can perform analyses that human being cannot. These machines also perform better than human beings. Like with machine learning, engineers train deep learning machines with large data-sets called the training data-set. They also use neural networks in the models.

How does Deep Learning attain such Impressive Results?

A deep learning model is very accurate, and it can derive these results because of the accuracy. Through various deep-learning techniques, an engineer can ensure that machines are very accurate. This helps the machine meet the demands of the customer, and it is crucial for devices like driverless cars to have this feature. The recent developments in deep learning allow machines to perform

548

some tasks, like the classification of images, better than human beings.

Although deep learning was studied in the early 1980s, it has only become a popular machine learning technique now for the following reasons:

- Deep learning uses large volumes of labeled data to train machines. For instance, an engineer will need to feed a car with thousands of hours of videos and trillions of images to train so it can perform well on the road without a driver.

- Deep learning also requires computing power. The parallel architecture that most machines have improves the functioning of a deep learning technique. When deep learning is combined with cloud computing or clusters, it helps to reduce the time that an engineer spends to train the machine from a few days to a few hours or even less.

Applications of Deep Learning

Deep learning techniques and applications are used in a wide range of industries.

Automatic translation

Deep neural networks can translate words, phrases or sentences from one language to another automatically. This application has been around for quite some time now, but the introduction to deep neural networks has helped this application achieve great results in the following areas:

1. Translation of images

2. Translation of text

For the translation of a text, the engineer does not have to feed the deep neural network with a pre-processing sequence. This allows the algorithm to identify the dependencies between the words in a sentence and map them to a new language. The stacked networks in a large LDTM recurrent neural network are used for this purpose.

You may have guessed from previous sections of the chapter that a CNN is used to verify if an image has letters, and where it can find those letters in the scene. Once the network identifies these letters, it can transform the letters into text, translate it into a different language and recreate the image with the translated text. This process is known as instant visual translation.

Object Detection and Classification in Images
In this application, the deep neural network identifies and classifies the objects in an image. The network classifies the images into a set of previously known objects. Very large CNN's have been used to achieve accurate results when compared to the benchmark examples of the problem.

Automated driving
As mentioned earlier, an engineer feeds a car with videos and images to help it detect objects like stop signs and traffic lights. Through deep learning, the car can also detect other vehicles and pedestrians, which helps to decrease the number of road accidents.

Defense and Aerospace
The military uses deep learning techniques to identify the safe and unsafe zones for its troops and people. These techniques also help the machine identify an area of interest when it uses satellite imagery.

Automatic Colorization of Images
Human beings tried their best to add colors to black and white photographs, and it was a difficult task to perform. Now, you can use deep learning networks to add color to photographs in less than a few seconds. A deep learning network will identify the objects in the image and their context within the photograph. It will add color

to the image based on the information it has obtained, and this is an impressive feat. This capability increases the use of large convolutional and high-quality neural networks like ImageNet. The approach involves the use of supervised layers and CNN's to recreate an image by adding color to it.

Medical research

Cancer researchers use deep learning techniques to detect cancer cells in the human body. Multiple teams at UCLA helped to build a microscope that uses some deep learning techniques. This microscope yields a high-dimensional data-set and can detect cancer cells in any part of the human body.

Industrial automation

Deep learning techniques help an organization improve the safety of the workers around some heavy machinery. The machine lets the supervisors know when an employee is at an unsafe distance from some heavy machinery.

Adding Sound to Silent Movies

In this task, the deep neural network must develop or recreate sounds that will match a silent video. Let us consider the following example. We need the network to add sounds to a video where people are playing drums. The engineer will provide the network with close to 1000 videos with the sound of the drum striking many surfaces. The network will identify the different sounds and associate the video frames from the silent video or movie with the pre-recorded sounds. It will then select the sound from the database that matches the video in the scene. This system is then evaluated using a Turing-test where human beings were asked to differentiate between the real and synthesized video. Both CNN and LSTM neural networks are used to perform this application.

Automatic handwriting generation

For this application, the engineer must feed the deep neural network with a few handwriting examples. This helps the network generate a new handwriting for a given word, phrase or sentence. The dataset that the engineer feeds the network should provide a sequence of coordinates that the writer uses when writing with a pen. From this dataset, the network identifies and establishes a relationship between the movement of the pen and the letters in the dataset. The network can then generate new handwriting examples. What is fascinating is that the network can learn different styles and mimic those styles whenever necessary.

Chapter Five

An Introduction to Neural Networks

Now that you know what deep learning, and some of its applications, let us look at what neural network architecture is. Engineers built artificial neural networks to help machines process information in the same way as the human brain. The most important feature of these networks is its layers that can process any kind of information. Every layer in the network consists of neutrons that are interconnected. These neutrons process information and work together to solve any problems. Since the neural network processes information, the same way as the human brain, a machine with neural network architecture will learn by example. Engineers develop these machines for special purposes like data classification or pattern recognition. Neural networks learn the same way that human beings do – when the neurons make some changes or adjustments, the network will learn.

Historical Background

Although neural networks were developed before the invention of computers, they suffered a setback since people were not fully adept at using these networks. It is because of this that the simulation of neural networks is a recent development. Any improvement made to the computer boosts the advances made in the development of neural networks. People threw themselves into research when the concept of neural networks gained importance. They were unable to obtain any information on how they can use neural networks to improve the accuracy and efficiency of machines. This led to a dip in the enthusiasm. Some researchers continued to study neural networks despite these failures. They worked hard to develop a neural network technology that most people in the industry accepted.

Warren McCulloch and Walter Pitts developed or produced the first artificial neural network in the year 1943, which is called the McCulloch-Pitts neuron. Since the technology to develop the network further was not available to them in that year, they did not use this network to perform or automate some complex tasks.

Why use Neural Networks?

Every industry today uses large volumes of data to improve the functioning of the industry. These datasets have many variables that make it difficult for human beings to understand the patterns in the dataset. Neural networks make it easier to identify these hidden patterns in the dataset. Some computers also find it difficult to identify the trends in the dataset if they do not have neural network architecture. An engineer can train the neural network using large datasets to help it become an expert in the field. The engineer can then use the network to predict the output for any future input. This gives the engineer a chance to answer some important questions about the future. Some advantages of neural networks include:

1. A neural network uses the supervised machine learning technique to learn and adapt to new tasks.

2. You can use the network to represent any information that you provide to it during the learning stage.

3. Neural networks can compute data in parallel, which means that machines with neural network architecture work faster to provide some results.

4. If the network is damaged, it will affect the performance, but the network will still retain some of its properties that

will make it easier for the engineer to fix the network and train it again.

Neural Networks versus Conventional Computers

Conventional computers and neural networks do not use the same approach to solve any problem. The former only use algorithms to solve a given problem. Conventional computers can also solve problems if they know what steps they should follow to identify the solution. This means that conventional computers often solve problems that human beings can solve. Computers are useful when they can solve problems that human beings do not know how to solve.

As mentioned earlier, neural networks function in the same way as the human brain, and the neurons in the network are interconnected. These neural networks always work in parallel to solve most problems. Since the network learns by example, the engineer cannot teach the network to perform a specific task. This makes it important for the engineer to choose the training datasets carefully. Otherwise, it will be difficult for the machine to learn how it should solve a problem correctly. Since the neural network learns from the dataset, it can solve a variety of problems including those that the engineer does not train the machine to solve. This makes these networks unpredictable.

Computers also solve problems using cognitive approaches. The computer should know the process it should follow to solve the problem, and this will only work when the engineer provides the computer with the correct instructions. The engineer can provide these instructions to the machine using a high-level programming language. The computer will decode the instructions into a language that it can understand. This process helps the engineer predict how a computer will work. If there is an issue with the result, the engineer knows that it is because of a hardware or software problem.

Neural networks and conventional computers complement each other. Some tasks like arithmetic calculations are better suited for conventional algorithmic computers while some complex tasks are more suited for neural networks. Most tasks require a combination of these approaches to ensure that the machine performs at maximum efficiency.

Types of Neural Networks

Fully connected neural network

The network layer is the most common type of neural network architecture. It has three layers of interconnected neurons. The first layer, known as the input layer, is connected to the hidden layer of neurons, which is connected to the output layer. The input layer represents the data or information that the engineer provides to the network. How the input layer views the raw data determines the weights that are placed on the neurons in the hidden layer and the weights that are placed on the nodes connecting the neurons in the input layer to the hidden layer. The behavior of the output layer is dependent on the weights placed on the neurons in the hidden layer and the weights placed on the nodes connecting the neurons in the hidden layer to the output layer.

This is the structure for a simple neural network and it is interesting since the hidden layers can choose to represent the data in any form. The weights present on the nodes connecting the input layer to the hidden layer determine when the hidden network layer must stay active. The engineer can modify the weights between the input and hidden layers to ensure that the hidden unit will represent what the engineer wants.

It is also easy to differentiate between a single-layer and a multi-layer architecture. In the single-layer architecture, the neurons are connected at their nodes. This means that every layer in the network is connected, which increases the computational power of the network. In the multi-layer architecture, the network is numbered by layers. This means that the layers and not the neurons are interconnected.

Perceptrons

Frank Rosenblatt coined the term perceptron in the year 1960. This was when there were significant developments being made in neural network architecture. Perceptrons are a type of McCulloch and Pitts model. Every model is assigned a pre-processing or fixed weight. This network is like the visual function or system in human beings, which makes it easier to use it in pattern recognition. You can use this network in other processes as well.

Feed-forward Networks

The feed-forward network is also called the bottom-up or top-down network. The signals will only travel in one direction in this network – only from the input to the output. There is no feedback loop in this network, which means that any output that is derived from one layer will not affect the output that is derived by another layer. The network is easy to construct since the input is associated with the output. This network is also used in pattern recognition.

Convolutional neural networks

Convolutional Neural Networks (CNNs) are similar to the fully connected neural networks. They are made up of multiple layers with many neurons. Each neuron in the network is assigned a weight based on the training data that the engineer uses to teach the network. When the neurons receive an input, they perform a dot product and then follow that product with a non-linearity. So, what is the difference between a convolutional neural network and a fully connected neural network? A CNN makes the assumption that every input in the training dataset is an image that allows the engineer to encode some properties into the network architecture. These make it easier for the network to apply the forward function and reduce the number of instances in the training dataset. Most deep learning applications use these types of neural networks.

Feedback networks

The signals in a feedback network will always move in both directions that introduce a loop in the network. It is difficult to build these networks, but they are extremely powerful. The state of a feedback network will constantly change until the signals reach equilibrium. The network will remain in this state of equilibrium until the input dataset changes. When the engineer feeds the network with a new data-set, the network must identify the new equilibrium point. It is for this reason that these networks are recurrent and interactive. The next section provides some information on recurrent neural networks.

Recurrent neural networks

In recurrent neural networks, the information always goes through a loop. When the network makes a decision, it will consider the current input and also assess what it has learned from the previous inputs. The usual RNN has a short-term memory, and when it is combined with the LSTM (Long Short-term memory) it will have a long-term memory. This is further discussed below.

A good way to illustrate the concepts of RNN is by using an example. Consider that you are using a regular feed-forward neural network and give the network the word "brain" as the input. This network will process that word character-by-character, and by the time it reaches the character "I," it will forget about the first three characters. This makes it impossible to use this model to predict what the next character will be. An RNN can remember the previous characters and also predict the next character since it has an internal memory. It produces outputs and copies those outputs back into the network. This means that the RNNs always add the immediate past information to the present information. Therefore, an RNN network has the following inputs:

1. The Present Data

2. The Recent Data

An engineer must be careful about the training dataset he uses to teach the model since the model uses the sequences to predict characters in the text. This means that an RNN can perform functions that most other algorithms cannot. A feed-forward neural network will assign weights to the neurons in every layer to produce the output. The RNN applies weight to the current and the previous input data and also tweaks the weights assigned to the neurons.

Generative adversarial network

In a generative adversarial network (GAN) two networks are pitted against each other, which is why this network is called adversarial. A GAN can learn to mimic any data-set or distribution, and it is because of this that most engineers use GAN in their system. You can use GAN to build a world that is similar to your own in many domains like prose, pictures and speech. The output from these networks is impressive.

In this network, you have a generator and a discriminator. The generator will generate every new instance in the data-set while the discriminator will evaluate the instances. The discriminator must then identify if the new instance belongs to an existing training data-set or not.

Let us consider the following example. We want to generate handwritten numerals from the MNIST dataset. You can download the dataset from the following location: http://yann.lecun.com/exdb/mnist/

The discriminator should identify whether the instances that the generator creates is authentic when compared to the MNIST dataset. This means that the generator will continue to develop newer instances of data, and the discriminator should identify whether the instance is valid or invalid. The generator has to try to lie to the discriminator without being caught. The discriminator must identify the fake instances that the generator creates. The steps that the GAN takes are as follows:

- The generator will choose random numbers in the data-set and return an image as a new instance.

- The engineer will send this new instance into the discriminator along with a stream of images in the training data-set.

- The discriminator will label the images with a degree of authenticity "1" and label the fake images "0."

Found this title interesting or useful? Then a review on Amazon will be highly appreciated!

Chapter Six

Building Your First Algorithm in Python

It is a rewarding experience to write an algorithm from scratch. This is only when the algorithm clicks and you understand what is happening inside the system. It is not going to be easy to write an algorithm from scratch even if you have built one in SciKit-learn. There are some algorithms that are more complicated than others, so let us take a look at a simple single layer algorithm.

This chapter covers the six steps that you will need to follow to write an algorithm, and we will be building a Perceptron model. You can translate this method to other machine learning algorithms with ease.

Understand the Algorithm

This goes back to what I mentioned earlier. You must understand all the basics before you begin to work on an algorithm. You must be able to answer the following questions before you build the algorithm in Python or any other language:

1. What is the algorithm?

2. What can I use this algorithm for?

3. Is there any reason why I cannot use this algorithm?

Let us answer these questions for the perceptron.

1. The perceptron is the most basic neural network that consists of one layer only. This neural network is used to find solutions for binary classification problems.

2. The perceptron is a linear classifier, which means that you can only use it when you need to make a linear decision. Some simple uses of this network are reinsurance default prediction ("reinsurer will pay," "reinsurer will not pay") or sentiment analyses (negative and positive responses). In both cases the boundary for the decisions is linear.

3. You can never use the perceptron if the boundary for the decision is non-linear. For non-linear problems, you will need to use a different algorithm.

Look for Different Learning Sources

Once you gather a basic understanding of the model, you should begin to research. There are many sources that you can use. Some people are capable of learning in a better way with videos, while others prefer textbooks. You should try to use different sources for the same. If you are learning more about the mathematical details, you should reach more texts, but you should use videos if you are working on some practical examples. You can find these videos on YouTube and blog posts. Here are some great resources that you can use for the perceptron:

Textbooks

1. Understanding Machine Learning: From Theory To Algorithms, Section 21.4

2. The Elements of Statistical Learning, Section 4.5.1

Videos

1. Perceptron Training:
   https://www.youtube.com/watch?v=5g0TPrxKK6o

2. The working of the algorithm: https://www.youtube.com/watch?v=1XkjVl-j8MM

Blogs

There are many machine learning blogs that you can read before you begin working on building a model. Some blogs you can look at are:

1. https://machinelearningmastery.com/implement-perceptron-algorithm-scratch-python/

2. https://sebastianraschka.com/Articles/2015_singlelayer_neurons.html

Break the Algorithm into Smaller Chunks

Once you have gathered the resources, you should start learning. Grab a paper and pencil and make notes of the important information that you read in a chapter or blog post. You should write down the points and outline the algorithm. Once you go through the sources linked above, you should break the algorithm for the perceptron into the following segments:

- Initialize weights.

- Multiply the weights with the inputs and sum the values up.

- Compare the results against your training dataset or threshold. This will allow you to derive the binary output.

- Update the weights.

- Repeat the process.

When you break the algorithm down into smaller chunks, it becomes easy for one to learn. You have broken the algorithm down into the pseudocode, which will help you fill in the finer details for the model.

563

Start with an example

Once you have put your notes together about the algorithm, you should work towards implementing that code. You should start off with a simple example before you begin to work on a complicated problem. For this algorithm, we will use the NAND gate data that you can find at the following location: https://en.wikipedia.org/wiki/NAND_gate

If both your inputs are true, the output is false; otherwise, the output will be true. The table below shows an example of the data-set.

x_1	x_2	y
0	0	1
0	1	1
1	0	1
1	1	0

You can build the algorithm that you outline in the third step now that you have the data-set. You should always write the algorithm in smaller pieces and test those sections before you test the full algorithm. This will make it easier for you to debug the program when you start out. You can always go back and make the algorithm look nicer.

Let us look at an example of the product part of the algorithm using the dot product that is outlined in step 3.

```
import numpy as np

w = [0,0,0]
x = [1,0,1]

print np.dot(w, x)

# Out: 0
```

Validate the algorithm with a trusted implementation

Once the code is written fully, and you have removed the bugs, you should test it on a large dataset. If you want to ensure that your code works correctly on a large dataset, you should always use a tested implementation. You can use an implementation from sci-kit learn for this algorithm.

```
clf = Perceptron(random_state=None, eta0= 0.1,
                 shuffle=False, fit_intercept=False)
```

When you test the code, you should look at the weights. If the algorithm is correct, the weights should match those of the sci-kit learn the implementation of the perceptron.

```
print "sklearn weights:"
print clf.coef_[0]

print "my perceptron weights:"
print w

#sklearn weights:
#[-0.5         -0.29850122  0.35054929]
#my perceptron weights:
#[-0.5         -0.29850122  0.35054929]
```

You will need to make some changes to the code if you want to test your new algorithm. You must remember to always be aware of the inputs that you give to the model. Make sure that you never use a model without questioning the assumptions and understanding what each input means.

Write your process

This is the last step of the process and is the most important one. You have done all your work – went through resources, made notes, wrote algorithms and also compared the algorithm with a trusted implementation. You should never let that work go to waste. It is important to write the process up for the following reasons:

1. Since you are explaining to people what you have just learned, you will gain a deeper understanding.

2. You can always show the developed model to employers. You can show them that you have used an existing machine learning library to build an algorithm. The most impressive part about it is that you built the algorithm from scratch.

You can create a GitHub portfolio and show the world what you have achieved.

Chapter Seven

How to Build an Algorithm in Python

Python is a powerful and popular interpreted language, and unlike R, it is a complete platform and language you can use for both development and research. You can also use python in developing production systems. There are many libraries and modules you can choose from. This means that there are different ways in which you can build your model. This may be overwhelming, and to avoid the fear of programming in python, you can build a small machine-learning project. When you build a project in Python, you will,

1. Install and begin to use the Python interpreter.

2. Have a bird's eye view of how you should progress through every step when you build the project.

3. Gain confidence, and start developing a project of your own.

You need an end-to-end Project

Courses and books become frustrating. You do get a lot of snippets and different recipes that you can use, but you will never know how to fit them together. When you apply a machine-learning concept to your data-set, you start working on a project. A machine-learning problem does not necessarily have to be linear, and there are many steps that you need to follow. These steps have been mentioned in the previous chapter.

The only way you can come to terms with using a new tool or platform is to work through a project and cover all the key steps. This means you need to start from loading the data and also make some predictions about the model. When you have this template stored in your head, you can use the model on different data-sets. You can fill the gaps, and improve on existing tasks. You can only do this when you are confident about your model.

Welcome to the World of Machine Learning

If you want to build your first machine-learning project, you should use the iris flowers data-set. Please find the data-set saved at the following location: https://archive.ics.uci.edu/ml/datasets/Iris. It is always a good idea to use this data-set since it is understood well by programmers in the machine learning community.

Let us look at a few properties of the iris data-set:

1. Since the attributes are numeric, you must learn how to load the data and then handle that data in Python.

2. The data-set represents a classification problem that will help you practice the supervised machine-learning algorithm.

3. If you use all the classes in the data-set for the purpose of the algorithm, it will become a multi-class classification problem, which will need some specialized handling.

4. There are 150 rows of data and only four attributes. This means that the data will fit easily into your system's memory.

5. The numeric attributes all have the same scale and units which means that you do not have to perform any special transformations or scaling to start working on your data.

Let us now build your machine learning project in Python.

Machine Learning in Python

In this secti0n, we will look at how you can build a small machine-learning project. Let us look at an overview of what we will cover in this chapter:

1. Installing Python and the SciPy platforms.

2. Loading the iris data-set into python.

3. Summarizing the iris data-set.

4. Visualizing the iris data-set.

5. Evaluating a few algorithms.

6. Predicting some outcomes.

You should take your time and work through every step. You should try to type the commands into the platform yourself. If you want to save time, you can copy the commands into the platform.

Downloading, Installing and Starting Python scipy

You should install the Python and SciPy platforms on your system if you do not have them already. This chapter does not cover them in great detail, but we will work on how you can install the SciPy libraries.

Install SciPy Libraries

In this tutorial, we will be using the 3.5+ version of Python. You must install the following libraries in your system for the purpose of this tutorial:

- SciPy

- Pandas

- Matplotlib

- Numpy

- Sklearn

You can install these libraries in different ways in your system. Experts suggest that you select one method and stick to that method when you install the different libraries in your system.

The SciPy installation page will provide you with excellent instructions that will help you install the libraries on different platforms, like Windows, mac OS X and Linux.

Start python and check the versions

It is always a good idea to ensure that the Python environment is successfully installed in the system. You should also ensure that it is working correctly. You can use the script below to help you test the environment. The script will import every library necessary and will print the version in the output window.

Open the command line and begin the python interpreter.

Python

Experts recommend that you work directly in the interpreter. Alternatively, you should write the scripts and run them on the command line, which is bigger than the IDEs and editors. You should always keep things simple and only focus on machine learning alone. Copy the script in the section below, and paste it in Python.

```
# Check the versions of libraries


# Python version
import sys
print('Python: {}'.format(sys.version))
# scipy
import scipy
print('scipy: {}'.format(scipy.__version__))
```

```
# numpy
import numpy
print('numpy: {}'.format(numpy.__version__))
# matplotlib
import matplotlib
print('matplotlib: {}'.format(matplotlib.__version__))
# pandas
import pandas
print('pandas: {}'.format(pandas.__version__))
# scikit-learn
import sklearn
print('sklearn: {}'.format(sklearn.__version__))
```

You will find the following output in your window.

Python: 2.7.11 (default, Mar 1 2016, 18:40:10)

[GCC 4.2.1 Compatible Apple LLVM 7.0.2 (clang-700.1.81)]

scipy: 0.17.0

numpy: 1.10.4

matplotlib: 1.5.1

pandas: 0.17.1

sklearn: 0.18.1

You should compare the above output to every version. The version that you are using should be more recent and always match. The API never changes quickly, so you should not worry if you are behind the latest version. Every step in this chapter will work for you regardless of the version. If you receive an error, you should stop and fix it. You cannot complete the steps in this chapter if the above script does not run cleanly.

Load the data

You will now need to sue the iris flower data-set. This data-set is the "hello world" version of a machine learning data-set. What I mean by this is that this data-set is used by almost everybody.

This data-set contains 150 observations or instances about the iris flowers. There are four attributes that carry information about various measurements of the iris flowers. The last column provides information about the species of the flower. The flowers in the data-set belong to three species.

Let us look at how you can load the CSV file that contains the iris data.

Import libraries

Let us first import the functions, objects and modules that we will use in this chapter.

```
# Load libraries

import pandas

from pandas.plotting import scatter_matrix

import matplotlib.pyplot as plt

from sklearn import model_selection

from sklearn.metrics import classification_report

from sklearn.metrics import confusion_matrix

from sklearn.metrics import accuracy_score

from sklearn.linear_model import LogisticRegression
```

572

```
from sklearn.tree import DecisionTreeClassifier

from sklearn.neighbors import KNeighborsClassifier

from sklearn.discriminant_analysis import
LinearDiscriminantAnalysis

from sklearn.naive_bayes import GaussianNB

from sklearn.svm import SVC
```

You should be able to load the data into Python without any errors. If there is an error, you should stop. You must ensure that the SciPy environment is in a working condition before you continue to work on the model. Learn how to set up the environment.

Load data-set

You can use the UCI Machine Learning repository to load the data directly into the platform. In this example, we will use pandas to load the data into python. You can use these pandas to explore the data using both data visualization and descriptive statistics. You should note that you are specifying the names of every column when you load the data. You can use this later when you explore the data.

```
# Load dataset

url =
"https://raw.githubusercontent.com/jbrownlee/Datasets/mast
er/iris.csv"

names = ['sepal-length', 'sepal-width', 'petal-length', 'petal-
width', 'class']

dataset = pandas.read_csv(url, names=names)
```

You can load the data-set into the platform without any incident or error. If you have any network trouble, you should download the data-set into a working directory and load that into the platform

573

using the same method. All you need to do is change the URL into a file name.

Summarize the data-set

Let us now look at the data-set. In this step, you will need to look at the data in the following ways:

1. The dimensions of the data-set

2. Look at the data-set

3. Derive a statistical summary of every attribute

4. Breaking the data down using a class variable

Do not let the data overwhelm you. You should look at the data in one command. There are some useful commands that you can use in future projects.

Dimensions of the data-set

You should always know how many instances are present in the data-set. You should know the number of rows and columns that are present in the data-set.

```
# shape

print(dataset.shape)
```

If you are using the iris data-set, you should see 5 attributes and 150 instances.

```
(150, 5)
```

Peek at the data

You should also look at the data and just surf through it to understand the structure.

```
# head

print(dataset.head(20))
```

When you do this, you will see the first twenty rows of the data.

	sepal-length	sepal-width	petal-length	petal-width	class
0	5.1	3.5	1.4	0.2	Iris-setosa
1	4.9	3.0	1.4	0.2	Iris-setosa
2	4.7	3.2	1.3	0.2	Iris-setosa
3	4.6	3.1	1.5	0.2	Iris-setosa
4	5.0	3.6	1.4	0.2	Iris-setosa
5	5.4	3.9	1.7	0.4	Iris-setosa
6	4.6	3.4	1.4	0.3	Iris-setosa
7	5.0	3.4	1.5	0.2	Iris-setosa
8	4.4	2.9	1.4	0.2	Iris-setosa
9	4.9	3.1	1.5	0.1	Iris-setosa
10	5.4	3.7	1.5	0.2	Iris-setosa
11	4.8	3.4	1.6	0.2	Iris-setosa
12	4.8	3.0	1.4	0.1	Iris-setosa
13	4.3	3.0	1.1	0.1	Iris-setosa
14	5.8	4.0	1.2	0.2	Iris-setosa
15	5.7	4.4	1.5	0.4	Iris-setosa
16	5.4	3.9	1.3	0.4	Iris-setosa
17	5.1	3.5	1.4	0.3	Iris-setosa
18	5.7	3.8	1.7	0.3	Iris-setosa
19	5.1	3.8	1.5	0.3	Iris-setosa

Statistical summary

Let us now look at the statistical summary of every attribute in the data-set. This includes the mean, minimum, maximum and count values. You can also calculate some percentiles if you want.

    # descriptions

    print(dataset.describe())

You will see that the numerical values are all in centimeters which means that they are in the same scale. The values also lie between zero and eight centimeters.

	sepal-length	sepal-width	petal-length	petal-width
count	150.000000	150.000000	150.000000	150.000000
mean	5.843333	3.054000	3.758667	1.198667
std	0.828066	0.433594	1.764420	0.763161
min	4.300000	2.000000	1.000000	0.100000
25%	5.100000	2.800000	1.600000	0.300000
50%	5.800000	3.000000	4.350000	1.300000
75%	6.400000	3.300000	5.100000	1.800000
max	7.900000	4.400000	6.900000	2.500000

Class distribution

You should now look at the number of rows, also called instances that belong to a class. This number can be viewed as an absolute count.

    # class distribution

```
print(dataset.groupby('class').size())
```

You will notice that every class has the same instance.

```
class

Iris-setosa        50

Iris-versicolor    50

Iris-virginica     50
```

Data Visualization

Now that you have a basic idea about the data-set, you should learn to visualize the results. We will now look at two different plots:

1. A univariate plot to understand the attributes individually.

2. A multivariate plot to understand the relationship between the attributes.

Univariate plot

Let us start with the univariate plots, which means that you have plots for each individual variable. Let us now create a box and whisper plot for each.

```
# box and whisker plots

dataset.plot(kind='box', subplots=True, layout=(2,2),
sharex=False, sharey=False)

plt.show()
```

This will give you a clear idea about the input attributes and their distributions.

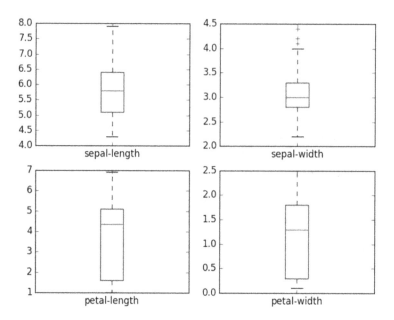

If you want to gather more information about the distribution of every input variable, you can create a histogram.

histograms

dataset.hist()

plt.show()

This will look like there are two input variables with a Gaussian or normal distribution. It is important to note that you can use these algorithms to exploit the assumption.

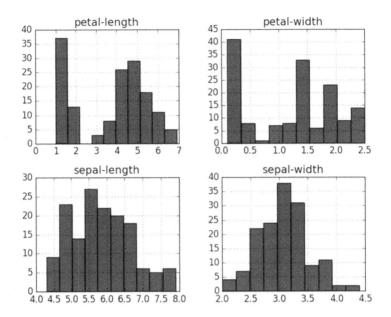

Multivariate plots

A multivariate plot helps you look at the interactions that exist between variables. Let us first look at a scatterplot for every attribute pair. This will help you spot a relationship between the input variables.

```
# scatter plot matrix

scatter_matrix(dataset)

plt.show()
```

You should note that there are some variables that have a diagonal grouping. This also suggests that there is a high correlation between the input variables. You can also predict the relationship between the variables if necessary.

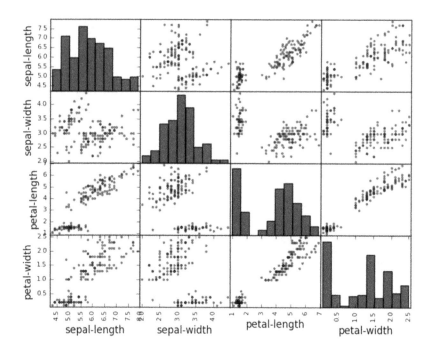

Evaluate the Algorithms

You should now learn to create some models and also estimate the accuracy of the models on any unseen data. In this step, we will cover the following:

- Create a separate validation data-set.

- Prepare the test harness and use the 10-fold cross validation technique.

- Build different models that will help you predict the species from different flower measurements.

- Choose the correct model.

Create a validation data-set

You need to verify if the model you have created is good. You can then use different statistical methods to identify and calculate the accuracy of the model that you create on any unseen data. You also need to obtain a concrete estimate of what the accuracy of the best model that you develop on unseen data. This means that you need to hold some data back from the algorithm, and then use that data to test the algorithm. This will help you test if the model will actually work well ad provides the desired result.

Let us split the data-set into two segments. We will use eighty percent of the data to train the model and twenty percent to test the model.

```
# Split-out validation dataset

array = dataset.values

X = array[:,0:4]

Y = array[:,4]

validation_size = 0.20

seed = 7

X_train, X_validation, Y_train, Y_validation =
model_selection.train_test_split(X, Y,
test_size=validation_size, random_state=seed)
```

You now have the training data to prepare the model in X_train and Y_train, while the X_validation and Y_validation to test the model.

Test harness

You can use the 10-fold cross validation technique to estimate the accuracy of the model. This means that you will split the data-set into ten parts, and then train the data using 9 parts of the data-set and one part to test the model.

```
# Test options and evaluation metric

seed = 7

scoring = 'accuracy'
```

The random seed that you use to build this model does not matter. You should, therefore, learn more about how to generate pseudorandom numbers in the following link:

https://machinelearningmastery.com/introduction-to-random-number-generators-for-machine-learning/.

You should use the accuracy metric to evaluate the model. The accuracy is a ratio of the number of instances that are predicted correctly to the total number of predictions that the model makes. You should multiply this by one hundred to obtain the percentage. You must use the scoring variable when you run and evaluate a model.

Build models

Since you do no know which algorithm is the right on to use for a problem or the right configuration you should use, you should use plots from some of the linearly separable classes in some dimensions. These will help you generate good results. Let us look at the six different algorithms:

1. Logistic Regression (LR)

2. Gaussian Naive Bayes (NB)

3. Classification and Regression Trees (CART)

4. Linear Discriminant Analysis (LDA)

5. K-Nearest Neighbors (KNN)

6. Support Vector Machines (SVM)

The above list is a mixture of non-linear and linear algorithms. You must reset the random number seed of right before a run to ensure that you evaluate the model perfectly. You can only do this when you use the exact same split. This will ensure that the results will be directly comparable. Let us now build and evaluate the five models:

```
# Spot Check Algorithms

models = []

models.append(('LR', LogisticRegression()))

models.append(('LDA', LinearDiscriminantAnalysis()))

models.append(('KNN', KNeighborsClassifier()))

models.append(('CART', DecisionTreeClassifier()))

models.append(('NB', GaussianNB()))

models.append(('SVM', SVC()))

# evaluate each model in turn

results = []

names = []

for name, model in models:

    kfold = model_selection.KFold(n_splits=10,
random_state=seed)

    cv_results = model_selection.cross_val_score(model,
X_train, Y_train, cv=kfold, scoring=scoring)

    results.append(cv_results)

    names.append(name)

    msg = "%s: %f (%f)" % (name, cv_results.mean(),
cv_results.std())

    print(msg)
```

Select the best model

Now that we have at least six models and also the accuracy estimations for each of these models, you should compare the models and select the one with the most accurate. Using the example above, you will obtain the following results:

LR: 0.966667 (0.040825)

LDA: 0.975000 (0.038188)

KNN: 0.983333 (0.033333)

CART: 0.975000 (0.038188)

NB: 0.975000 (0.053359)

SVM: 0.981667 (0.025000)

You should remember that your results will differ. If you want to learn more about how you can embrace the randomness in the data, please access the following link:
https://machinelearningmastery.com/randomness-in-machine-learning/

It will look like the KNN has the best accuracy score. You can also create a plot that will help you evaluate and compare the results of the models. You can compare the mean and spread of every model. It is important to remember that the algorithm was evaluated at least ten times.

```
# Compare Algorithms

fig = plt.figure()

fig.suptitle('Algorithm Comparison')

ax = fig.add_subplot(111)

plt.boxplot(results)

ax.set_xticklabels(names)
```

plt.show()

Now, you can see that the whisker and box plots are squashed at the top with many of the samples achieving at least a hundred percent accuracy.

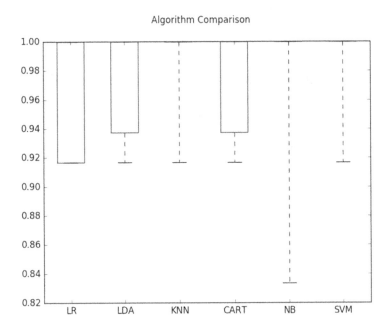

Make Predictions

So far, we have tested the most accurate model, which is the KNN model. You also want to assess the accuracy of the model using the validation set. This will help you check the accuracy of the model you need to use. You should always build a validation set if you have made any slips when you were training the model, like a data leak or overfitting the training data-set. These will result in an output that is overly optimistic. You can always run the validation data-set through the model and summarize the results. You can use different metrics to calculate the accuracy. We will discuss these in the next chapter.

```
# Make predictions on validation dataset

knn = KNeighborsClassifier()

knn.fit(X_train, Y_train)

predictions = knn.predict(X_validation)

print(accuracy_score(Y_validation, predictions))

print(confusion_matrix(Y_validation, predictions))

print(classification_report(Y_validation, predictions))
```

You will notice that the accuracy is 90% or 0.9. You can identify the errors that the model can make by using the confusion matrix. You can then use the classification report to provide a detailed explanation of the precision and also show the best results.

0.9


```
[[ 7  0  0]
 [ 0 11  1]
 [ 0  2  9]]
```


	precision	recall	f1-score	support
Iris-setosa	1.00	1.00	1.00	7
Iris-versicolor	0.85	0.92	0.88	12
Iris-virginica	0.90	0.82	0.86	11
avg / total	0.90	0.90	0.90	30

If you want to learn more about how you can make predictions and also predict the probabilities, please go to the following link: https://machinelearningmastery.com/make-predictions-scikit-learn/

You can Build Machine Learning Models in Python

Go through the tutorial above, and replicate the steps. You will only take half an hour to replicate the process. The process may overwhelm you, but you should keep the following points in mind.

You do not have to Understand Everything

At the moment, you do not have to worry about understanding everything. Your goal should be to run through the tutorial and ensure that you obtain the desired result. You do not have to understand everything initially. You must remember to list any of the questions you may as you go. If you are unsure of a function in Python, you should use the help function to learn more about the function.

You do not need to know how the Algorithm Works

You should know what your limitations are and also learn how you can configure some machine learning algorithms. You can learn more about algorithms later. You can only build on this language over a period of time. All you should do now is familiarize yourself with the platform.

You do not need to be a Python Programmer

If you are new to Python, the syntax of the language is intuitive. You should always focus on function calls and the assignments, just like every other language. You will learn more about the language. Since you are a developer, you can learn the basics of the language quickly. All you need to do is get started and then dive into the details.

You do not need to be a Machine Learning Expert

In the previous book, I covered the benefits and limitations of the many machine-learning algorithms. You can read many blog posts or books to brush up on the different machine learning steps. You can also evaluate the importance and accuracy of a machine-learning algorithm.

What about the other Steps in a Machine Learning Project

Since this is your first project, this chapter does not cover every step you must follow to develop a machine-learning project. We are only covering loading data, analyzing data and making any predictions.

Chapter Eight

How to Evaluate Machine Learning Algorithms in Python?

This chapter demonstrates different methods to evaluate machine-learning algorithms in Python using SciKit-learn. Every program in this chapter is a standalone program, and you can simply copy this program into your system if you want to use them immediately. The metrics in this chapter are for both the regression and classification types of machine learning problems.

In the examples below, we are using the following datasets:

1. The Pima Indians Onset of Diabetes Dataset is used to demonstrate the classification metrics. This data-set can be used for binary classification problems. The data are all numeric values. You can download the dataset from the following location: https://raw.githubusercontent.com/jbrownlee/Datasets/master/pima-indians-diabetes.data.csv

2. The Boston House Price Data-set is used to demonstrate the regression metrics. This data-set represents a regression problem. The input variables in this data-set are also unique. You can download the data-set from the following location: https://raw.githubusercontent.com/jbrownlee/Datasets/master/housing.data

We will download the data-set from the UCI Machine Learning Repository for all the examples given in this chapter. The programs are used to evaluate the same models – linear regression for regression problems and logistic regression for classification problems. We will use a 10-fold cross-validation test to demonstrate every metric since this is the most likely scenario that you will incorporate in different evaluation metrics.

The cross_val_score() function will report the performance of every model. It will allow you to use different scoring methods that we will discuss in this chapter. All the scores will be reported so you can sort them in an ascending order. There are some vectors that produce descending scores. You need to remember this since there are some scores that are reported as negative values, but these are not negative by definition.

Classification metrics

A common type of machine learning problem is the classification problem, and it is for this reason that there are many metrics that you can use to evaluate a classification model. This section covers five common metrics used:

1. Classification Accuracy

2. Logarithmic Loss

3. Area Under ROC Curve

4. Confusion Matrix

5. Classification Report

Classification accuracy

The classification accuracy is a ratio. This value is calculated as the ratio of the number of correct predictions to the total number of predictions made by the model. The classification accuracy is a common evaluation metric for most classification problems. It is also the most misused metric. This value is suitable when you have equal number of observations in every class. You must also remember that the prediction errors and predictions are important, which is usually not the case.

Let us look at an example of how you can calculate the classification accuracy in Python.

```
# Cross Validation Classification Accuracy

import pandas

from sklearn import model_selection

from sklearn.linear_model import LogisticRegression

url =
"https://raw.githubusercontent.com/jbrownlee/Datasets/master/p
ima-indians-diabetes.data.csv"

names = ['preg', 'plas', 'pres', 'skin', 'test', 'mass', 'pedi', 'age',
'class']

dataframe = pandas.read_csv(url, names=names)

array = dataframe.values

X = array[:,0:8]

Y = array[:,8]

seed = 7

kfold = model_selection.KFold(n_splits=10,
random_state=seed)

model = LogisticRegression()

scoring = 'accuracy'

results = model_selection.cross_val_score(model, X, Y,
cv=kfold, scoring=scoring)
```

```
print("Accuracy: %.3f (%.3f)") % (results.mean(), results.std())
```

The output shows the ratio. You can multiply this ratio by 100 to convert it to a percentage. This will give you a score of 77%.

Accuracy: 0.770 (0.048)

Logarithmic loss

The logloss or logarithmic loss is a measure that you can use to evaluate the predictions of some probabilities based on the memberships that you give some class. The probability between zero and one is seen as a measure of confidence for any prediction that the algorithm makes. The predictions are either incorrect or correct, and depending on the accuracy of the prediction, the algorithm is either punished or rewarded. This punishment or reward is directly proportional to the confidence of that prediction.

The example below calculates the logarithmic loss of some logistic regression predictions.

```
# Cross Validation Classification LogLoss

import pandas

from sklearn import model_selection

from sklearn.linear_model import LogisticRegression

url =
"https://raw.githubusercontent.com/jbrownlee/Datasets/mast
er/pima-indians-diabetes.data.csv"

names = ['preg', 'plas', 'pres', 'skin', 'test', 'mass', 'pedi', 'age',
'class']

dataframe = pandas.read_csv(url, names=names)

array = dataframe.values
```

```
X = array[:,0:8]

Y = array[:,8]

seed = 7

kfold = model_selection.KFold(n_splits=10,
random_state=seed)

model = LogisticRegression()

scoring = 'neg_log_loss'

results = model_selection.cross_val_score(model, X, Y,
cv=kfold, scoring=scoring)

print("Logloss: %.3f (%.3f)") % (results.mean(),
results.std())
```

The value zero represents a model with a perfect logloss. It is always better to have a smaller logloss. As mentioned in the previous section, the measure is always inverted so that the values are ascending. You can use the cross_val_score() function to calculate the loss.

Logloss: -0.493 (0.047)

Area under roc curve

You can use the area under the ROC curve allows you to test the performance metric for any binary classification problems. The area under the curve will represent the model or algorithm's ability to differentiate between negative and positive classes. If the output of the model is 1.0, the model has made the predictions perfectly. If the area is 0.5, it means that the model is random.

You can break the ROC down into specificity and sensitivity. A classification problem is mostly a trade-off between specificity and sensitivity.

- Specificity or the true negative rate is the number of instances in the second or negative class that the model predicted accurately.

- Sensitivity or the true positive rate, also called recall, represents the number of instances in the first class or the positive class that the model predicted accurately.

The example below will show you how you can calculate the AUC in Python.

```
# Cross Validation Classification ROC AUC

import pandas

from sklearn import model_selection

from sklearn.linear_model import LogisticRegression

url =
"https://raw.githubusercontent.com/jbrownlee/Datasets/mast
er/pima-indians-diabetes.data.csv"

names = ['preg', 'plas', 'pres', 'skin', 'test', 'mass', 'pedi', 'age',
'class']

dataframe = pandas.read_csv(url, names=names)

array = dataframe.values

X = array[:,0:8]

Y = array[:,8]

seed = 7

kfold = model_selection.KFold(n_splits=10,
random_state=seed)

model = LogisticRegression()

scoring = 'roc_auc'
```

```
results = model_selection.cross_val_score(model, X, Y,
cv=kfold, scoring=scoring)

print("AUC: %.3f (%.3f)") % (results.mean(), results.std())
```

The value of the AUC is greater than zero and close to one, which suggests that the model made many predictions.

AUC: 0.824 (0.041)

Confusion matrix

If you build a machine learning algorithm with more than two classes in it, you should use the confusion matrix to represent the model's accuracy. The table will present the accuracy outcomes on the y-axis and the predictions on the x-axis. The number of cells in the table depends on the predictions that the machine learning algorithm will make.

For instance, you can build an algorithm that will either predict zero and one for an instance, and each prediction outcome could either be zero or one. The predictions that were supposed to be zero and actually zero will appear in the cells for the actual = 0 and prediction = 0, while the predictions that were supposed to be one and are actually one appear in the actual = 1 and prediction = 1.

Let us now look at how you can calculate the confusion matrix for some predictions that a model makes using test data.

```
# Cross Validation Classification Confusion Matrix

import pandas

from sklearn import model_selection

from sklearn.linear_model import LogisticRegression

from sklearn.metrics import confusion_matrix
```

```
url =
"https://raw.githubusercontent.com/jbrownlee/Datasets/mast
er/pima-indians-diabetes.data.csv"

names = ['preg', 'plas', 'pres', 'skin', 'test', 'mass', 'pedi', 'age',
'class']

dataframe = pandas.read_csv(url, names=names)

array = dataframe.values

X = array[:,0:8]

Y = array[:,8]

test_size = 0.33

seed = 7

X_train, X_test, Y_train, Y_test =
model_selection.train_test_split(X, Y, test_size=test_size,
random_state=seed)

model = LogisticRegression()

model.fit(X_train, Y_train)

predicted = model.predict(X_test)

matrix = confusion_matrix(Y_test, predicted)

print(matrix)
```

The output will not have any headings. You can however, see that the majority of the predictions made by the model fall on the diagonal.

```
[[141  21]

 [ 41  51]]
```

Classification report

You can use a convenience report in Scikit-learn when you work with classification problems. These reports will provide a quick idea on whether the model you are using is accurate using different classification measures. You can display the precision of the algorithm using the classification report() function. You can use this for every class. The program below shows how you can derive a report for a binary classification problem.

```
# Cross Validation Classification Report

import pandas

from sklearn import model_selection

from sklearn.linear_model import LogisticRegression

from sklearn.metrics import classification_report

url =
"https://raw.githubusercontent.com/jbrownlee/Datasets/mast
er/pima-indians-diabetes.data.csv"

names = ['preg', 'plas', 'pres', 'skin', 'test', 'mass', 'pedi', 'age',
'class']

dataframe = pandas.read_csv(url, names=names)

array = dataframe.values

X = array[:,0:8]

Y = array[:,8]

test_size = 0.33

seed = 7
```

```
X_train, X_test, Y_train, Y_test =
model_selection.train_test_split(X, Y, test_size=test_size,
random_state=seed)

model = LogisticRegression()

model.fit(X_train, Y_train)

predicted = model.predict(X_test)

report = classification_report(Y_test, predicted)

print(report)
```

The output will show you a good prediction and recall for the algorithm.

	precision	recall	f1-score	support
0.0	0.77	0.87	0.82	162
1.0	0.71	0.55	0.62	92
avg / total	0.75	0.76	0.75	254

Regression Metrics

This section reviews three of the most common metrics that we use to evaluate the prediction derived from regression machine learning programs.

1. Mean Absolute Error

2. Mean Squared Error

3. R Squared Error

Mean absolute error

The MAE or the mean absolute error is calculated as the sum of the absolute differences between the actual and predicted values. This will give you an estimate of how wrong the prediction values were. This measure will only give you an idea about the magnitude about the error but not the direction of the error. The example below uses the Boston house price data-set to calculate the mean absolute error.

```
# Cross Validation Regression MAE

import pandas

from sklearn import model_selection

from sklearn.linear_model import LinearRegression

url =
"https://raw.githubusercontent.com/jbrownlee/Datasets/master/housing.data"

names = ['CRIM', 'ZN', 'INDUS', 'CHAS', 'NOX', 'RM', 'AGE', 'DIS', 'RAD', 'TAX', 'PTRATIO', 'B', 'LSTAT', 'MEDV']

dataframe = pandas.read_csv(url, delim_whitespace=True, names=names)

array = dataframe.values

X = array[:,0:13]

Y = array[:,13]

seed = 7

kfold = model_selection.KFold(n_splits=10, random_state=seed)

model = LinearRegression()
```

```
scoring = 'neg_mean_absolute_error'

results = model_selection.cross_val_score(model, X, Y,
cv=kfold, scoring=scoring)

print("MAE: %.3f (%.3f)") % (results.mean(), results.std())
```

If the predictions are perfect, which means that there is no error, the function will return a value of zero. This metric is inverted by using the cross_val_score() function.

```
MAE: -4.005 (2.084)
```

Mean squared error

The mean squared error is like the mean absolute error which provides an idea of what the magnitude of the error is. When you take the square root of the mean squared error, you will convert the units to the original units of the variables. You can then use this measure to derive meaningful insights about the model. This variable is called the root mean squared error (RMSE). The section below depicts how you can calculate the mean squared error in Python.

```
# Cross Validation Regression MSE

import pandas

from sklearn import model_selection

from sklearn.linear_model import LinearRegression

url =
"https://raw.githubusercontent.com/jbrownlee/Datasets/mast
er/housing.data"

names = ['CRIM', 'ZN', 'INDUS', 'CHAS', 'NOX', 'RM',
'AGE', 'DIS', 'RAD', 'TAX', 'PTRATIO', 'B', 'LSTAT',
'MEDV']
```

```
dataframe = pandas.read_csv(url, delim_whitespace=True,
names=names)

array = dataframe.values

X = array[:,0:13]

Y = array[:,13]

seed = 7

kfold = model_selection.KFold(n_splits=10,
random_state=seed)

model = LinearRegression()

scoring = 'neg_mean_squared_error'

results = model_selection.cross_val_score(model, X, Y,
cv=kfold, scoring=scoring)

print("MSE: %.3f (%.3f)") % (results.mean(), results.std())
```

The results increase since the metric is inverted. You should remember to calculate absolute value of the results before you calculate the square root. This is only if you want to calculate the RMSE.

MSE: -34.705 (45.574)

R^2 metric

The R Squared or R^2 metric will indicate whether the predicted values lie in the same distribution of the actual values. This term is called the coefficient of determination in statistical terms. The value of the coefficient should either be zero, meaning the values do not fit, or 1, meaning the values fit perfectly. You can use many sources to learn more about the R Squared coefficient. The example below shows how you can calculate the R Squared value for a set of predictor variables.

```
# Cross Validation Regression R^2

import pandas

from sklearn import model_selection

from sklearn.linear_model import LinearRegression

url = "https://raw.githubusercontent.com/jbrownlee/Datasets/master/housing.data"

names = ['CRIM', 'ZN', 'INDUS', 'CHAS', 'NOX', 'RM', 'AGE', 'DIS', 'RAD', 'TAX', 'PTRATIO', 'B', 'LSTAT', 'MEDV']

dataframe = pandas.read_csv(url, delim_whitespace=True, names=names)

array = dataframe.values

X = array[:,0:13]

Y = array[:,13]

seed = 7

kfold = model_selection.KFold(n_splits=10, random_state=seed)

model = LinearRegression()

scoring = 'r2'

results = model_selection.cross_val_score(model, X, Y, cv=kfold, scoring=scoring)

print("R^2: %.3f (%.3f)") % (results.mean(), results.std())
```

If you look carefully, the predictions have a very poor fit to the actual values. This is because the value is close to zero and less than 0.5.

R^2: 0.203 (0.595)

Chapter Nine

How to Develop a Neural Network in Python using Keras

In the previous chapter, we looked at the different libraries that you need to set up in Python to build your machine learning model. Let us now look at how we can build our very own neural network in Python using Keras.

Load Data

In order to build a machine learning algorithm that always uses a stochastic approach to generate output, you should use a seed. This seed will ensure that you can run the code repeatedly and generate the same output or result. You must use this method if you want to compare the results from different algorithms or models for the same data-set. You can also use this seed to debug a part of the program.

You can initialize a random number generator with any number as the seed. For example,

from keras.models import Sequential

from keras.layers import Dense

import numpy

numpy.random.seed(7)

In the last statement in the code above, you can fix a random seed that you can use to reproduce the results innumerable times.

Now, you can load the data into Python. For the examples in this chapter, we will use a dataset from the UCI Machine Learning Repository. The dataset we will be using is the Pima Indians onset of diabetes. This dataset contains medical records of multiple patients for Pima India and provides information on whether they developed diabetes in five years or not.

This data is very simple to use since it poses a binary classification problem. All you need to do is check whether a patient has developed diabetes or not. In this problem, we will label the onset of diabetes as 2 and no diabetes as 0. Since the input variables are numerical, you can use this data-set when you want to train your neural network to only provide numeric values as the output when you feed it numerical input values. This is an ideal example to use for your first neural network. Please download the dataset from the following location: https://raw.githubusercontent.com/jbrownlee/Datasets/master/pima-indians-diabetes.data.csv

You should move the dataset to a working directory where you have the Python files saved. Save the data-set with a file name, and load it into Python by using the function loadtxt(). This is a NumPy function. As mentioned in the previous chapter, you should go through the data-set and make sense of the different variables in the set.

The dataset has one output variable in the last column and eight input variables. Once you load the data into Python, you can split the data into input and output variables.

```
dataset = numpy.loadtxt("file_name.csv", delimiter=",")

X = dataset[:,0:8]
```

$$Y = dataset[:,8]$$

In the first statement of the code above, you are loading the dataset into Python. Remember to name the dataset once you download it. The second and third statements of the code split the data into the input (X) and output (Y) variables. There are nine columns in the dataset, and the range in the second line of the code, 0:8, will select the columns with their index between 0 and 7.

In the first part of this section, we defined the seed. Now, you can define the neural network model.

Define the Model

When it comes to defining a model in Keras, you will need to use a sequence of layers. This section will teach you how you should build a sequential model and add layers to that model one at a time. When you are happy with how the network looks, you can stop adding more layers to the model.

You will first need to ensure that the input layer in your model has the correct number of inputs. You should specify this when you create the first layer in the model using the keywords input dim. Set the number to 8 for every input variable. You may wonder how you will know the number of layers and what their types are. It is difficult to answer this question, but you can use the trail and error method to understand the network better. Al you need to worry about is building the model that will understand the network and capture the problem.

In the example in this section, we will use a network structure that has three layers and is fully connected.

Using the Dense Class, you can define a fully connected neural network in Python. You have the liberty to specify how many neurons you want in every layer as the first argument and use the second argument to talk about the activation function you want Python to use.

In the example below, we will assign weights to the network using a small number generated from the uniform distribution. The weight is between the numbers 0 and 0.05 in the example below since that is the default weight assigned to the neurons in Keras. An alternative would be to generate a random number from the Normal or Gaussian distribution.

In this example, we will use the sigmoid function and the rectifier function for the output and input layers respectively. In the past, the tanh and sigmoid functions were used for all layers. Engineers have now moved to using a rectifier function instead of the tanh function since it improves the performance of the system.

The sigmoid function is used to ensure that the output in the last layer are only between zero and one. This function makes it easy for the network to map the variables in the data-set into different classes with probabilities 0 and 1 using a threshold of 0.5.

```
model = Sequential()

model.add(Dense(12, input_dim=8, activation='relu'))

model.add(Dense(8, activation='relu'))

model.add(Dense(1, activation='sigmoid'))
```

In the model we have created above, the first layer has 8 input variables and 12 neurons, the second layer, which is the hidden layer, has 8 neurons and the output layer has only one neuron to predict whether the patient has diabetes or not.

Compile the Model

When you define the model, you should compile it. There are many libraries in Python that you can use for this purpose like

TensorFlow and Theano. These libraries have many numerical libraries, which make them efficient to test the model. Since the libraries lie at the back end of the system, they determine how a system can represent a network. These libraries will also determine how an engineer should train the model. The backend will decide if the system should distribute the functions of the network evenly between the CPU and GPU or if it should only use the CPU or GPU.

You can define additional properties when you build the model if you want to compile it when you are done. These properties will help you train the network better. When I say train the network, I am talking about letting the model identify the weights that it should assign to different neurons to ensure that it can predict the results of the problem. You should also specify the loss function that you will use to evaluate the calculated weights, the optimizer to search for different weights in the network and any other metrics that you want to collect during the training.

In the example below, we use logarithmic loss, which is defined as "binary_crossentropy" in Keras for a binary classification problem. We will also use "adam" which is the gradient descent algorithm since it is an efficient default. The accuracy will be reported as a metric since we are working on a classification problem.

```
model.compile(loss='binary_crossentropy',
optimizer='adam', metrics=['accuracy'])
```

The code above is used to compile the model.

Fit the Model

Once you have defined the model and compiled it, you can use it to perform some analysis. Enter the data into the model and either fit or train your model using that data-set. You need to enter the fit() function to begin the training process. When you train the network, it will run through a predetermined number of epochs or iterations.

You can specify the number of iterations using the nepochs statement. The model will run through the dataset and assign weights to the different layers in the network. You can set the number of instances that the model can evaluate using the batch size argument.

In the example below, we will run 150 iterations and use a batch size of 10. This means that we will only allow the model to define 10 instances. You can either increase or decrease the size once you have run the model a few times.

```
model.fit(X, Y, epochs=150, batch_size=10)
```

The code above fits the model.

Depending on what the model decides, the work will happen either on the CPU or GPU. For the above example, we do not need to use the GPU since the data-set is small. If you use a larger data-set, you should use the GPU hardware that is available in the cloud.

Evaluate the Model

Now that you have trained the neural network, and let it run through the 150 epochs or iterations, you can evaluate the performance of the network. This will give you an idea of whether the model understands the data-set well. You will, however, not gather information about whether the model will perform well on a new data-set. In the example that we will use the same data-set to train and evaluate the model to help you understand how you can test the model with new data. You can split the dataset into training datasets and test datasets to train and evaluate your model.

You can evaluate the model with the training data-set and the evaluate() function. All you need to do is pass the same training input and output to the model, and allow the model to generate predictions for every input and output pair. This model will also collect scores on the different metrics that you have defined like accuracy or average loss. You can use the following code to evaluate the model.

```
scores = model.evaluate(X, Y)
print("\n%s:      %.2f%%"      %      (model.metrics_names[1],
scores[1]*100))
```

Tie it All Together

Since you know how to create neural networks in Keras, let us tie the steps up and write the complete code. The sentences that begin with '#' represent the comments which will help you understand what the statement in the codes means.

```
# Create your first network in Keras
from keras.models import Sequential
from keras.layers import Dense
import numpy
# fix random seed to reproduce the results
numpy.random.seed(7)
# load the dataset
dataset = numpy.loadtxt("file_name.csv", delimiter=",")
# split the data into input and output class variables
X = dataset[:,0:8]
Y = dataset[:,8]
# create the model
model = Sequential()
model.add(Dense(12, input_dim=8, activation='relu'))
model.add(Dense(8, activation='relu'))
model.add(Dense(1, activation='sigmoid'))
```

```
# Compile the model
model.compile(loss='binary_crossentropy',
optimizer='adam', metrics=['accuracy'])
# Fit the model
model.fit(X, Y, epochs=150, batch_size=10)
# Evaluate the model
scores = model.evaluate(X, Y)
print("\n%s: %.2f%%" % (model.metrics_names[1],
scores[1]*100))
```

You should always read the message you receive when you run the model. You will receive a message at the end of every epoch or iteration, and this message will let you know how accurate the data is. It will also provide information about the trained model. If you use a Theano backend on your CPU, this code will take 15 seconds to run. The output below is for the iteration number 145.

Epoch 145/150

768/768 [==================] - 0s - loss: 0.5105 - acc: 0.7396

Epoch 146/150

768/768 [==================] - 0s - loss: 0.4900 - acc: 0.7591

Epoch 147/150

768/768 [==================] - 0s - loss: 0.4939 - acc: 0.7565

Epoch 148/150

768/768 [==================] - 0s - loss: 0.4766 - acc: 0.7773

Epoch 149/150

768/768 [==================] - 0s - loss: 0.4883 - acc: 0.7591

Epoch 150/150

768/768 [==================] - 0s - loss: 0.4827 - acc: 0.7656

32/768 [>..........................] - ETA: 0s

acc: 78.26%

If you use Jupyter notebook or IPython to run this program, you will receive an error since the output progress on these platforms are barred during training. You can turn off the output progress bars by making a change to the function verbose when you fit the model. You should also remember that the skill of your model will vary.

Neural networks are stochastic algorithms, which means that you can train a different model with a different skill using the same data and algorithm. This is not an error or a bug, but a feature of the neural network. You should not worry if you do not receive the same output like the one above, although we did fix the same seed.

Make Predictions

Once you train the model, it becomes easy to use that model to predict the output for new data-sets. You can use the example in this chapter to generate any predictions about the training data-set. You can always instruct the model to make some predictions. You only need to use the function model.predict(). You use the sigmoid function to activate the output layer to ensure that the results are only between 0 and 1. You can convert the results into a binary prediction by using the rounding function on the data. You can use the following code to make predictions:

```python
# Create your first network in Keras
from keras.models import Sequential
from keras.layers import Dense
import numpy
# fix random seed to reproduce the results
numpy.random.seed(7)
# load the dataset
dataset = numpy.loadtxt("file_name.csv", delimiter=",")
# split the data into input and output class variables
X = dataset[:,0:8]
Y = dataset[:,8]
# create the model
model = Sequential()
model.add(Dense(12, input_dim=8, activation='relu'))
model.add(Dense(8, activation='relu'))
model.add(Dense(1, activation='sigmoid'))
# Compile the model
model.compile(loss='binary_crossentropy',
optimizer='adam', metrics=['accuracy'])
# Fit the model
model.fit(X, Y, epochs=150, batch_size=10)
# Evaluate the model
scores = model.evaluate(X, Y)
print("\n%s: %.2f%%" % (model.metrics_names[1],
scores[1]*100))
# Making predictions
```

```
predictions = model.predict(X)

rounded = [round(x[0]) for x in predictions]

print(rounded)
```

In the above example, we are rounding the predictions to obtain whole numbers as results.

When you run the complete program, you will receive an output for every input pattern. You can use these predictions in your application if necessary.

Conclusion

Thank you for purchasing the book.

Machine learning and artificial intelligence have taken over almost every industry. Every business wants to use the different machine learning algorithms to improve its operations. This book provides information on the different applications of machine learning. You will also gather information about how you can build machine learning algorithms. You will also gather information about deep learning and artificial neural networks.

I hope you gather the information you are looking for.

Hi there, avid reader! If you have extra time on your hands, I would really, really appreciate it if you could take a moment to click my author profile in Amazon. In there, you will find all the titles I authored and who knows, you might find more interesting topics to read and learn!

If it's not too much to ask, you can also leave and write a review for all the titles that you have read – whether it's a positive or negative review. An honest and constructive review of my titles is always welcome and appreciated since it will only help me moving forward in creating these books. There will always be room to add or improve, or sometimes even subtract certain topics, that is why these reviews are always important for us. They will also assist other avid readers, professionals who are looking to sharpen their knowledge, or even newbies to any topic, in their search for the book that caters to their needs the most.

If you don't want to leave a review yourself, you can also vote on the existing reviews by voting Helpful (Thumbs Up) or Unhelpful (Thumbs Down), especially on the top 10 or so reviews.

If you want to go directly to the vote or review process, just visit on any of the titles below:

Machine Learning For Beginners : A Comprehensive, Step-by-Step Guide to Learning and Understanding Machine Learning Concepts, Technology and Principles for Beginners . Audiobook format is also available in www.audible.com

Excel VBA : A Step-By-Step Tutorial For Beginners To Learn Excel VBA Programming From Scratch

Excel VBA : Intermediate Lessons in Excel VBA Programming for Professional Advancement

Again, I truly appreciate the time and effort that you will be putting in leaving a review for my titles or even just for voting. This will only inspire me to create more quality content and titles in the future.

Thank you and have a great day!

Peter Bradley

Resources

https://www.kdnuggets.com/2016/08/10-algorithms-machine-learning-engineers.html

https://www.kdnuggets.com/2018/09/6-steps-write-machine-learning-algorithm.html

https://www.toptal.com/machine-learning/machine-learning-theory-an-introductory-primer

https://machinelearningmastery.com/machine-learning-in-python-step-by-step/

https://machinelearningmastery.com/metrics-evaluate-machine-learning-algorithms-python/

https://ujjwalkarn.me/2016/08/09/quick-intro-neural-networks/

https://towardsdatascience.com/a-gentle-introduction-to-neural-networks-series-part-1-2b90b87795bc

https://becominghuman.ai/artificial-neuron-networks-basics-introduction-to-neural-networks-3082f1dcca8c

https://towardsdatascience.com/how-to-build-a-neural-network-with-keras-e8faa33d0ae4

https://machinelearningmastery.com/tutorial-first-neural-network-python-keras/

https://medium.com/app-affairs/9-applications-of-machine-learning-from-day-to-day-life-112a47a429d0

https://www.analyticsindiamag.com/6-types-of-artificial-neural-networks-currently-being-used-in-todays-technology/

https://medium.com/@datamonsters/artificial-neural-networks-for-natural-language-processing-part-1-64ca9ebfa3b2

https://medium.com/intro-to-artificial-intelligence/deep-learning-series-1-intro-to-deep-learning-abb1780ee20

https://blog.algorithmia.com/introduction-to-deep-learning/

https://towardsdatascience.com/a-weird-introduction-to-deep-learning-7828803693b0

Machine Learning

A Comprehensive, Step-by-Step Guide to Learning and Applying Advanced Concepts and Techniques in Machine Learning

Introduction

Thank you for purchasing the book, *'Machine Learning - A Comprehensive, Step-by-Step Guide to Learning and Applying Advanced Concepts and Techniques in Machine Learning.'*

The first two parts of the series covered the basics of machine learning, deep learning and neural networks. In the second book, readers learnt how to build a machine-learning model in Python using Sci-kit learn and some panda libraries. We also learnt how to build a neural network in Python using Keras.

In this book, you will learn to build some supervised and unsupervised machine-learning algorithms in Python using some panda libraries. Before you learn about the different algorithms, we will look at why we use Python to build machine-learning algorithms and artificial neural networks. Since we learnt how to build a neural network in the previous book, we will need to learn to evaluate that network. This book will show you different ways in which you can evaluate the performance of a neural network.

Over the course of the book, you will also gather information on saving and loading neural networks on your system. It is easier to do this since it saves time, and you can make the necessary changes to the program with ease.

I hope this book guides you on your journey to mastering machine-learning and deep learning. I wish you luck on your journey.

Chapter One

Machine-Learning versus Deep Learning

The first chapter covers the basics of artificial intelligence, and the first two books in the series provide information about machine-learning and deep learning. An algorithm to calculate the shortest path can also be an example of artificial intelligence. The two categories of artificial intelligence, namely machine-learning and deep learning are often mixed up. These two categories refer to the statistical modeling of variables in the data set to extract useful information to make informed decisions or predictions. This chapter provides some insight on why these two methods are difference. The information will also help you improve your understanding of these models.

An Overview

Machine learning is a statistical learning model where every instance in the data set is identified by a set of attributes and features. On the other hand, deep learning is a method that extracts the attributes and features from the data set. The latter algorithm does this by using neural networks with many hidden layers, powerful computational resources and big data. The terms are interchangeable, but deep learning algorithms always identify a way to represent the data set automatically. In machine learning, data representation is taught to the machine using training data sets. This means that you need to include some features in the algorithm that will tell the machine to extract some features and select some features depending on the data set.

These terms are in contrast to the rule-based systems, which are a type of classic artificial intelligence algorithm. In these algorithms, a decision is like a statistical model, and every decision is programmed into the algorithm. In both machine-learning and deep learning, there are many models that you can use. These models fall into the categories of supervised and unsupervised learning. In unsupervised learning algorithms like hierarchical clustering, k-means clustering and Gaussian mixture models are used. These models try to derive a meaningful structure in the data set. Supervised learning algorithms assign an output label to every instance in the data set. The machine and engineer can categorize the input as a categorical or discrete variable. Supervised learning algorithms include regression and classification. The former type of algorithm will estimate real-valued outputs, while the latter looks at discrete-valued outputs. We have covered some of the common machine-learning algorithms in the first part of the series.

Data Size

Machine-learning and deep learning can handle and work with large data sets. Machine-learning algorithms however, work best on small data sets. For example, if you were to use a data set with 200 data points, you can use k-nearest neighbors, regression or decision trees to learn more about the data set instead of fitting a deep learning neural network to the data. This is because of the interpretability of the models.

Interpretability

It is difficult to interpret some machine learning and deep learning algorithms like support vector machines and Naïve Bayes, because of which both machine and deep learning receive criticism. For instance, if you use a convolutional neural network, and see that it has given you an output of fruit in a fruit versus vegetables problem, you will never know why it did that. It is easier to understand the output of a machine-learning algorithm, since you know what to expect from the model.

Decision trees are a classic example of interpretability. In this algorithm, you will need to follow some steps and reach the node of the tree until you can make an informed decision. Another algorithm that you can use is the k-nearest neighbors algorithm. It is because of the interpretability of these algorithms that make it easier to use machine-learning algorithms on smaller data sets instead of using deep learning algorithms.

For example, consider a raw data set in the form of sin waves in an audio file or pixels in an image. It is difficult for a machine-learning algorithm to read this data and develop an association between the variables or data points. Therefore, it is better to use deep learning models for such methods. One can use deep learning in many applications in which classic machine learning cannot be used.

Choosing between Deep Learning and Machine-learning

Machine-learning algorithms offer different models and techniques that the engineer can choose from depending on the application, the type of problem the machine should solve and the data that it is processing. Deep neural networks require a huge volume of data that the engineer can use to train the model, as well as a graphics processing units or GPUs, which will process the data quickly.

When you need to choose between deep neural networks and machine learning, you should consider whether you have labeled data and a high-performance GPU. If you do not have either, you should stick to machine-learning algorithms. Since deep learning is more complex, you will need at least a few thousands of variables to ensure that the algorithm provides the necessary output. If you have GPU with high performance, you can be certain that the model will analyze the data quickly.

Hi there! If you found the topic or information useful, it would be a great help if you can leave a quick review on Amazon. Thanks a lot!

Chapter Two

Steps in Building
a Machine-Learning System

In the second book of the series, we learnt how you could build a machine-learning algorithm in Python. Regardless of the type of algorithm you are building, there are some steps that you need to follow. This chapter will provide a snapshot of those steps.

Define Objective

Like every other task, it is important that you define the reason behind developing the machine-learning algorithm. Your predictions will determine the type of data you use, the algorithm you will use and what type of system you will need to use.

Collect Data

This is one of the most tedious steps when it comes to building a machine-learning algorithm. You as an engineer must collect the right data to ensure that you train the algorithm to function correctly.

Prepare Data

This is a step that most people overlook. What they forget is that this can be a costly affair if they do not take care of the step properly. It is always important to clean the data and prepare it well to ensure that the predictions or output is accurate.

Select Algorithm

In the first section of the book, we covered the different algorithms one can use when building a machine-learning system. Therefore, it is important that you choose the appropriate algorithm to achieve the objective of the model.

Train Model

Once you have developed the model, you should set aside some data called the training data set. You must use this data set to train your model.

Test Model

When you have trained the model, you can use it to generate an output. You can test the model with some data, and check if it is working according to your expectations.

Predict

You can run multiple iterations, and there are times when you can send feedback to the system.

Deploy

When you have tested the model and identified that it works correctly, you can integrate the model into an application, and then deploy it to other companies.

The order of the steps will vary depending on the application and type of algorithm that you want to use. You can choose to implement either a supervised or unsupervised machine-learning algorithm, but this template is a good one to use since it involves all the steps that you need to consider when developing a machine-learning algorithm. You can use different tools and languages, but Python is used often since it supports every system. The next chapter provides information on why we should use Python to build a machine-learning algorithm.

Chapter Three

Why Use Python
for Machine-Learning

Python has fast become one of the most popular programming languages in the world as it can be used to write simple and efficient applications. Python is one of the most beginner friendly languages, with its simplicity and readability making it easy to understand and grasp. The numerous libraries and packages that are available to it simplify the achievement of complex functions with minimal code. Machine-learning applications typically work with large data sets and inbuilt libraries like NumPy, SciPy and TensorFlow, which make Machine-learning and Deep Learning applications much easier to build.

Since Python can be extended to work best for different programs, data scientists have begun to use it to analyze data. It is best to learn how to code in Python since it will help you analyze and interpret data and efficiently identify the best solutions for your business. Python is a well-designed programming language with very clean and simple syntax that was developed to work across multiple devices, and it is very intuitive and easy to learn for anyone.

Python is a high-level programming language developed by Guido van Rossum in the late 1980s, and it is highly popular within the developer community, with beginners and pros alike due to its design philosophy. Before we look at why we use Python for machine-learning models, let us look at how you can set it up on your system.

Running Python

You can install Python on many operating systems including Mac OS X, Linux, Unix, Windows or OS/2. Most GNU/Linux systems or Mac OS X systems already come installed with Python. It is always a good idea to work on systems that already have Python installed.

Installing on Windows

You will need to install Python if you are using Windows. You will also need to change some settings to ensure that the language will work well in your system. You will need to follow the instructions given on the different web pages listed below:

http://wiki.python.org/moin/BeginnersGuide/Download

http://www.python.org/doc/faq/windows/

http://docs.python.org/dev/3.0/using/windows.html

You should first download the installer from http://www.python.org/download/. You should save this file in your working directory or folder and double-click on this to begin the installation wizard. This will take you through the process of installation. It is always a good idea to choose default settings if you do not know what works best for your system.

Installing on Other Systems

You can also install Python in other systems. For systems that use Unix and Linux, you can find the instructions in the following links:

http://docs.python.org/dev/3.0/using/unix.html

If you're using OS X, your instructions are here:

http://www.python.org/download/mac/

http://docs.python.org/dev/3.0/using/mac.html

Advantages of Using Python

Some of the reasons why the python philosophy makes it a truly brilliant language are listed in the chapter below.

Simple and Easy to Learn

Python is developed to be simple and minimalistic, with any program written by python looking like a pseudocode written in English, making it easier for anyone to understand the program. Syntax and keywords that are more English-like also make it easier to learn. This quality of it is actually the real power of the language, as it allows the programmer to focus on solving the problem rather than trying to learn the syntax and how to use it, a barrier that most of the other high-level languages come with.

High-level Language

Python is a high-level programming language. This means that as a developer there are some internal details like memory management that you do not need to worry about. These details are hidden from you and are taken care of by the language itself. This makes it a language that is easy for every beginner and non-programmer to use.

Open Source

Python is an open source programming language that is free for anybody to use. This means that you can write and distribute any code that you write with Python. This allows every user of the Python language to share his or her models with the community. It is for this reason that this language is well maintained, improved and reused by different developers across the world.

Portable

As mentioned earlier, one of the reasons why Python is great as a first programming language to learn is not only due to its simplicity, but also due to it being very powerful, considering that it is designed to work on multiple platforms without requiring any new changes when moving between devices, as long as necessary care is taken to avoid any system-dependent coding. The range of platforms on which Python code can run includes Windows, Solaris, Macintosh, FreeBSD, VMS, Palm OS, Linux, VxWorks and even PlayStation!

Interpreted

Python is an interpreted language like Java - this means that any program written in Python does not need to be compiled every time it needs to be executed. Instead, it can be compiled once and then executed on any number of devices. For example, a program written in C or C++, which are compiler based, gets converted from the source code (in human-readable format) to binary code (0's or 1's machine-readable format) using various platform-specific flags and options. This binary code is then loaded to the device's memory using what we call the linker/loader, and then it starts running. The compiler/ linker/ loader is therefore additional overhead, which can be avoided by using languages like Python, as it does not compile source code to binary format; instead, it is designed to be directly executed from the source code.

Internally, the source code gets converted to an intermediate form called the bytecode, which is then interpreted and executed by the device. This feature is what makes Python a useful powerful language, by allowing users to create code once and then use it across a plethora of devices without worrying about compilation and library linking overloads; all you need to do is copy the program files to the device to get started.

Object Oriented

Like every other language, Python also allows you to use the object-oriented programming approach. In this approach, the code is organized or broken down into classes that will act as an object or template. These objects are instances of the classes. Objects are essentially the building blocks of an Object-Oriented Programming language program that combines data and the methods that perform functions upon this data. Unlike the object-oriented programming in C++ and Java, the system is easy to use in Python. There are no complicated concepts that you will need to learn more about.

Fast and Efficient to Use

Another factor, which makes Python an efficient language to use is that it is easy to execute the language regardless of the action. Any piece of code that you write in Python can be used in different scripts and languages. Alternatively, one can write simple python scripts to execute C/ C++ programs.

Batteries Included

The speed of the execution and writing code, as well as the numerous inbuilt libraries and data types available, enable a lot of complex operations to be achieved in fewer lines of code than with any other programming language, thus simplifying the programmer's job. This aspect of pre-loaded libraries that come bundled within Python is popularly referred to as "Batteries Included".

The Python library is so vast that it allows the developer to focus on thinking of a solution to a problem, rather than thinking about how to implement the data Structures and other low-level details involved in finding a solution. The libraries cover almost everything, from working with Hypertext Markup Language, to databases, to audio files (.wav), to Graphical User Interface and to security using cryptography and other utilities.

There are many libraries in Python that you can use to build strong machine-learning models. These libraries reduce the complexity of the model that allows the user to focus on the model instead of the code. This will allow him or her to achieve the objective of the system.

Python Libraries

As mentioned in the previous chapter, a primary step in machine learning is data analysis. There are many packages in Python that will allow you to analyze the data with ease. You can use all the libraries mentioned in the chapter below when you build machine-learning models.

NumPy

NumPy is a package that is used most often when developing a machine-learning model in Python. This is because this package has amazing computing application. You can use this package to develop some logical and mathematical operations that involve the generation of random numbers, shape transformations, Fourier transforms and linear algebra. A key feature of this package is its support for array data structures, particularly multi- dimensional arrays and operations on each element.

Pandas

Pandas is a popular open source package in Python that allows the user to develop high-performance data analysis tools and data structures. This will reduce implementation time by a large factor. The key structure that is supported by this package is the data frame, panel or series.

Matplot Lib

The Matplot Library comes in handy when you want to visualize the output of the data. You can use this library to build some graphs and charts. Some other charts that you can build are scatter plots, histograms, bar graphs, pie charts, etc. You can also use a sophisticated library called "seaborn" which allows you to generate some visualization. This library provides a more accurate design. The star among all the library packages available in Python is "SciKit Learn", and it is probably one of the key reasons for Python being the most favored machine-learning application.

SciKit Learn

The SciKit learn package is built using the Matplotlib and NumPy packages. This package offers the user the option to use a comprehensive way to build a simple and efficiently data mining and analysis model for a variety of applications including regression, clustering, classification and dimensionality reduction.

To summarize, Python offers an end-to-end solution for building machine-learning systems from data wrangling to feature extraction, modeling, training and evaluating the system to visualizations. Also, it is able to easily integrate with BigQuery, Kafka, pubsub, redshift etc. for data pipeline.

Data wrangling can be achieved using Panda, NumPy and Pyspark, which can be integrated from other big data engines, with Dask being Python's own big data engine. Python offers a large inbuilt image and video library that comes in handy in the feature extraction phase. This aspect is another one of the many reasons why Python is the preferred language for Machine-learning systems.

You can also use the SciKit learning package in various stages of the process. This package can be used to train the model or build it to evaluate an existing system allowing the process to fit together seamlessly. Pytorch is a good alternative for beginners. TensorFlow is another key package used in Deep Learning applications, and it is more mature than libraries available in R, the main competitor.

Once this is all used to build, train and test the system, Python offers equally effortless options to deploy these systems to production, and creating a REST-API and serializing the model is quite simple with Python.

Therefore, this philosophy, which stresses on a minimalist approach by giving clear syntaxes and keywords in simple English enables the same task to get done in fewer lines of code than with other programming languages such as Java or C++. The ease of readability of code and the availability of a loaded library of predefined functions, as well as the vast variety of data types such as dictionaries and lists make it a very popular choice to work with.

Found this title interesting or useful? Then a review on Amazon will be highly appreciated!

Chapter Four

Supervised Algorithms Implementation

In the first and second parts of the series provide information on machine learning. You also read about the different supervised machine-learning algorithms like regression and classification. The same can be said about unsupervised machine-learning algorithms.

In this chapter, we will look at the different supervised machine-learning algorithms, and also how you can build the model in Python. Let us first look at some examples of the linear regression and multiple regression models. We will then look at a classification model with some examples.

Supervised machine-learning models are the most commonly used models in machine learning. Of the different supervised machine-learning models, the regression and classification algorithms are used often.

Before we look at the different ways to build a supervised machine-learning model in Python, let us look at a simple linear regression model and understand this fully. The idea of a machine-learning algorithm is to train the machine using a training data set, and show it what types of outputs you expect. When you give the machine this information, it will learn from the data set and try to identify the relationship between the variables in the data set, and the input and output values. Using this information, it will predict the output values for new data sets.

The next section will provide a simple example, which explains the process. In this example, we will check if a user will need to carry an umbrella or not depending on what the weather will be. Let us assume that the following table contains some sample information about the training data set.

Outside Temperature	Carry an umbrella
30 degrees Celsius	No
25 degrees Celsius	No
20 degrees Celsius	No
15 degrees Celsius	Yes
10 degrees Celsius	Yes

Human beings are always trained to look at the input temperatures and then determine the output. Let us look at how you can model this process to make a decision about whether or not a user should carry an umbrella. You can provide the machine with an input data set through which you can help the machine make an informed decision about such instances.

For this, we will need the use of the trusted Python Library for machine-learning implementations: SciKit Learn. Consider the following sample data set:

X1	X2	X3	Y
1	2	3	14
4	5	6	32
11	12	13	74
21	22	23	134
5	5	5	30

Looking at the table, one can infer the mathematical model or algebraic equation for getting the output y =

(x1 + 2*x2 + 3*x3).

To generate the training data set from random import randint

TRAIN_SET_LIMIT = 1000

TRAIN_SET_COUNT = 100

TRAIN_INPUT = list()

TRAIN_OUTPUT = list()

for i in range(TRAIN_SET_COUNT):

    a = randint(0, TRAIN_SET_LIMIT)

    b = randint(0, TRAIN_SET_LIMIT)

    c = randint(0, TRAIN_SET_LIMIT)

    op = a + (2*b) + (3*c)

TRAIN_INPUT.append([a, b, c])

TRAIN_OUTPUT.append(op)

Train the model:

from sklearn.linear_model import LinearRegression

predictor = LinearRegression(n_jobs=-1)

predictor.fit(X=TRAIN_INPUT, y=TRAIN_OUTPUT)

When the system is ready, you can pass a test data set into the model using the following format [[20, 30, 10]]. You can then observe the output. This output should be 20+30*2+10*2, and the output should be 100.

```
X_TEST = [[10, 20, 30]]

outcome = predictor.predict(X=X_TEST)

coefficients = predictor.coef_

print('Outcome : {}\nCoefficients : {}'.format(outcome,
coefficients))
```

Output

Outcome = [140]

Coefficients = [1.2.3]

You have now successfully implemented the model, trained the model and seen the model predict the output for a new input data set. This is based on a mathematical equation.

Simple Linear Regression

Regression is a supervised learning algorithm and in this model, when given an input, we get an output that is normally a numerical value. Our interest here is not to learn the class but the numeric function that best describes the data. The objective is then to use this model to generate estimations. The simplest form of the regression algorithm is the simple linear regression algorithm,. You should use this algorithm when you are developing a model to identify a prediction function when you know what the level of correlation is in the data set. This correlation value, called the correlation coefficient predicts the events in the data set.

We will use Python to create a scatter plot of the data based on the training data set, and this will create a straight line. This linear regression is also the preferred method to show the linear relationship between two variables. This is a simple formula that you can use to calculate the slope of a line in geometry.

$$Y = mx + c$$

This is a common and largely popular simple algebraic equation, which can also be used to explain the linear regression concept in machine learning. In the above equation, you have a dependent variable, which is a function of another variable, which is the independent variable. The objective of the model is to calculate a function that will allow you to determine how the variables are related to each other. In the data set, you are normally given values in a tabular format. These values are plotted on the X and Y-axes of a graph.

Linear regression or relationship is basically observing that when one or more independent variable increases or decreases, the corresponding dependent variable also increases or decreases in tandem resulting in a slope as seen above. You should also remember that the linear relationship can either be positive or negative. The relationship is dependent on whether the line has a positive or negative slope.

Positive Slope

When the value of the independent variable increases, the value of the dependent variable also increases, and vice versa the slope of the line will be positive. This means that the variables are directly proportional to one another.

Negative Slope

When the value of the independent variable increases and causes a decrease in the dependent variable, and vice versa, the slope of the line will be negative. This means that the variables are indirectly proportional to one another.

Let us now go back to the earlier equation to see how you can implement a regression model in Python. We have seen that X and Y will have a relationship, however, in real life, this isn't necessarily true. In the case of a Simple Linear regression on SLR, the model you build depends only on the data. In this case, the y-axis and the slope is calculated using the data. Also, the relationship between the x and y variables does not have to be strictly linear, since there is a probability of an error. These errors are calculated as residuals.

The objective is to simply take continuous data, find an equation that best fits the data and extrapolate and forecast or, in the future, predict a specific value. In the case of SLR or simple linear regression, we do exactly this by creating a best-fit line as shown in the scatter graph below.

A popular application of a regression model is to calculate the real estate prices or the stock prices. Since this is a type of supervised machine learning, the engineer will need to train the machine using a training data set, which will contain a set of features and the corresponding answers to those features. You will need to train the model repeatedly to ensure that it knows what to predict when a similar input is given to the machine.

There are several data sets available that you can use for the same. Let us look at an example where we will use a stock data set to write a program. To do this, one needs to install and import the quandl package.

The code to pull stock data set is as below - please create a Python script with the following code and execute it from the terminal.

import pandas as pd

import Quandl

```
df = Quandl.get("WIKI/GOOGL")

print(df.head())
```

Please note to look for the library "quandl" or "Quandl" depending on the version of Python you are using.

Open High Low Close Volume Ex-Dividend \

Date

2004-08-19 100.00 104.06 95.96 100.34 44659000 0

2004-08-20 101.01 109.08 100.50 108.31 22834300 0

2004-08-23 110.75 113.48 109.05 109.40 18256100 0

2004-08-24 111.24 111.60 103.57 104.87 15247300 0

2004-08-25 104.96 108.00 103.88 106.00 9188600 0

 Split Ratio Adj. Open Adj. High Adj. Low Adj. Close \

Date

2004-08-19 1 50.000 52.03 47.980 50.170

2004-08-20 1 50.505 54.54 50.250 54.155

2004-08-23 1 55.375 56.74 54.525 54.700

2004-08-24 1 55.620 55.80 51.785 52.435

2004-08-25 1 52.480 54.00 51.940 53.000

Adj. Volume

Date

2004-08-19 44659000

2004-08-20 22834300

2004-08-23 18256100

2004-08-24 15247300

2004-08-25 9188600

This sample data is pulled from the internet.

In the previous chapter, we looked at the many steps you will need to follow when you are building a model in Python. Now, that you have decided what model to use, you should learn now scrub, clean and prepare the input data set. You will see that there are some redundancies that are in the data, and will also identify some discrepancies. You can rectify these by including the following line in the Python script:

```
df = df[['Adj. Open', 'Adj. High', 'Adj. Low', 'Adj. Close',
'Adj. Volume']]
```

You will learn that the input data set is not always useful when it is in its raw form. When you clean the data set, you can transform the data better to give you the desired results. Use the code below for the same:

```
df['HL_PCT'] = (df['Adj. High'] - df['Adj. Low']) / df['Adj.
Close'] * 100.0
```

The following piece of code defines data frames and interprets the data output.

```
df['PCT_change'] = (df['Adj. Close'] - df['Adj. Open']) /
df['Adj. Open'] * 100.0

df = df[['Adj. Close', 'HL_PCT', 'PCT_change', 'Adj.
Volume']]

print(df.head())
```

The output will look like this

Adj. Close HL_PCT PCT_change Adj. Volume

Date

2004-08-19 50.170 8.072553 0.340000 44659000

2004-08-20 54.155 7.921706 7.227007 22834300

2004-08-23 54.700 4.049360 -1.218962 18256100

2004-08-24 52.435 7.657099 -5.726357 15247300

2004-08-25 53.000 3.886792 0.990854 9188600

We now have our data set ready, which we will now have to convert to array format so that it is understood by the SciKit library, which we will be used to perform actual regression functions.

To proceed further, add the following lines of code to the Python script file. These lines essentially import these libraries, which will be required for further functionalities.

```
import Quandl, math

import numpy as np

import pandas as pd

from sklearn import preprocessing, cross_validation, svm

from sklearn.linear_model import LinearRegression
```

At this point, the Python script file must look something like this:

```
import Quandl, math

import numpy as np

import pandas as pd

from sklearn import preprocessing, cross_validation, svm

from sklearn.linear_model import LinearRegression

df = Quandl.get("WIKI/GOOGL")
```

```
df = df[['Adj. Open', 'Adj. High', 'Adj. Low', 'Adj. Close',
'Adj. Volume']]

df['HL_PCT'] = (df['Adj. High'] - df['Adj. Low']) / df['Adj.
Close'] * 100.0

df['PCT_change'] = (df['Adj. Close'] - df['Adj. Open']) /
df['Adj. Open'] * 100.0

df = df[['Adj. Close', 'HL_PCT', 'PCT_change', 'Adj.
Volume']]

print(df.head())
```

Now, if we remember, we are at the stage where we need to cross-validate our cleaned and prepared data, for which we need to add the following lines that will feed the data as a feature and label tuple to the classifier machine-learning model. The feature can be defined as descriptive attributes and labels are the values that we are looking to predict with our machine-learning models.

```
forecast_col = 'Adj. Close'

df.fillna(value=-99999, inplace=True)

forecast_out = int(math.ceil(0.01 * len(df)))

df['label'] = df[forecast_col].shift(-forecast_out)
```

With the few lines of code above we've defined what we want to forecast. The next step is to train and test our model.

At this point, we can use the dropna function and then proceed to convert the data to numpy array format, which is the expected data format by the SciKit library functions that we will subsequently be using.

```
df.dropna(inplace=True)
```

```
X = np.array(df.drop(['label'], 1))

y = np.array(df['label'])

X = preprocessing.scale(X)

y = np.array(df['label'])
```

We have now created the label, array and preprocessed the dataset. We will now use the svm model and classifier model clf available in the SciKit toolkit to predict and print how robust the model is, as well as its accuracy and reliability using the confidence functions.

```
X_train, X_test, y_train, y_test =
cross_validation.train_test_split(X, y, test_size=0.2)

clf = svm.SVR()

clf.fit(X_train, y_train)

confidence = clf.score(X_test, y_test)

print(confidence)
```

One can rerun the same script using the linear regression classifier instead of svm like the following:

```
clf = LinearRegression()
```

The next steps are to forecast and predict, for which the following lines of code need to be added to an existing script.

```
forecast_set = clf.predict(X_lately)

print(forecast_set, confidence, forecast_out)
```

The output:

```
[    745.67829395    737.55633261    736.32921413
717.03929303 718.59047951
```

731.26376715 737.84381394 751.28161162 756.31775293
756.76751056

763.20185946 764.52651181 760.91320031 768.0072636
766.67038016

763.83749414 761.36173409 760.08514166 770.61581391
774.13939706

768.78733341 775.04458624 771.10782342 765.13955723
773.93369548

766.05507556 765.4984563 763.59630529 770.0057166
777.60915879] 0.956987938167 30

The next step is to import and use Matplotlib to plot the scatter graph, which is beyond the scope of this book.

Therefore, linear regression is used in varied applications and domains ranging from economics to biology, to predicting trend lines in oil prices, to GDP, to house prices, to import spending, etc.

You can use correction formulae to check how close the prediction is to the training data set. Let us take another example to understand the linear regression model better.

Let us use the example from above, where we needed to determine if someone needs to carry an umbrella depending on what the weather is outside.

Outside Temperature	Carry an umbrella
30 degrees Celsius	No
25 degrees Celsius	No
20 degrees Celsius	No
15 degrees Celsius	Yes
10 degrees Celsius	Yes

As mentioned earlier, human beings always look at the weather outside and determine if they should carry an umbrella since that is how the mind is trained. Let us assume that the temperature outside is 10 degrees Celsius. You will want to carry an umbrella since you expect the weather conditions to be bad. Let us see how you can model this using a simple linear model. This way you can train the machine to provide the output depending on the input data set.

For this, we will need to use the trusted Python Library for machine-learning implementations - sci-kit learn. Let's consider the following sample data set.

x1	x2	x3	y
1	2	3	14
4	5	6	32
11	12	13	74
21	22	23	134
5	5	5	30

Looking at the table, one can infer the mathematical model or algebraic equation to get the output $y = (x1 + 2*x2 + 3*x3)$.

Steps To Build the Model

To generate the training data set

```
from random import randint

TRAIN_SET_LIMIT = 1000

TRAIN_SET_COUNT = 100

TRAIN_INPUT = list()

TRAIN_OUTPUT = list()
```

```
for i in range(TRAIN_SET_COUNT):

a = randint(0, TRAIN_SET_LIMIT)

b = randint(0, TRAIN_SET_LIMIT)

c = randint(0, TRAIN_SET_LIMIT)

op = a + (2*b) + (3*c)

TRAIN_INPUT.append([a, b, c])

TRAIN_OUTPUT.append(op)
```

Train the model

```
from sklearn.linear_model import LinearRegression

predictor = LinearRegression(n_jobs=-1)

predictor.fit(X=TRAIN_INPUT, y=TRAIN_OUTPUT)
```

Once the system is ready, pass a sample test data in the following format of a tuple [[10, 20, 30]] and observe the output. According to our algebraic equation, this must be 10+20*2+30*2 and the output must be 140.

```
X_TEST = [[10, 20, 30]]

outcome = predictor.predict(X=X_TEST)

coefficients = predictor.coef_

print('Outcome: {}\nCoefficients: {}'.format(outcome,
coefficients))
```

Output

Outcome = [140]

Coefficients = [1.2.3]

We have successfully implemented a model, trained the system, and seen it predict the output for new input based on the mathematical linear equation.

Multiple Regression

In the previous section, we looked at regression modeling using simple linear regression where we considered a single predictor variable and a single response variable. We also look at how the data are correlated. Let us assume that we do not look at the presence of correlation within the data set, but performed the regression analysis on the data set. Is there a way you can use the results to see if there is multicollinearity in the data set? The answer to that question is yes. You can calculate variance inflation factors or VIFs, and report those values. You will need to standardize all the variables that you involve in the process to avoid great variability. If there is one variable that varies too much, it will affect the values of every other variable in the system.

Consider a dataset with p features (or independent variables) and one response (or dependent variable). This data set will also contain n observations or rows. We will define the data set as follows:

X (feature matrix) = a matrix of size n X p where x_{ij} denotes the values of jth feature for ith observation. So,

import matplotlib.pyplot as plt

import numpy as np

from sklearn import datasets, linear_model, metrics

load the boston dataset

boston = datasets.load_boston(return_X_y=False)

defining feature matrix(X) and response vector(y)

X = boston.data

```python
y = boston.target

# splitting X and y into training and testing sets

from sklearn.model_selection import train_test_split

X_train, X_test, y_train, y_test = train_test_split(X, y,
test_size=0.4, random_state=1)

# create linear regression object

reg = linear_model.LinearRegression()

# train the model using the training sets

reg.fit(X_train, y_train)

# regression coefficients

print('Coefficients: \n', reg.coef_)

# variance score: 1 means perfect prediction

print('Variance score: {}'.format(reg.score(X_test, y_test)))

# plot for residual error

## setting plot style

plt.style.use('fivethirtyeight')

## plotting residual errors in training data

plt.scatter(reg.predict(X_train), reg.predict(X_train) -
y_train, color = "green", s = 10, label = 'Train data')

## plotting residual errors in test data

plt.scatter(reg.predict(X_test), reg.predict(X_test) - y_test,
color = "blue", s = 10, label = 'Test data')

## plotting line for zero residual error
```

```
plt.hlines(y = 0, xmin = 0, xmax = 50, linewidth = 2)

## plotting legend

plt.legend(loc = 'upper right')

## plot title

plt.title("Residual errors")

## function to show plot

plt.show()
```

You can add the code above to a .py file and then execute the script from the terminal. You can also save the downloaded data set into the same working directory or folder as the output, including the generation of a scattered plot.

Decision Trees

Decision trees are one of the most ubiquitous and powerful classification algorithms available. This falls under the category of supervised learning algorithms and works for both continuous as well as categorical output variables. As we know, classification algorithms are the category of algorithms used to predict the category of the given input data. Other popular algorithms in this category include the k-nearest algorithm, however, in this book we will focus on the supervised learning algorithm of Decision Trees. The objective is to create a model that predicts the value of a target based on simple decision rules that are inferred from the data features.

In simple words, it is very similar to the common -if.. then.. else.. conditional statements that are commonly used as part of programming languages. This is more like a flow chart and it's a branch-based decision system. The algorithm is something that is very basic and easy to understand, like looking at an incoming email and classifying it as personal, work or spam based on certain predefined rules. This is as a very simple use case of decision trees.

A decision tree is a tree where one can take either route of the branches based on the answer to the conditional question at each node, with each branch representing a possible course action. Below is a simple decision tree example from real-life, where the tree can be used to determine whether a person is fit or unfit.

Simple to understand and interpret and easy to visualize

This model requires little to no data preparation while other techniques require various steps such as normalizing the input data set, creating dummy variables, cleaning up blank or null values as well as scrubbing and reducing activity which isn't normally required. The use of this machine-learning model significantly reduces the time and cost of execution. It is important to remember that this model requires missing data to be filled up, or else will it will throw an error and won't be able to proceed with further computation.

The number of data points determines the cost of execution, and the relationship of cost to the number of data is logarithmic to train the data model.

The other unique strength of this data model is that it works well with both numerical as and categorical data, while several other techniques are usually specially designed to work with one format of data or the other.

Ability to handle multi-output problems

The white box model says that if any solution is observable in a model, the explanation for this condition can be easily explained using a Boolean logic equation. In the case of algorithms based on a black box model like a synthetic neural network, the outcome could be tough to understand.

The other advantage is the ability to evaluate the model by using statistical trials, which makes the model more reliable than the others.

This model also performs well if the assumption is that datasets are slightly violated when applying the actual model, which ensures flexibility and accurate results irrespective of variance.

Disadvantages of Decision Trees

This section will cover some of the disadvantages of using decision trees.

1. There are times when you can create a complex tree, which will not generalize the data. This will lead to overfitting. You can overcome this by using some techniques like pruning. Pruning is similar to pruning the branch of a tree, but this feature is not present in Python. Therefore, you can include a small section to the program where you will set up a few samples of what every node must look like and how deep the tree is allowed to grow. The model will use this information to fit the data, and this will reduce the probability of overfitting.

2. Since there will be some variations in the data set, the tree will become unstable which will lead to the generation of a completely different tree. You can overcome this issue by using a decision tree only inside an ensemble.

3. It is difficult to compute some concepts like parity, multiplexer issues and XOR when you use decision trees.

4. If there are some classes that dominate others, the tree learners will create a biased learner. Therefore, it is

important o strike a balance within the data set before you fit it using a decision tree.

5. NP-Complete problem - a very common theoretical computer science problem can be a hindrance in the attempt to design the most optimal decision tree because under several aspects, the optimality can become affected. As a result, heuristic algorithms such as greedy algorithms with local optimal decisions at each node may become an issue. Teaching multiple trees to a collaborative learner can again reduce the effect of this issue and the feature and samples can randomly be sampled with replacements.

6. It is important to be conscious that decision trees tend to overfit data with a large number of features, and it is important to get the right sample and number of features in order for it not to become too highly dimensional.

7. Decision trees are used extensively in designed intelligent automation systems for homes and offices. Let us assume that the humidity, temperature and some other factors are at a certain level in the system. You can use the system to control these factors. These systems are designed on the basis of decision trees.

Key Factors

There are two factors that a decision tree is dependent on:

1. Entropy: This is the measure of impurity or randomness in the data set. The value must be very low.

2. Information Gain: This is also known as entropy reduction. It is the measure of the how the entropy has changed once the data is split into a tree. The value of this factor should be high.

Modeling a Decision Tree in Python

You will need to know the following concepts when you are developing a decision tree model in Python.

Importing a csv file into the script using pandas

from __future__ import print_function

import os

import subprocess

import pandas as pd

import numpy as np

from sklearn.tree import DecisionTreeClassifier, export_graphviz

Visually Drawing the tree

def visualize_tree(tree, feature_names):

"""Create tree png using graphviz.

Args

----

tree -- SciKit-learn DecsisionTree.

feature_names -- list of feature names.

"""

with open("dt.dot", 'w') as f:

export_graphviz(tree, out_file=f,

feature_names=feature_names)

657

```python
command = ["dot", "-Tpng", "dt.dot", "-o", "dt.png"]

try:

subprocess.check_call(command)

except:

exit("Could not run dot, ie graphviz, to "

"produce visualization")
```

Using panda's library to prep the data set for the SciKit-learn decision tree code

```python
def get_iris_data():

"""Get the iris data, from local csv or pandas repo."""

if os.path.exists("iris.csv"):

print("-- iris.csv found locally")

df = pd.read_csv("iris.csv", index_col=0)

else:

print(" downloading rom github")

fn = "https://raw.githubusercontent.com/pydata/pandas/" + \

"master/pandas/tests/data/iris.csv"

try:

df = pd.read_csv(fn)

except:

exit("Unable to download iris.csv")

with open("iris.csv", 'w') as f:
```

```
print("writing to local iris.csv file")

df.to_csv(f)

return df
```

Producing pseudocode that represents the tree

```
def get_code(tree, feature_names, target_names,

spacer_base=" "):

"""Produce psuedo-code for decision tree.

Args

----

tree -- SciKit-leant DescisionTree.

feature_names -- list of feature names.

target_names -- list of target (class) names.

spacer_base -- used for spacing code (default: " ").

Notes

-----

based on http://stackoverflow.com/a/30104792.

"""

left = tree.tree_.children_left

right = tree.tree_.children_right

threshold = tree.tree_.threshold

features = [feature_names[i] for i in tree.tree_.feature]
```

```python
value = tree.tree_.value
def recurse(left, right, threshold, features, node, depth):
    spacer = spacer_base * depth
    if (threshold[node] != -2):
        print(spacer + "if (" + features[node] + " <= " + \
        str(threshold[node]) + ") {")
        if left[node] != -1:
            recurse(left, right, threshold, features,
            left[node], depth+1)
        print(spacer + "}\n" + spacer +"else {")
        if right[node] != -1:
            recurse(left, right, threshold, features,
            right[node], depth+1)
        print(spacer + "}")
    else:
        target = value[node]
        for i, v in zip(np.nonzero(target)[1],
        target[np.nonzero(target)]):
            target_name = target_names[i]
            target_count = int(v)
            print(spacer + "return " + str(target_name) + \
```

" (" + str(target_count) + " examples)")

recurse(left, right, threshold, features, 0, 0)

Fitting the decision tree using sci kit learn library

y = df2["Target"]

X = df2[features]

dt = DecisionTreeClassifier(min_samples_split=20, random_state=99)

dt.fit(X, y)

Example

In the example below, we will build a sample decision tree classifier program using the SciKit learn package in Python.

>>> from sklearn import tree

>>> X = [[0, 0], [1, 1]]

>>> Y = [0, 1]

>>> clf = tree.DecisionTreeClassifier()

>>> clf = clf.fit(X, Y)

>>> clf.predict([[2., 2.]])

array([1])

>>> from sklearn.datasets import load_iris

>>> from sklearn import tree

>>> iris = load_iris()

>>> clf = tree.DecisionTreeClassifier()

```
>>> clf = clf.fit(iris.data, iris.target)

>>> import graphviz

>>> dot_data = tree.export_graphviz(clf, out_file=None)

>>> graph = graphviz.Source(dot_data)

>>> graph.render("iris")

>>> dot_data = tree.export_graphviz(clf, out_file=None,

... feature_names=iris.feature_names,

... class_names=iris.target_names,

... filled=True, rounded=True,

... special_characters=True)

>>> graph = graphviz.Source(dot_data)

>>> graph
```

K-Nearest Neighbor Algorithm

Apart from decision trees, the k-Nearest Neighbor Algorithm is a commonly used classification algorithm. The section below provides a sample code in Python where you will build a classification algorithm using supervised machine-learning techniques.

```
import numpy as np

import matplotlib.pyplot as plt

from matplotlib import style

import warnings

from collections import Counter
```

662

```python
#dont forget this

import pandas as pd

import random

style.use('fivethirtyeight')

def k_nearest_neighbors(data, predict, k=3):

 if len(data) >= k:

 warnings.warn('K is set to a value less than total voting
groups!')

 distances = []

 for group in data:

 for features in data[group]:

 euclidean_distance = np.linalg.norm(np.array(features)-
np.array(predict))

 distances.append([euclidean_distance,group])

 votes = [i[1] for i in sorted(distances)[:k]]

 vote_result = Counter(votes).most_common(1)[0][0]

 return vote_result


df = pd.read_csv('breast-cancer-wisconsin.data.txt')

df.replace('?',-99999, inplace=True)

df.drop(['id'], 1, inplace=True)

full_data = df.astype(float).values.tolist()
```

```
random.shuffle(full_data)


test_size = 0.2

train_set = {2:[], 4:[]}

test_set = {2:[], 4:[]}

train_data = full_data[:-int(test_size*len(full_data))]

test_data = full_data[-int(test_size*len(full_data)):]


for i in train_data:

 train_set[i[-1]].append(i[:-1])


for i in test_data:

 test_set[i[-1]].append(i[:-1])


correct = 0

total = 0


for group in test_set:

 for data in test_set[group]:

 vote = k_nearest_neighbors(train_set, data, k=5)

 if group == vote:
```

```
        correct += 1

        total += 1

    print('Accuracy:', correct/total)
```

Chapter Five

Unsupervised Learning Algorithms

Clustering

The last chapter covered some supervised learning algorithms, like classification and regression. In a similar way, we will cover two common unsupervised machine-learning algorithms. We will also learn how you can model these algorithms in Python.

In the first book of the series, we learnt that an unsupervised machine-learning algorithm can be used to derive some meaningful inferences from unlabeled data. You do not need to tell the model what the target variable is or what it should predict. You will instead ask if to infer or understand the model using the training data set.

Simply put, in supervised learning, we were looking for an answer "y" based on the input data "x", however in unsupervised learning, we are looking to find what the model can say based on the given "x."

In the data science domain, we often think about how to use the data available to us to make predictions on new data points, which is "supervised learning." Rather than 'making predictions', there are times when instead, we want to categorize the available data into categories. This is called "unsupervised learning."

Let's look at an example to understand this - say you are employed at a pizza outlet and have the task of creating a new feature for the order management software, which should be able to predict delivery times for customers based on historical data of previous deliveries, such as the distance traveled, the time that it took and other parameters such as the day of the week, time of the day etc. With this information, we can predict future delivery times.

Now, let's add a requirement to this - you are still employed at the same pizza outlet, but you are now tasked with segmenting your customers in order to run a targeted coupon campaign. Similarly, we have access to various historical data such as customer name, age, order, area and other details. Classifying these customers into clusters like young, old and other factors is an example of "unsupervised learning", where we are not making predictions but merely categorizing the customers into various groups.

Real Life Applications of Clustering

Some real-life applications of unsupervised learning include domains that deal with humongous and complex data sets such as genomics, to form clusters of genes with similar patterns. Also, it is commonly used in astronomy, to classify different families of stars or celestial objects based on various factors such as their color, size, distance, materials etc.

It is also extensively used to predict earthquake zones based on epicenter clusters, as well as in the following businesses:

1. Market segmentation
2. In driving targeted advertisements
3. Image segmentation
4. Medical image detection
5. Image segmentation
6. Social media analysis
7. In Netflix recommendations
8. Search result grouping

9. Anomaly detection

10. Recommendation engines

Classification of Clustering Algorithms

Clustering is one of the most commonly use type of unsupervised machine-learning algorithm. You can classify a clustering algorithm in two ways alone. These types are based on the type of input, meaning the type of data, you will be using to train and test your algorithm. This section provides information on the two types of clustering algorithms:

Hard Clustering

A hard clustering algorithm is the type of algorithm where the input data set should belong to at least one type of cluster. This is a binary classification problem, where the data set either belongs to one type of cluster or not.

Soft Clustering

It is always a good idea to include soft clustering algorithms in a real-time application. This is a more pragmatic approach, since the data set that you use is often in a grey area, which means that it does not necessarily have to belong to a specific cluster. Therefore, this is not a binary classification problem like the hard clustering algorithm. Instead of categorizing the data set, you will need to attach a probability value to indicate the likelihood of the input data belonging to a specific cluster. In this way, you can predict if a specific customer will buy a specific product or not. The model will not come to the conclusion that the customer will buy a specific product.

Types of Clustering Algorithms

The different types of clustering algorithms are as follows.

Flat Clustering

In this type of clustering the engineer will tell the model the number of categories it should assign the data to. This means that the user will define the value of k, which determines the number of clusters that can be used in the model.

Hierarchical clustering

The second type of clustering algorithm is Hierarchical Clustering where the user does not define the k value. The engineer allows the machine to decide the number of clusters it can create based on the iterations that the mode runs.

Model of Clustering

Based on the model of clustering, you can classify clustering algorithms into different categories. This is because the task of clustering is subjective. This section throws some light on the different approaches that an engineer can use to cluster different data sets.

Density Model

The data points or variables in the input data set is plotted on the graph, and there are some points that will vary in the data space. This variation is due to the density, which is the basis of clustering the data points or variables for the different clustering algorithms that fall under a density model. These models function by isolating multiple density regions and identifying the data points from every region using some models like OPTICS and DBSCAN.

Connectivity models

As the name suggests, this model of algorithms is based on the notion that the data points that are closer in data space are more likely to exhibit similarity than those that are farther away. These algorithms take one of the following two approaches when trying to cluster the input data – they start with classifying the data points and then proceed to aggregate them as the distance decreases. In the alternative, second approach, it is the polar opposite, where the partitioned data are clustered as the distance between them increases. The distance function is subjective and this class of algorithms is generally not suitable for scalable solutions and to handle larger data sets. Hierarchical clustering and other similar variants of this fall under this category.

Centroid Models

A centroid model is a type of clustering model that uses an iterative approach. The idea behind this model is to calculate the distance between a data point and variable and the centroid of a cluster. The k means algorithm is an example of this type of clustering since the algorithm depends on the centroid of the cluster. We will cover this model in the next part of this chapter. The user or engineer will need to define the many clusters in the data set which makes it important for him to know the data set well. This is a limitation of the application that you are developing since the model cannot respond dynamically. The model will need to run many iterations to calculate the centroid which is the optimal central point.

Distribution Models

This type of classification is always based on the probability that a data point or variable will fall under a cluster with the same distribution like Gaussian or binomial. These models often overfit the data. Th expectation maximization algorithm is the most popular type of algorithm in this class. This model is used on data that follows a multivariate normal distribution.

Implementation of Clustering Algorithms

In this book, we'll explore two of the most common forms of clustering: k-means and hierarchical.

K-Means Clustering Algorithm

Clustering, which is sometimes called unsupervised classification, is one of the most popular algorithms; the k in the name refers to how many different unique clusters one wishes to generate from the given data set. The value of k is defined by the user and each cluster formed has a centroid. The centroid is the central point of all the points that form any given cluster and the number of centroid is equal to k - the number of clusters. This algorithm primarily works with numerical values and all other symbolic data type are excluded.

This algorithm is used to build many models since it is easy for one to understand and is simple to build. You can also see how well this model is executed when you write it. The input data that you feed the model is automatically divided into clusters. This makes it easier for you to use the model. The only disadvantage is that you need to specify the number of clusters that the data should be categorized into. This does not allow you to make any dynamic adjustments to the data if necessary.

Also, the output can be significantly influenced by the seed data that is initially fed to the model. The algorithm tends to converge to the local minimal and it is therefore recommended to reset and rerun the algorithm with different random seeds to ensure minimal error. It is not most efficient when working with large data sets, and is therefore not scalable for large real-time applications. Sampling can at times help in making the runs quicker on large datasets.

671

Another disadvantage of this algorithm is that it is sensitive to outliers. A single value can alter the efficiency of the model. The mean value in the model will be skewed if the input data set has large values. The engineer can use the median value of the data set instead of the mean to overcome this issue.

K-Means Steps of the algorithm

You will need to code the following steps in Python to build your algorithm:

1. Choose a random value for k. Here k is the number of clusters you want to build.

2. Assign a data point to the center of the cluster using different methods. In the example below, we will use the Euclidean distance. This distance calculates the center that is closest to a data point.

3. The position of every centriole must be updated by calculating the average of every point in the data set.

You will need to repeat the second and third steps, which means that you need to iterate through the data set. This is done until you reach the point of convergence. The point of convergence is when the clusters have reached an optimal state, and further iterations will not affect the position of the clusters. Let us now look at how you can implement this algorithm in Python. In the code below, we will create the many cluster blobs or bars in Python using the make_blobs function. This function is in the sci kit library. You can use the code in the section below to create a random cluster on a graph.

```
# import statements
from sklearn.datasets import make_blobs
import numpy as np
```

```
import matplotlib.pyplot as plt

# create blobs

data = make_blobs(n_samples=200, n_features=2,
centers=4, cluster_std=1.6, random_state=50)

# create np array for data points

points = data[0]

# create scatter plot

plt.scatter(data[0][:,0], data[0][:,1], c=data[1],
cmap='viridis')

plt.xlim(-15,15)

plt.ylim(-15,15)
```

The above piece of code will create 4 different colored blobs on the scattered plot, that overlap with each other. Two of these blobs are placed at the top of the chart, and two at the bottom. You must understand that four clusters are being created since we defined the value of k to be four. The next step is to measure the Euclidean distance. You can calculate this value using the norm function in the numpy package in Pyhton. After that iteration, the new plot will show the cluster centroid in new updated positions. You should repeat these iterations until you identify the optimal cluster position for the data set.

```
# import K Means

from sklearn.cluster import K Means

# import statements

from sklearn.datasets import make_blobs

import numpy as np

import matplotlib.pyplot as plt
```

```
# create blobs

data = make_blobs(n_samples=200, n_features=2, centers=4,
cluster_std=1.6, random_state=50)

# create np array for data points

points = data[0]

# create scatter plot

plt.scatter(data[0][:,0], data[0][:,1], c=data[1], cmap='viridis')

plt.xlim(-15,15)

plt.ylim(-15,15)

# create kmeans object

kmeans = KMeans(n_clusters=4)

# fit kmeans object to data

kmeans.fit(points)

# print location of clusters learned by kmeans object

print(kmeans.cluster_centers_)

# save new clusters for chart

y_km = kmeans.fit_predict(points)

plt.scatter(points[y_km ==0,0], points[y_km == 0,1], s=100,
c='red')

plt.scatter(points[y_km ==1,0], points[y_km == 1,1], s=100,
c='black')

plt.scatter(points[y_km ==2,0], points[y_km == 2,1], s=100,
c='blue')
```

```
plt.scatter(points[y_km ==3,0], points[y_km == 3,1], s=100,
c='cyan')
```

The statement from sklearn.cluster import K Mean is a reference to the actual k means algorithm. The k means algorithm is based on an algorithm called Lloyds algorithm, which used to have a cluster of cells called the Voronoi cells. A key concept that you need to keep in mind when you use the clustering algorithm is to understand the concepts of boundaries. These boundarie define the range of the data set, which helps to identify the outliers. After importing the sci kit learn library inbuilt in the k mean algorithm, we will then need to plot the data set. You can use the following lines of code for the same.

```
x = [1, 5, 1.5, 8, 1, 9]

y = [2, 8, 1.8, 8, 0.6, 11]

plt.scatter(x,y)

plt.show()
```

Once the graph is plotted, the following set of lines can be written to convert the data into array - which is the acceptable input data structure format for scikit library.

```
X = np.array([[1, 2],

[5, 8],

[1.5, 1.8],

[8, 8],

[1, 0.6],

[9, 11]])
```

In the next section of the code, we will initialize the value of k, and map the k means algorithm to the k means type of cluster alone.

```
kmeans = KMeans(n_clusters=2)

kmeans.fit(X)

centroids = kmeans.cluster_centers_

labels = kmeans.labels_

print(centroids)

print(labels)

colors = ["g.","r.","c.","y."]

for i in range(len(X)):

print("coordinate:",X[i], "label:", labels[i])

plt.plot(X[i][0], X[i][1], colors[labels[i]], markersize = 10)

plt.scatter(centroids[:, 0],centroids[:, 1], marker = "x",
s=150, linewidths = 5, zorder = 10)

plt.show()
```

K-means ++ is an algorithm that you can implement if you want to use a seed to improve the accuracy of the model.

Hierarchical Clustering Algorithm

In this algorithm, every data point or variable in the training data set is assigned to a cluster or category. These points find the closest data points in the set, and then create a dendogram. This plot will help an analyst or engineer determine the number of clusters in the data set. One can also use this dendogram to calculate the distance between the clusters. It is for this reason that this algorithm is known to produce more accurate results when compared to the k-means algorithms when the user does not specify the value of k.

```
# import hierarchical clustering libraries

import scipy.cluster.hierarchy as sch

from sklearn.cluster import AgglomerativeClustering

# create dendrogram

dendrogram = sch.dendrogram(sch.linkage(points,
method='ward'))

# create clusters

hc = Agglomerative Clustering(n_clusters=4, affinity =
'euclidean', linkage = 'ward')

# save clusters for chart

y_hc = hc.fit_predict(points)

plt.scatter(points[y_hc ==0,0], points[y_hc == 0,1], s=100,
c='red')

plt.scatter(points[y_hc==1,0], points[y_hc == 1,1], s=100,
c='black')

plt.scatter(points[y_hc ==2,0], points[y_hc == 2,1], s=100,
c='blue')

plt.scatter(points[y_hc ==3,0], points[y_hc == 3,1], s=100,
c='cyan')
```

You can use the clustering algorithms as both an unsupervised and supervised learning algorithm. When you use these algorithms with other supervised learning algorithms, you can increase the accuracy of the output that is generated by those algorithms.

Chapter Six

Python Environment for Deep Learning

This chapter will provide information on the environment that you need to set up to use Python for deep learning. You must install the following software to build deep learning algorithms in Python.

1. Python 2.7+

2. Matplotlib

3. SciPy with NumPy

4. Theano

5. Keras

6. TensorFlow

In the third chapter of the book, we covered some of the most important libraries in Python. Experts recommend that you install Python and all of those libraries using the Anaconda distribution since that comes with every package. You should ensure that different libraries and tools you download are installed correctly in your system. To import the libraries from the software listed above into Python, type the following commands in the command line program in Python.

$ python

Python 3.6.3 |Anaconda custom (32-bit)| (default, Oct 13 2017, 14:21:34)

[GCC 7.2.0] on Linux

Now, import the necessary libraries and print the versions in the output window.

import numpy

print numpy.__version__

You will receive the version number of the installed software.

Installation of Keras, TensorFlow and Theano

You should always check if the system you use has a pip installed before you install the Keras, TensorFlow and Theano packages in your system. A pip is a package management system in the Anaconda distribution. You should type in the following command in Python to confirm if the pip has been installed.

$ pip

When Python confirms that the pip has been installed, you should install Keras and TensorFlow using the following command:

$pip install theano

$pip install tensorflow

$pip install keras

To confirm if Theano has been installed in Python, you should type the following code:

$python –c "import theano: print (theano.__version__)"

Once you obtain the version number of Theano that has been installed in your system, you should confirm if TensorFlow has been installed in Python by executing the following line of code:

$python   -c   "import   tensorflow: print tensorflow.__version__"

Now, to confirm the installation of Keras on your system, execute the following line of code:

$python -c "import keras: print keras.__version__"

Using TensorFlow backend

You will receive the version number of TensorFlow that is installed in your system.

Chapter Seven

How to Evaluate the Performance of a Deep Learning Model

You will need to make a lot of decisions when you design and configure the deep learning models. Most of the decisions you make should be resolved through the trial and error method. You should then evaluate the model on real data or test data. Therefore, it is important that you identify a robust way to evaluate the performance of a deep neural network. This chapter will provide some information on the different ways you can evaluate the model you building using Keras.

Empirically Evaluate Network Configurations

There are many decisions that are you should make when you design and configure deep learning models. You can make most of these decisions by copying a pre-existing model and making changes to the model depending on your requirement. The best technique is to design small segments of the model and evaluate the smaller segments using real data. If the model performs well, you can combine the small segments of the model to develop the final model.

All the decisions that you will need to make include the number of layers in the network, the size of the network, the type of layers included, epochs or number of iterations, activation function, optimization procedure and choice of loss function.

Deep learning models are often used to solve different problems where the input data set is large with at least a million variables or instances. It is for this reason that you need to identify different criteria, which will allow you to estimate the performance of a variety of configurations of the network on any new data.

Data Splitting

If you use large volumes of complex data sets you need to allow the deep neural network to learn from the data set. You should therefore, avoid using a large data set. Instead, split the data into two sets – training data and the validation or testing data set. Keras libraries allow you to evaluate a deep learning algorithm using the following methods:

1. Use a manual dataset for verification

2. Use an automatic dataset for verification

Use an Automatic Dataset for Verification

You can use Keras to split the dataset into a training dataset and validation dataset. Once you have developed the model, you can use the validation data set to validate every output after an epoch. The large data set can be split using the validation split function in the fit() function of the code. You can tell Python how much of the data should be split into the validation data set. For instance, you can ask Python to use at least 30% of the training data set as the validation data set.

The example in this section shows how you can use Keras to split the training dataset into a validation dataset. The dataset used in the examples below is the same as the one we used to build the neural network in the second series of the book.

Neural network with an automatic validation set

from keras.models import Sequential

```
from keras.layers import Dense

import numpy

# fix random seed to reproduce results

numpy.random.seed(7)

# load pima indians dataset

dataset = numpy.loadtxt("file_name.csv", delimiter=",")

# split into input (X) and output (Y) variables

X = dataset[:,0:8]

Y = dataset[:,8]

# create model

model = Sequential()

model.add(Dense(12, input_dim=8, activation='relu'))

model.add(Dense(8, activation='relu'))

model.add(Dense(1, activation='sigmoid'))

# Compile model

model.compile(loss='binary_crossentropy',
optimizer='adam', metrics=['accuracy'])

# Fit the model

model.fit(X, Y, validation_split=0.33, epochs=150,
batch_size=10)
```

When you run the example above, you will receive the following output for each iteration or epoch. This epoch will show the accuracy and loss on both the validation and training datasets.

Epoch 145/150

514/514 [================================] - 0s - loss: 0.5252 - acc: 0.7335 - val_loss: 0.5489 - val_acc: 0.7244

Use a Manual Dataset for Verification

Using Keras, you can split the data set manually as the validation data set and training data set. In the example below, we will use the train_test_split() fuction in the scikit library and separate the data into a training and validation dataset. The model will use 67% of the dataset for training and the remaining 33% for validation. You can specify the validation dataset in the fit() function using the validation data argument. This argument takes the tuple of both the input and output datasets.

```
# Neural network with manual validation set

from keras.models import Sequential

from keras.layers import Dense

from sklearn.model_selection import train_test_split

import numpy

# fix random seed to reproduce results

seed = 7

numpy.random.seed(seed)

# load the dataset

dataset = numpy.loadtxt("file_name.csv", delimiter=",")

# split into input (X) and output (Y) variables

X = dataset[:,0:8]

Y = dataset[:,8]
```

684

split into 67% for train and 33% for validation

X_train, X_test, y_train, y_test = train_test_split(X, Y, test_size=0.33, random_state=seed)

create model

model = Sequential()

model.add(Dense(12, input_dim=8, activation='relu'))

model.add(Dense(8, activation='relu'))

model.add(Dense(1, activation='sigmoid'))

Compile model

model.compile(loss='binary_crossentropy', optimizer='adam', metrics=['accuracy'])

Fit the model

model.fit(X_train, y_train, validation_data=(X_test,y_test), epochs=150, batch_size=10)

Like the earlier example, you will receive an output for every epoch which includes the accuracy and loss for every model for both the training and validation datasets.

Epoch 145/150

514/514 [==============================] - 0s - loss: 0.4847 - acc: 0.7704 - val_loss: 0.5668 - val_acc: 0.7323

Manual k-Fold Cross-Validation

One of the best ways to evaluate a deep learning model is using the k-fold cross-validation method. This method provides the designer with an estimate of how the model performs on unseen data. In this method, the data is split into k sets, and the training data is run through these sets, except for the one set that it does not use. The process runs through many iterations, and an average of the estimates and takes that as the performance measure. This method is often not used to evaluate a deep learning model since it is expensive. For instance, you can use the k-cross validation method to either fold the data into five or ten folds. This means that Python will need to construct and evaluate either five or ten models. This will increase the time taken to evaluate the model. If the data set is small, and you have enough resources to use this method, you can identify a less biased estimate of the model.

In the example below, we will use the StratifiedKFold class from the scikit library in Python to split the training data set into 10 folds. The algorithm tries to maintain a balance between the number of instances in each class in every fold. In this example, we will create and evaluate the ten models and use the ten splits of data to collect the scores.

The algorithm will print the performance for every model and will store that in the memory. Once the cycle is run, the algorithm will calculate the average and variation of the performance and print that value in the output window after every epoch. This will provide a robust performance estimate of the model.

```
# Neural network for dataset with 10-fold cross validation

from keras.models import Sequential

from keras.layers import Dense

from sklearn.model_selection import StratifiedKFold

import numpy

# fix random seed to reproduce the results

seed = 7
```

```python
numpy.random.seed(seed)
# load pima indians dataset
dataset = numpy.loadtxt("file_name.csv", delimiter=",")
# split into input (X) and output (Y) variables
X = dataset[:,0:8]
Y = dataset[:,8]
# define 10-fold cross validation test harness
kfold = StratifiedKFold(n_splits=10, shuffle=True,
random_state=seed)
cvscores = []
for train, test in kfold.split(X, Y):
  # create model
  model = Sequential()
  model.add(Dense(12, input_dim=8, activation='relu'))
  model.add(Dense(8, activation='relu'))
  model.add(Dense(1, activation='sigmoid'))
  # Compile model
  model.compile(loss='binary_crossentropy',
optimizer='adam', metrics=['accuracy'])
  # Fit the model
  model.fit(X[train], Y[train], epochs=150, batch_size=10,
verbose=0)
  # evaluate the model
```

```
scores = model.evaluate(X[test], Y[test], verbose=0)

print("%s: %.2f%%" % (model.metrics_names[1],
scores[1]*100))

cvscores.append(scores[1] * 100)

print("%.2f%% (+/- %.2f%%)" % (numpy.mean(cvscores),
numpy.std(cvscores)))
```

You will receive the following output when you run the algorithm.

acc: 77.92%

acc: 68.83%

acc: 72.73%

acc: 64.94%

acc: 77.92%

acc: 35.06%

acc: 74.03%

acc: 68.83%

acc: 34.21%

acc: 72.37%

64.68% (+/- 15.50%)

Chapter Eight

How to Save and Load
Deep Learning Models

It takes days, hours, weeks and years to train some deep learning models. Therefore, it is important that you know how you can save your models to load them off the disk or storage space whenever you need to use them. This chapter provides information on how you can save a Keras model to your disk and load it into Python when you need to make any predictions. With Keras, you do not have to worry about saving the architecture and model weights. The model weights are always saved in the HDF5 format, which is the grid format that Python uses to store multivariate or multi-dimensional data. You can save the model structure using the following formats – JSON and YAML. We will look at the following examples in this chapter:

1. Save the Model in the JSON format

2. Save the Model in the YAML format

The examples in the chapter will also demonstrate how you can save and load the model weights to the HDF5 format. We will continue to use the dataset we used in the previous chapter for these examples. You will first need to install h5py in Python.

sudo pip install h5py

Save Your Neural Network Model to JSON

JSON is a simple format that allows you to use a hierarchy to describe the data. Keras allows you to save the file and later load the file using the model_from_json() function. This will create a new model using the JSON specification or format. The weights that you use in the model are saved directly using the save weights() function and these are loaded once again into Python using the load weights() function.

The weights in the model are saved directly using the following function: save_weights(). These weights are later loaded into the model using the load weights() function. In the example below, we will load the model and then used the saved files to develop a new model. It is important that you compile the loaded model before you begin to use it. This is done to ensure that the predictions made use the efficient and appropriate computations from the Keras backend.

```
# Neural network for the dataset Serialize to JSON and
HDF5

from keras.models import Sequential

from keras.layers import Dense

from keras.models import model_from_json

import numpy

import os

# fix random seed to reproduce results

numpy.random.seed(7)

# load pima indians dataset

dataset = numpy.loadtxt("file_name.csv", delimiter=",")

# split into input (X) and output (Y) variables

X = dataset[:,0:8]
```

```python
Y = dataset[:,8]
# create model
model = Sequential()
model.add(Dense(12, input_dim=8,
kernel_initializer='uniform', activation='relu'))
model.add(Dense(8, kernel_initializer='uniform',
activation='relu'))
model.add(Dense(1, kernel_initializer='uniform',
activation='sigmoid'))
# Compile model
model.compile(loss='binary_crossentropy',
optimizer='adam', metrics=['accuracy'])
# Fit the model
model.fit(X, Y, epochs=150, batch_size=10, verbose=0)
# evaluate the model
scores = model.evaluate(X, Y, verbose=0)
print("%s: %.2f%%" % (model.metrics_names[1],
scores[1]*100))
 # serialize model to JSON
model_json = model.to_json()
with open("model.json", "w") as json_file:
   json_file.write(model_json)
# serialize weights to HDF5
model.save_weights("model.h5")
print("Saved model to disk")
 # load json and create model
json_file = open('model.json', 'r')
```

```python
loaded_model_json = json_file.read()
json_file.close()
loaded_model = model_from_json(loaded_model_json)
# load weights into new model
loaded_model.load_weights("model.h5")
print("Loaded model from disk")
 # evaluate loaded model on test data
loaded_model.compile(loss='binary_crossentropy',
optimizer='rmsprop', metrics=['accuracy'])
score = loaded_model.evaluate(X, Y, verbose=0)
print("%s: %.2f%%" % (loaded_model.metrics_names[1],
score[1]*100))
```

When you run the example, you will obtain the following output:

acc: 78.78%

Saved model to disk

Loaded model from disk

acc: 78.78%

The format of the model in JSON looks as follows:

```json
{
  "keras_version":"2.0.2",
  "backend":"theano",
  "config":[
    {
      "config":{
        "dtype":"float32",
```

"bias_regularizer":null,

"activation":"relu",

"bias_constraint":null,

"use_bias":true,

"bias_initializer":{

  "config":{

  },

  "class_name":"Zeros"

},

"kernel_regularizer":null,

"activity_regularizer":null,

"kernel_constraint":null,

"trainable":true,

"name":"dense_1",

"kernel_initializer":{

  "config":{

    "maxval":0.05,

    "minval":-0.05,

    "seed":null

  },

  "class_name":"RandomUniform"

},

"batch_input_shape":[

  null,

693

8
    ],
    "units":12
  },
  "class_name":"Dense"
},
{
  "config":{
    "kernel_regularizer":null,
    "bias_regularizer":null,
    "activation":"relu",
    "bias_constraint":null,
    "use_bias":true,
    "bias_initializer":{
      "config":{

      },
      "class_name":"Zeros"
    },
    "activity_regularizer":null,
    "kernel_constraint":null,
    "trainable":true,
    "name":"dense_2",
    "kernel_initializer":{
      "config":{

```
        "maxval":0.05,

        "minval":-0.05,

        "seed":null

      },

      "class_name":"RandomUniform"

    },

    "units":8

  },

  "class_name":"Dense"

},

{

  "config":{

    "kernel_regularizer":null,

    "bias_regularizer":null,

    "activation":"sigmoid",

    "bias_constraint":null,

    "use_bias":true,

    "bias_initializer":{

      "config":{

      },

      "class_name":"Zeros"

    },

    "activity_regularizer":null,

    "kernel_constraint":null,
```

```
      "trainable":true,

      "name":"dense_3",

      "kernel_initializer":{

        "config":{

          "maxval":0.05,

          "minval":-0.05,

          "seed":null

        },

        "class_name":"RandomUniform"

      },

      "units":1

    },

    "class_name":"Dense"

  }

 ],

 "class_name":"Sequential"

}
```

Save Your Neural Network Model to YAML

The example in this section is the same as the one above, except for the fact that we will use the YAML format to specify the model. The model described below uses YAML, saves the model to the file named neural_yaml and loads the new model using the function model_from_yaml(). The weights are handled in the same way as the example above in the HDF5 format as model.h5.

```
# Neural network for the Pima Indians Dataset to serialize to
YAML and HDF5
```

```python
from keras.models import Sequential
from keras.layers import Dense
from keras.models import model_from_yaml
import numpy
import os
# fix random seed to reproduce results
seed = 7
numpy.random.seed(seed)
# load pima indians dataset
dataset = numpy.loadtxt("file_name.csv", delimiter=",")
# split into input (X) and output (Y) variables
X = dataset[:,0:8]
Y = dataset[:,8]
# create model
model = Sequential()
model.add(Dense(12, input_dim=8,
kernel_initializer='uniform', activation='relu'))
model.add(Dense(8, kernel_initializer='uniform',
activation='relu'))
model.add(Dense(1, kernel_initializer='uniform',
activation='sigmoid'))
# Compile model
model.compile(loss='binary_crossentropy',
optimizer='adam', metrics=['accuracy'])
# Fit the model
model.fit(X, Y, epochs=150, batch_size=10, verbose=0)
```

```python
# evaluate the model
scores = model.evaluate(X, Y, verbose=0)
print("%s: %.2f%%" % (model.metrics_names[1],
scores[1]*100))


# serialize model to YAML
model_yaml = model.to_yaml()
with open("model.yaml", "w") as yaml_file:
    yaml_file.write(model_yaml)
# serialize weights to HDF5
model.save_weights("model.h5")
print("Saved model to disk")
 # Load YAML to create the model
yaml_file = open('model.yaml', 'r')
loaded_model_yaml = yaml_file.read()
yaml_file.close()
loaded_model = model_from_yaml(loaded_model_yaml)
# Load weights into the new model
loaded_model.load_weights("model.h5")
print("Loaded model from disk")
 # Evaluate the model using test data
loaded_model.compile(loss='binary_crossentropy',
optimizer='rmsprop', metrics=['accuracy'])
score = loaded_model.evaluate(X, Y, verbose=0)
print("%s: %.2f%%" % (loaded_model.metrics_names[1],
score[1]*100))
```

When you run the program above, you will receive the following output:

acc: 78.78%

Saved model to disk

Loaded model from disk

acc: 78.78%

The model that you described in the YAML format will look like this:

```yaml
backend: theano

class_name: Sequential

config:

- class_name: Dense

  config:

    activation: relu

    activity_regularizer: null

    batch_input_shape: !!python/tuple [null, 8]

    bias_constraint: null

    bias_initializer:

      class_name: Zeros

      config: {}

    bias_regularizer: null

    dtype: float32

    kernel_constraint: null

    kernel_initializer:

      class_name: RandomUniform

      config: {maxval: 0.05, minval: -0.05, seed: null}
```

kernel_regularizer: null

name: dense_1

trainable: true

units: 12

use_bias: true

- class_name: Dense

  config:

    activation: relu

    activity_regularizer: null

    bias_constraint: null

    bias_initializer:

      class_name: Zeros

      config: {}

    bias_regularizer: null

    kernel_constraint: null

    kernel_initializer:

      class_name: RandomUniform

      config: {maxval: 0.05, minval: -0.05, seed: null}

    kernel_regularizer: null

    name: dense_2

    trainable: true

    units: 8

    use_bias: true

- class_name: Dense

  config:

activation: sigmoid

activity_regularizer: null

bias_constraint: null

bias_initializer:

  class_name: Zeros

  config: {}

bias_regularizer: null

kernel_constraint: null

kernel_initializer:

  class_name: RandomUniform

  config: {maxval: 0.05, minval: -0.05, seed: null}

kernel_regularizer: null

name: dense_3

trainable: true

units: 1

use_bias: true

keras_version: 2.0.2

Chapter Nine

Reducing Dropouts in Deep Learning Models

O ne of the most powerful and simple techniques you can use to regularize a neural network and deep learning is the dropout. In this chapter, you will gather information on what the dropout regularization technique is and how you can apply it to your deep learning models in Python using Keras.

Dropout Regularization for Neural Networks

Srivastava and his team proposed the use of dropouts to regularize neural networks. They explained the concept of dropouts and how they help to regularize neural networks in the paper 'Dropout: A Simple Way to Prevent Neural Networks from Overfitting.'

Dropout is a technique where the model ignores some neurons in every iteration during the training period. These neurons are "dropped-out" at random. This means that these neurons do not contribute to obtaining the results. Their contribution is not taken into account on the forward pass, and any updates made during the iteration are not pushed back towards these neurons.

As the neural network learns, every neuron in the network is assigned a weight. Some neurons in the network will be assigned an additional weight to represent a special feature in the training dataset. The neighboring neurons will rely on this special weight, and if this weight is too high, it can result in a sensitive model that is specialized to the training data. The phenomenon where many neurons rely on one neuron in the network is known as co-adaptation.

If neurons are dropped out of the network at random during training, other neurons will need to step up and handle the problem. They should learn to make predictions even if one neuron is missing. This ensures that the network learns to make multiple independent internal representations of the dataset.

The effect of this is that the neurons in the network will become less sensitive to a change in the specific weights of other neurons. This will help you develop a model that can make better predictions. These models will not overfit the training data which will reduce the effect of co-adaptation.

Regularizing Dropouts in Keras

You can easily implement dropouts be selecting, at random, which notes should be dropped-out given a specific probability in each epoch or weight cycle. This is how you can implement dropouts in Keras. It is important to remember that dropouts can only be used when you are training the model and not when you want to evaluate the model.

We will now look at different ways to use Dropout in Keras. The examples use the Sonar dataset. You can download this dataset from the following location:
http://archive.ics.uci.edu/ml/datasets/Connectionist+Bench+(Sonar,+Mines+vs.+Rocks)

The dataset is taken from the UCI Machine-learning repository. Like the examples used above, this dataset provides a binary classification problem. The model needs to differentiate between mock-mines and rocks from the sonar chirp returns in the data. This is a good training dataset to use since the input values have the same scale and are numerical.

The dataset has one single output value and sixty input values. You must standardize these input values before you use the dataset in the network. The neural network model has an input layer, two hidden layers and one output layer. The first hidden layer has 60 units and the second has 30 units. We train the model with a low momentum and learning rate using the stochastic gradient descent.

Once you download the data, move it to the working directly and give the file a name. In the example below, we will evaluate the model using the scikit-learn method and a 10-fold cross validation. This will help you identify the differences in the results. The following code will develop the neural network model.

```
# Baseline Model on the Sonar Dataset

import numpy

from pandas import read_csv

from keras.models import Sequential

from keras.layers import Dense

from keras.layers import Dropout

from keras.wrappers.scikit_learn import KerasClassifier

from keras.constraints import maxnorm

from keras.optimizers import SGD

from sklearn.model_selection import cross_val_score

from sklearn.preprocessing import LabelEncoder

from sklearn.model_selection import StratifiedKFold

from sklearn.preprocessing import StandardScaler

from sklearn.pipeline import Pipeline
```

```python
# fix random seed for reproducibility

seed = 7

numpy.random.seed(seed)

# load dataset

dataframe = read_csv("file_name.csv", header=None)

dataset = dataframe.values

# split into input (X) and output (Y) variables

X = dataset[:,0:60].astype(float)

Y = dataset[:,60]

# encode class values as integers

encoder = LabelEncoder()

encoder.fit(Y)

encoded_Y = encoder.transform(Y)

# baseline

def create_baseline():

    # create model

    model = Sequential()

    model.add(Dense(60, input_dim=60,
kernel_initializer='normal', activation='relu'))

    model.add(Dense(30, kernel_initializer='normal',
activation='relu'))

    model.add(Dense(1, kernel_initializer='normal',
activation='sigmoid'))
```
705

```
# Compile model

sgd = SGD(lr=0.01, momentum=0.8, decay=0.0,
nesterov=False)

model.compile(loss='binary_crossentropy',
optimizer=sgd, metrics=['accuracy'])

return model

numpy.random.seed(seed)

estimators = []

estimators.append(('standardize', StandardScaler()))

estimators.append(('mlp',
KerasClassifier(build_fn=create_baseline, epochs=300,
batch_size=16, verbose=0)))

pipeline = Pipeline(estimators)

kfold = StratifiedKFold(n_splits=10, shuffle=True,
random_state=seed)

results = cross_val_score(pipeline, X, encoded_Y,
cv=kfold)

print("Baseline: %.2f%% (%.2f%%)" %
(results.mean()*100, results.std()*100))
```

The code will generate results with an 86% estimated classification accuracy.

Using Dropout on the Visible Layer

You can always use a dropout in the visible layers of the neural network. The example below uses a dropout layer between the visible layers of the network and the first hidden layer. The rate is set to 20%, which means that one in five inputs will be excluded from every update cycle. The input will be selected at random. Additionally, we have imposed a constraint on the weights in every hidden layer. This ensures that the maximum of the weights in the layers does not exceed three. This is done by using the kernel constraint argument in the Dense class when you start building the model. The momentum is increased to 0.9 and the learning rate is increased by one. The paper mentioned in the first section of the book recommends that you always increase the learning rate when you want to use dropouts in your model.

Continuing from the example above, the code includes an input dropout for the same network.

```
# dropout in the input layer with weight constraint

def create_model():

  # create model

  model = Sequential()

  model.add(Dropout(0.2, input_shape=(60,)))

  model.add(Dense(60, kernel_initializer='normal',
activation='relu', kernel_constraint=maxnorm(3)))

  model.add(Dense(30, kernel_initializer='normal',
activation='relu', kernel_constraint=maxnorm(3)))

  model.add(Dense(1, kernel_initializer='normal',
activation='sigmoid'))

  # Compile model

  sgd = SGD(lr=0.1, momentum=0.9, decay=0.0,
nesterov=False)

  model.compile(loss='binary_crossentropy',
optimizer=sgd, metrics=['accuracy'])
```

```
    return model

  numpy.random.seed(7)

  estimators = []

  estimators.append(('standardize', StandardScaler()))

  estimators.append(('mlp',
  KerasClassifier(build_fn=create_model, epochs=300,
  batch_size=16, verbose=0)))

  pipeline = Pipeline(estimators)

  kfold = StratifiedKFold(n_splits=10, shuffle=True,
  random_state=seed)

  results = cross_val_score(pipeline, X, encoded_Y,
  cv=kfold)

  print("Visible: %.2f%% (%.2f%%)" % (results.mean()*100,
  results.std()*100))
```

When you run the example above, you will notice that the classification accuracy has reduced in at least one test run. You will receive the following output when you run the code:

Visible: 83.52% (7.68%)

Using Dropout on Hidden Layers

You can also apply a dropout to the hidden neurons and layers in the neural network. This section gives you an example that will show you how you can apply a dropout between the different layers in the neural network. The dropout rate that we are using in the example below is 20%, and we are placing an additional constraint on the weights that you use in those layers.

```
  def create_model():

    # create model
```

```
model = Sequential()

model.add(Dense(60, input_dim=60,
kernel_initializer='normal', activation='relu',
kernel_constraint=maxnorm(3)))

model.add(Dropout(0.2))

model.add(Dense(30, kernel_initializer='normal',
activation='relu', kernel_constraint=maxnorm(3)))

model.add(Dropout(0.2))

model.add(Dense(1, kernel_initializer='normal',
activation='sigmoid'))

# Compile model

sgd = SGD(lr=0.1, momentum=0.9, decay=0.0,
nesterov=False)

model.compile(loss='binary_crossentropy',
optimizer=sgd, metrics=['accuracy'])

return model

numpy.random.seed(7)

estimators = []

estimators.append(('standardize', StandardScaler()))

estimators.append(('mlp',
KerasClassifier(build_fn=create_model, epochs=300,
batch_size=16, verbose=0)))

pipeline = Pipeline(estimators)

kfold = StratifiedKFold(n_splits=10, shuffle=True,
random_state=seed)

results = cross_val_score(pipeline, X, encoded_Y,
cv=kfold)
```

```
print("Hidden: %.2f%% (%.2f%%)" % (results.mean()*100,
    results.std()*100))
```

The output for the above code is,

Hidden: 83.59% (7.31%)

You will find that using dropouts for the problem and the chosen network did not improve the performance of the model. The performance was worse than the benchmark. It is possible that you may need to increase the number of epochs during the training stage. Alternatively, you may need to fine-tune the learning rate in the code.

Tips for using Dropout

In the paper mentioned above, you will obtain information about the many machine-learning problems. The paper also provides information on what you should look at when you want to implement dropouts in your machine-learning model.

1. Always use a small dropout value. It is ideal to use a value between 20% and 40%. Always stick to 20% if you are using dropouts for the first time in your model. It is best to avoid using extremes since the network will not enough about the data.

2. If you want to include dropouts in your model, you should use a large model since you will get better performance. Dropouts help the model learn how to represent the data without the use of some neurons in the layers.

3. You must use dropouts on both hidden and visible units.

4. To obtain good results, you should apply dropout at each layer in the network.

5. When you use dropouts in your model, you should include a large learning rate with a large momentum and decay. Increase the learning rate in the model by a factor of 100 and use a momentum value of 0.99 or 0.9.

6. You should always maintain the size or volume of the weights of every neuron in the network. If the learning rate is high, it will result in a high weight. It is always good to maintain the weight on every neuron to improve the result of the model.

Conclusion

With that, we have come to the end of this book and the series on Machine Learning. I sincerely hope you found the books in this series informative.

This is the third book in the series, and provides further information on what machine-learning and deep learning are. I hope the book provides all the information you are looking for.

Good luck on building your very own machine learning and deep learning models.

Hi there, avid reader! If you have extra time on your hands, I would really, really appreciate it if you could take a moment to click my author profile in Amazon. In there, you will find all the titles I authored and who knows, you might find more interesting topics to read and learn!

If it's not too much to ask, you can also leave and write a review for all the titles that you have read – whether it's a positive or negative review. An honest and constructive review of my titles is always welcome and appreciated since it will only help me moving forward in creating these books. There will always be room to add or improve, or sometimes even subtract certain topics, that is why these reviews are always important for us. They will also assist other avid readers, professionals who are looking to sharpen their knowledge, or even newbies to any topic, in their search for the book that caters to their needs the most. Will you help me?

If you don't want to leave a review yourself, you can also vote on the existing reviews by voting Helpful (Thumbs Up) or Unhelpful (Thumbs Down), especially on the top 10 or so reviews.

If you want to go directly to the vote or review process for my titles , please visit on any of the titles below:

Machine Learning For Beginners: A Comprehensive, Step-by-Step Guide to Learning and Understanding Machine Learning Concepts, Technology and Principles for Beginners . Audiobook format is also available here.

Machine Learning : A Comprehensive, Step-by-Step Guide to Intermediate Concepts and Techniques in Machine Learning

Excel VBA : A Step-By-Step Tutorial For Beginners To Learn Excel VBA Programming From Scratch . Audiobook format is also available here.

Excel VBA : Intermediate Lessons in Excel VBA Programming for Professional Advancement . Audibook format is also available here.

Excel VBA: A Step-By-Step Comprehensive Guide on Advanced Excel VBA Programming Techniques and Strategies

Again, I truly appreciate the time and effort that you will be putting in leaving a review for my titles or even just for voting. This will only inspire me to create more quality content and titles in the future.

Thank you and have a great day!

Peter Bradley

Resources

https://pythonprogramming.net/regression-introduction-machine-learning-tutorial/

https://machinelearningmastery.com/visualize-machine-learning-data-python-pandas/

https://machinelearningmastery.com/machine-learning-in-python-step-by-step/

https://diwashrestha.com/2017/09/18/machine-learning-on-iris/

https://stackoverflow.com/questions/25900341/what-does-the-n-mean-in-this-block-of-python-code

https://towardsdatascience.com/machine-learning-vs-deep-learning-62137a1c9842

https://www.datascience.com/blog/regression-and-classification-machine-learning-algorithms

https://towardsdatascience.com/introduction-to-machine-learning-algorithms-linear-regression-14c4e325882a

https://www.analyticsvidhya.com/blog/2016/11/an-introduction-to-clustering-and-different-methods-of-clustering/

https://stackoverflow.com/questions/44300789/invalid-literal-for-float-in-k-nearest-neighbor

https://home.deib.polimi.it/matteucc/Clustering/tutorial_html/

https://www.datascience.com/blog/k-means-clustering

https://www.datacamp.com/community/tutorials/k-means-clustering-python

https://www.kaggle.com/andyxie/k-means-clustering-implementation-in-python

https://machinelearningmastery.com/evaluate-performance-deep-learning-models-keras/

https://medium.com/codebagng/basic-analysis-of-the-iris-data-set-using-python-2995618a6342

https://machinelearningmastery.com/save-load-keras-deep-learning-models/

Machine Learning

A Complete Exploration of Highly Advanced Machine Learning Concepts, Best Practices and Techniques

Introduction

In the last three parts of this series, we covered the basics of Machine Learning and the different subjects and algorithms that one can use to build a Machine Learning model. You also learned how to build a Machine Learning model in Python using the clustering and regression models.

Over the course of this book, you will gather information on some statistical concepts that one uses in Machine Learning. You will also learn about the different fields that are linked to Machine Learning. It is important to learn how these different concepts are intertwined, so you can build better models. You will also learn how you can build a genetic algorithm in Python and how to build a Neural Network in R.

Thank you for purchasing the book, *'Machine Learning - A Complete Exploration of Highly Advanced Machine Learning Concepts, Best Practices and Techniques'* and I hope you find the book as useful as you considered the previous books in the series to be.

I hope you gather all the information you are looking for.

Chapter One

An introduction to Descriptive Statistics

This chapter deals with descriptive statistics, that is, the methodology for describing or summarizing a set of data using tables, diagrams and numerical measures.

Presenting the data in a descriptive form is usually the first stage in any statistical analysis, as it allows us to spot any patterns in the data. The numerical measures mentioned are the 'average' of the data (i.e., mean, median, and mode) and the 'spread' of the data (i.e., range, IQR, and variance).

Types of Data

Batch data are a set of related observations, such as the current inflation rates of EU countries. Sample data are a set of observations selected from a population and designed to be representative of that population, such as the sums assured for a sample of 100 policies selected from a company's whole-life business.

The "sum assured" for a life insurance policy is the amount of benefit that is paid when the policyholder dies or the policy matures. "Whole-life business" refers to a particular type of policy. These terms are not important here. The objectives of an analysis involving batch data will usually be to extract the important features by summarizing the data. For an analysis involving sample data, the objectives will be the same plus the main objective of making inferences about the population.

In other words, we can use sample data to determine certain properties of the underlying population from which the sample was taken. This might be useful, for example, in setting up a model, which could then be used to predict future behavior. For example, estimating the number of claims that will be made on a certain type of policy in a given time period.

Data involve the values of a variable, and there are several types of variables.

Numerical

Numerical data can be classified into two types: discrete and continuous. The distinction between discrete and continuous data is that discrete data can only take one of a set of particular values, whereas continuous data can take any value within a specified range (or the possible values are so close together that they can be considered to occupy a continuous range).

Discrete data arise from counting. For example, numbers of actuaries, numbers of claims.

It is also possible to have discrete data that take negative or fractional values. To take a non-statistical example, data obtained from measuring the spins of subatomic particles, which can take any "half-integer" value (..., ½, ½, - - - + + + 1½, 1 0 1 1½,), would also be discrete.

Continuous data arise from measuring. For example, height, amount, age.

In statistical work, an "amount" often refers to an amount of money - for example, an employee's annual salary. "Age" here refers to a person's "exact age," not age last birthday, for example, your age might be 21.85 years.

Categorical

Dichotomous Data

Attribute (or dichotomous) data have only two categories. Some examples are yes/no, claim/no claim, make/female, etc.

Nominal Data

Nominal data have several unordered categories. Some examples of nominal data are types of policies, nature of claims, type of event occurred, etc.

Ordinal Data

Ordinal data have several ordered categories. An example of ordinal data would be questionnaire responses like strongly in favor // strongly against.

It is important to differentiate between discrete and continuous data since you will always use different statistical methods to deal with a specific type of data.

Frequency Distributions

You can summarize the data from in a discrete distribution using frequency distributions, that is, by counting the number of 0s, 1s, 2s, etc. For example, the number of children in a sample of 80 families might be summarized as follows:

Number of children under 16	Number of Families in the Sample
0	8
1	12
2	28
3	19
4	7
5	4
6	1
7	1
8 or more	0

A bar chart is used to represent the data.

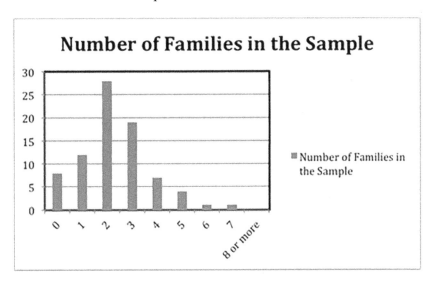

Histogram and Grouped Frequency Distributions

The next example involves a typical continuous variable and will introduce the idea of a grouped frequency distribution and a histogram. The data involve cash amounts given to the nearest £1. Cash amounts are actually discrete, being measured in whole numbers of pence, but here the sums are so large that they can be considered as continuous. In practice, all variables are discrete due to the fact that they will be rounded to certain accuracy and nothing can be measured to infinitesimal accuracy.

For example, a sample of 100 claims for damage due to water leakage on an insurance company's household contents policies might be as follows:

243 306 271 396 287 399 466 269 295 330 425 324 228 113 226
176 320 230 404 487 127 74 523 164 366 343 330 436 141 388 293
464 200 392 265 403 372 259 426 262 221 355 324 374 347 261
278 113 135 291 176 342 443 239 302 483 231 292 373 346 293
236 223 371 287 400 314 468 337 308 359 352 273 267 277 184
286 214 351 270 330 238 248 419 330 319 440 427 343 414 291
299 265 318 415 372 238 323 411 494

These data might be summarized in the following grouped frequency distribution:

Group	Frequency
50-99	1
100-149	5
150-199	4
200-249	14
250-299	22
300-349	20
350-399	14
400-449	13
450-499	6
500-549	1

A histogram is similar to a bar chart, but with a continuous scale.

In other words, a bar chart is called a histogram when it is used to present continuous numerical data. So the responses to any of the six questions on the dating agency questionnaire could be represented as a bar chart, but only Question 2 could be shown as a histogram.

Histograms are usually presented with vertical rectangles, but the one given below is unusual as it is in horizontal form.

In this histogram, the continuous scale has been broken down into categories by dividing the data values into £50 bands.

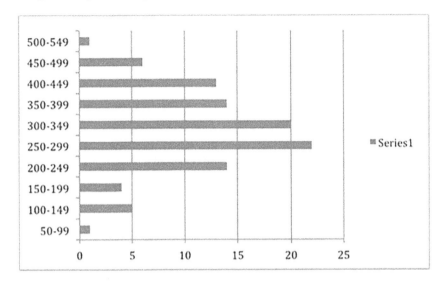

The above-grouped frequency distribution and histogram have equal group widths. In some situations, it may be convenient to have one or two wider groups at the extremes of the distributions. For such cases, it should be noted that it is the areas of the rectangles that are proportional to the frequencies, not their heights.

This is an important point to note, and you may wonder why this is the case. Think of a histogram as a 'fairer' bar chart: if a group has twice the width, it should only be half the height for a given frequency.

Measures of Location

There are a number of different quantities, which can be used to estimate the central point of a sample. These are called measures of central tendency or measures of location.

Mean

The quantities described in this section are just different ways of calculating the "average" value of the data set.

By far the most common measure for describing the location of a set of data is the mean.

For a set of observations denoted by x1, x2, x3, ..., xn, the mean is defined by:

> Mean (x- bar) = (sum of all observations)/(total number of observations)

For a frequency distribution with possible values x1, x2, x3, ..., xn, with corresponding frequencies f1, f2, f3, ..., fn, the mean is defined by:

> Mean = (sum of observation * frequency of observation) / (total number of observations)

For example, for the family size distribution data, the mean number of children in the sample is, from the frequency distribution,

> Mean = 186 / 80 = 2.235

Median

Another useful measure of location is the median. Consider placing the n observations in order of magnitude. The median is a value, which splits the data set into two halves so that half the observations are less than the median and half is greater than the median. This definition uses the words "a value," and not "the value," since there will be a range of values that may satisfy this condition. If the number of variables is odd, the median is the observation that lies in the middle. If the number of variables is even, the median is the average of the observations in the middle. This is expressed as the + (1)/2 n Th observation. The value of the median is robust or resistant in the sense that any extreme variables or outliers do not affect it, which is an advantage of using this measure.

Extreme observations (outliers) can cause problems because they can have a disproportionate effect on the calculated value of some of the quantities we have been looking at. The word "robust" is used with this special meaning in statistics. An area of statistics called robust statistics deals with the issue mentioned above.

For the family size distribution data, the 40th and 41st observations are both 2. So the median number of children is 2.

If we were asked to calculate the median of grouped data we would use interpolation.

The median is that value corresponding to a cumulative frequency of 50%, and it can be read from a plot of the cumulative frequency distribution.

Mode

The third measure of location is the mode. It is defined as the value that occurs with the greatest frequency or the most typical value. Its use in practice is limited, but there are occasions when, for example, a company is interested in the most typical policyholder.

For the family size distribution data the largest frequency is 28, so the modal number of children in the sample is 2.

Symmetry and Skewness

The next feature of interest is the shape of the distribution of a data set, that is, whether it is symmetric or skewed to one side or the other.

The approximate shape of a distribution can be determined by looking at a histogram, stem and leaf display or dot plot.

It should be noted that for sample data, a small data set of 10 observations is unlikely to show up the skewness of a population unless its skewness is very severe, whereas a large data set of 200 observations will reflect the shape of the population quite well.

The reason for describing these as positively or negatively skewed is that the skewness can be measured numerically by calculating the third central moment. For a positively (negatively) skewed distribution, this works out to a positive (negative) answer. For a symmetrical, distribution it equals zero.

You may wonder why the skewness is called positive when the 'hump' is on the left of the X-Axis. This is due to the fact that there are more data points to the right (on the positive side) of the 'hump' than the left and vice versa for negative skewness.

Positively skew distributions are most common in statistical work because we are often dealing with quantities, such as claim amounts, which must be positive but have no upper limit.

Probability

Probability is a numerical way of describing how likely something is to happen. This chapter looks at calculating probabilities using set theory. We also look at various rules for calculating 'or,' 'and' and 'conditional' probabilities, including Bayes' Theorem.

Fundamental Axioms

Let us take a look at the various axioms that are used in machine learning to understand the math that supports the model. One of the most fundamental axioms can be expressed as follows:

$$0 < P(A) < 1$$

This states that the probability of any event occurring is always going to be greater than zero but less than one, both inclusive. This implies that the probability of the occurrence of any event can never be negative. This makes sense since the probabilities can never be more certain than hundred percent and least certain than zero percent.

Additive Property

The next axiom that is important to note can only be true when both events A and B are mutually exclusive.

$$P(A+B) = P(A) + P(B)$$

This axiom states that the probability of both events A and B occurring is the same as the sum of the individual probabilities of the events occurring if and only if both events exclude each other. For example, if A is the event that we get a six on rolling a die and B is the event that we get a five rolling a die, then this axiom hold. But, if B were assumed to be the event where we get an even number, this set would include the number six making the axiom false.

Joint Probability

This property can be expressed as follows:

$$P(a, b) = P(A=a, B=b)$$

This property can be read as the probability of a and b is the same as the probability that event A turns out in state 'a' and event B turns out in state 'b.'

Conditional Probability

Consider the two events, A and B. We might wish to know the probability that event A occurred, given the occurrence of the event B. This is known as a conditional probability and is denoted thus:

P (A|B)

P (A|B) is read as "the probability that the event A occurs given that the event B has already occurred" or "probability of A given B" for short. This is called a conditional probability as the probability depends (i.e., is conditional) on event B.

Bayes' Rule

This rule is often used to identify the conditional probability when P (A, B) is not known. The equation used is as follows:

$$P (A|B) = [P (B|A)*P (A)]/P (B)$$

These various axioms are a great way to understand the logic behind Markov Models. Let us now take a look at the mathematical aspects of the Markov Model. As mentioned above, Markov Models was discovered in the year 1916 by Andreevich Markov, a scientist who was studying and analyzing the frequency of different types of words in Pushkin's poems. These models have now become an integral model to use while working with data science, artificial intelligence, and machine learning.

Understanding Random Variables and Expectations

You are on holiday in Las Vegas and have decided to go to a casino. You have settled into your favorite chair at the roulette table and have just turned the wheel. You have understood that there is an equal chance that the ball can fall into any of the slots in the cylinder. The slot where the ball can fall is random, and the probability or likelihood of that happening is the same for each slot on the table. Since there is an equal probability of the ball landing in any slot, the random variable would follow the uniform distribution.

But, not every slot on the wheel is the same – there are twenty slots that are either red or green, and there are 18 that are black. This would mean that there is an 18/38 probability that your ball will land on a black slot. You plan to make successive bets on your ball landing on the black slot.

Your net winnings can be considered to be a random variable here. A random variable is a measure of a value or trait that is associated with a place, person or an object. This is something that is unpredictable. That being said, it does not mean that one does not know anything about the random variable. You can use what you know about the random variable to help you make an informed decision.

You can take a weighted average – an average value over a large number of data points – of your winnings across the distribution, which yields the expectation of the random variable. This expectation is the expected value of all your winnings over a number of bets made. If you had to describe it formally, you would need to remember that an expectation is a weighted average of any measure that is associated with the random variable that is being considered. If you are trying to derive a model for an unpredictable variable, you can always use probability and random variables.

Let us assume that a data scientist is walking down a street in California and is looking at the eye color of the people walking past him. She would notice people with green eyes, brown eyes, blue eyes and so forth. She will not have an idea about the eye color of the person she will see next. But, she has identified that brown and blue eyes are the most common. Since she has observed this, you will make an educated guess on what the eye color of the next person can be. The random variable here would be the eye color, and her guess on what the eye color of the next person would be based on the probability that distribution of the eye color of people walking along the street.

Are you ready to dig a little deeper? Let us get a little more quantitative. If the data scientist sat down and recorded how many people were observed with the same eye color, she would be able to create a frequency distribution that will help her understand what the percentage is. These percentages, called percentiles in statistics will help her make an informed decision about the eye color of the population. These percentiles represent the probability distribution and the expectation calculated would be similar to how we calculated it in the roulette wheel example above.

There are a number of probability distributions that you would need to understand. However, you do not need to become a master at understanding these distributions since you can use programming languages like Python and R to identify the right distribution for your data.

Hi there! If you found the topic or information useful, it would be a great help if you can leave a quick review on Amazon. Thanks a lot!

Chapter Two

An introduction to Artificial Intelligence

An amazing development has taken place over the last few years. You may have watched how robots in Star Wars were able to perform so many actions and maybe, just maybe, you would have wondered how wonderful it would have been if this were to happen in this decade. You may not have seen it coming, but this was an inevitable turn of events – the emergence of Artificial Intelligence (AI). Everywhere we look today, we come across a number of intelligent systems that talk to us – Siri, Google Assistant – offering us advice and also offering us recommendations. These systems improve almost every year to improve its interpretation of images, voice recognition and also to drive cars based on different techniques used by Facebook and Google's Deep Learning Efforts. Other work always aims to understand and generate machines that would understand our language and communicate with us.

The reemergence of AI has caused a lot of confusion since there are so many companies that have begun to explore the scene. How do we make sense of any of it?

Let us start with a simple definition of AI. Artificial Intelligence or AI is a field of computer science that is aimed at developing computers that are capable of performing tasks that can be done by people, especially those tasks that are considered to be performed by intelligent people.

AI has had a number of excellent runs. In the early sixties, there were great promises that were made about what a machine could do. In the eighties, it was said to revolutionize the way businesses were run. But in those eras, the promises that were made were too difficult to deliver. So what makes the latest developments in AI any different? What makes the systems developed now any different from the diagnostic programs and neural nets of the past? There are a number of reasons why the developments in this era are different from the last.

Increased Computational Resources

The computers we have in this era are faster and can think harder thereby increasing the computational power. The techniques used earlier worked well only in the past, but now there would be a necessity to improve the computational grid and also expand it.

Growth of Data

Over the years, the data collected has increased by a vast amount and this data is being made available to the machines. This increase in the data has given machines much more to think about. This goes to say that learning systems get better at understanding more data and would now be able to look at thousand examples as opposed to only a few hundred.

Deeper Focus

AI has shifted away from looking at smaller aspects of data to look at specific problems. The systems now are capable of thinking about a particular problem as opposed to daydreaming without any problem. Systems like Cortana and Siri work well within limited domains that can be focused and modeled on pulling specific words that you would have said instead of understanding the entire sentence spoken by you.

Knowledge Engineering

The problem and issues with knowledge engineering have been transformed into different aspects of learning. The systems developed these days use their own ways to learn. The bottleneck in the systems in the past helped us add more rules to avoid such bottlenecks in the further processing of data. Most approaches in the modern times focus on learning these rules automatically.

Alternative Reasoning Models

Alternative reasoning models have been adopted which are based on the assumption that the systems do not have to reason like human beings in order to be smart. The machine is allowed to think like a machine.

It is these factors put together that have given the world the first renaissance of intelligent machines that have become a part of our lives and have been adopted in different tools and in workplaces.

Exploring AI

The goal for some developers and researchers is to build a system that has the ability to act and think intelligently the way human beings do. Most others do not care if the system does think like human beings – they are only worried about whether or not the system would do the right thing. Apart from these two schools of thought, there are others that are somewhere in between. If we were to use human reasoning in systems, it would help computers do things similar to human beings.

Strong AI

The work that is aimed at stimulating human reasoning in a machine is what is called strong AI. This implies that any machine created would need to have the capabilities of obtaining the results and also explain how a human being would think. Genuine models of AI systems that are simulations of the human mind and cognition have to be built.

Weak AI

The work that was done within the second school of thought, aimed towards just getting structures to work, is commonly known as weak AI in that even as we might be able to build structures which can behave like people, the outcomes tell us nothing about how human beings think or feel. One of the best examples of this is IBM's Deep Blue, a gadget that became a master chess player but absolutely did not play in the same manner that human beings do and informed us very little about cognition in general.

Anything in Between

The systems in between Weak and Strong AI are those that are informed and understand human reasoning but are not slaves to it. This is where most of the powerful work is happening in AI today. This work uses human emotion and reasoning as a guide, but it does not use it as a goal to model the system. If only one were able to come up with a name for this school of thought – maybe Practical AI.

The important takeaway is that a system does not have to be smart the way human beings are smart in order for it to be AI. The system would just need to be smart.

Chapter Three

The Artificial Intelligence Ecosystem

Interest in the field of Artificial Intelligence keeps increasing and decreasing. However, the fact of the matter is that we have had AI systems around us for a very long time now. Since many of these systems are narrow AI systems, and because they function exactly as expected, these systems are often not considered to be AI. However, they are smart and efficient and that is what matters when it comes to AI. In case you have forgotten the meaning of narrow AI, refer to Chapter 1.

Understanding that AI is everywhere

When websites like Amazon and eBay give suggestions to their customers, they are actually implementing something that is very close to human cognition. These websites use data mining in order to generate the suggestion list. They look at what you have purchased in the past and the products you have viewed or bookmarked and suggest similar products that have not been viewed before. These engines sometimes look at profiles of people that are "similar" to you and suggest products that they have purchased, to you. Although it may not be exactly like human thinking, notice that it is very similar to it. For instance, if you were to buy something for a friend, you would think of his or her likes and dislikes and choose a gift based on that information. Or, you would think of someone you consider similar to your friend and pick a gift based on that person's likes and dislikes.

At this moment in time, let us not get too worried about how these recommendation engines work and how to grade them as good or bad. Instead, let us appreciate the capability of these engines to generate profiles, identify similarities between different profiles and generate suggestion lists based on these similarities.

What makes human beings so smart?

In layman terms, the concept of intelligence and thinking can be reduced to three main stages: taking information in, thinking about it and finally, acting on it based on the thinking. These stages could be considered to be sensing, reasoning, and acting. Further distinctions can be made within these three broad areas. Let us look at each of these tasks in further detail.

Sensing

This stage is essentially just imbibing information from the world around us. Two of the most common methods of doing this are image sensing and speech sensing.

Image Processing

Human beings can take in the information that they see. This is how they can differentiate between objects, people, etc.

Speech Recognition

Human beings take in the information that they hear, and this is the only way we can understand what someone else is saying to us.

Other Sensors

There are many other sensory methods such as radar, sonar, speedometers, weighing machines, oscilloscopes, etc.

Reasoning

In reasoning, historical information or past information is used to relate to the information that is provided now. Let us look at some of the inference systems:

Natural Language Generation

If a human being is given the task to communicate with another object or human being, this method will allow the human being to generate the language you needs to use to complete the task.

Logic-Based Inference

This will help the human being decide whether anything is logically true.

Learning

Through learning, the human being can develop some new knowledge using some examples or using a training information. This loosely translates to machine learning.

Evidence-Based Inference

This type of inference lets the human being use some evidence to decide whether the answer to a specific question is true or false.

Situation Assessment

Here, human beings will need to identify what is happening in the world at a broad level.

Language Processing

This will allow the human beings to convert the words it hears into relations or ideas.

Planning/problem solving

The human being should identify what needs to be done to solve a problem.

Acting

After thinking about the information that we receive, we perform some action. Let us look at some examples.

Speech Generation

If a human being is given some text, and he or she needs to read it out or act according to that information, he or she can do it easily.

Robotic Control

This is analogous to muscular movement. You can do this either through an action or a reaction.

Examining the Components of AI

Research in the field of Artificial Intelligence looks to mimic various aspects of machine reasoning and human cognition. The AI systems that are being created these days, especially the consumer products such as Google's Now and Apple's Siri use all of the three layers mentioned above.

These AI systems are a new kind of organism in the AI ecosystem and they are considered to be complete. These systems use speech recognition and generation. They utilize language processing to understand what the user has spoken and interpret the language to run some decision model. This model then figures out the task that needs to be performed. If the response has a speech component, the system generates the speech after the task is performed. The best part about these systems is that they are very fast and the transition between the layers is seamless and this provides the best functionality to the users. Let us go into further detail into how the three areas of intelligence – sensing, reasoning and acting- come together in these AI systems.

Sensing

The two systems that were mentioned above are speech recognition systems. This means that they function based on the words that are spoken by the user. They achieve this by listening to the user through a microphone and then examine the waveforms to identify the words that are being spoken. Different systems use different voice recognition software. Apple uses a product designed by Nuance for Siri whereas Google uses a product that it creates.

These systems capture the words through the microphone, but they do not instantly interpret them and understand what they mean. They interpret these words in a very similar manner to how they interpret words when you type them in. The input waveform is analyzed and the system interprets it by comparing it to other waveforms.

The output of this process is a series of words. For these words to make sense to the system, it has to analyze them further and reason them. This step includes the system understanding what the words mean, seeing if it can provide the service and if so, deciding how to provide it. This is done through natural language processing.

Reasoning

Every intelligent system has its own way of analyzing a problem; they all perform very similar activities at the reasoning phase. In the example mentioned earlier, systems may record the use of the word pizza and mark it as food and see that the term recipe does not exist in that text where it has been indicated that the speaker wanted more information on how to make a pizza. It then deduces that the speaker wants to go to a restaurant where they serve pizza.

This type of processing, called lightweight language processing, is driven by simple relationships and definitions, which allow the system to determine whether an individual wants to visit a restaurant or learn how to make a pizza. The other alternative inference that the system can make is that the speaker would like to know where he or she could find a pizza. Knowing how to do it and what to do are very different from each other.

The transition from sounds to words to ideas to understanding user needs, provide every system with the necessary information to plan to satisfy those very needs. In this case, the system would look at the GPS and identify restaurants that would serve the user with pizza and rank those options based on certain rules – proximity, price, and rating. If there is user history, the system will provide the user with information on restaurants that he or she already likes.

The reasoning involved with choosing and deciding on different plans of action is artificial intelligence. However, the plans tend to be scripts that are used by the system to gather information. The simplicity of the script should not reduce its importance in an artificial intelligence system. An intelligent being is called an expert when he or she knows what to do and when to do it.

Acting

Once reasoning and sensing have been enabled within an artificial intelligence system, the results that are obtained would need to be communicated to the users. This often results in segregating the ideas into sets that can be communicated to the user easily and then mapping those ideas into words and sentences and then turning those words and sentences into sounds.

Assessing Data using AI

Consumer systems always try to assess human beings. For examples, Amazon puts together a picture of who you are and what products interest you and also assesses you against other similar customers and makes predictions about you. The data that is used to make this prediction is transactional – what you look at and what you purchase. Amazon's recommendation engines use all this information to come to a conclusion of what products should be recommended to you.

Profile data is only a small part of the picture. To this data, information about different categories – cluster objects (DIY books), Customers and other information – would need to be assessed to make an informed decision. The area you live in and the amount of money you would be willing to spend can be pulled in to refine the assumptions made about you.

The results are always a set of characterizations:

1. Based on what collections you like, you have a lot in common with a person across the globe that has a similar interest in science fiction, DIY books, and cookbooks and so on.

2. Based on a set of things you were looking at, you could be someone who loves to garden.

3. You just bought gardening tools to create your own kitchen garden.

For retailers, the information that is of utmost importance is transactions, product categories and the clusters of people. For search engines, the important information is the history of the information you have looked for and also the items you have clicked on and at which location those clicks were made.

Predicting Outcomes with AI

Prediction is one of the most important outcomes of reasoning. It is important to make a guess about what may happen in the future so that we can always deal with the outcomes of those events and AI systems also have the same focus.

How do managers in retail stores know what their customers would like to buy next? They look at what products a group of customers have bought or looked at and then project the actions of those customers onto ours. They reason in the following way, "*You and Ginny like reading novels, especially science fiction novels. I also know that Ginny likes picking up classics occasionally, and I bet you would too.*" Now, multiply Ginny with over 300 million customers – that is how a company can predict what a customer may like.

The combination of identifying the similarity and projecting that similarity forward is called collaborative filtering. This type of filtering is what most transactional recommendation systems are based on. These systems use intuition to identify people who are similar to each other based on set criteria.

Prediction can also be used to classify individuals and their behavior into groups with similar characteristics using their profiles. Target had used one such method to map the shopping behavior of pregnant women. They used this mapping to advertise to women who they believed were pregnant with products like breast pumps, blankets, and cribs. This was a fairly accurate technique – however, they did receive some flack about it. Target discovered that women did not want their family members to know that they were pregnant through a retail store.

Features and actions are linked so tightly that it is difficult to predict one from the other. If you watch Star Wars, it is true that you will view The Empire Strikes Back. If you were to buy a coffee maker, you will definitely need to buy filters. If you open a savings or checking account, you will definitely be making some deposits in the near future. Such predictions enhance the need to categorize things into groups and find similar individuals.

The goal of prediction is to identify a problem that may occur in the future and how that problem can be avoided. The target is not to find the person who is receiving it but to predict what the person may choose.

Some systems use machine learning and data mining when they need to focus more on outcomes rather than make recommendations or predictions. These systems connect visible characteristics and features at a point in time with events that will need to be predicted in the future by looking at the frequency of the features when compared to the examples of what the system is predicting. This process of prediction gives rise to the following question, "What feature or behavior will predict this?"

The feature or behavior in question can be anything from buying a particular product to a cyber-attack or a virus attack. Using techniques such as regression analysis, predictive analysis, data mining, they build rules that can be used to predict the events we care about before they occur.

Dynamic assessing, predicting, and inferring lie at the core of most intelligent systems especially at the core of the systems we interact with most. The reason behind this is very clear. For an intelligent system, the ability to identify what events are occurring right now, make inferences about the event and predict what will happen in the future is crucial because we would need to be able to anticipate the events that may occur in the future and plan for those.

Have a minute to spare? Please visit Amazon and leave a 5 star review

Chapter Four

Big Data and Artificial Intelligence

Most artificial intelligence and machine learning systems use assessing, predicting and inferring. These are components of human reasoning. There are a number of questions that would need to be answered every day – what is happening around us, what it means, what will happen next and so on. When we push the call button, walk towards and elevator or wait for a taxi, we are trying to assess, infer and predict. AI systems have started to do the same thing, although they would not wait in line to catch a taxi.

In the world of Big Data, where at least 2.5 quintillion bytes of data are collected or produced every single day, it important to know how AI Systems would capture that data, synthesize it and use it to drive their reasoning. The use of AI systems in issues like Big Data allows us to transform the world of numbers and unstructured data into knowledge that can be used by human beings.

The trick to understanding these systems is to understand that the processes that underlie the intelligence are smart. The systems are built on a foundation that processes are not only simple but also understandable. It is important to remember that AI is not magic, but it is the application of algorithms that are powered by data, processing power and scale.

What is Big Data?

Data that is obtained from two significantly different sources is grouped under the banner of Big Data. The first source of data is the data that is found within the organization or business and that is shared across a vast network. This data includes PDF documents, blogs, emails, work documents, business events, internal files, process events and any other structured data, unstructured or semi–structured data that can be found within the organization. The second source of data would be the data that is available outside the organization. Most of this information is available for free, but there is some information that would require a certain payment to be made in order to obtain it. Most of this information is available to the general public, but there is some information that is considered confidential and is kept within the organization itself. This information includes literature on products that is distributed by the competitors, information available on social media, hints from third parties, certain organization hierarchies and also any complaints that may have been posted by customers on regulatory sites.

You may begin to wonder what makes Big Data any different from the data that is being used since the ancient times. There are four characteristics of Big Data that make is very different from other kinds of data – Volume, Velocity, Variety, and Veracity. There are a number of other characteristics that differentiate Big Data from other types of data, but these are the most important and prominent characteristics to consider.

Volume

Numerous organizations have started to struggle with the amount of data that is being stored in their data warehouses since big data took the world by a storm. It was noted in the Fortune magazine that the world had already created close to 10 exabytes of data by the year 2006 and that this number would double by the year 2015. It has also been identified that this amount of data can now be collected within a few nanoseconds thereby increasing the data collected by trillion gigabytes every hour, which is a scary amount of data.

A few years ago, there were organizations that would count their data storage space for any type of analytics in terabytes. Now, they can only do the same in petabytes since the data collected has doubled or tripled since then. The amount of data does cause a strain on the analytics architecture for different organizations in different industries. For instance, let us consider an organization that is in the communication industry. You know that this organization would definitely have a hundred million customers. If data were collected for these customers on a daily basis, there would be at least 5 petabytes of data in a hundred days. Most companies try to get rid of data daily, but regulators have asked most companies in the communication industry to store records about calls made or the data used by each customer.

Velocity

Velocity can be understood from two different perspectives – one that represents latency while the other represents the throughput of data. Let us first take a look at latency. The analytics infrastructure was once a store – and – report environment where the data that was collected the previous day was used to make reports and this data was represented as "D-1". Over the last decade, the analytics infrastructure has been used in different business processes that there was a necessity to change the infrastructure to cater to the needs of all businesses. For example, some advertising agencies are trying to conduct analytics to help them place advertisements on online platforms within 10 milliseconds.

Let us now consider the second measure of velocity – the throughput of data. This represents the data that is flowing through the pipes of the analytics infrastructure. The amount of global mobile data is growing at the rate of 80 percent, which is said to compound annually implying that the data that is collected annually is set to increase by 12 – 14 exabytes per year as users begin to share more images and videos with the world. In order to analyze this data, many corporates are seeking analytical infrastructure that will help them process information in parallel.

Variety

It was in the late 1990s that Data Warehouse Technology was introduced to create and represent data using Meta–models that would help to simplify data and also help to represent data collected in one form, irrespective of whether or not the data was structured.

The data was often compiled from multiple sources and was then transformed using either ETL (Extract, Transform, Load) or ELT (Extract data, load it into the warehouse and transform the data within the warehouse). The idea was to narrow down the variety and ambiguity in the data collected and also structure that data to put it to good use. Big Data has helped to expand our horizons by enabling new data integration and solutions infrastructure and data analytics technology. A number of call center analytics constantly seek solutions that would help them attend to their customers better. These solutions would also help them understand the conversation that takes place between them and the disgruntled customer, which would then give them an idea of how to proceed further. The source data that is obtained from call centers are only unstructured data like audio, sound, or text and some structured data. Different applications gather different types of data from blogs, emails, and documents. For example, Slice, a company used to provide analytics for online orders, uses raw data that comes from a number of different organizations like online bookstore purchases, airline tickets, parking tickets, music download receipts and any other purchases that may have hit your email. How can this information be normalized into creating product catalogs and also analyze any purchases made?

Veracity

Internal data is often carefully governed while Big Data comes from a number of sources that are outside the control of the company and this data often comes with a lot of inaccuracies and incorrectness, which would hamper the analysis made. Veracity represents the sustainability of the data obtained and also looks for the credibility of the sources of data that is obtained for a target audience.

Let us try to see how we can understand the credibility of the sources of data. If organizations began to collect information on their own products using third parties and then provide that information to their customer care support or their contact center employees in order to support the queries that customers have, the organizations providing the information would need to be assessed and screened before trusting the information that is provided by them. Otherwise, there can be a possibility of the organization making a wrong offer to the customer thereby affecting the revenue. Numerous social media responses to different campaigns could come from unhappy customers or disgruntled employees, which would definitely impact the decisions made by the company. For instance, if there was a survey conducted by companies on the products provided by them and customers happened to like the product, this would be taken into consideration. However, if the customer were to select an option that did not show that they liked the product, it is important to know why before taking this unstructured piece of data into account.

We have to always consider the amount of truth that can be shared with an audience. The veracity of the data that is collected or created within a given organization is often considered to be well-intentioned. However, some of that data cannot be shared with the public since there could be some threat to the company. This would reduce the chance of having a wider communication network. For instance, if customer service has provided the manufacturing and engineering department with the shortcomings of a particular product based on the feedback given by customers, the data shared should be selective and on a need – to – know basis only. Other data can be shared with some customers who have certain prerequisites or contracts.

Big Data makes it possible for numerous businesses to process all the information that is collected on the simple learning systems. They would need to identify one signal from all the noise. It is only through this way of learning that it is possible to translate sentences from one language to the other. Parallelism and processing enable systems to take up thousands of pieces of evidence and then test them independently before adding up the results.

Chapter Five

Building a Genetic Algorithm in Python

In this chapter, we will look at how we can implement a genetic algorithm in Python. We will use a simple example where we are trying to maximize the solution or output for equations. This tutorial will use a decimal representation of the genes, a one-point crossover and a mutation. This mutation is over a uniform distribution.

The figure below shows a flowchart of the genetic algorithm. You must remember that every step involved in a genetic algorithm has some variations.

Genetic Algorithm(GA)

→ Population
↓
Fitness Calculation
↓
Mating Pool
↓
Parents Selection
↓
Mating ⟨ Crossover
        Mutation
↓
Offspring

(https://www.kdnuggets.com/2018/07/genetic-algorithm-implementation-python.html)

A gene can be represented in different ways – binary, integer, decimal or other similar types. There are numerous types of mutation you can use when you build a genetic algorithm – swap, bit flap, uniform, non-uniform, inverse, shrink, Gaussian and others. There are also different types of crossovers like one point, blend, uniform, two point and others. We will only look at how to implement one of these types in the algorithm we are now building. In this chapter, we will use the decimal representation of genes, uniform mutation and one point crossover. The first part of the series introduced genetic algorithms and explained how they work. If you do not remember too much about the genetic algorithms, please read the following articles:

1. **LinkedIn**: https://www.linkedin.com/pulse/introduction-optimization-genetic-algorithm-ahmed-gad/

2. **KDnuggets**:
   https://www.kdnuggets.com/2018/03/introduction-optimization-with-genetic-algorithm.html

3. **TowardsDataScience**:
   https://towardsdatascience.com/introduction-to-optimization-with-genetic-algorithm-2f5001d9964b

4. **SlideShare**:
   https://www.slideshare.net/AhmedGadFCIT/introduction-to-optimization-with-genetic-algorithm-ga

Before we look at the genetic algorithm, let us look at the equation we will be representing.

$$Y = w1x1 + w2x2 + w3x3 + w4x4 + w5x5 + w6x6$$

There are six input variables in the above equation (x1 – x6) and six weights for each input variable (w1 – w6). Let us define the input variables as (x1, x2, x3, x4, x5, x6) = (4, -2, 7, 5, 11, 1). We now need to find the weights or the parameters that will maximize this equation. The idea behind maximizing these equations is simple. You have to multiply the positive numbers by the largest positive number and the negative numbers by the smallest negative number. What we want to do is to ensure that the genetic algorithm does this for you. Therefore, you need to teach the algorithm that it is always a good idea to use positive inputs and positive weights or negative inputs and negative weights. Let us now start implementing the genetic algorithm.

Let us first create the list of inputs and the variables that will hold the number of weights.

Inputs of the equation.

equation_inputs = [4,-2,3.5,5,-11,-4.7]

Number of the weights we are looking to optimize.

num_weights = 6

Now, we should define the initial population that we want to use. Since you have assigned six weights, every chromosome, individual or solution, will have six genes. This means that there is one gene assigned for each weight. The question you may be wondering about is how many solutions can exist per population. There is no fixed number of solutions that the algorithm should provide, and you can choose the value or solution that will fit well with the problem. This means that you can leave it generic or make a change in the code. We will then create three variables – one to hold the number of solutions for every population, one for the size of the population and the last to hold the actual population.

import numpy

sol_per_pop = 8

Defining the population size.

pop_size = (sol_per_pop,num_weights) # The population will have sol_per_pop chromosome where each chromosome has num_weights genes.

#Creating the initial population.

new_population = numpy.ram.uniform(low=-4.0, high=4.0, size=pop_size)

Once you import the numpy library, you can create the initial population using the numpy.random.uniform function. Based on the parameters you select, the shape of the function will be (8,6) where eight indicates the number of chromosomes that every solution should have, and six indicates the number of genes. When you run this code, you will obtain the following population:

[[-2.19134006 -2.88907857 2.02365737 -3.97346034
3.45160502 2.05773249]

[2.12480298 2.97122243 3.60375452 3.78571392
0.28776565 3.5170347]

[1.81098962 0.35130155 1.03049548 -0.33163294
3.52586421 2.53845644]

[-0.63698911 -2.8638447   2.93392615 -1.40103767 -
1.20313655 0.30567304]

[-1.48998583 -1.53845766 1.11905299 -3.67541087
1.33225142 2.86073836]

[1.14159503 2.88160332 1.74877772 -3.45854293
0.96125878 2.99178241]

[1.96561297 0.51030292 0.52852716 -1.56909315 -
2.35855588 2.29682254]

[3.00912373 -2.745417   3.27131287 -0.72163167
 0.7516408   0.00677938]]

You should remember that this is a random solution, and will change when you run the code again.

When you are preparing the population, the next step is to stick to the flowchart in the figure above. Using the fitness function, you will select the individual sets from the population set that you want to use as a parent for the purpose of mating. The next step is to apply the genetic algorithm crossover and mutation to develop or derive the offspring in the next generation. This will create a new population when you append the parents and the offspring. You can repeat these steps numerous times. We will apply these steps in the next set of the code:

```
import GA
num_generations = 5
num_parents_mating = 4
for generation in range(num_generations):
    # Measuring the fitness of each chromosome in the population.
    fitness = GA.cal_pop_fitness(equation_inputs, new_population)
    # Selecting the best parents in the population for mating.
    parents = GA.select_mating_pool(new_population, fitness,
                      num_parents_mating)
    # Generating next generation using crossover.
    offspring_crossover = GA.crossover(parents,
                    offspring_size=(pop_size[0]-
parents.shape[0], num_weights))
    # Adding some variations to the offsrping using mutation.
    offspring_mutation = GA.mutation(offspring_crossover)
```

Creating the new population based on the parents and offspring.

new_population[0:parents.shape[0], :] = parents

new_population[parents.shape[0]:, :] = offspring_mutation

The number of generations that you have selected is five. We have selected a small number for the purpose of this chapter. You can use the GA module to implement these changes. You must first calculate the fitness value for every solution in the population. This can be done by using the GA.cal_pop_fitness. This is implemented as follows in the genetic algorithm as follows:

def cal_pop_fitness(equation_inputs, pop):

Calculating the fitness value of each solution in the current population.

The fitness function calculates the sum of products between each input and its corresponding weight.

fitness = numpy.sum(pop*equation_inputs, axis=1)

return fitness

This fitness function will accept both the input values and the population values. It will calculate a fitness value which is calculated as the sum of the products of every input and the corresponding weights or genes. These values are based on the function you have written. Based on the number of values or solutions you want per population, there will be many sums of products. We have set the number of solutions to eight in the previous section of the code. This number is set in the sol_per_pop variable.

[-63.41070188 14.40299221 -42.22532674 18.24112489 - 45.44363278 -37.00404311 15.99527402 17.0688537]

You should note that the solution is better if it has a higher fitness value. When you calculate the fitness value for every solution, you should then select the solution as a parent in the mating pool. You can define this in the GA.select_mating_pool. This function will accept the fitness value, population and the number of parents that you want to use. This function will return the parent selected. The implementation will be done inside the genetic algorithm model:

```
def select_mating_pool(pop, fitness, num_parents):
    # Selecting the best individuals in the current generation
    as parents for producing the offspring of the next
    generation.
    parents = numpy.empty((num_parents, pop.shape[1]))
    for parent_num in range(num_parents):
        max_fitness_idx = numpy.where(fitness ==
    numpy.max(fitness))
        max_fitness_idx = max_fitness_idx[0][0]
        parents[parent_num, :] = pop[max_fitness_idx, :]
        fitness[max_fitness_idx] = -99999999999
    return parents
```

The function will create an array to hold the number of parents in them. The number of parents is defined in the num_parents_mating variable.

```
parents = numpy.empty((num_parents, pop.shape[1]))
```

When you loop through the current population, the function will calculate the index of the largest fitness value, as this is the best solution that you must select.

```
max_fitness_idx = numpy.where(fitness ==
numpy.max(fitness))
```

You can use the following line of code to retrieve the solution which will correspond to the fitness value:

parents[parent_num, :] = pop[max_fitness_idx, :]

If you do not want to select this solution, you should set the fitness value to a number that is too small. This means that the algorithm will not select the parent again. The following array is returned based on the example:

[[-0.63698911 -2.8638447 2.93392615 -1.40103767 -
1.20313655 0.30567304]

[3.00912373 -2.745417   3.27131287 -0.72163167
0.7516408   0.00677938]

[1.96561297 0.51030292 0.52852716 -1.56909315 -
2.35855588 2.29682254]

[2.12480298 2.97122243 3.60375452 3.78571392
0.28776565 3.5170347]]

You must note that the parents in the list above are the best to choose from the current population. This is based on the fitness value which is 18.24112489, 17.0688537, 15.99527402, and 14.40299221, respectively. The next step is to select these parents for the process of crossover and mutation to generate offspring. This process will start with the crossover operation based on the GA.crossover function, which will the size of the parents and the offspring. This function will use the offspring to define the number of offspring it should produce from the parents. This function is used within the genetic algorithm module.

```
def crossover(parents, offspring_size):

    offspring = numpy.empty(offspring_size)

    # The point at which crossover takes place between two
    parents. Usually, it is at the center.
```

```
crossover_point = numpy.uint8(offspring_size[1]/2)
for k in range(offspring_size[0]):
    # Index of the first parent to mate.
    parent1_idx = k%parents.shape[0]
    # Index of the second parent to mate.
    parent2_idx = (k+1)%parents.shape[0]
    # The new offspring will have its first half of its genes
    taken from the first parent.
    offspring[k, 0:crossover_point] = parents[parent1_idx,
    0:crossover_point]
    # The new offspring will have its second half of its
    genes taken from the second parent.
    offspring[k, crossover_point:] = parents[parent2_idx,
    crossover_point:]
```

The function will first create an empty array based on the size of the offspring based on the following line:

```
offspring = numpy.empty(offspring_size)
```

Since we use a single point crossover, you should specify the point in the algorithm where the crossover will take place. This point will be selected to divide the solution into two equal parts based on the following line:

```
crossover_point = numpy.uint8(offspring_size[1]/2)
```

You will now need to select two parents to build a crossover. You will select the indices of the parents using the following lines of code:

```
parent1_idx = k%parents.shape[0]

parent2_idx = (k+1)%parents.shape[0]
```

You will select the parents in the same way that you select a ring. The parents with the indices zero and one will be selected first to produce offspring. If you need to produce more offspring, you will need to select the parents with the indices one and two. If you want more offspring, you can choose the parent algorithms with the indices two and three. When you reach the index three, you have reached the last parent. This means you will need to go back to the parent with the index zero if you want to produce more offspring.

When you apply the crossover operation to the parents, the genetic algorithm will store the solutions in the offspring variable. The solution is as follows:

[[-0.63698911 -2.8638447 2.93392615 -0.72163167
0.7516408 0.00677938]

[3.00912373 -2.745417   3.27131287 -1.56909315 -
2.35855588 2.29682254]

[1.96561297 0.51030292 0.52852716 3.78571392
0.28776565 3.5170347]

[2.12480298 2.97122243 3.60375452 -1.40103767 -
1.20313655 0.30567304]]

You should now apply the second variant and mutation to the result of the crossover that is stored in the final variable. This is done using the mutation function within the genetic algorithm module. This function will accept the crossover offspring and will then return the offspring once the mutation function is applied. This function will be implemented as follows:

```
def mutation(offspring_crossover):

    # Mutation changes a single gene in each offspring
    randomly.

    for idx in range(offspring_crossover.shape[0]):
```

The random value to be added to the gene.

random_value = numpy.random.uniform(-1.0, 1.0, 1)

offspring_crossover[idx, 4] = offspring_crossover[idx, 4] + random_value

The function will loop through the individual offspring, and will add a random number between the range (-1,1) based on the following line of code:

random_value = numpy.random.uniform(-1.0, 1.0, 1)

Such random number is then added to the gene with index 4 of the offspring according to this line:

offspring_crossover[idx, 4] = offspring_crossover[idx, 4] + random_value

You must remember that the index will always change to another value when you run the code. The solution or offspring are as follows:

[[-0.63698911 -2.8638447 2.93392615 -0.72163167 1.66083721 0.00677938]

[3.00912373 -2.745417   3.27131287 -1.56909315 - 1.94513681 2.29682254]

[1.96561297 0.51030292 0.52852716 3.78571392 0.45337472 3.5170347]

[2.12480298 2.97122243 3.60375452 -1.40103767 - 1.5781162   0.30567304]]

You need to add these results to the offspring_crossover variable to obtain newer results.

We have successfully developed four offspring using the four selected parents. We are now ready to develop the new population for the next generation.

You must note that the genetic algorithm is based on a random optimization technique. This technique will try to enhance a current solution by applying some changes to the variables. Since these changes are random, you can never be sure if you will obtain the best solutions. It is for this reason that you use the previous solutions as the parents for the next generation. In a worst case scenario, if you have the worst offspring, you will continue to use the parents. When you do this, you can guarantee that at least some part of the new generation will preserve the earlier results. The new population will have the first four solutions from the previous parents, while the last four solutions come after you apply mutation and crossover.

new_population[0:parents.shape[0], :] = parents

new_population[parents.shape[0]:, :] = offspring_mutation

The fitness values for all solutions for both the parents and offspring in the first generation is as follows:

[18.24112489 17.0688537   15.99527402 14.40299221 - 8.46075629 31.73289712 6.10307563 24.08733441]

The output of the first generation had a fitness value of 18.24112489, but the fitness value now is 31.7328971158. This means that every random change always moves towards a more accurate solution. This is great news, but every result should be enhanced as it passes through more generations. In the sections below, we will look at the results for four more generations.

Generation: 1

Fitness values:

[18.24112489 17.0688537   15.99527402 14.40299221 -
8.46075629 31.73289712   6.10307563 24.08733441]

Selected parents:

[[3.00912373 -2.745417   3.27131287 -1.56909315 -
1.94513681 2.29682254]

[2.12480298 2.97122243 3.60375452 -1.40103767 -
1.5781162   0.30567304]

[-0.63698911 -2.8638447   2.93392615 -1.40103767 -
1.20313655 0.30567304]

[3.00912373 -2.745417   3.27131287 -0.72163167
0.7516408   0.00677938]]

Crossover result:

[[3.00912373 -2.745417   3.27131287 -1.40103767 -
1.5781162   0.30567304]

[2.12480298 2.97122243 3.60375452 -1.40103767 -
1.20313655 0.30567304]

[-0.63698911 -2.8638447   2.93392615 -0.72163167
0.7516408   0.00677938]

[3.00912373 -2.745417   3.27131287 -1.56909315 -
1.94513681 2.29682254]]

Mutation result:

[[3.00912373 -2.745417   3.27131287 -1.40103767 -
1.2392086   0.30567304]

[2.12480298 2.97122243 3.60375452 -1.40103767 -
0.38610586 0.30567304]

764

[-0.63698911 -2.8638447   2.93392615 -0.72163167
1.33639943 0.00677938]

[3.00912373 -2.745417   3.27131287 -1.56909315 -
1.13941727 2.29682254]]

Best result after generation 1 : 34.1663669207

Generation : 2

Fitness values:

[31.73289712 24.08733441 18.24112489 17.0688537
34.16636692 10.97522073 -4.89194068 22.86998223]

Selected Parents:

[[3.00912373 -2.745417   3.27131287 -1.40103767 -
1.2392086   0.30567304]

[3.00912373 -2.745417   3.27131287 -1.56909315 -
1.94513681 2.29682254]

[2.12480298 2.97122243 3.60375452 -1.40103767 -
1.5781162   0.30567304]

[3.00912373 -2.745417   3.27131287 -1.56909315 -
1.13941727 2.29682254]]

Crossover result:

[[3.00912373 -2.745417   3.27131287 -1.56909315 -
1.94513681 2.29682254]

[3.00912373 -2.745417   3.27131287 -1.40103767 -
1.5781162   0.30567304]

[2.12480298 2.97122243 3.60375452 -1.56909315 -
1.13941727 2.29682254]

[3.00912373 -2.745417   3.27131287 -1.40103767 -
1.2392086 0.30567304]]

Mutation result:

[[3.00912373 -2.745417   3.27131287 -1.56909315 -
2.20515009 2.29682254]

[3.00912373 -2.745417   3.27131287 -1.40103767 -
0.73543721 0.30567304]

[2.12480298 2.97122243 3.60375452 -1.56909315 -
0.50581509 2.29682254]

[3.00912373 -2.745417   3.27131287 -1.40103767 -
1.20089639 0.30567304]]

Best result after generation 2: 34.5930432629

Generation : 3

Fitness values:

[34.16636692 31.73289712 24.08733441 22.86998223
34.59304326 28.6248816   2.09334217 33.7449326]

Selected parents:

[[3.00912373 -2.745417   3.27131287 -1.56909315 -
2.20515009 2.29682254]

[3.00912373 -2.745417   3.27131287 -1.40103767 -
1.2392086 0.30567304]

[3.00912373 -2.745417   3.27131287 -1.40103767 -
1.20089639 0.30567304]

[3.00912373 -2.745417   3.27131287 -1.56909315 -
1.94513681 2.29682254]]

Crossover result:

[[3.00912373 -2.745417   3.27131287 -1.40103767 -
1.2392086   0.30567304]

 [3.00912373 -2.745417   3.27131287 -1.40103767 -
1.20089639 0.30567304]

 [3.00912373 -2.745417   3.27131287 -1.56909315 -
1.94513681 2.29682254]

 [3.00912373 -2.745417   3.27131287 -1.56909315 -
2.20515009 2.29682254]]

Mutation result:

[[3.00912373 -2.745417   3.27131287 -1.40103767 -
2.20744102 0.30567304]

 [3.00912373 -2.745417   3.27131287 -1.40103767 -
1.16589294 0.30567304]

 [3.00912373 -2.745417   3.27131287 -1.56909315 -
2.37553107 2.29682254]

 [3.00912373 -2.745417   3.27131287 -1.56909315 -
2.44124005 2.29682254]]

Best result after generation 3: 44.8169235189

Generation : 4

Fitness values

[34.59304326 34.16636692 33.7449326   31.73289712
44.81692352

33.35989464 36.46723397 37.19003273]

Selected parents:

[[3.00912373 -2.745417   3.27131287 -1.40103767 -
2.20744102 0.30567304]

[3.00912373 -2.745417   3.27131287 -1.56909315 -
2.44124005 2.29682254]

[3.00912373 -2.745417   3.27131287 -1.56909315 -
2.37553107 2.29682254]

[3.00912373 -2.745417   3.27131287 -1.56909315 -
2.20515009 2.29682254]]

Crossover result:

[[3.00912373 -2.745417   3.27131287 -1.56909315 -
2.37553107 2.29682254]

[3.00912373 -2.745417   3.27131287 -1.56909315 -
2.20515009 2.29682254]

[3.00912373 -2.745417   3.27131287 -1.40103767 -
2.20744102 0.30567304]]

Mutation result:

[[3.00912373 -2.745417   3.27131287 -1.56909315 -
2.13382082 2.29682254]

[3.00912373 -2.745417   3.27131287 -1.56909315 -
2.98105233 2.29682254]

[3.00912373 -2.745417   3.27131287 -1.56909315 -
2.27638584 2.29682254]

[3.00912373 -2.745417   3.27131287 -1.40103767 -
1.70558545 0.30567304]]

Best result after generation 4: 44.8169235189

Once the model provides the results for all five generations, the best result will now have a fitness value of 44.8169235189. You must remember that the fitness value changes in every generation.

The following weights provide the best solution:

[3.00912373 -2.745417   3.27131287 -1.40103767 -2.20744102 0.30567304]

The code below will implement the genetic algorithm in Python:

```
import numpy
import GA
"""

The y=target is to maximize this equation ASAP:

    y = w1x1+w2x2+w3x3+w4x4+w5x5+6wx6
    where (x1,x2,x3,x4,x5,x6)=(4,-2,3.5,5,-11,-4.7)


    What are the best values for the 6 weights w1 to w6?

    We are going to use the genetic algorithm for the best possible values after a number of generations.
"""


# Inputs of the equation.
equation_inputs = [4,-2,3.5,5,-11,-4.7]


# Number of the weights we are looking to optimize.
num_weights = 6
```

```
"""
Genetic algorithm parameters:
    Mating pool size
    Population size
"""




sol_per_pop = 8

num_parents_mating = 4


# Defining the population size.

pop_size = (sol_per_pop,num_weights) # The population will have
sol_per_pop    chromosome    where    each    chromosome    has
num_weights genes.

#Creating the initial population.

new_population = numpy.random.uniform(low=-4.0,
high=4.0, size=pop_size)

print(new_population)


num_generations = 5


for generation in range(num_generations):
    print("Generation : ", generation)
```

```python
    # Measing the fitness of each chromosome in the
population.

    fitness = GA.cal_pop_fitness(equation_inputs,
new_population)


    # Selecting the best parents in the population for mating.

    parents = GA.select_mating_pool(new_population,
fitness,

                    num_parents_mating)


    # Generating next generation using crossover.

    offspring_crossover = GA.crossover(parents,

                    offspring_size=(pop_size[0]-
parents.shape[0], num_weights))

    # Adding some variations to the offsrping using mutation.

    offspring_mutation = GA.mutation(offspring_crossover)


    # Creating the new population based on the parents and
offspring.

    new_population[0:parents.shape[0], :] = parents

    new_population[parents.shape[0]:, :] =
offspring_mutation


    # The best result in the current iteration.

    print("Best result : ",
numpy.max(numpy.sum(new_population*equation_inputs,
axis=1)))
```

\# Getting the best solution after iterating finishing all generations.

\#At first, the fitness is calculated for each solution in the final generation.

fitness = GA.cal_pop_fitness(equation_inputs, new_population)

\# Then return the index of that solution corresponding to the best fitness.

best_match_idx = numpy.where(fitness == numpy.max(fitness))

print("Best solution : ", new_population[best_match_idx, :])

print("Best solution fitness : ", fitness[best_match_idx])

The following is the module you should write to build the genetic algorithm.

import numpy

def cal_pop_fitness(equation_inputs, pop):

    \# Calculating the fitness value of each solution in the current population.

    \# The fitness function calculates the sum of products between each input and its corresponding weight.

    fitness = numpy.sum(pop*equation_inputs, axis=1)

    return fitness

def select_mating_pool(pop, fitness, num_parents):

```python
    # Selecting the best individuals in the current generation
as parents for producing the offspring of the next
generation.

    parents = numpy.empty((num_parents, pop.shape[1]))

    for parent_num in range(num_parents):

        max_fitness_idx = numpy.where(fitness ==
numpy.max(fitness))

        max_fitness_idx = max_fitness_idx[0][0]

        parents[parent_num, :] = pop[max_fitness_idx, :]

        fitness[max_fitness_idx] = -99999999999

    return parents

def crossover(parents, offspring_size):

    offspring = numpy.empty(offspring_size)

    # The point at which crossover takes place between two
parents. Usually it is at the center.

    crossover_point = numpy.uint8(offspring_size[1]/2)


    for k in range(offspring_size[0]):

        # Index of the first parent to mate.

        parent1_idx = k%parents.shape[0]

        # Index of the second parent to mate.

        parent2_idx = (k+1)%parents.shape[0]
```

```python
    # The new offspring will have its first half of its genes
taken from the first parent.

    offspring[k, 0:crossover_point] = parents[parent1_idx,
0:crossover_point]

    # The new offspring will have its second half of its
genes taken from the second parent.

    offspring[k, crossover_point:] = parents[parent2_idx,
crossover_point:]

    return offspring


def mutation(offspring_crossover):

    # Mutation changes a single gene in each offspring
randomly.

    for idx in range(offspring_crossover.shape[0]):

    # The random value to be added to the gene.

    random_value = numpy.random.uniform(-1.0, 1.0, 1)

    offspring_crossover[idx, 4] = offspring_crossover[idx,
4] + random_value
```

Found this title interesting or useful? Then a review on Amazon will be highly appreciated!

Chapter Six

Activation Functions Used
to Develop Deep Learning Models

In the previous book, we built a neural network in Python. We used an activation function to build the network, and it is important to include these functions since they decide whether every neuron in a layer should be used when it creates an output. This function will also decide if there is any information that the network should pass to the neuron, or if the output of those neurons should be used. An activation function is a non-linear transformation that is performed over the input layer. The input layer's output is used as an input for the other layers in the network.

Popular Activation Functions

Binary Step Function

A binary step function is a threshold-based classifier that decides whether the network should include a neuron in the calculation process. If the output value from the neuron is higher than a given threshold, the neuron is activated. Otherwise, the neuron should remain deactivated.

The function is defined as: $f(x) = 1, x >= 0$.

The binary function is a simple example of an activation function. This function can be used when you need to create a binary classifier.

Sigmoid Function

The sigmoid function is an activation function that most engineers use when they develop a deep neural network. The examples in the book use a sigmoid activation function to activate the layers of the neural network. The function is of the form: $f(x) = 1/(1+e^{-x})$.

The Sigmoid function is smooth, non-linear and continuously differentiable. When I say that the function is non-linear it means that you receive a non-linear output when you multiply neurons that have a sigmoid function. The output values for a sigmoid function lie in the range [0,1] where 0 and 1 are included, and the curve of the function has an S-shape.

Tanh

The tan h and sigmoid functions are similar. The tanh function is only a scaled version. The function is scaled using the following function: $tanh(x) = 2sigmoid(2x)-1$.

Alternatively, you can write the function in the following way: $tanh(x)=2/(1+e^{(-2x)})-1$. The tanh function, unlike the sigmoid function is symmetric. This solves the problem that the values derived as the output will have the same sign. Like the sigmoid function, the tanh function is differentiable and continuous at all points. Since the function is non-linear, it makes it easy for the engineer to backpropagate the errors.

ReLU

The Rectified Linear Unit or ReLU function is defined as follows: $f(x)=max(0,x)$. Most engineers use this function to design networks. The ReLU function is a non-linear function, which means that you can backpropagate errors and activate many layers of neurons. The advantage of the ReLU function is that it does not activate every neuron in the network. This means that if the output from one neuron is negative, it will deactivate that neuron and convert the output to zero. In this situation, the network is sparse which makes it easier to compute the problem.

Choosing the Right Activation Function

Now that you have seen a few activation, you should know which activation function can be used and in which situation. You can make a choice of the activation depending on the properties of the problem.

1. A Sigmoid function and its combinations work if you want to solve a classification problem

2. Avoid the Sigmoid and Activation functions if you want to avoid the vanishing gradient problem

Chapter Seven

Building a Neural Network in R

In this chapter, we will work on building a neural network in R in the same way that we did in Python. This code will only be focused on understandability and simplicity. We are not looking at how to write an elegant or efficient code at the moment. We will build a neural network with only two layers. Below is a pictorial representation of the neural network.

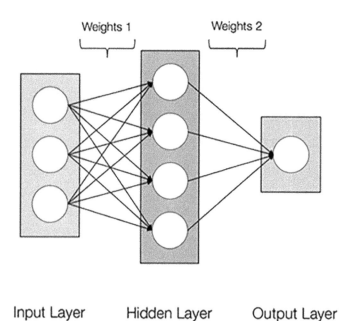

Input Layer   Hidden Layer   Output Layer

(https://www.r-bloggers.com/how-to-build-your-own-neural-network-from-scratch-in-r/)

To understand the model better, you should look at the second and third book of the series. You can also compare some parts of the Python code with the R code below.

Create Training Data

We will first need to create the data set to train the network.

```
# predictor variables
X <- matrix(c(
  0,0,1,
  0,1,1,
  1,0,1,
  1,1,1
),
  ncol = 3,
  byrow = TRUE
)
# observed outcomes
y <- c(0, 1, 1, 0)
# print the data so we can take a quick look at it
cbind(X, y)
##           y
## [1,] 0 0 1 0
## [2,] 0 1 1 1
## [3,] 1 0 1 1
## [4,] 1 1 1 0
```

There are four observations in the above data. You must remember that every type represents an observation. The first three columns from the left are the input while the column labelled y is the output. We will use there columns to train the model. When the model is trained, you can pass on new variables to predict the outcome values that the model has not observed yet.

Create an object to store the state of our neural network

Let us now create a model. We should first create an object which will store the state of the model.

```
# generate a random value between 0 and 1 for each

# element in X.  This will be used as our initial weights

# for layer 1

rand_vector <- runif(ncol(X) * nrow(X))

# convert above vector into a matrix

rand_matrix <- matrix(

  rand_vector,

  nrow = ncol(X),

  ncol = nrow(X),

  byrow = TRUE

)

# this list stores the state of our neural net as it is trained

my_nn <- list(

  # predictor variables

  input = X,

  # weights for layer 1

  weights1 = rand_matrix,
```

```
# weights for layer 2
weights2 = matrix(runif(4), ncol = 1),
# actual observed
y = y,
# stores the predicted outcome
output = matrix(
  rep(0, times = 4),
  ncol = 1
)
)
```

Activation Function

Now that we have decided what data we want to work with, and also know what the state of the model is, let us look at the different functions that we should use to train the model.

We will now define the activation function. This function will transform one layer's inputs into outputs. These outputs will then move to the next layer. We will use the Sigmoid activation function in the model.

```
#' the activation function
sigmoid <- function(x) {
  1.0 / (1.0 + exp(-x))
}
#' the derivative of the activation function
sigmoid_derivative <- function(x) {
  x * (1.0 - x)
}
```

Loss Function

We will use the loss function to determine if the model we have constructed fits the data set well. In this example, we will use the Sum-of-Squares error as the loss function.

```
loss_function <- function(nn) {

  sum((nn$y - nn$output) ^ 2)

}
```

The objective of the neural network is to identify or calculate the weight for every layer in the network. These weights should help to reduce or minimize the value of the loss function.

Feedforward and Back Propagation

The objective is to minimize the value of the loss function as the number of iterations increase. We will use the feedforward and backpropagation functions for this purpose. The former will use an activation function on the layers and produce an output.

```
feedforward <- function(nn) {

  nn$layer1 <- sigmoid(nn$input %*% nn$weights1)

  nn$output <- sigmoid(nn$layer1 %*% nn$weights2)

  nn

}
```

The backpropagation function will use the result from the feedforward function to adjust the weights placed on the model. This will help to reduce the loss function.

```
backprop <- function(nn) {
```

```r
# application of the chain rule to find derivative of the loss
function with

# respect to weights2 and weights1

d_weights2 <- (

  t(nn$layer1) %*%

  # `2 * (nn$y - nn$output)` is the derivative of the sigmoid
loss function

  (2 * (nn$y - nn$output) *

  sigmoid_derivative(nn$output))

)

d_weights1 <- ( 2 * (nn$y - nn$output) *
sigmoid_derivative(nn$output)) %*%

  t(nn$weights2)

d_weights1 <- d_weights1 *
sigmoid_derivative(nn$layer1)

d_weights1 <- t(nn$input) %*% d_weights1

# update the weights using the derivative (slope) of the loss
function

nn$weights1 <- nn$weights1 + d_weights1

nn$weights2 <- nn$weights2 + d_weights2

nn

}
```

Train the Model

The final step is to train the model. We are going to use the functions feedforward() and backprop() to reduce the value of the loss function as the number of iterations increase.

```
# number of times to perform feedforward and
backpropagation

n <- 1500

# data frame to store the results of the loss function.

# this data frame is used to produce the plot in the

# next code chunk

loss_df <- data.frame(

  iteration = 1:n,

  loss = vector("numeric", length = n)

)

for (i in seq_len(1500)) {

  my_nn <- feedforward(my_nn)

  my_nn <- backprop(my_nn)

  # store the result of the loss function.  We will plot this
later

  loss_df$loss[i] <- loss_function(my_nn)

}

# print the predicted outcome next to the actual outcome

data.frame(
```

```
  "Predicted" = round(my_nn$output, 3),

  "Actual" = y

)
```

Predicted Actual

1   0.017   0

2   0.975   1

3   0.982   1

4   0.024   0

You can see from the output that the values that the network predicted are close to the actual values.

Now that the model is trained, you can plot the results of the loss function on a graph. When you build a model, your objective should be to minimize the results of the loss function as the number of iterations increase. If you look at the graph below, you will notice that the value of the loss function, plotted on the y axis, will approach zero.

```
# plot the cost

library(ggplot2)

ggplot(data = loss_df, aes(x = iteration, y = loss)) +

  geom_line()
```

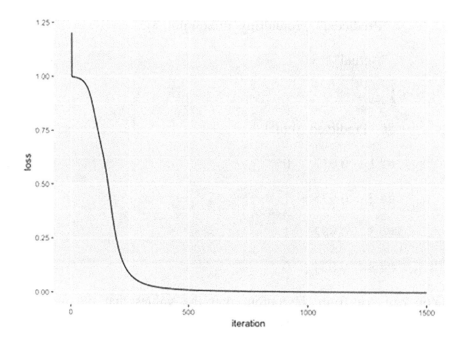

(https://www.r-bloggers.com/how-to-build-your-own-neural-network-from-scratch-in-r/)

In the previous book, we built a neural network on python. That chapter will allow you to explore how a neural network functions and what you will need to do to ensure that the network fits together. When you convert the code from Python to R, you will gather more information and understand how the code in Python works.

The example used in this chapter is very simple, and the predictions of the data set may not be meaningful. You can, however, use a different data set and predict the necessary output.

Chapter Eight

Fitting a Neural Network

Over the course of this chapter, we will fit a simple neural network and fit a linear model to use as a comparison. We will use the neuralnet package in R.

For the purpose of this model we will be using the Boston data set in the MASS package. This data set is a collection of information about the value of housing in Boston. The objective of this model is to identify or calculate the median value of the occupied homes, based on the assumption that all the other variables are continuous.

    set.seed(500)

    library(MASS)

    data <- Boston

We will first need to verify that no data point a variable is missing in the data set. If there is a missing variable we will need to use a proxy or dummy value.

    apply(data,2,function(x) sum(is.na(x)))

    crim   zn indus chas   nox   rm   age   dis   rad
    tax ptratio

     0   0   0   0   0   0   0   0   0   0   0

    black lstat   medv

     0   0   0

Run the above function to verify that there is no missing data points or variables. We will now split the data set into a training and testing data set. After the data is split we will fit a linear regression model using the training data set and test that model using the testing data set. Please note that we will be using the glm() function instead of the lm() function. The glm function is useful when you cross validate the linear model.

```
index <- sample(1:nrow(data),round(0.75*nrow(data)))

train <- data[index,]

test <- data[-index,]

lm.fit <- glm(medv~., data=train)

summary(lm.fit)

pr.lm <- predict(lm.fit,test)

MSE.lm <- sum((pr.lm - test$medv)^2)/nrow(test)
```

The function sample(x, size) extracts a smaller vector of the specified size from the vector named x. The sampling does not replace any numbers from the main vector. The vector index is a random vector with the indeces. We will calculate the mean square error to test the neural network. The mean square error will provide information on how far off the predictions are from the training data set.

Preparing to fit the neural network

Before you fit a neural network, you must prepare the data, as it is difficult to train a neural network. The first thing you will need to do is process the data you have.

It is always a good idea to normalize the data set before you begin to train the model. Experts always stress on the importance of this step. If you do not normalize the data, the output will not be accurate since the algorithm will never converge regardless of the number of iterations. There are many methods you can choose from to normalize your data, of which the z-normalization method and min-max scale are most popular. In this exercise, we will use the min-max scale method to scale the variables between the closed interval 0 and 1. It is always a good idea to use the intervals [-1,1] and [0,1] since they provide better results. Therefore, we will scale the data and then split it before we move on.

```
maxs <- apply(data, 2, max)

mins <- apply(data, 2, min)

scaled <- as.data.frame(scale(data, center = mins, scale = maxs - mins))

train_ <- scaled[index,]

test_ <- scaled[-index,]
```

The function scale will return a matrix that the model will need to coerce into the data frame.

Parameters

In the second book of the series, we learned about the different types of neural networks. We also learned that you can include many neurons and layers in the network. It is important to remember that one hidden layer is enough for numerous applications. The number of neurons you include should be at least two-thirds of the size of the input layer. It is always a good idea to test the products since there is no guarantee that these rules will apply to your model.

We will use the following configuration in the toy example and include two hidden layers: 13:5:3:1. This configuration implies that there are thirteen input layers, two hidden layers with five and three neurons and an output layer. Since we are performing regression, there will only be one layer.

Let us now fit the neural network.

> library(neuralnet)
>
> n <- names(train_)
>
> f <- as.formula(paste("medv ~", paste(n[!n %in% "medv"], collapse = " + ")))
>
> nn <-
> neuralnet(f,data=train_,hidden=c(5,3),linear.output=T)

Some additional points that you must note are:

1. The neuralnet package does not allow you to use the y~ formula. To overcome this issue, you should first write the formula, and then use it as an argument in the fitting function.

2. You can include a vector in the hidden argument. This vector should indicate the number of neurons you want to use in the hidden layers. You can then use the linear.output argument to specify if you want to perform a classification function (linear.output=FALSE) or regression (linear.output=TRUE).

You can use the plot (nn) function in the neuralnet package to plot the network.

plot(nn)

The following is a graphical representation of the neural network. It also shows the weights that are placed on each node in the network.

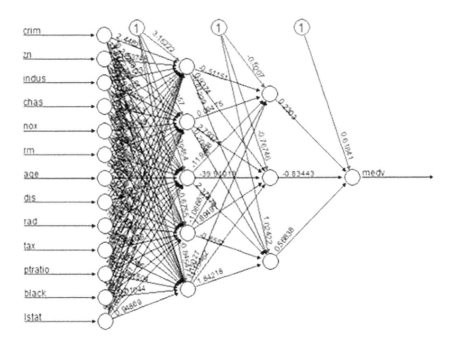

(https://datascienceplus.com/fitting-neural-network-in-r/)

The diagram about uses black lines to show how each layer is connected. It also shows how the weights have been added for each connection. The blue lines will show how much is a base has been added in every step. This base is analogous to the intercept in a linear model.

Since the neural network is a black box it is difficult to make comments about the fitting, the model and the weights. You can now use the model since the changing algorithm has worked.

Predicting medv using the neural network

The next step is to predict the value of the test data set and then calculate the mean square error. You must remember that the neural network will give you an output that has gone through the process of normalization. Therefore you must scale the numbers back if you want to make a simple prediction or a meaningful comparison.

791

```
pr.nn <- compute(nn,test_[,1:13])

pr.nn_ <- pr.nn$net.result*(max(data$medv)-
min(data$medv))+min(data$medv)

test.r <- (test_$medv)*(max(data$medv)-
min(data$medv))+min(data$medv)

MSE.nn <- sum((test.r - pr.nn_)^2)/nrow(test_)
```

We will now compare the two mean square errors.

```
print(paste(MSE.lm,MSE.nn))

"21.6297593507225 10.1542277747038"
```

You will notice that the network is better at predicting the median value when compared to the linear model. You must remember that this result is heavily dependent on how you split the data set. Once we look at the visual plot, you will perform a cross validation on the data set. This will help you understand if the results are accurate.

The following section depicts the performance of the linear model and the network using a scatter plot.

```
par(mfrow=c(1,2))

plot(test$medv,pr.nn_,col='red',main='Real vs predicted
NN',pch=18,cex=0.7)

abline(0,1,lwd=2)

legend('bottomright',legend='NN',pch=18,col='red', bty='n')

plot(test$medv,pr.lm,col='blue',main='Real vs predicted
lm',pch=18, cex=0.7)

abline(0,1,lwd=2)
```

legend('bottomright',legend='LM',pch=18,col='blue', bty='n',
cex=.95)

The output plot

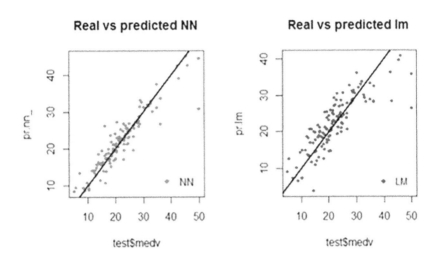

(https://datascienceplus.com/fitting-neural-network-in-r/)

When you inspect the plot you will notice that the predictions that the neural network makes are concentrated around the specific line. If the values are perfectly aligned with the straight line it will indicate that the mean square error is zero. This means that the output variables have been predicted directly by the network when compared to the linear model.

plot(test$medv,pr.nn_,col='red',main='Real vs predicted NN',pch=18,cex=0.7)

points(test$medv,pr.lm,col='blue',pch=18,cex=0.7)

abline(0,1,lwd=2)

legend('bottomright',legend=c('NN','LM'),pch=18,col=c('red','blue'))

The graph below shows a visual comparison.

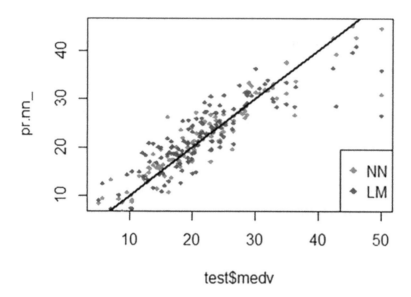

Real vs predicted NN

test$medv

(https://datascienceplus.com/fitting-neural-network-in-r/)

A (fast) cross validation

If you want to build a predictive model you must also incorporate cross validation. There are numerous cross validation methods that you can use, but the idea is to repeat the following processes multiple times.

1. Split the data into the training data set and the testing data set

2. Fit the neural network using the training data set

3. Test the functioning of the model using the testing data set

4. Calculate the prediction error

5. Repeat the process n times (iterations)

Once you calculate the mean square error you can understand how your model is working.

Since we want to use a fast cross validation we will use of for loop in the neural network. Occasionally, we will also need to use the cv.glm() function for the linear model. Since there is no built in function in r we will need to build a model for cross-validation. Let us look at how we can build a ten-fold cross validation model.

```
library(boot)

set.seed(200)

lm.fit <- glm(medv~.,data=data)

cv.glm(data,lm.fit,K=10)$delta[1]

23.83560156
```

Now we will work on building the network. We will use 90% of the data as the training set and the remaining 10% as a testing set. If you want to check the status of the process you can use the plyr library to initialize a progress bar because it takes some time to fit a neural network.

```
set.seed(450)

cv.error <- NULL

k <- 10

library(plyr)

pbar <- create_progress_bar('text')

pbar$init(k)

for(i in 1:k){

    index <- sample(1:nrow(data),round(0.9*nrow(data)))
```

```
train.cv <- scaled[index,]

test.cv <- scaled[-index,]

nn                                                      <-
neuralnet(f,data=train.cv,hidden=c(5,2),linear.output=T)

pr.nn <- compute(nn,test.cv[,1:13])

pr.nn        <-        pr.nn$net.result*(max(data$medv)-
min(data$medv))+min(data$medv)

test.cv.r       <-       (test.cv$medv)*(max(data$medv)-
min(data$medv))+min(data$medv)

cv.error[i] <- sum((test.cv.r - pr.nn)^2)/nrow(test.cv)

pbar$step()

}
```

Once the process is complete we will calculate the mean square error and plot the output as a box plot.

```
mean(cv.error)

cv.error

10.32697995

17.640652805  6.310575067 15.769518577  5.730130820
10.520947119 6.121160840

6.389967211 8.004786424 17.369282494 9.412778105
```

The code for the box plot:

```
boxplot(cv.error,xlab='MSE CV',col='cyan',

    border='blue',names='CV error (MSE)',
```

main='CV error (MSE) for NN',horizontal=TRUE)

The above code will give you the following output:

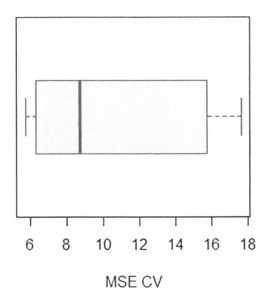

CV error (MSE) for NN

MSE CV

(https://datascienceplus.com/fitting-neural-network-in-r/)

From above you can see that the average mean square error for the neural network is low when compared to the mean square error of the linear model. You can also see that there is some variation in the mean square error for Cross validation. This is heavily dependent on how you split the data. It is also dependent on how you initialise weights in the network. You can get a precise estimate of the average mean square error if you run the simulation multiple time with different seeds.

A final note on model interpretability

A neural network and the Black box have a lot in common. It is difficult to explain the outcome of a neural network when compared to a linear model. It is for this reason that you need to verify if the model is indeed worth designing for the type of application you are building. You have to be very careful when you fit the neural network since a small change can lead to a different result.

Conclusion

Thank you for purchasing the book. The first three books of the series covered the basics of machine learning, and you learned how to build your first machine learning model in Python. You also learned how to build your very own neural network in Python, and the different types of neural networks. This book will delve into some concepts that are linked to machine learning, and also looks at how you can build some algorithms in Python and R.

I hope you gather all the information you are looking for, and wish you luck on your journey!

If you don't mind, please drop a short review of my title on Amazon and feel free to tell me what you think! Thanks a lot!

Will you help me?

Hi there, avid reader! If you have extra time on your hands, I would really, really appreciate it if you could take a moment to click my author profile in Amazon. In there, you will find all the titles I authored and who knows, you might find more interesting topics to read and learn!

If it's not too much to ask, you can also leave and write a review for all the titles that you have read – whether it's a positive or negative review. An honest and constructive review of my titles is always welcome and appreciated since it will only help me moving forward in creating these books. There will always be room to add or improve, or sometimes even subtract certain topics, that is why these reviews are always important for us. They will also assist other avid readers, professionals who are looking to sharpen their knowledge, or even newbies to any topic, in their search for the book that caters to their needs the most.

If you don't want to leave a review yourself, you can also vote on the existing reviews by voting Helpful (Thumbs Up) or Unhelpful (Thumbs Down), especially on the top 10 or so reviews.

If you want to go directly to the vote or review process, please visit Amazon on any of the titles below:

Machine Learning For Beginners : A Comprehensive, Step-by-Step Guide to Learning and Understanding Machine Learning Concepts, Technology and Principles for Beginners . Audiobook format is also available at www.audible.com

Machine Learning : A Comprehensive, Step-by-Step Guide to Intermediate Concepts and Techniques in Machine Learning

Machine Learning : A Comprehensive, Step-by-Step Guide to Learning and Applying Advanced Concepts and Techniques in Machine Learning

Excel VBA : A Step-By-Step Tutorial For Beginners To Learn Excel VBA Programming From Scratch . Audiobook format is also available at www.audible.com

Excel VBA : Intermediate Lessons in Excel VBA Programming for Professional Advancement . Audi0book format is also available at www.audible.com

Excel VBA: A Step-By-Step Comprehensive Guide on Advanced Excel VBA Programming Techniques and Strategies

Again, I truly appreciate the time and effort that you will be putting in leaving a review for my titles or even just for voting. This will only inspire me to create more quality content and titles in the future.

Thank you and have a great day!

Peter Bradley

Resources

https://www.kdnuggets.com/2018/07/genetic-algorithm-implementation-python.html

https://www.r-bloggers.com/how-to-build-your-own-neural-network-from-scratch-in-r/

https://datascienceplus.com/fitting-neural-network-in-r/

https://www.analyticsvidhya.com/blog/2017/09/creating-visualizing-neural-network-in-r/

https://conferences.oreilly.com/strata/strata-ny-2018/public/schedule/detail/69255

www.ingramcontent.com/pod-product-compliance
Lightning Source LLC
Chambersburg PA
CBHW071353050326
40689CB00010B/1625